Crowdsourcing and Knowledge Management in Contemporary Business Environments

Regina Lenart-Gansiniec
Jagiellonian University, Poland

A volume in the Advances in Logistics, Operations, and Management Science (ALOMS) Book Series

IGI Global
DISSEMINATOR OF KNOWLEDGE

Published in the United States of America by
IGI Global
Business Science Reference (an imprint of IGI Global)
701 E. Chocolate Avenue
Hershey PA, USA 17033
Tel: 717-533-8845
Fax: 717-533-8661
E-mail: cust@igi-global.com
Web site: http://www.igi-global.com

Library of Congress Cataloging-in-Publication Data

Names: Lenart-Gansiniec, Regina, 1978- editor.
Title: Crowdsourcing and knowledge management in contemporary business environments / Regina Lenart-Gansiniec, editor.
Description: Hershey : Business Science Reference, [2018]
Identifiers: LCCN 2017030760| ISBN 9781522542001 (hardcover) | ISBN 9781522542018 (ebook)
Subjects: LCSH: Knowledge management. | Human computation. | Organizational learning.
Classification: LCC HD30.2 .C786 2018 | DDC 658.4/038--dc23 LC record available at https://lccn.loc.gov/2017030760

This book is published in the IGI Global book series Advances in Logistics, Operations, and Management Science (ALOMS) (ISSN: 2327-350X; eISSN: 2327-3518)

British Cataloguing in Publication Data
A Cataloguing in Publication record for this book is available from the British Library.

All work contributed to this book is new, previously-unpublished material.
The views expressed in this book are those of the authors, but not necessarily of the publisher.

For electronic access to this publication, please contact: eresources@igi-global.com.

Advances in Logistics, Operations, and Management Science (ALOMS) Book Series

ISSN:2327-350X
EISSN:2327-3518

Editor-in-Chief: John Wang, Montclair State University, USA

MISSION

Operations research and management science continue to influence business processes, administration, and management information systems, particularly in covering the application methods for decision-making processes. New case studies and applications on management science, operations management, social sciences, and other behavioral sciences have been incorporated into business and organizations real-world objectives.

The **Advances in Logistics, Operations, and Management Science** (ALOMS) Book Series provides a collection of reference publications on the current trends, applications, theories, and practices in the management science field. Providing relevant and current research, this series and its individual publications would be useful for academics, researchers, scholars, and practitioners interested in improving decision making models and business functions.

COVERAGE

- Organizational behavior
- Finance
- Services management
- Information management
- Production management
- Political science
- Operations management
- Marketing engineering
- Risk Management
- Computing and information technologies

IGI Global is currently accepting manuscripts for publication within this series. To submit a proposal for a volume in this series, please contact our Acquisition Editors at Acquisitions@igi-global.com or visit: http://www.igi-global.com/publish/.

The Advances in Logistics, Operations, and Management Science (ALOMS) Book Series (ISSN 2327-350X) is published by IGI Global, 701 E. Chocolate Avenue, Hershey, PA 17033-1240, USA, www.igi-global.com. This series is composed of titles available for purchase individually; each title is edited to be contextually exclusive from any other title within the series. For pricing and ordering information please visit http://www.igi-global.com/book-series/advances-logistics-operations-management-science/37170. Postmaster: Send all address changes to above address.

Titles in this Series

For a list of additional titles in this series, please visit:
https://www.igi-global.com/book-series/advances-logistics-operations-management-science/37170

Handbook of Research on Intrapreneurship and Organizational Sustainability in SMEs
Rafael Perez-Uribe (EAN University, Colombia) Carlos Salcedo-Perez (EAN University, Colombia) and David Ocampo-Guzman (EAN University, Colombia)
Business Science Reference • ©2018 • 475pp • H/C (ISBN: 9781522535430) • US $295.00

Entrepreneurship, Collaboration, and Innovation in the Modern Business Era
Mehdi Khosrow-Pour, D.B.A. (Information Resources Management Association, USA)
Business Science Reference • ©2018 • 367pp • H/C (ISBN: 9781522550143) • US $215.00

Developing Organizational Maturity for Effective Project Management
Gilbert Silvius (LOI University of Applied Sciences, The Netherlands & University of Johannesburg, South Africa) and Gamze Karayaz (Isik University, Turkey)
Business Science Reference • ©2018 • 349pp • H/C (ISBN: 9781522531975) • US $225.00

Organizational Leadership for the Fourth Industrial Revolution Emerging Research and...
Peter A.C. Smith (The Leadership Alliance Inc., Canada) and John Pourdehnad (University of Pennsylvania, USA)
Business Science Reference • ©2018 • 125pp • H/C (ISBN: 9781522553908) • US $165.00

Management Techniques for a Diverse and Cross-Cultural Workforce
Naman Sharma (Amity University, India) Vinod Kumar Singh (Gurkul Kangri University, India) and Swati Pathak (Invertis University, India)
Business Science Reference • ©2018 • 381pp • H/C (ISBN: 9781522549338) • US $225.00

Improving Business Performance Through Effective Managerial Training Initiatives
Luisa dall'Acqua (Scientific Lyceum TCO, Italy & Live Editions Inc., USA) and Dickson Lukose (GCS Agile Pty. Ltd, Australia)
Business Science Reference • ©2018 • 316pp • H/C (ISBN: 9781522539063) • US $215.00

For an entire list of titles in this series, please visit:
https://www.igi-global.com/book-series/advances-logistics-operations-management-science/37170

IGI Global
DISSEMINATOR OF KNOWLEDGE

701 East Chocolate Avenue, Hershey, PA 17033, USA
Tel: 717-533-8845 x100 • Fax: 717-533-8661
E-Mail: cust@igi-global.com • www.igi-global.com

List of Reviewers

Alireza Amrollahi, *Griffith University, Australia*
Prasenjit Choudhury, *National Institute of Technology, India*
Neema Nicodemus, *Sokoine University of Agriculture, Tanzania*
Saurabh Pal, *Bengal Institute of Technology, India*
Pijush Dutta Pramanik, *National Institute of Technology, India*
Gadaf Rexhepi, *South European University, Macedonia*
Mansour Esmaeil Zaei, *University of Warsaw, Poland*

Table of Contents

Detailed Table of Contents

Crowdsourcing is a relatively new concept, which was defined for the first time only in 2006. The growing interest in crowdsourcing has been observed since 2010. As of that moment, the number of publications on crowdsourcing has been systematically increasing. The researchers' attention is frequently focused on the benefits possible to be obtained by the organization owing to crowdsourcing. Not without importance is the issue of cooperation with the crowd. Despite the growth tendency, it may still be ascertained that the multitude and diversity of approaches to crowdsourcing does not increase the chances for clarification and transparency. In their majority these papers are of a theoretical nature and rather dispersed and fragmentary. As a whole they do not make reference to the achievements of the predecessors. The subject of this chapter is searching for an answer to the question whether crowdsourcing displays the features of a public management fashion.

Knowledge is power, and when managed efficiently, it generates optimum outcomes. Knowledge management is an established phenomenon, applied across various disciplines for transformational growth. In the year 2015, the Government of India launched Digital India Programme with the vision to "transform India into a digitally

shorten the new drugs pipelines. One of the most "open" dimensions of innovation activity in pharmaceutical industry is crowdsourcing: a specific sourcing model, an internet-enabled business model that harnesses the creative ability of agents external to organization.

The growing importance of knowledge sharing is promoting individual innovative work behavior (IWB) to create new products or services for innovative business systems. Also, the key challenges faced by individuals in their knowledge sharing behavior (KSB) are personal perceptions and environmental influences. Thus, this chapter provides a research model using an extension of social cognitive theory that comprises environmental factors (subjective norms, trust), personal factors (knowledge self-efficacy, enjoyment in helping others, organizational rewards, reciprocal benefits, and psychological ownership of knowledge), KSB, and IWB. The authors advance to implement mixed-methods approaches to evaluate the proposed model. The authors believe that this research will contribute to deeper understanding of the effects of personal and environmental factors and KSB on IBW within organizations. The model is also expected to be tested in any organizations in which future researchers or practitioners wish to test this model.

The main objective of the chapter is to provide an insight into the motivation mechanisms for the crowd to participate in crowdsourcing projects. For this to happen, the authors investigate the factors which have been suggested in the literature as influencing the motivation of the crowd and the task type in each study in the related literature and contrasted the motivation factors in various contexts. The systematic literature review method has been used for the purpose of this study. This involved a comprehensive search in five scientific databases which resulted in 575 papers. This initial pool of studies has been refined in various rounds and ended in identification of 37 studies which directly targeted the topic of motivation in crowdsourcing. The study introduces various categories of motivations and investigates the factors which have been utilized in each context. Finally, possible implications for practice and potential research gaps are discussed.

The aim of the study is to analyze case studies of selected organizations in terms of their achievements in the use of social media. The profiling method applied in the study facilitated evaluating the model of the selected organization. It is an efficient technique for exploring data. Graphic objects show the individual characteristics of selected organizations. Graphical visualization makes it easy to gauge the trajectory, the direction of your company's social media strategy, and helps to make a decision to change it. Further analysis of the structure of these models may facilitate the discovery of relevant relationships between the analyzed variables.

This chapter aims to make the case that analytics methods must respond to the significant changes that big data challenges are bringing to operationalizing the production of information and knowledge. More specifically it discusses the analytics dimension of big data challenges and its contribution for value creation. It shows that data analytics tools and methods offer strong support in knowledge acquisition and discovery. This suggests that the effectiveness of an analytics method must be measured based on how it promotes and enhances knowledge, how it improves patterns and understanding of the decision makers, and thereby how it improves their decision making and hence organization performance. This chapter explores the synergies between big data analytics and knowledge discovery by identifying challenges and opportunities in data analytics applications for knowledge acquisition.

The power of crowd always has brought wonders. The same applies to the computing as well. The accumulated idle CPU cycles of millions of personally owned devices are capable of producing huge computing capacity. We have termed it as crowd computing. Though this very concept has been nurtured in the past through grid

Preface

INTRODUCTION

In the era of economy based on knowledge and Web 2.0 technology, knowledge is the basis for improving the decision-making processes and relations between people in the organisation and with the environment. Knowledge enables fast reacting to changes, foreseeing, and outrivaling competitors' actions as well as undertaking adaptive-corrective and reparative actions. Thanks to knowledge it is possible for the whole organisation to self-organise and learn. Knowledge enables the organisation to translate its strategic goals to each functional area and in addition it leads the processes of reconfiguring other resources, enables designing the organisational structure, is the source of innovation, and gives a possibility to shape competitive advantage. However, the organisation's dependence only on its own resources seems to be inadequate. The more the knowledge possessed by the organisation is diversified and comes from various sources, the bigger the possibilities of making changes are. Therefore, it is important to search by the organisation for new, unique sources of knowledge, particularly beyond its borders, in the environment.

The number of Internet users has been growing year by year. According to Internet World Stats, by the end of 2009 the number of Internet users worldwide was close to 2 billion, whereas in Poland over 20 million. What is more this number has been increasing every year. By the end of 2015 the number of Internet users around the world was almost 3 billion, while in Poland close to 26 million – which constitutes 67.5% of the entire population.

It is assumed in the literature that virtual communities have ceased to be passive Internet members, having accounts in the social media, looking through job offers, listening to the music, watching films, or reading articles. These communities more and more frequently begin to interact and they are interested in participating in the business environments. They are not just a big group of people. As self-defining networks of interactive communication, they concentrate around groups of interest or goals. The Internet is becoming for them an important means of communication, while what joins them are common values, interests, and creating groups based on trust.

Organisations seem to perceive the importance of the virtual communities. More and more often they try to engage them in various endeavours, particularly based on an open call – through the so-called crowdsourcing platforms. It appears that knowledge, experience, or potential, which is possessed by the virtual communities may become useful and advantageous for the functioning of the organisation. First, in the business aspect, knowledge possessed by the virtual communities may contribute to creating new products or improving the existing ones. Second, the virtual communities are interested in assessing, recommending, reviewing of the ideas of others. They are becoming demanding and educated participants.

STATE-OF-THE-ART CROWDSOURCING

In recent years in the literature on management, including strategic management, one may observe an increased interest in the problems of crowdsourcing. This interest also appears in business practice. It began in 2006 as a result of Howe's publication. This author introduced and defined the term "crowdsourcing". He named in such way actions consisting in taking over tasks traditionally executed by workers, by undefined, large groups of people. At the same time, the significance of virtual communities and making use of crowd wisdom are emphasised. Such actions lead to obtaining the best solutions to a given problem (Majchrzak & Malhotra, 2013) or building of competitive advantage (Rigby &Zook, 2002). This gains significance particularly in the context of open innovations (Afuah & Tucci, 2012; Boudreau & Lakhani, 2013; Marjanovic et al., 2012; Wikhamn & Wikhamn, 2013).

Crowdsourcing is one of the new subjects, which has appeared in the last decade. It may be said that it strengthens its position in management sciences; in addition in business practice it has become a megatrend, which drives innovations, collaboration in the area of scientific studies, business, or society. More and more organisations reach for it, for instance taking into account its potential business value (Leimeister, et al., 2009) in the scope of innovative solving of problems (Afuah & Tucci, 2013). Creative effects possible to be achieved owing to crowdsourcing are based not only on individual features, motivation, experience, and capabilities of virtual communities (Paulus & Dzindolet, 2008). It is also important to note the role of the initiator, namely the organisation, which directs questions and demands to the virtual communities (Schemmann et al., 2016). It seems that the multitude and large number of obtained ideas is important and valuable for the organisation. Owing to that the organisation may expand its existing activity and offer, create its own image, optimise its operational costs, modify the business processes (Malone et al., 2010), and achieve the intended results at lower costs in a shorter time.

The term crowdsourcing appeared in literature for the first time in 2006, owing to Howe. He defined crowdsourcing as "the act of a company or institution taking a function once performed by employees and outsourcing it to an undefined (and generally large) network of people in the form of an open call. This can take the form of peer-production (when the job is performed collaboratively), but is also often undertaken by sole individuals" (Howe, 2006). With time, the author expanded this definition with using the rules of an open source, not only in the scope of software, but also ordering tasks to the crowd, matching talent and knowledge of the crowd to the needs of an organisation. According to this approach crowdsourcing is a blend of the following words: outsourcing, crowd, and sourcing (Rouse, 2010). The principal building material of crowdsourcing is crowd wisdom (Surowiecki, 2004) and making use of ideas, resources, and competencies of people who are interested in solving problems or creating new products (Burger-Helmchen & Penin, 2010; Jain, 2010). He acknowledges that a group is able to achieve and gain more benefits than any expert (Jeppesen & Lakhani, 2010).

The principal building material of crowdsourcing is crowd wisdom and making use of ideas, resources, and competencies of people who are interested in solving problems or creating new products (Jain, 2010). He acknowledges that a group is able to achieve and gain more benefits than any expert (Jeppesen & Lakhani, 2010; Leimeister, 2010). Therefore, taking over of the tasks performed by professionalists by those interested in solving various types of problems or creating innovations whether laymen or amateurs, takes place.

Technological evolution will remain the main enabler of changes in communication behaviour over the next five years. The number of global Internet users is likely to triple by 2012. The average time spent in front of the computer will grow. The amount of data transmitted will multiply; within four years it is expected to be seven times the level of today. For the public organisations it means the need to search for new ways for increasing co-participation or engagement of the citizens in decision making and making use of their knowledge and skills to more effective problem solving. What is more, it is suggested that these organisations should reach for modern digital technological and communication tools.

KNOWLEDGE MANAGEMENT

Knowledge is defined in various ways, using many different perspectives. The Polish Language Dictionary considers knowledge to be "a generality of information obtained owing to research learning, an resource of information in a given field and knowledge of something" (www.sjp.pwn.pl). On the basis of management sciences knowledge is perceived as:

Table 1. Definitions of crowdsourcing

Date	Author(s)	Definition
2006	Reichwald & Piller	Interactive creation of values: collaboration between the organisation and the users in the development of a new product
2008	Chanal & Caron-Fasan	Opening of the innovation process in the organisation in order for integration through a competence network
2008	Howe	Act of a company or institution taking a function once performed by employees and outsourcing it to an undefined (and generally large) network of people in the form of an open call. This can take the form of peer-production (when the job is performed collaboratively), but is also often undertaken by sole individuals
2008	Kleeman et al.	Form of integration of users or consumer in internal processes of value creation. The essence of crowdsourcing is an intended mobilisation with allocation of commercial exploration of creative ideas and other form of work performed by the consumer
2008	Yang et al.	Making use of a virtual community to transfer tasks
2009	DiPalantino & Vojnovic	Methods while using an open call to encourage communities to solve problems
2009	Poetz &Schreier	Outsourcing of the phase of generating ideas to potentially large and unknown groups of people in the form of an open call
2009	Vukovic	A new production model widespread on the Internet in which people collaborate in order to complete a task
2009	Whitla	The process of outsourcing of an organisation's activity to the virtual community. The process of organising work in which the organisation offers payment for realisation of tasks by the crowd members
2010	Buecheler et al.	A specific case of collective intelligence
2010	Burger-Helmchen & Penin	The way in which the organisation gains access to external knowledge
2010	Heer & Bostok	A relatively new phenomenon in which Internet workers carry out one or more micro-tasks, often for a micro- payment ranging from $ 0.01 to $ 0.10 for the tasks
2010	La Vecchia & Cisternino	Tools for solving problems in the organisation
2010	Mazzola & Distefano	Purposeful mobilisation through web 2.0, creation of innovative ideas, incentives for problem solving, where users coming forward voluntarily are taken into account by the organisation in the process of solving internal problems
2010	Oliveira et al.	A way of outsourcing to the crowd of tasks related to creating of intellectual assets, often together in order for an easier to access to the necessary palette of skills and experience
2011	Alonso & Lease	Outsourcing of tasks to a large group of people rather than assigning these tasks to the employees or contractors at home
2011	Bederson & Quinn	People devote themselves to perform Internet tasks manager by organisations
2011	Grier	A way of making use of the Internet to employ a large number of dispersed workers
2011	Heymann & Garcia-Molina	Acquiring one or more Internet users to remote performance of work
2013	Brabham	Way of problem solving as well as a production model, in which in order to achieve goals characteristic for an organisation collective intelligence of Internet communities is used

Source: own elaboration.

- Effective use of information in action (Drucker, 1999),
- Information used for solving a given problem (Applehans, Globe, Laugero, 1999),
- A specific type of an organisation's resource (Galata, 2004).
- An open-ended mixture of contextual experiences, values, information, and skills which creates a framework of evaluation, understanding, and absorbing new experiences and information (Tiwana, 2003).

Examples of other ways to define knowledge are presented in the table below. The diversification in understanding this concept stems mainly from the fact that knowledge is an immaterial resource, and such resources are open-ended, underspecified, and changeable (table 2).

Table 2. Knowledge definitions

Date	Author/Authors	Knowledge Definitions
1993	Hall	A special, ephemeral resource that is difficult to be defined
1993	Wiig	Truths, beliefs, views and concepts, judgments and expectations, methodology, and know-how
1994	Davis & Botkin	Distinction between data, information, and knowledge
1995	Blackler	Exhaustive and comprehensive, explicit and hidden, shared and personal, physical and mental, static and dynamic, verbal and encrypted
1998	Cleveland	Information put in order, implemented by the owners
1998	Davenport & Prusak	Smooth combination of expressed experience, values, appropriately selected information and expert insight into a random issue that provides a framework for assessing and integrating new experiences and information
1998	Urlich	Direct competitive advantage for companies offering ideas and relationships
1999	Steward	An intangible asset
1999	McDermott	The effect of using information and experience in the thinking process
1999	Beckman	The ability to use data and information for a specific action
2000	Buckley & Carter	Quality that is in the hands of people, a catalyst for action that makes people aware of opportunities and how to use knowledge
2000	Nonaka & Takeuchi	A confirmed conviction, a dynamic and deeply humanistic process of verifying the truth of personal imagination
2001	Vorbeck & Finke	The result of the process of learning about some facts, their quality and relationships with other parts and quality
2002	Probst, Raub, & Romhardt	It is created by placing information on the web and using it in specific areas of activity
2003	Amstrong	Information submitted for productive use

Source: own elaboration.

Knowledge is defined in the literature including three perspectives. The first one, connects it with data and information (Davenport & Prusak, 1998). The next one, which connects knowledge with the effect of processing information, experiences, was formulated as a relic of the thought process (McDermott, 1999). The third perspective brings down knowledge to the totality of information and skills used by individuals to solve problems (Probst, Raub, & Romhardt, 2002). J.B. Barney proposes expanding the semantic range of the knowledge definition. He acknowledges that knowledge has a unique, individual, and organised character. It is a strategic resource which is not subject to the right of decreasing profits and its value increases as it is used, which leads to increasing market share, financial results, and the organisation's position (Barney, 2001). The above-mentioned definitions of knowledge and their perspectives indicated that knowledge is personalised and connected with the human factor.

The carried out literature review indicates that knowledge is a combination of information with experience, context, interpretation, reflection and perspective. It is a flexible and dynamic intangible substance that arises as a result of the mental processing of information possessed by man and the information sets obtained from the environment, while the creative entities and the carriers of its core are people. Knowledge arises through the processing of information coming from outside the organisation and the organisation's other resources and the development of their values.

Knowledge is considered an organisational resource that can contribute to building competitive advantage (Wang & Noe, 2010), solving organisational problems, adjusting key organisation's resources to market requirements (Faulkner & Bosman, 1996) and increasing effectiveness and productivity (Cummings, 2004). Knowledge is also perceived as a source of innovation (Kogut & Zander, 1992), an economic pension (Stańczyk-Hugiet, 2009). It is also a strategic resource of the organisation and a success factor (Nahapiet & Ghosal, 1998), which is an element of the organisation's survival in a dynamic and competitive era (Asrar-ul-Haq & Anwar, 2016).

In order for knowledge to contribute to building competitive advantage, it should be renewed, updated, modified, which determines its usefulness and value. The ability to allocate these resources and assimilation is important. It boils down to the fact that the organisation should create a balance between exploited and explored knowledge, define knowledge that is to be the strategic asset of the organisation and create a synergy effect and become valuable for it (Levitt, 1991). Knowledge is considered an excellent resource that requires proper treatment, "care and unconventional solutions" (Kowalczyk & Nogalski, 2007). Independent knowledge creation concentrates risk and extends the time of creating the knowledge base. For knowledge to be used effectively, it must be managed. This means that knowledge management is just as important for the organisation as managing other resources. Knowledge that is not well managed, easily corrodes.

Knowledge management is the result of a reflection on the productivity factors of knowledge workers and knowledge-based organisations, being a synthesis of quality management regarding the internal client, open processes and common goals; strategic management as an attempt to formalise processes connected with the management of intellectual capital; human resource management, focused on individual competences; information management, dealing with information in separation from technology and economics, in which the concept of learning in action was created. Bukowitz and Williams (2000) define knowledge management as a process owing to which the organisation generates wealth of knowledge based on intellectual and knowledge-based organisational assets, and PF Drucker emphasises that knowledge management is primarily about people, and its goal is to achieve such cooperation of people that will neutralise weaknesses and make the most of the talents and strengths of the organisation's participants. In practice, knowledge management comes down to taking care of knowledge.

In the literature three directions of knowledge management development have been distinguished: Japanese, resource, and process. The Japanese approach accentuates the aspect of the so-called knowledge spiral. Knowledge management is a recurring cycle that involves processes. Silent and formal knowledge is juxtaposed in knowledge management. After their juxtaposition, the processes of knowledge conversion arise: - socialisation involving the conversion of silent knowledge into silent knowledge, - externalisation, or the exchange of silent knowledge into formal knowledge, - combination, or the creation of formal knowledge from formal knowledge, - internalisation corresponding to changing the formal knowledge into silent knowledge.

The resource approach assumes that key skills are essential for skilful knowledge management, which consist of: physical and technical systems, management, skills, and knowledge of employees and standards and values, joint problem solving, implementation and integration of new tools and technologies, experimenting and importing knowledge. Knowledge management focuses on key competences, skills, and knowledge of employees as well as standards and implementation of technologies that will facilitate the transfer of knowledge from the environment to the organisation.

The process approach is influenced by the subprocesses that make up knowledge management. In this approach, knowledge management is all the processes that enable the creation, dissemination, and use of knowledge for the purposes of the organisation. The knowledge management model, developed by Davenport and Prusak (1988), is based on three processes: creation, codification, and knowledge transfer. The knowledge creation process involves increasing the amount of knowledge that is inside and outside the organisation. The codification of knowledge consists in giving knowledge a new form which is accessible to the users. The knowledge transfer process includes its transmission and absorption.

It is emphasised in the literature that knowledge management is a complex concept, because it consists of many processes. Most often, three processes are indicated, i.e. knowledge acquisition, dissemination of knowledge, and the use of knowledge. Acquisition of knowledge comes down to analysis, reconstruction, synthesis, and creation of knowledge. It is important to ensure the transparency of internal and external knowledge resources and enable employees to locate them. Dissemination of knowledge means coordination, providing access, sparing, and knowledge transfer. In turn, the use of knowledge focuses on review, knowledge description, selection, observation, analysis, evaluation, decision making, and knowledge implementation.

The main goal of knowledge management is to facilitate management staff search for practical applications of knowledge (Probst, Raub & Romhardt, 2002). In addition, it allows reorientation of the organisation's ways of functioning, absorption of new experiences and information, gaining knowledge transparency, identifying areas of ignorance, codifying knowledge, changing organisational culture, improving communication and cooperation, educational processes, training and networking, as well as employee development. It also helps to reduce costs, improve innovation management, improve quality, increase loyalty, establish and strengthen long-term relationships with customers, employees, shareholders and suppliers, shorten implementation time and modernise the offer and increase decision-making effectiveness

Crowdsourcing and Knowledge Management

The search for relationships between knowledge management and crowdsourcing is a relatively new topic. However, the relationship between knowledge management and crowsourcing is increasingly being pointed out. Crowdsourcing is considered a knowledge management tool (Trudell, 2014). Crowdsourcing allows not only gathering knowledge, but also to store, process and share it, and track changes and links in information and distribution of the obtained solutions within the organisation.

First, acquiring knowledge. In literature on knowledge management, crowdsourcing is often presented as a new source of external knowledge. So far, the following external sources have been pointed out in the literature: new employees, literature studies, stakeholders, clients, benchmarking, purchase of licenses and patents, business intelligence, cooperation with consulting companies, training, visits, knowledge obtained from government agencies and legal provisions. An exogenous source is also the possibilities that will allow the creation of new knowledge, including: alliances, market analysis, establishing knowledge gaps, cooperation with R&D organisations, outsourcing, and staff turnover. Thus, crowdsourcing allows the organisation to increase access to new sources of knowledge in the form of experience and skills found in virtual communities (Chi & Bernstein, 2012). It is considered to be a tool for creating knowledge and generating new solutions by the virtual communities (Burger-Helmchen & Penin, 2010). This is done through externalisation. In this perspective, crowdsourcing has become a computational tool for collecting and expanding knowledge resources.

Second, knowledge sharing. The literature recognises a connection between crowdsourcing and knowledge sharing through a common platform on which participants interact and enter into discussions (Mazzolini & Maddison, 2007). The exchange of knowledge takes place through joint activities of the virtual communities (Kapur & Kinzer, 2007). Here, researchers focus on assessing the propensity to trust (Colquitt et al., 2007), defining the level of motivation (Budhathoki & Haythornthwaite, 2012) both internal (Roberts et al., 2006) and external (Ryan & Decy, 2000), evaluating the mental model (Fuller et al., 2007), ideas reported by the virtual community (Schall, 2012; Archak, 2010; Heipke, 2010), comparing answers with the ideas of other users (Karger, Shah, 2011), implemented incentive mechanisms (Heipke, 2010) for cooperation and coordination (Gao et al., 2011), posting comments by members of the virtual community (Sloane, 2011), participation duration, and the organisation's response time to the behaviours of the virtual community (Chen, Marsden & Zhang, 2012).

Thirdly, the use of knowledge. Many authors believe that crowdsourcing promotes a learning culture. Crowdsourcing is related to the so-called "collective intelligence" (Chi & Bernstein, 2012). It boils down to the fact that many people cooperate in making decisions, creating new products, or solving problems. This allows creating, through the joint effort of many people, new dynamic knowledge. Creating it through crowdsourcing platforms fosters the further development and using of knowledge, because it is generated and shared by people through dialogue, for example with the help of questions and answers.

In conclusion, many authors are convinced about the relationships between crowdsourcing and knowledge management – however there is a lack of in-depth research in this regard, in particular it is difficult to find research studies about the impact of crowdsourcing on knowledge-related processes. The formulated statements are rather general in their nature and they do not explore the subject. Moreover, it is pointed out in the literature that "although crowdsourcing is an effective way to collect ideas from large communities of heterogeneous users, our study shows that companies need to think about user-knowledge management in a more holistic way to complement and make benefit of users' knowledge" (Rajala, Westerlund, Vuori & Hares, 2013).

Crowdsourcing: Research Problems

Crowdsourcing is referred to in the literature as an organisational business process. Therefore, there are a number of actions that make it up. The typology that is referred to the most in the subject literature is the one introduced by Marjanovic et al., (2012). One may distinguish here: input, process, output, and outcome. A distinguishing feature for these actions is the level of interaction with the crowd. In input the problem is defined, the platform is advertised, calling forth and identifying potential suppliers of ideas or knowledge. The significance of this stage is emphasized here due to the fact that appropriate members of the crowd are selected as well as choosing incentives and motivators (Sloane, 2011). At this stage there a division of tasks into smaller elements also takes place. In the process there is organising, managing, coordination of actions, and focusing on building a crowd community, encouraging them to share knowledge and skills (Saxton & Kishore, 2013). Therefore, all of the actions should be oriented on building dependency and relations between the organisation and the crowd, which, as the authors point out, have impact on ensuring bilateral benefits. Therefore, constant monitoring and evoking the crowd to be active are indicated. In the action of the "output" members of the crown transfer ready-to-use solutions to the problem. Whereas, in the action of the "outcome" bilateral benefits are generated: both for the organisation and members of the crowd (Zwass, 2010). The main assumption here is the so-called value of co-creation – measured as the level of contribution and quality of involvement.

Other authors (Muhdi et al., 2011) point out to the following stages: deliberation (getting the organisation interested, establishing internal procedures, promoting platforms), preparation (establishing the expectations of the organisation, formulating tasks, planning internal resources), execution (grouping of the obtained ideas, monitoring progress, communication with the crowd), assessment (evaluation and selection and awarding the best ideas) post-processing (interpretation, preparing for implementation, realizing selected ideas). The authors underline that knowledge of processes and actions included in them may contribute to a success of crowdsourcing actions and obtaining benefits from them.

Crowdsourcing has gained on popularity in management sciences owing to its potential (Afuah & Tucci, 2013; Gassenheimer, Siguaw, & Hunter, 2013), among others: business process improvement (Balamurugan & Roy, 2013), creating open innovations (Brabham, 2008; Burger-Helmchen & Penin, 2010), building of competitive advantage (Leimeister & Zogaj, 2013), access to experience, innovativeness, information, crowd skills and work, which are located outside the organisation (Aitamurto, Leiponen, & Tee, 2011; Brabham, 2008; Vukovic & Bartolini, 2010). It started to be linked to initiating collaboration and relations with virtual communities (Yang et. al., 2008), further on using their wisdom (Surowiecki,

2004) to solve problems (Vukovic, 2009), participation management, increasing transparency and openness of public organisations (Brabham, 2015).Crowdsourcing also enables crisis management, expand existing activity and offer of the organisation, create the organisation's image, improve communication with the surroundings, and optimise costs of the organisation's activity. It also enables access to knowledge and creativity resources, facilitates acquiring of new contents and data (Kowalska, 2015; Chesbrough & Crowther, 2006; Chesbrough, 2010; Huston & Sakkab, 2006; Feller et al., 2012). Few researchers point out that studying the connections between crowdsourcing and organisational learning may be considered "an exciting new line of research" (Schlagwein & Bjørn-Andersena, 2014). It may constitute a new contribution and mechanism of learning by an organisation (Schlagwein & Bjørn-Andersena, 2014), a complement of the traditional one (Feller et. al., 2012).

Crowdsourcing: The Challenges

Crowdsourcing is an interdisciplinary phenomenon and a relatively new one. The growing interest in crowdsourcing has been observed since 2010. As of that year the number of publications has been constantly growing. This subject is undertaken by in the literature by representatives of various scientific disciplines: medical, technical, and economic sciences. Despite such dispersion, it is the object of researchers' interest in the context of open innovations, problem solving, executing tasks, optimising the costs of organisation activity, or as a tool of marketing and collaboration with the customer. However, it may continually be ascertained that research on this subject is difficult because its investigation is still relatively poor.

Currently a rapid interest in crowdsourcing of both researchers and practitioners can be observed. What is more, crowdsourcing is beginning to play a very important role in several areas, inter alia: medical sciences, technical sciences, and management sciences. It is becoming more and more frequently the subject of theoretical considerations and empirical research. As a consequence of such evolution various solutions are considered an expression of crowdsourcing. However, the multitude and diversity of approaches to crowdsourcing does not facilitate the chances to clarify and for transparency. Thus, it may lead to many misunderstandings.

Despite the proliferation of considerations on crowdsourcing there is no unanimity related to the definition of crowdsourcing. It is interpreted not only as a way to solve problems or a method of collecting ideas, but also as a term which accompanies all expressions of Web 2.0 technology. In the literature it is pointed out that crowdsourcing is a difficult concept, often obscure, capacious, and complex, moreover there is talk about the possibilities of defining a conceptual framework, common features, or elements of crowdsourcing. Sivula and Kantola (2015) aptly formulated the issue of defining crowdsourcing acknowledging that it encompasses the human element, which in this connection constitutes a challenge for researchers. Thus, it may be acknowledged that crowdsourcing is a social phenomenon and so such that exists owing to the actions of a social collectivity. As it is indicated by Gummesson (1993), social phenomena are not precise. In addition, a lack of consensus and a certain semantic confusion may be observed among researchers. Many terms such as open innovations, outsourcing, open resources are many a time used interchangeably. Nevertheless, crowdsourcing is recognised based on management sciences as a significant, highly up-to-date interesting, but relatively new, poorly structurised area of scientific research. A conviction even appears that crowdsourcing is a new, exciting research area, which in the next years will be a dynamic and live area of study.

The fact that crowdsourcing is a complex and multidimensional concept does not facilitate research on it. That is why not much is known in the literature. The existing investigations in the area of crowdsourcing focus, inter alia, on the following: acknowledging crowdsourcing as a new, emerging paradigm of online learning the coming into being of which took place along with introducing digital and online technologies. Other research concentrated on the assessment of crowdsourcing importance to open innovations, problem solving, cost optimising, organisational activity, and business process improvement. Definitely the majority of them are of a theoretical nature and placed in the American and Northern European reality, this particularly concerns the United States and Finland.

First, the crowd. Most authors agree that the principal substance of crowdsourcing is crowd wisdom (Surowiecki, 2004). Nonetheless, up until recently the notion of the "crowd" in sociology has been defined as a large collectivity of people who have found themselves in direct spatial contact and they react spontaneously, unreflectively, and imitatively to common stimuli and the co-presence of others (Sztompka, 2007). In this approach the crowd is irrational, aggressive, and threatening. In crowdsourcing the crowd is wise, rational, kind, investing in social capital, useful, and ready to solve problems (Wexler, 2011). It demonstrates a will to react and get involved. It is becoming a specific virtual community. The basis here is interaction, building relations, and common knowledge. It is acknowledged that a group is able to achieve and work out more benefits than any expert. The crowd's role is to carry out tasks, solve problems, or undertake any activity (Burger-Helmchen & Penin, 2010).

Second, importance to the organisation. Sparse research studies place crowdsourcing at the same level with an additional, routine resource or intraorganisational capabilities, a "floating" workforce for the organisation. Other definitions define crowdsourcing as a simple tool for collecting data (Fink et al., 2014). In their research Afuah and Tucci (2012) rightly paid attention to the need for differentiating between crowdsourcing and economic exchange. Economic exchange as a simple transaction ignores the need for possessing solid knowledge, absorptive ability or capability – which is necessary in crowdsourcing. In addition, it is hard to boil down crowdsourcing to the methods of recruitment or ways of acquiring knowledge because it may be useful in order to get access to diverse resources. Crowdsourcing is not limited to creating works of art. As it is written by Chesbrough (2010), crowdsourcing combines knowledge, creativity, and capabilities of the whole world. It may be helpful in anticipating sales, supply chain management, foreseeing the results of presidential elections, increasing the customer's experience in products and services of a given organisation. However, it cannot be considered as a cure-all – the lack of appropriate management may lead to negative results. The author points out that crowdsourcing may be mainly helpful in improving and achieving better results by the organisation.

Third, crowdsourcing and the levels of analysis. The next emerging problem for researchers dealing with the subject of crowdsourcing is the issue of a lack of coherence among the authors connected with locating this concept on different levels (Zhu & Zhao, 2012), i.e. organisation, intermediary, user, system, as well as application and assessment. From the organisation's perspective, the organisations are crowdsourcing initiators and applicants. It is presented from the position of organisational implementation, challenges, and possibilities of being used in the business environment. In the intermediary perspective the customers, the crowd, and technology (Zogaj et al., 2014), process requirements, assessment, managerial challenges that an intermediary may come across in connection with software development are studied. The system perspective assumes that crowdsourcing is a social and technical system. The authors identify here requirements connected with designing crowdsourcing platforms and software. The user's perspective includes motivation of the online community members. The perspective of applying assessing concerns evaluation of the efficiency or possibility of applying crowdsourcing in different contexts and at various stages of software development.

Crowdsourcing at the organisational level is noticeably dominant and widespread in management sciences. The researchers have also focused on the issue of crowd motivation and technical issues in the case of crowdsourcing platforms. Nonetheless, the multitude of diverse conceptualisations and approaches to crowdsourcing introduces a specific chaos. Some levels overlap. Certain researchers use the system and process level interchangeably. However, the main areas of the researchers' interest are crowdsourcing benefits and crowd motivation. Moreover, despite the postulates (Louis, 2013) there is a lack of in-depth and comprehensive multidimensional studies in this scope.

Fourth, crowdsourcing and the limit of providing its analysis with particulars. Integration of the basic assumptions of the conducted research on crowdsourcing enables ascertaining that generally in management sciences two conceptualisations are used, namely that of Howe and Brabham. The most frequently cited work related to crowdsourcing defines it as an "act of a company or institution taking a function once performed by employees and outsourcing it to an undefined (and generally large) network of people in the form of an open call. This can take the form of peer-production (when the job is performed collaboratively), but is also often undertaken by sole individuals". In his definition, Howe points out that crowdsourcing is connected with outsourcing and partner production. Nevertheless, Howe's conceptualisation seems to have some constraints. In outsourcing a provider selected by the organisation transfers services or products according to the requirements and an agreement. In crowdsourcing we are dealing with the crowd which is difficult to specify or define. Second, partner production. It assumes decentralisation of tasks, large dispersion of the team, independent choice of tasks based on self-assessment of skills and interests and treating the outcoming products or services as common goods available to a broader circle of recipients. Crowdsourcing should, however, be considered a broader concept: the crowd may also concentrate its actions on other activities. Third, open call. Differences appear, however, between crowdsourcing and open access. In crowdsourcing, organisations make use of their intellectual property rights, for instance, they implement the awarded ideas, whereas in open access they cannot be used.

ORGANISATION OF THE BOOK

The book fits in the trend of transformations that are currently taking place in the functioning of contemporary organisations, which more and more often reach for modern solutions, including crowdsourcing. The proposed book is the first item on the market, which reading will give at the same time theoretical and practical knowledge on the novelty, which knowledge management in crowdsourcing is. Its goal is better understanding and development of knowledge about the mechanisms of knowledge management in crowdsourcing. It should be emphasised that the state of knowledge on the management of knowledge in crowdsourcing is quite modest and fragmentary. This publication will contribute to eliminate the research gap in this scope and develop knowledge on the management of knowledge in crowdsourcing projects.

The book is divided into ten chapters. Below there is a short description of each chapter.

Chapter Descriptions

Chapter 1 takes up the subject of management fashion and an answer to the question whether crowdsourcing displays the features of management fashion is being sought in it.

Chapter 2 highlights the multi-dimensional aspects of deploying KM for e-Governance in a Federal Government system, along with its key objectives, core features moving on to framework and implementation structure.

Chapter 3 focuses on knowledge management in NGOs. NGOs are recognised as knowledge-intensive organisations in nature.

Chapter 4 focuses on crowdsourcing in Innovation Activity of Enterprises.

Chapter 5 provides a research model using an extension of social cognitive theory that comprises environmental factors (subjective norms, trust), personal factors (knowledge self-efficacy, enjoyment in helping others, organisational rewards, reciprocal benefits, and psychological ownership of knowledge), knowledge sharing behaviour and individual innovative work behaviour.

The goal of Chapter 6 is to provide an insight into the motivation mechanisms for the crowd to participate in crowdsourcing projects.

The aim of Chapter 7 is to analyse case studies of selected organisations in terms of their achievements in the use of social media. The profiling method applied in the study, facilitated evaluating the model of the selected organisation.

Chapter 8 makes the case that analytics methods must respond to the significant changes that big data challenges is bringing to operationalising the production of information and knowledge.

Chapter 9 presents crowd computing in a modern approach. Readers will be able to gain a fair comprehension of the various aspects of Crowd Computing and have an insight of the ecosystem of this computing paradigm.

Chapter 10 proposes development of a crowdsourcing platform as an essential step towards combating corruption, misuse, and embezzlement of funds. The developed system provides an up-to-date status of projects based on key indicators set and from this information a member can monitor and evaluate the progress of a given project.

Regina Lenart-Gansiniec
Jagiellonian University, Poland

REFERENCES

Afuah, A., & Tucci, C. L. (2012). Crowdsourcing As a Solution to Distant Search. *Academy of Management Review*, *37*(3), 355–375. doi:10.5465/amr.2010.0146

Aitamurto, T., Leiponen, A., & Tee, R. (2011). The promise of idea crowdsourcing: Benefits, contexts, limitations. *White Paper June*, *2*(30)

Andriole, S. J. (2010). Business impact of Web 2.0 technologies. *Communications of the ACM*, *53*(12), 67. doi:10.1145/1859204.1859225

Applehans, W., Globe, A., & Laugero, G. (1999). *Managing Knowledge. A Practical Web-Based Approach.* Addison-Wesley.

Archak, N. (2010). *Money, Glory and Cheap Talk: Analyzing Strategic Behavior of Contestants in Simultaneous Crowdsourcing Contests on Topcoder.Com*. Retrieved from http:// pages.stern.nyu.edu/~narchak/wfp0004-archak.pdf

Asrar-ul-haq, M., & Anwar, S. (2016). A systematic review of knowledge management and knowledge sharing: Trends, issues, and challenges. *Cogent Business & Management*, *3*(1), 1–17. doi:10.1080/23311975.2015.1127744

Balamurugan, Ch., & Roy, S. (2013). Human computer interaction paradigm for business process task crowdsourcing. *Proceedings of the 11th Asia Pacific Conference on Computer Human Interaction*, 364-273. 10.1145/2525194.2525294

Barney, J. (1991). Firm resources and sustained competitive advantage. *Journal of Management*, *17*(1), 99–120. doi:10.1177/014920639101700108

Bernhard, S. (Ed.). (2010). *Leveraging Applications of Formal Methods, Verification, and Validation.* Berlin: Springer.

Boudreau, K. J., & Lakhani, K. R. (2013). Using the crowd as an innovation partner. *Harvard Business Review*, *91*(4), 60–69. PMID:23593768

Brabham, D. C. (2008). Moving the crowd at iStockphoto: The composition of the crowd and motivations for participation in a crowdsourcing application. *First Monday*, *13*(6). doi:10.5210/fm.v13i6.2159

Brabham, D. C. (2015). *Crowdsourcing in the Public Sector*. Georgetown University Press.

Budhathoki, N. R., & Haythornthwaite, C. (2012). Motivation for Open Collaboration: Crowd and Community Models and the Case of OpenStreetMap. *The American Behavioral Scientist*, *57*(5), 548–575. doi:10.1177/0002764212469364

Bukowitz, W. R., & Williams, R. L. (2000). *The Knowledge Management Fieldbook, Financial Time*. London: Prentice Hall.

Burger-Helmchen, T., & Pénin, J. (2010). The limits of crowdsourcing inventive activities: What do transaction cost theory and the evolutionary theories of the firm teach us? *Workshop on Open Source Innovation*, France.

Burger-Helmchen, T., & Pénin, J. (2010). The Limits of Crowdsourcing Inventive Activities: What Do Transaction Cost Theory and the Evolutionary Theories of the Firm Teach Us? *Workshop on Open Source Innovation*, Strasbourg, France.

Cacciattolo, K. (2015). *Understanding Social Phenomenon, An Analysis of the Combination of Qualitative and Quantitative Methods to Understand Social Phenomenon*. Academic Press.

Callaghan, Ch. W. (2015). Crowdsourced R&D and medical research. *British Medical Bulletin*, *115*(1), 1–10. doi:10.1093/bmb/ldv035 PMID:26307550

Chen, L., Marsden, J. R., & Zhang, Z. (2012). Theory and analysis of company-sponsored value cocreation. *Journal of Management Information Systems*, *29*(2), 141–172. doi:10.2753/MIS0742-1222290206

Chesbrough, H. W. (2010). Business Model Innovation: Opportunities and Barriers. *Long Range Planning*, 43.

Chesbrough, H. W., & Crowther, A. K. (2006). Beyond High Tech: Early Adopters of Open Innovation in other Industries. *R & D Management*, *36*(3), 229–236. doi:10.1111/j.1467-9310.2006.00428.x

Chi, E. H., & Bernstein, M. S. (2012). Leveraging Online Populations for Crowdsourcing. *IEEE Internet Computing*, *16*(5), 10–12. doi:10.1109/MIC.2012.111

Colquitt, J. A., Scott, B. A., & LePine, J. A. (2007). Trust, trustworthiness, and trust propensity: A meta-analytic test of their unique relationships with risk taking and job performance. *The Journal of Applied Psychology*, *92*(4), 909–927. doi:10.1037/0021-9010.92.4.909 PMID:17638454

Cummings, J. N. (2004). Work groups, structural diversity, and knowledge sharing in a global organization. *Management Science*, *50*(3), 352–364. doi:10.1287/mnsc.1030.0134

Davenport, T. H., & Prusak, L. (1988). *Working Knowledge - How Organisations Manage What They Know*. Boston: Harvard Business School Press.

Doan, A., Ramakrishnan, R., & Halevy, A. Y. (2011). Crowdsourcing systems on the World-Wide Web. *Communications of the ACM*, *54*(4), 86–96. doi:10.1145/1924421.1924442

Drucker, P. F. (1999). *Społeczeństwo prokapitalistyczne*. Warszawa: PWN.

Estellés-Arolas, E., & González-Ladrón-de-Guevara, F. (2012). Towards an integrated crowdsourcing definition. *Journal of Information Science*, *38*(2), 1–14. doi:10.1177/0165551512437638

Faulkner, D., & Bowman, C. (1996). Strategie konkurencji. Gebethner i s-ka, Warszawa.

Feller, J., Finnegan, P., Hayes, J., & O'Reilly, P. (2012). Orchestrating sustainable crowdsourcing: A Characterisation of Solver Brokerages. *The Journal of Strategic Information Systems*, *21*(3), 216–232. doi:10.1016/j.jsis.2012.03.002

Fink, D., Hochachka, W., Zuckerberg, B., Winkler, D., Shaby, B., Munson, M., ... Kelling, S. (2010). Spatiotemporal Exploratory Models for Broad-Scale Survey Data. *Ecological Applications*, *20*(8), 2131–2147. doi:10.1890/09-1340.1 PMID:21265447

Fuller, A., Unwin, L., Felstead, A., Jewson, N., & Kakavelakis, K. (2007). Creating and using knowledge: An analysis of the differentiated nature of workplace learning environments. *British Educational Research Journal*, *33*(5), 743–759. doi:10.1080/01411920701582397

Galata, S. (2004). *Strategiczne zarządzanie organizacjami. Wiedza intuicja strategie etyka*. Warszawa: Difin.

Gao, S., Li, L., Li, W., Janowicz, K., & Zhang, Y. (2014). Constructing gazetteers from volunteered big geo-data based on Hadoop. *Computers, Environment and Urban Systems*, *61*, 172–186. doi:10.1016/j.compenvurbsys.2014.02.004

Gassenheimer, J. B., Siguaw, J. A., & Hunter, G. L. (2013). Exploring motivations and the capacity for business crowdsourcing. *Academy of Marketing Science*, *3*, 205–216.

Gummesson, E. (1993). Quality Management in Service Organisational. International Service Quality Association.

Halder, B. (2014). Evolution of crowdsourcing: Potential data protection, privacy and security concerns under the new Media Age. *Democracia Digital e Governo Eletrônico, Florianópolis*, *10*, 377–393.

Heipke, C. (2010). Crowdsourcing geospatial data. *ISPRS Journal of Photogrammetry and Remote Sensing*, *65*(6), 550–557. doi:10.1016/j.isprsjprs.2010.06.005

Howe, J. (2006). The Rise of Crowdsourcing. *Wired Magazine, 14*(6).

Howe, J. (2008). *Crowdsourcing: Why the Power of the Crowd Is Driving the Future of Business*. New York: Crown Publishing Group.

Huston, L., Sakkab, N. (2006). Connect and Develop. Inside Procter&Gamble's New Model for Innovation. *Harvard Business Review*.

Jain, R. (2010). *Investigation of Governance Mechanisms for Crowdsourcing Initiatives*. AMCIS Proceed.

Jeppesen, L. B., & Lakhani, K. R. (2010). Marginality and Problem Solving Effectiveness in Broadcast Search. *Organization Science, 21*(5), 1016–1033. doi:10.1287/orsc.1090.0491

Kapur, M., & Kinzer, C. (2007). Examining the effect of problem type in a synchronous computer-supported collaborative learning (CSCL) environment. *Educational Technology Research and Development, 55*(5), 439–459. doi:10.100711423-007-9045-6

Karger, D. R., Oh, S., Shah, D. (2011). Iterative. Learning for Reliable Crowdsourcing Systems. *Neural Information Processing Systems*, 1953-1961.

Kleeman, F., Voss, G. G., & Rieder, K. (2008). Un(der)paid Innovators: The Commercial Utilization of Consumer Work through crowdsourcing. Science. *Technology and Innovation Studies, 4*(1), 5–26.

Kogut, B., & Zander, U. (1992). Knowledge of the firm, combinative capabilities and the replication of technology. *Organization Science, 3*(3), 383–397. doi:10.1287/orsc.3.3.383

Kowalczyk, A., & Nogalski, B. (2007). *Zarządzanie wiedzą. Koncepcja i narzędzia*. Warszawa: Difin.

Kowalska, M. (2015). *Crowdsourcing internetowy – pozytywny wymiar partycypacji społecznej. Konteksty – istota – uwarunkowania*. Warszawa: Wydawnictwo Stowarzyszenie Bibliotekarzy Polskich.

Leimeister, J.M. (2012). Crowdsourcing: Crowdfunding, Crowdvoting, Crowdcreation. *Zeitschrift für Controlling und Management*, 56.

Leimeister, J. M., Huber, M., Bretschneider, U., & Krcmar, H. (2009). Leveraging Crowdsourcing: Activation-Supporting Components for IT-Based Ideas Competition. *Journal of Management Information Systems, 26*(1), 197–224. doi:10.2753/MIS0742-1222260108

Leimeister, J.M. & Zogaj S. (2013). Neue Arbeitsorganisation durch Crowdsourcing. *Hans-Böckler-Stiftung Arbeitspapier Arbeit und Soziales*, 287.

Levitt, T. (1991). *Marketing Imagination*. New York: The Free Press.

Louis, C.A. (2013). Organizational Perspectives of Open Innovation in Government. *iConference Proceedings*.

Majchrzak, A., & Malhotra, A. (2013). Towards an Information Systems Perspective and Research Agenda for Open Innovation Crowdsourcing. *The Journal of Strategic Information Systems*, 22.

Malone, T. W., Laubacher, R., & Dellarocas, C. (2010). The collective intelligence genome. *IEEE Engineering Management Review*, *38*(3), 38–52. doi:10.1109/EMR.2010.5559142

Marjanovic, S., Fry, C., & Chataway, J. (2012). Crowdsourcing based business models: In search of evidence for innovation 2.0. *Science & Public Policy*, *39*(3), 318–332. doi:10.1093cipolcs009

Mazzolini, M., & Maddison, S. (2007). When to jump in: The role of the instructor in online discussion forums. *Computers & Education*, *49*(2), 193–213. doi:10.1016/j.compedu.2005.06.011

McDermott, R. (1999). Why information technology inspired but cannot deliver knowledge management. *California Management Review*, *41*(4), 103–117. doi:10.2307/41166012

Muhdi, L., Daiber, M., Friesike, S., & Boutellier, R. (2011). The crowdsourcing process: An intermediary mediated idea generation approach in the early phase of innovation. *International Journal of Entrepreneurship and Innovation Management*, *14*(4), 315–332. doi:10.1504/IJEIM.2011.043052

Nahapiet, J., & Ghoshal, S. (1998). Social Capital, Intellectual Capital, and the Organizational Advantage. *Academy of Management Review*, *23*(2), 242–266.

Paulus, P. B., & Dzindolet, M. (2008). Social Influence, Creativity and Innovation. *Social Influence*, *3*(4), 228–247. doi:10.1080/15534510802341082

Probst, G., Raub, S., & Romhardt, K. (2002). *Zarządzanie wiedzą w organizacji*. Kraków: Oficyna Ekonomiczna.

Rajala, R., Westerlund, M., Vuori, M., & Hares, J. P. (2013, December). From Idea Crowdsourcing to Managing User Knowledge, Technology Innovation. *Management Review*.

Rigby, D. & Zook, C. (2002, October). Open-market innovation. *Harvard Business Review*.

Roberts, B. W., Walton, K. E., & Viechtbauer, W. (2006). Patterns of mean-level change in personality traits across the life course: A metaanalysis of longitudinal studies. *Psychological Bulletin, 132*(1), 3–27. doi:10.1037/0033-2909.132.1.1

Rouse, A. C. (2010). A preliminary taxonomy of crowdsourcing. *21st Australasian Conference on Information Systems*.

Ryan, R. M., & Deci, E. L. (2000). Self-determination theory and the facilitation of intrinsic motivation, social development, and well-being. *The American Psychologist, 55*(1), 68–78. doi:10.1037/0003-066X.55.1.68 PMID:11392867

Saxton, G. D., Oh, O., & Kishore, R. (2013). Rules of Crowdsourcing: Models, Issues, and Systems of Control. *Information Systems Management, 30*(1), 2–20. doi:10.1080/10580530.2013.739883

Schall, D. (2012). *Service-Oriented Crowdsourcing - Architecture, Protocols and Algorithms. Springer Briefs in Computer Science*. Springer.

Schemmann, B., Herrmann, A. M., Chappin, M. M. H., & Heimeriks, G. J. (2016). Crowdsourcing ideas: Involving ordinary users in the ideation phase of new product development. *Research Policy, 45*(6), 1145–1154. doi:10.1016/j.respol.2016.02.003

Schlagwein, D. & Bjorn-Andersen, N. (2014). Organizational Learning with Crowdsourcing: The Revelatory Case of LEGO. *Journal of the Association for Information Systems, 15*(11).

Sivula, A., & Kantola, J. (2015). Ontology focused crowdsourcing management. *Procedia Manufacturing, 3*, 632–638. doi:10.1016/j.promfg.2015.07.286

Sloane, P. (2011). *A Guide to Open Innovation and Crowdsourcing: Advice from Leading Experts*. Kogan Page Publishers.

Stańczyk-Hugiet, E. (2007). Strategiczny kontekst zarządzania wiedzą. Wydawnictwo Akademii Ekonomicznej we Wrocławiu, Wrocław.

Surowiecki, J. (2004). *The Wisdom of Crowds: Why the Many Are Smarter Than the Few and How Collective Wisdom Shapes Business, Economies, Societies, and Nations*. New York: Doubleday.

Tiwana, A. (2003). *Przewodnik po zarządzaniu wiedzą: e-biznes i zastosowania CRM*. Warszawa: Placet.

Trudell, E. (2014). *Crowdsourcing as a Tool for Knowledge Management*. Retrieved from https://web.jinfo.com/go/blog/71903

Vukovic & Bartolini. (2010). Towards a research agenda for enterprise crowdsourcing. *Leveraging applications of formal methods, verification, and validation*, 425-434.

Vukovic, M. (2009). Crowdsourcing for Enterprises. In SERVICES '09 Proceed of the 2009 Congr on Services - I (pp. 686-692). Los Angeles, CA: Academic Press.

Wang, S., & Noe, R. A. (2010). Knowledge sharing: A review and directions for future research. *Human Resource Management Review*, *115*, 20–22.

West, J., Salter, A., Vanhaverbeke, W., & Chesbrough, H. (2014). Open innovation: The next decade. *Research Policy*, *43*(5), 805–811. doi:10.1016/j.respol.2014.03.001

Wexler, M. N. (2011). Reconfiguring the sociology of the crowd: Exploring crowdsourcing. *The International Journal of Sociology and Social Policy*, *31*(1/2), 6–20. doi:10.1108/01443331111104779

Wikhamn, B. R., & Wikhamn, W. (2013). Structuring of the Open Innovation Field. *Journal of Technology Management & Innovation*, *8*(3), 173–185.

Yang, J., Adamic, L., & Ackerman, M. (2008). Crowdsourcing and knowledge sharing: strategic user behavior on Taskcn. *Proceedings of the 9th ACM International Conference on Electronic Commerce*. 10.1145/1386790.1386829

Zhao, Y., & Zhu, Q. (2012). *Exploring the Motivation of Participants in Crowdsourcing Contest*. ICIS Association for Information Systems.

Zogaj, S., Bretschneider, U., & Leimeister, J. M. (2014). Managing crowdsourced software testing: A case study based insight on the challenges of a crowdsourcing intermediary. *Journal of Business Economics*, *84*(3), 375–405. doi:10.100711573-014-0721-9

Zwass, V. (2010). Co-creation: Toward a taxonomy and an integrated research perspective? *International Journal of Electronic Commerce*, *15*(1), 11–48. doi:10.2753/JEC1086-4415150101

Acknowledgment

The editor would like to acknowledge the help of all the people involved in this project and, more specifically, to the authors and reviewers that took part in the review process. Without their support, this book would not have become a reality.

First, the editor would like to thank each one of the authors for their contributions. Our sincere gratitude goes to the chapter's authors who contributed their time and expertise to this book.

Second, the editor wish to acknowledge the valuable contributions of the reviewers regarding the improvement of quality, coherence, and content presentation of chapters. Most of the authors also served as referees; we highly appreciate their double task.

Regina Lenart-Gansiniec
Jagiellonian University, Poland

Chapter 1
Crowdsourcing as an Example of Public Management Fashion

Regina Anna Lenart-Gansiniec
Jagiellonian University, Poland

ABSTRACT

Crowdsourcing is a relatively new concept, which was defined for the first time only in 2006. The growing interest in crowdsourcing has been observed since 2010. As of that moment, the number of publications on crowdsourcing has been systematically increasing. The researchers' attention is frequently focused on the benefits possible to be obtained by the organization owing to crowdsourcing. Not without importance is the issue of cooperation with the crowd. Despite the growth tendency, it may still be ascertained that the multitude and diversity of approaches to crowdsourcing does not increase the chances for clarification and transparency. In their majority these papers are of a theoretical nature and rather dispersed and fragmentary. As a whole they do not make reference to the achievements of the predecessors. The subject of this chapter is searching for an answer to the question whether crowdsourcing displays the features of a public management fashion.

INTRODUCTION

It is stated more and more often in the literature on management sciences that the ideas of management are subject to fashion swings in the same way as the aesthetic aspects of life such as clothing styles, hair length, music tastes, furniture designs, or paint colours. They are characterised by a growth of popularity, and next by their decline. Such an approach is mainly justified by a neoinstitutional perspective, a lack of strong roots and institutionalisation of management, uncertainty about the

DOI: 10.4018/978-1-5225-4200-1.ch001

state and value of academic knowledge, but also admiration and quick abandoning of various techniques by the organisations. The term "fashion" refers to a generally accepted custom, which is subject to frequent changes. Fashion is characterised by a lack of stability, changeability, a transitory nature, opposition to existing tradition, unreflectiveness, dependency, superficiality, shallowness, an imitative character, originality, and a promise of rationality and progress (Abrahamson, 1996). The appearing novelties quickly gain on importance, but they also lose their popularity. It is their superficiality which causes that the changes introduced along with a fashion do not have their own identity, coherence, they are dependent and they refer to akin terms. This does not, however, boil down to creating new, import ant ideas or values. It stems from the fact that old customs, solutions become less attractive for their recipients and they receive new names, packaging, intended use, and rhetoric. Linking of elements of different models takes place in order to create new or add new elements to the existing fashion and thanks to that they are perceived as new concepts (Sturdy, 1997).

Fashion does not bypass management as well. Management fashion may be determined as "a relatively transitory collective belief, disseminated by management fashion setters that a management technique leads to rational management progress" (Abrahamson, Fairchild, 1999). Management fashions result from demand and supply on the market of knowledge, innovations, willingness to test and implement new ideas, but also refreshing forgotten ideas. This gives managers a chance to implement in the organisation innovations (Carson et al., 2000), which are offered by advisors and have received a high level of acceptance in other leading organisations across the globe.

The subject of this chapter is an attempt to answer the following question: does crowdsourcing show features of a management fashion? The starting point for the assumed considerations is the ascertainment that crowdsourcing is an interdisciplinary and relatively new concept. It has been taken up in the literature by representatives of various scientific disciplines, starting with medical sciences, through technical sciences, and ending with economic sciences. Despite such dispersion, it is the object of researchers' interest in the context of open innovations, problem solving, performing tasks, optimising costs of the organisation's activity, or as a tool of marketing and cooperation with the customer.

The chapter is composed of four parts. In the first one the definitions of management fashion and fad have been presented. The second part contains examples of applying crowdsourcing in the public sector. The third part includes considerations on crowdsourcing as a public management fashion. In the last, fourth part focus has been made on the future of crowdsourcing. To realise the goal of this chapter, a bibliometric analysis of publications from 2006 to 2017 published in the ProQuest scientific base was used.

MANAGEMENT FASHION

Management fashion is defined in various ways, inter alia, as a transitory collective belief (Abrahamson & Fairchild, 1999), "the production and consumption of temporarily intensive management discourse, and the organizational changes induced by and associated with this discourse" (Benders & van Veen, 2001, pp. 48-49). It is also defined as "managerial interventions which appear to be innovative, rational, and functional and are aimed at encouraging better organizational performance (Carson et al., 1999).

According to a market model of management fashions (Abrahamson, 1996) the creation, development, and dissemination of fashion is dependent on the ideas of fashion setters and the needs of its consumers (Lang & Ohana, 2012). As it is written by Abrahamson, "Management fashion setters disseminate management fashions, transitory collective beliefs that certain management techniques are at the forefront of management progress". The above-mentioned management fashion setters may include the authors of guidebooks, managers, advisors, consultants, the media, and business schools.

Searching for the causes of the attractiveness of the alternating management fashions, it is possible to indicate a radical detachment from the existing rules and practices, pressure, and need to increase effectiveness, the expectations of the stakeholders, and looking for solutions, which will enable the organisation to solve its ongoing problems (Crandall et al., 2006). This means that management fashions stem from the supply and demand on the market of knowledge, innovation, willingness to test and implement new ideas, but also refreshing the forgotten ones (Carson et 2000). This gives the managers an opportunity to implement new solutions, which the advisors offer and which have received a high level of acceptance in other, leading organisations worldwide. They are connected with an unreflective enchantment, fascination, and implementation of new approaches to management, considering them to be universal and useful for solving all of the organisation's problems (Abrahamson, 1996). Kieser (2001) acknowledges that management fashion allows for maintaining balance between simplicity and uncertainty, it becomes a simplification. It is not, however, simplicity – it is located between tradition and revolution. The need for an internal legitimisation is also one of the premises of introducing fashion into the organisation (Wilhelm & Bort, 2013; Staw & Epstein, 2000).

The notion of "fashion" may have pejorative connotations, which is connected with passive mimicking and quick fascination. Abrahamson presented fashion as a destructive phenomenon which has a negative impact on management practice (Abrahamson, 1991; Abrahamson, 1996; Kieser, 1996). He states that fashion leads to treating management sciences as an arena or catwalk where the setters promote further solutions – which drives sales of bestseller guidebooks (Micklethwait &

Wooldridge, 2000, p. 55). Management fashion may, however, be treated in a less critique way and it may be considered as a contribution to knowledge development and dissemination. For example Swanson and Ramiller (1997) emphasised the importance of fashion for creating the "organising vision", whereas Czarniawska and Joerges (1995) deemed fashion as a mechanism of diffusing ideas and concepts among organisations and their implementation.

It is also pointed out in the literature that in order for fashion not to be a negative phenomenon it should meet two conditions. Firstly, making reference to its roots – novelties contain elements of the previous concept that have been updated or given in a different form. It may be observed that reaching to the roots of a fashionable concept facilitates a critical analysis of the genuineness and originality of the proposed recommendations. The result of this condition is that there is a need for continuous modernising and improving the concept. Secondly, the usefulness for the organisation and justification for implementing a given fashion. In this case an attempt to determine the usefulness, making reference to the organisation's priorities, adaptation to its needs, potential benefits and possible threats connected with implementing the fashion in the organisation are important.

It is pointed out in the literature that fashions "exist in large part as linguistic artifacts" (Abrahamson & Eisenman, 2008), which in practice boils down to a rhetoric construction and not empirical analyses (p. 46). Benders and van Veen explain that the nature of the message is decisive to the possibilities of accepting a fashion. This means that the appearing novelties are translated from action to linguistic artefacts and *vice versa* (Czarniawska & Joerges, 1995), which appeal to managers more than scientific theories. As it is emphasised by Giroux "identifying and analyzing the particular trajectory of collections of texts is not a poor substitute for studying" (Giroux, 2006). Kieser (2001) acknowledges that we can thus speak of fashion when both terms, i.e. *buzzword* and *label* become the key words. In addition he ascertains that the means of persuasion used by the fashion setters have a mythical meaning. Openness to a myth is connected with a feeling of uncertainty about the future and a loss of control over what will come (Kieser, 1997).

The management fashion rhetoric, its attractiveness, pragmatic ambiguity (Giroux, 2006), incoherence, variation of interpretation, controversy, selectivity, positive connotations, easiness of memorising contribute to constituting, increasing the range and "interpretational viability of fashion" (Benders & van Veen, 2001; Røvik, 2011). Abrahamson, Eisenman (2008, pp. 719-744) ascertain that the language changeability depends on the course of fashion's life cycle and what strategy has been used by the fashion's protagonists. The greater the diversification in rhetoric (towards the previous fashion) the greater conviction about innovation and novelty. This diversification (Giroux, 2006) facilitates adaptation in situations of different and contradictory interests, coping with the complexity and variability of managerial problems (Astley & Zammuto, 1992).

A fashion's life cycle resembles the life cycle of a product and it comprises the following stages: introduction, mimicking, mass-scale, and decline (Abrahamson & Fairchild, 1999; Kieser, 1997; Perkman & Spicer, 2008; Rost & Osterloh, 2009). This means that fashions are subject to cyclic changes, according to which, first the fashion setters propagate a given fashion during lectures, in books, or through the rendered consulting services. Next, articles appear in the press which inform about the successes of those organisations which make use of a given fashion. In the next stage we can observe a massive interest in the novelty, which appears to be a cure-all for the organisation's every problem – which translates to a sudden increase in the number of publications and implementation of the novelty in the organisations. Gill and Whittle (1993) point out that management fashions are of a sudden nature – they disseminate by imitation, quick fascination, sudden interest, appreciation, and a growth of popularising events.

According to the life cycle of fashion, a situation may occur when its impact on practice is maintained a lot longer than the terminology connected with it – the terminology which remains in the consumers' consciousness (Nicolai & Dautwiz, 2010). The determinant of a given stage of fashion is the intensity of discourse in scientific and trade publications and managers' willingness to apply it (Lang & Ohana, 2012; Abrahmson & Eisenman, 2008). It may also happen that the number and intensity of the publications is not commensurate with the fashion's impact on management practice (Perkmann & Spicer, 2008; Madsen & Stenheim, 2014) – a quick increase in the number of publications may lead to quick abandonment. It is then when publications that overthrow a given fashion appear (Abrahamson & Fairchild, 1999). The second situation may be connected with disappointment, abandonment, and transition into another fashion – a decrease if social acceptance is observed at that point. Consequently, taking into account the arising difficulties connected with implementing the novelties, blurring of the whole concept, fashions are abandoned and make room for the next, seasonal ones. However, the decline of a fashion is not always connected with disappointment or appearance of a new fashion. Another reason is its institutionalisation and transition to another fashion. For the last fifty years the fashion's life cycle has been gradually shortened (Carson et al., 2000).

The possible institutionalisation of fashion is dependent on specific types of action. The more differentiated they are, the higher is the probability of the fashion's strengthening. According to Perkmann and Spicer (2008) political, technical, and cultural actions are discerned. Political actions are connected with creating a system of support, forming coalitions of entities interested in strengthening of a given fashion and institutional barriers related to applying a given fashion, for example examining or certifying. Within the framework of these actions, thematic conferences, workshops, training sessions, and symposiums sponsored by consulting firms are organised. The technical actions include formalisation, the effect of which is creating models, standards, procedures, and tools. The aim of cultural actions is linking fashion with the adopted standards and models, which leads to professionalisation of fashion. In connection with the fact that fashion is a social phenomenon (Ansari et al., 2010; Abrahamson, 1996) not without importance are the psycho-social factors connected with willingness to be distinguished or to imitate. The institutionalisation of fashion is also influenced by potential possibilities of obtaining advantages. The new concept, however, has to be consistent with the "standards of rationality and progress" (Abrahamson, 1996).

Management fashions mat be divided into two categories: ephemeral, quickly fading (Abrahamson, 2016) and relative stable (Madsen & Stenheim, 2014). Some researchers call the ephemeral and transitory fashions – a fad. Van der Wiele (1998) acknowledges that we may speak of a fad in a situation when there is a small group of people in the organisation who believe in the efficiency and sense of a given method, however, the interest in it is expanding and includes a bigger and bigger group of the organisation's members. They concern poorly defined aspects of management, which are not innovations, but only old ideas placed in a new packaging. Abrahamson and Eisenman (2008) think that fads result from a need to imitate the behaviours caused by three factors: (1) social tensions connected with a feeling of threat or appearing opportunity, (2) simplified and erroneous thinking which leads to making choices of management techniques under the influence of emotions and stress, (3) a decline of the previous fad. Fads, as seasonal fashions, constitute an accidental joining of forces that cause their diffusion (Abrahamson, 1991; Strang & Soule, 1998). They are distinguished by simplicity, possibility of simple and partial implementation, poor impact and dissemination, and a lack of social acceptance. Fads come and go equally fast and thus they have a minor impact on the management techniques (Cole, 1989) and organisational practices (Ghaziani & Ventresca, 2005). According to Stanga (2001) the dissemination of a fad may be explained by the mechanism of pluralist ignorance. According to it, the management staff do not privately agree with a given fad, they reject it, however, they do not present their negative attitudes, suppress their scepticism and assume that the majority of the employees accepts this fad.

This does not mean that fads are detrimental to the organisation. In the opinion of Cole, the organisation's interest in every novelty makes sense since it exercises the role of a mobilising factor which counteracts inertia in its life. Therefore, fads may be a value to the organisation. Adopting them enables the organisation to achieve an image of and innovative organisation. In the case of innovations, adopting fads may be less costly than rejecting them. Nonetheless, passive mimicking, limited information on the method itself and its potential threats may lead to excessive concentration on maximising the benefits and foster cognitive errors. Organisations will not be willing to admit their failures.

Undoubtedly, despite the attributed features, the scientific considerations on management fashion are justified. Klincewicz thinks that "management fashions are a natural element of the organisational reality, which is difficult to eliminate and which does not justify the critique of those who engage in the »fashionable« areas of the organisation" (Klincewicz, 2016). Analysing them enables perceiving the contribution of the concept in the development of research studies being aware of their features and ways of creation. On the one hand, the growth in popularity of a given method, approach in management practice, puts pressure and constitutes a serious challenge for researchers who deal with the problematic aspects connected with management sciences. Thus, it is a source o inspiration for them. Many a time fashion reveals the shortcomings both in the organisation's competences and management sciences. It is a natural method of developing the management concept, a stimulator of organisational changes and a creator of artefacts, which contribute to its institutionalisation – which may either lead to a gradual abandonment of the fashion or searching for new characteristics that would stimulate it. On the other hand, the growth of a scientific fashion decreases scientific reliability in favour of enthusiasm and emotions. Taking up an argumentative and substantive discussion after the interest in a given fashion diminishes may turn out to be helpful. This takes place after a sudden increase in popularising publications and the activity of consulting firms. In this context, scientific research becomes a reaction to a fading fashion. However, taking into account the complexity of the context in which fashions come into being and function – the dominant method connected with researching them is bibliometric research and an analysis of the writings' contents (Abrahamson, 1996).

CROWDSOURCING IN PUBLIC MANAGEMENT

The beginning of crowdsourcing may be dated back to 2006 when the editor of "Wired" magazine - Howe published an article entitled "The Rise of Crowdsourcing". He described how organisations make use of the Internet to establish cooperation with the customers and engage them in creating innovations. After consulting it with his editorial colleague Robinson, he published the definition of crowdsourcing on his blog one month after the article had appeared. He also developed and published the so-called "White Paper Version", in which he said that "crowdsourcing is the act of taking a job traditionally performed by a designated agent (usually an employee) and outsourcing it to an undefined, generally large group of people in the form of an open call" (Howe, The White Paper Version, www.crowdsourcing.com). With time, the author expanded this definition by applying the rules of the open source

(Howe, The Soundbyte Version, www.crowdsourcing.com). The author acknowledged crowdsourcing as a tool or method that helps organisations in acquiring free or cheap labour force.

The continuator of Howe's concept is Brabham. He proposed his first definition, following a cycle of numerous publications between 2008 and 2012, in his book entitled "Crowdsourcing" published in 2013. He stated that crowdsourcing is an online, dispersed model for solving problems and production, a tool for social participation, planning for the governments, and a method for building common resources or processing their great amount. It is also deliberate combining of a bottom-up, open, and creative process with the top-down organisational goals.

Since 2008 we have been observing tendencies to include crowdsourcing by local government units in their activity. Although in Poland it is in the phase of early development, overseas, in particular in the United States and the United Kingdom, it is becoming almost an obligation. Most often public organisations reach for crowdsourcing potential related to generating by the crowd of new ideas, testing products, services, and solving all kinds of problems. Crowdsourcing seems to facilitate the process of common designing. Moreover, it is a solution which helps local government units implement the postulates of open government. Crowdsourcing was used for the very first time by the government of the United Sates President Barack Obama and by the same token it became its specific precursor. It was then when several crowdsourcing projects were implemented: "Open Data", "Dear Mr. President", or "Challenge.gov". For example "Open Data" was a repository in which the virtual community had an opportunity to give examples of solutions to various problems. The "Dear Mr. President" platform enabled Internet users to write a letter to President Barack Obama in the form of a postcard. It was possible to describe their ideas for solving a nationwide problem. In the "Challenge.gov" project more than 80 governmental agencies have been able to place and address requests to the crowd for indicating innovative solutions to problems as well as improving ideas, products, or processes in public organisations. The winning ideas received awards and have been implemented. Since the moment of launching the portal more than 640 problems to be solved have been handed over to the crowd, over 220 million dollars have been spent on awards, more than 250 thousand users have participated, and more than 4.5 million people have visited the website.

It is possible to observe the interest in crowdsourcing in other countries as well. The city of Sao Paulo is using crowdsourcing to search among the crowd for ideas for the advancement of spatial development plans. Whereas, Santa Catarina in the Plamus project (http://www.plamus.com.br) asked the virtual community to solve problems connected with movement and transport. The presented selected examples of crowdsourcing initiatives indicate that crowdsourcing may and is more and more often used by local government units.

CROWDSOURCING IN FASHION, CROWDSOURCING AS A FASHION

Undoubtedly, we are currently able to observe a rapid interest in crowdsourcing, both by scientists and practitioners (West et al., 2014). The Google Trends service (https://trends.google.pl) indicates a growing trend for the entry - "crowdsourcing". This is also confirmed by an analysis of the number of publications devoted to crowdsourcing. In line with it, it can be acknowledged that crowdsourcing has been enjoying a greater interest among researchers. The publication trend figure in the case of publications found in English language bases, which is equal to R^2=0.668, proves a growing tendency of these publications. This result clearly shows that the number of publications has been increasing for the last 10 years.

Figure 1 presents the results of a bibliometric analysis for the entry *crowdsourcing* in the ProQuest base. Additional limitations have been imposed: full-text, reviewed publications, *crowdsourcing* in the title, abstract, and key words. Publications related to information technology, social, technical, mathematical, humanistic, and medical were excluded. Duplicating publications, books, dissertations, and book chapters were also eliminated. Articles in their full version published in journals and the so-called proceedings were included. The research covered English language publications. The graph suggests that the greatest interest, supported by the number of scientific publications, was reached in 2016. However, it is difficult to talk about a declining

Figure 1. Number of selected publications on crowdsourcing in the ProQuest base
Source: Own elaboration.

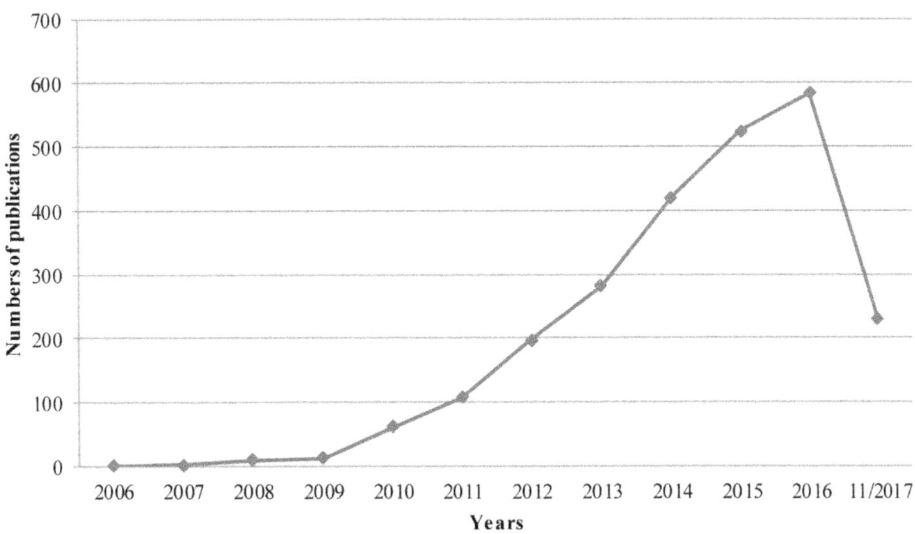

tendency. According to the management fashion life cycle by Abrahamson and Fairchild (1999), it signifies a long period of popularity.

Apart from the gradually growing interest of scientists in crowdsourcing, it is also possible to note various efforts which condition crowdsourcing institutionalisation, inter alia, conferences, sponsored by consulting and IT firms (e.g. "Crowdsourcing Week") are organised as well as workshops, symposiums, training sessions, most often ended with awarding a certificate or attestation of participation. Apart from this reports and papers are published (e.g. Deloitte's "Accenture Technology Vision" and "Tech Trends" reports). The phrase "crowdsourcing specialist" appears in announcements and requirements for certain posts (e.g. "Community & social media specialist" or "Community Manager"). Guidebooks appear on the publishing market (e.g. "Crowdsourcing for Dummies") and articles which popularise crowdsourcing (e.g. "Jak ugryźć crowdsourcing?" ("How to Grasp Crowdsourcing?") in the „Marketing w Praktyce" ("Marketing in Practice") journal, or "Crowd Wisdom" as the leitmotif in the "Harvard Business Review" magazine). In addition, there is a growing number of crowdsourcing platforms – at present there are over 150 platforms in operation in 28 thematic categories.

Although the interest in crowdsourcing has been intensifying for the last five years, according to some researchers reference can be made to it as far back as the 18th century: in 1714 the British government established the Longitude reward amounting to 20 thousand pounds for helping in elaborating simple and practical methods for determining the position of vessels on the sea. Another example is the announcement by Louis XVI in 1791 of a competition for developing a method of producing alkalies. In 1795, the French government announced a competition for developing a cheap and effective method for storing large quantities of food. Again, the French government, at the end of the 19th century established a prize for finding a substitute for butter that could be used by the armed forces. Another example of a crowdsourcing initiative was the call for developing an Oxford English language dictionary at the end of the 19th century. Crowdsourcing was also used for creating logotypes: in 1916 a company dealing with peanut production called "Planters" announced a competition for developing a logotype, whereas in 1936 Toyota also invited the public to design their logo. Governmental organisations also reached for the ideas of the society: in 1957 the Australian government organised a competition for designing the Sydney Opera House.

Opposite voices are also appearing: as it is stated by Afuah and Tucci crowdsourcing has been known for a long time, however it was only the arriving of the Internet and other communications technologies which opened many opportunities for this phenomenon (Afuah & Tucci, 2012). In the opinion of Brabham crowdsourcing is not "just old wine in new bottles". The author acknowledges that the examples from the 18th or 19th century are not examples of crowdsourcing because in crowdsourcing the organisation has a task to perform, while the online community carries it out voluntarily. The result of these actions are mutual benefits (Brabham, 2013). In addition, technologies and new media create the basis for participation and making use of knowledge found in online communities.

Therefore, a question appears whether crowdsourcing may turn out to be a fad or fashion. Bayus (2013) points out that crowdsourcing is innovative, inspired by crowd wisdom and has a long history that goes back to 1714 and the Longitude reward. The author thinks that the Internet has caused that reaching for the crowd's ideas and knowledge has become less expensive and easier to implement and it enables reaching a greater number of people. However, "crowdsourcing won't replace R&D departments anytime soon (…). While it can give valuable information in certain situations, the research I'm doing shows there are some issues to be aware of". Bayus emphasises, however, that the endeavours of various companies became the grounds for initiating theoretical and research work by scientists. However, he notices that not many crowdsourcing systems or platforms had lasted a few years, "they have no established history of successes or failures, so little is known about their long-term effectiveness" (Bayus, 2013). This may give evidence of a fad.

The next noticeable premise of a fad is the possibility of easy implementation. Tutorials and guidebooks of the "do it yourself" type give instructions on crowdsourcing implementation, i.e.: project definition, data preparation, project implementation, and its evaluation (Sabou et al., 2014). However, it is difficult to acknowledge the easiness of implementation Since more and more often it is mentioned that it is important to take into consideration the intraorganisational conditions (Dimitrova, 2013).

One of fad's symptoms is also a tendency to simplify. Crowdsourcing is a complex, multidimensional concept which is described by many theories and it is connected with many aspects fragmentarily identified by management sciences. Over the years crowdsourcing has been variously defined, which undoubtedly was a consequence of the growing interdisciplinary nature of the issue. This is reflected in different research perspectives. Furthermore, crowdsourcing is becoming to play a very important role in several areas, inter alia: medical sciences (Callaghan, 2015), technical sciences (Halder, 2014), and management sciences (Balamurugan & Roy, 2013). The existing research in the area of crowdsourcing focus on, inter alia: recognising crowdsourcing as a new emerging network learning paradigm (Albors et al., 2008), which appearance occurred along with the introduction of digital and network technologies. Other research studies concentrated on an evaluation of crowdsourcing importance to open innovations, problem solving, optimising the costs of the organisation's activity, and improving business processes. Most of them are of a theoretical nature and they are embedded in American and Northern European relations, this particularly concerns the United States and Finland.

THE FUTURE OF CROWDSOURCING

Opinions have been appearing that crowdsourcing may be detrimental to the organisation. Its greatest critics are those organisations in which the endeavour ended in failure. Many of them consider it to be a useless and harmful novelty. This results, above all, from the fact that crowdsourcing is based on virtual community. The crowd in crowdsourcing is not an unorganised, chaotic group, but it is rather a collectivity, which demonstrates a will to react and be engaged. It becomes a characteristic virtual community, which is united by interactions, relations, and common knowledge (Rheingold, 1993; Hsu et. al., 2007; Lin et al., 2008). This constitutes a confirmation that in crowdsourcing, a group may achieve and work out more benefits than any expert (Jeppesen & Lakhani, 2010; Leimeister, 2012). Its function is carrying out tasks, solving problems, or undertaking any activity (Burger-Helmchen & Penin, 2010; Jain, 2010; Basto et al., 2010). These communities are characterised by the following conditions: repeated involvement, active participation, strong emotional bonds, and common actions, access to common resources and defining the rules of access to them, mutuality of information, support, common context of social convention, language, and protocol, willingness to interact in order to satisfy one's needs, common interests, norms, which lead the relations, computer systems, which assure support, and integrity among members. And so, the members of the virtual community are interested in co-creating, initiating ideas, and assessing ideas of others who participate in crowdsourcing (Schemmann et al., 2016). Seemingly, it may appear that from the point of view of the initiator of crowdsourcing a large number of acquired ideas and active members of the virtual communities are invaluable. However, paraphrasing the statement "every excess becomes a vice" – a broad user base can also have negative effects on user engagement. It was stated in the literature that when a community surpasses a certain number of active users, idea generation is negatively affected (Chan et al., 2015).

The supporters of crowdsourcing think that discarding crowdsourcing is unjustified and detrimental.

Klososky (2011) ascertains that crowdsourcing is a new tool which may not be ignored. This is supported by the benefits which organisations can obtain when they implement it. Sherman (2011) thinks that crowdsourcing is not a temporary fashion or fad and sees in it a new method of working, acquiring knowledge from others. She recognises that the current online form of crowdsourcing may change with the appearance of new technologies, such as online networks, or actions in the "cloud". New applications of crowdsourcing may also appear, e.g. for crime detection (https://www.cnet.com/news/wisdom-of-the-crowd-jeremy-piven-solving-crimes-crowdsourcing-a-dangerous-game), in the cultural heritage (https://cdh.princeton.edu/events/2017/10/crowdsourcing-cultural-heritage-communitiesprozhito-project-perspective), agriculture (http://documents.worldbank.org/curated/en/455701468340165132/ICT-in-agriculture-connecting-smallholders-to-knowledge-networks-and-institutions), and medicine (www.malariaspot.org). The justification for orientation on crowdsourcing is underlined by Majchrzak and Malhotra (2013). They think that "the community of scholars that succeeds at this reorientation may be doing nothing less than defining a new basis for strategic competition in the years to come".

According to the "The State of Crowdsourcing 2015" report the organisations' interest in crowdsourcing has been growing from year to year, the effect of which is that using company websites and the social media has decreased in the last years. The authors of the report concluded that it is three times more likely that a crowdsourcer (an organisation, which initiates crowdsourcing) will use a crowdsourcing platform than company websites or the social media to contact the customers. Zhao and Zhu (2014) state that crowdsourcing is one of the trends based on Web 2.0, which should be analysed by scientists. They think that "a good opportunity for scholars is to pay more attention to this research area and contribute to what is likely to be not only a significant scholarly endeavour, but also one with important implications to benefit people, organizations, and societies. It should be noted that although we identify several essential research directions for future investigation, the list is by no means complete. Some social, cultural, and ethical issues are also very important to investigate in future studies" (Zhao & Zhu, 2014). According to J. Howe (2006) "crowdsourcing is outsourcing on steroids", which means that it is not a new concept, but with new possibilities of application and development perspectives. This is confirmed by the results of research conducted by Gartner company, which say that within 2018, 75% of worldwide companies will be using crowdsourcing. This is supported by the benefits that are possible to be obtained.

FUTURE RESEARCH DIRECTIONS

From a methodological point of view a bibliometric analysis, as every other method, has some limitations, which stem from accessibility and completeness of the databases. Moreover, the language of the publications poses a constraint. In connection with the imposed limitations only English language publications were the subject of analysis. This leads to dependency on the quality and accessibility of the scientific publications. A useful step for conducting studies connected with crowdsourcing as a management fashion would be to use the discourse life-cycle analysis. It is an approach used for studying the volume and nature of a discourse on a fashion in a given period of time. This usually takes place through a bibliographic and content analysis, separating different modes of discourse – the mass media, the Internet, trade/business press, and academic press (journals and dissertations). Such usage of the term "discourse" significantly differs from the post-modernist theories of discourse analysis (see: Brown & Yule, 2003). In addition, it would be important to take a look at the actual dissemination of the key issues connected with crowdsourcing both by an analysis of the secondary data from other research studies and in field observation to observe the current acceptance of crowdsourcing in the commercial and public sectors. Not without importance would be research on the understanding of the nature and process of accepting by the organisations of management fashion, the role of the fashion setters in its dissemination, and finally at present little is known about the impact of management fashion on the public organisation managers.

CONCLUSION

Crowdsourcing is a relatively new concept in public management; nonetheless it has been raising more and more interest. The constant growth of the number of theoretical publications and empirical research and their intensity confirm the coevolution of the discourse and practical applications of crowdsourcing in public organisations. Its popularisation started with the trend setters i.e. people from the advisory and consulting companies' environment. It is also possible to note may actions oriented on crowdsourcing institutionalisation: workshops, conferences, guidelines, and certificates. This has led to a very quick interest, implementing in organisations and considering crowdsourcing as a remedy to all of the organisation's problems. However, despite the growing interest, knowledge about it is still fragmentary and dispersed and the number of theoretical and empirical papers is still relatively low. This may lead to a conclusion that at the present development stage it is not possible to exclude a chance that crowdsourcing will grow strong and become permanently embedded in practice and theory. The above-mentioned premises aim at giving crowdsourcing the name of public management fashion.

ACKNOWLEDGMENT

This project was financed from the funds provided by the National Science Centre, Poland awarded on the basis of decision number DEC-2016/21/D/HS4/01791.

REFERENCES

Abrahamson, E. (1991). Managerial Fads and Fashions: The diffusion and rejection of innovations. *Academy of Management Review*, *16*, 586–612.

Abrahamson, E. (1996). Management fashion, academic fashion, and enduring truths. *Academy of Management Review*, *21*(3), 616–618.

Abrahamson, E., & Eisenman, M. (2008). Employee-management techniques: Transient fads or trending fashions? *Administrative Science Quarterly*, *53*(4), 719–744. doi:10.2189/asqu.53.4.719

Abrahamson, E., & Fairchild, G. (1999). Management fashion: Lifecycles, triggers, and collective learning processes. *Administrative Science Quarterly*, *44*(4), 708–740. doi:10.2307/2667053

Afuah, A., & Tucci, C. L. (2012). Crowdsourcing as a solution to distant search. *Academy of Management Review*, *37*(3), 355–379. doi:10.5465/amr.2010.0146

Albors, J., Ramos, J. C., & Hervas, J. L. (2008). New learning network paradigms: Communities of objectives, crowdsourcing, wikis and open source. *International Journal of Information Management*, *28*(3), 194–202. doi:10.1016/j.ijinfomgt.2007.09.006

Ansari, S. M., Fiss, P. C., & Zajac, E. J. (2010). Made to fit: How practices vary as they diffuse. *Academy of Management Review*, *35*(1), 67–92. doi:10.5465/AMR.2010.45577876

Astley, W. G., & Zammuto, R. F. (1992). Organization Science, Managers and Language Games'. *Organization Science*, *3*(4), 443–460. doi:10.1287/orsc.3.4.443

Basto, D., Flavin, T., & Patino, C. (2010). *Crowdsourcing Public Policy Innovation*. Working Paper, Heinz College Carnegie Mellon University.

Bayus, B. L. (2012). *Crowdsourcing New Product Ideas Over Time: An Analysis of Dell's Ideastorm Community*. UNC Kenan-Flagler Research Paper 5.

Benders, J., & van Veen, K. (2001). What's in a fashion? Interpretative viability and management fashions. *Organization*, *8*(1), 48–49. doi:10.1177/135050840181003

Brabham, D. C. (2013). *Using crowdsourcing in government*. Washington, DC: IBM Center for the Business of Government.

Brown, G., & Yule, G. (2003). *Discourse Analysis*. Cambridge, UK: Cambridge University Press.

Burger-Helmchen, T., & Pénin, J. (2010). The limits of crowdsourcing inventive activities: What do transaction cost theory and the evolutionary theories of the firm teach us? *Workshop on Open Source Innovation*, France.

Callaghan, C. W. (2015). Crowdsourced 'R&D' and medical research. *British Medical Bulletin*, *115*(1), 1–10. doi:10.1093/bmb/ldv035 PMID:26307550

Carson, P. P., Lanier, P. A., Carson, K. D., & Birkenmeier, B. J. (1999). A historical perspective on fad adoption and abandonment. *Journal of Management History*, *5*(6), 320–333. doi:10.1108/13552529910288109

Carson, P. P., Lanier, P. A., Carson, K. D., & Guidry, B. N. (2000). Clearing a path through the management fashion jungle: Some preliminary trailblazing. *Academy of Management Journal*, *43*(6), 1143–1158. doi:10.2307/1556342

Chan, K., Li, S., & Zhu, J. (2015). Fostering Customer Ideation in Crowdsourcing Communities: The Role of Online Interactions with Peers and Firm. *Journal of Interactive Marketing*, *31*, 42–62. doi:10.1016/j.intmar.2015.05.003

Cole, R. E. (1989). *Strategies for Learning: Small Group Activities in American, Japanese, and Swedish Industry*. Berkeley, CA: University of California Press.

Crandall, W. R., Crandall, R. E., & Ashraf, M. (2006). *The perilous world of management fashion: An examination of their life cycles and the problem of scholarly lags*. Atlanta, GA: Academy of Management Proceedings.

Czarniawska-Joerges, B. (1995). Narration or Science? Collapsing the division in organization studies. *Organization*, *2*(1), 11–33. doi:10.1177/135050849521002

Dimitrova, S. G. (2013). *Implementation of Crowdsourcing into Business and Innovation Strategies: A Case Study at Bombardier Transportation, Germany*. Retrieved December 1, 2017, from https://publications.polymtl.ca/1311/1/2013_Sylvia_GueorguievaDimitrova.pdf

Ghaziani, A., & Ventresca, M. J. (2005). Keywords and Cultural Change: Frame Analysis of Business Model Public Talk, 1975-2000. *Sociological Forum*, *20*(4), 523–559. doi:10.100711206-005-9057-0

Gill, J., & Whittle, S. (1993). Management by panacea: Accounting for transience. *Journal of Management Studies*, *30*(2), 281–295. doi:10.1111/j.1467-6486.1993.tb00305.x

Giroux, H. (2006). It was such a handy term: Management fashions and pragmatic ambiguity. *Journal of Management Studies*, *43*(6), 1227–1260. doi:10.1111/j.1467-6486.2006.00623.x

Halder, B. (2014). Evolution of crowd sourcing: Potential data protection, privacy and security concerns under the new media age. *Revista Democracia Digital e Governo Eletrônico*, *1*(10), 377–393.

Howe, J. (2006). The Rise of Crowdsourcing. *Wired Magazine*, *14*(6), 1–4.

Howe, J. (n.d.a). *The Soundbyte Version*. Retrieved December 1, 2017, from http://www.crowdsourcing.com

Howe, J. (n.d.b). *The White Paper Version*. Retrieved December 1, 2017, from http://www.crowdsourcing.com

Jain, R. (2010). Investigation of Governance Mechanisms for Crowdsourcing Initiatives. *AMCIS Proceedings*.

Jeppesen, L. B., & Lakhani, K. R. (2010). Marginality and Problem-Solving Effectiveness in Broadcast Search. *Organization Science*, *21*(5), 1016–1033. doi:10.1287/orsc.1090.0491

Kieser, A. (1996). Moden und Mythen des Organisierens. *Die Betriebswirtschaft*, *56*, 21–40.

Kieser, A. (1997). Rhetoric and my thin management fashion. *Organization*, *4*(1), 49–74. doi:10.1177/135050849741004

Klincewicz, K. (Ed.). (2016). *Zarządzanie, organizacje i organizowanie – przegląd perspektyw teoretycznych*. Warszawa: Wydawnictwo Naukowe Wydziału Zarządzania Uniwersytetu Warszawskiego. doi:10.7172/978-83-65402-29-5.2016.wwz.9

Klososky, S. (2011). *Enterprise social technology*. Austin, TX: GreenLeaf Book Group Press.

Lang, G., & Ohana, M. (2012). Are management fashions dangerous for organizations? *International Journal of Business and Management*, *7*(20), 81–89. doi:10.5539/ijbm.v7n20p81

Leimeister, J. M. (2012). Crowdsourcing, Crowdfunding, Crowdvoting, Crowdcreation. *Zeitschrift für Controlling und Management*, *56*(6), 388–392. doi:10.136512176-012-0662-5

Madsen, D. O., & Stenheim, T. (2014). Perceived benefits of balanced scorecard implementation: Some preliminary evidence. *Problems and Perspectives in Management, 12*(3), 81–90.

Majchrzak, A., & Malhotra, A. (2013). Towards an Information Systems Perspective and Research Agenda on Crowdsourcing for Innovation. *The Journal of Strategic Information Systems, 22*(4), 257–268. doi:10.1016/j.jsis.2013.07.004

Micklethwait, J., & Wooldridge, A. (2000). *Szamani zarządzania*. Poznań: Zysk i S-ka.

Nicolai, A. T., & Dautwiz, J. M. (2010). Fuzziness in Action: What Consequences Has the Linguistic Ambiguity of the Core Competence Concept for Organizational Usage? *British Journal of Management, 21*(4), 874–888. doi:10.1111/j.1467-8551.2009.00662.x

Perkmann, M., & Spicer, A. (2008). How are management fashions institutionalized? The role of institutional work. *Human Relations, 61*(6), 811–844. doi:10.1177/0018726708092406

Rost, K., & Osterloh, M. (2009). Management Fashion Pay-for-Performance for CEOs. *Schmalenbach Business Review, 61*(2), 119–149. doi:10.1007/BF03396781

Røvik, K. A. (2011). From fashion to virus: An alternative theory of organizations' handling of management ideas. *Organization Studies, 32*(5), 631–653. doi:10.1177/0170840611405426

Roy, S., Balamurugan, C., & Gujar, S. (2013). Sustainable employment in India by crowdsourcing enterprise tasks. *Proceedings of the 3rd ACM Symposium on Computing for Development*. 10.1145/2442882.2442904

Sabou, M., Bontcheva, K., Derczynski, L., & Scharl, A. (2014). Corpus Annotation through Crowdsourcing: Towards Best Practice Guidelines. *Proceedings of the Conference on Language Resources and Evaluation (LREC).*

Schemmann, B., Herrmann, A. M., Chappin, M. M. H., & Heimeriks, G. J. (2016). Crowdsourcing Ideas: Involving Ordinary Users in the Ideation Phase of New Product Development. *Research Policy, 45*(6), 1145–1154. doi:10.1016/j.respol.2016.02.003

Sherman, A. (2011). *How 3 Cities Are Crowdsourcing for Community Revitalization*. Retrieved December 1, 2017, from http://mashable.com/2011/07/20/crowdsourcing-city-tech/

Staw, B., & Epstein, L. (2000). What bandwagons bring: Effects of popular management techniques on corporate performance, reputation, and CEO pay. *Administrative Science Quarterly, 45*(3), 553–556. doi:10.2307/2667108

Strang, D., & Soule, S. A. (1998). Diffusion in Organizations and Social Movements: From Hybrid Corn to Poison Pills. *Annual Review of Sociology, 24*(1), 265–290. doi:10.1146/annurev.soc.24.1.265

Sturdy, A. (1997). The consultancy process – An insecure business? *Journal of Management Studies, 34*(3), 389–413. doi:10.1111/1467-6486.00056

Swanson, E. B., & Ramiller, N. C. (1997). The organizing vision in information systems innovation. *Organization Science, 8*(5), 458–474. doi:10.1287/orsc.8.5.458

West, J., Salter, A., Vanhaverbeke, W., & Chesbrough, H. (2014). Open innovation: The next decade. *Research Policy, 43*(5), 805–811. doi:10.1016/j.respol.2014.03.001

Wiele, van der A. (1998). *Beyond Fads: Management Fads and Organizational Change with Reference to Quality Management.* Delft: Eburon Publishers.

Wilhelm, H., & Bort, S. (2013). How managers talk about their consumption of popular management concepts: Identity, rules and situations. *British Journal of Management, 24*(3), 428–444. doi:10.1111/j.1467-8551.2012.00813.x

Zhao, Y. Ch., & Zhu, Q. (2014). Effects of Extrinsic and Intrinsic Motivation on Participation in Crowdsourcing Contest. *Online Information Review, 38*(7), 896–917. doi:10.1108/OIR-08-2014-0188

KEY TERMS AND DEFINITIONS

Crowdsourcing: The act of taking a job traditionally performed by a designated agent (usually an employee) and outsourcing it to an undefined, generally large group of people in the form of an open call.

Management Fad: A transitory fashion, the interest in which does not last longer than 5 years.

Management Fashion: A relatively transitory collective conviction, knowledge disseminated by entrepreneurs that a certain management technique will contribute to management progress.

Web 2.0: A collective term for certain applications of the Internet and the World Wide Web, including blogs, wikis, video sharing services, and social media websites such as Facebook and MySpace, which focus on interactive sharing and participatory collaboration rather than simple content delivery.

Chapter 2
Knowledge Management System for Governance:
Transformational Approach Creating Knowledge as Product for Governance

Shilohu Rao N. J. P.
Digital India Corporation, India

Ravi Shankar Chaudhary
Digital India Corporation, India

Dhrubajit Goswami
Digital India Corporation, India

ABSTRACT

Knowledge is power, and when managed efficiently, it generates optimum outcomes. Knowledge management is an established phenomenon, applied across various disciplines for transformational growth. In the year 2015, the Government of India launched Digital India Programme with the vision to "transform India into a digitally empowered society and knowledge economy." The program aims to benefit every section and sector of the country by creating an ecosystem for delivery of user centric and qualitative digital services. It weaves together a large number of ideas and thoughts into a single, comprehensive vision so that each of them is seen as part of a larger goal. To foster such knowledge economy, Capacity Building Scheme Phase II has been approved under Digital India Programme with one of the key components being knowledge management (KM) in the area of e-governance. This chapter highlights the multi-dimensional aspects of deploying KM for e-governance in a federal government system, along with its key objectives, core features moving on to framework and implementation structure.

DOI: 10.4018/978-1-5225-4200-1.ch002

INTRODUCTION

Acquiring knowledge is a continuous process which involves analyzing and identifying the patterns in pieces of information. It is in the higher echelon composed of data, information and knowledge. As a matter of fact, knowledge is an intellectual asset of any organization. The transformation from information societies to knowledge societies has begun to empower and enhance the self-development capacities of individuals, communities and societies as a whole. It helps people in utilizing the facilities available through digital infrastructure.

Knowledge Societies are identified as societies based on the creation, dissemination and utilization of information and knowledge. They are societies with economies through which knowledge is acquired, created, disseminated and applied to enhance economic and social development (GESCI, 2012). According to UNESCO, "Knowledge Societies are societies in which people have the capabilities not just to acquire information but also to transform it into knowledge and understanding, which empowers them to enhance their livelihoods and contribute to the social and economic development of their communities" (Engida, 2016). Knowledge Societies can also be defined as human-structured organizations based on contemporary knowledge and representing new quality of life support systems. This implies the need for understanding of distribution of knowledge, access to information and capability to transfer information into knowledge (Afgan & Carvalho, 2010).

KM has been defined by Davenport (1994) as the process of capturing, distributing, and effectively using knowledge. A later definition was provided by Duhon (1998) as "KM is a discipline that promotes an integrated approach to identifying, capturing, evaluating, retrieving, and sharing all of an enterprise's information assets. These assets may include databases, documents, policies, procedures, and previously un-captured expertise and experience in individual workers."

One of the most commonly used definitions on KM is provided by Nonaka and Takeuchi (1995), who defined KM as the substantiated understandings and beliefs in an organization about the organization and its environment. They also differentiated between two types of knowledge: explicit and tacit. Explicit knowledge is codified, easily translated and shared facts and information. It exists in reports and other documents. Tacit knowledge is personal knowledge that is hard to confirm and share with others. It is the private understanding and knowledge that people have about issues, problems, solutions, services, and products etc. A major area of KM is to turn tacit knowledge into explicit knowledge.

Three converging trends are behind the drive by organizations to gain better control of their information infrastructure and management of the tacit and explicit knowledge held by their personnel and the knowledge repositories in the organization. The first trend is the expected increased turnover of knowledge workers. The second trend is the push of Government to implement e-Governance at all levels – there has been increase in the amount and variety of online services available to citizens. Many Government agencies are also providing mobile communications capability to their knowledge workers, thus enabling them to communicate as information is gathered. The third trend is continued emphasis on shared services to achieve greater operational efficiencies (McNabb, 2007).

The Knowledge Management envisioned by National e-Governance Division (NeGD) is unique in its own kind under Digital India flagship programme. It is a transformational multi-phase approach adopted to establish a knowledge sharing culture for growth in the Government system. The initial phase of Knowledge Management implementation covers inter-departmental i.e. NeGD, followed by Knowledge Management at Ministry of Electronics & Information Technology (MeitY) and finally reaching out to Mission Mode Projects (MMPs) under e-Kranti mission (e-Kranti is an e-Governance plan initiated by the Government of India) of other ministries and departments in the federal Government of India.

In order to spearhead these initiatives for managing knowledge resources, NeGD conceptualized the broad framework for implementing the KM System for e-Governance with a view to harvest innovative & effective methods/ tools for enabling ease of adoption and operationalisation. This initiative has progressed with development of a responsive Knowledge Management System (KMS) in both web portal as well as mobile application has been completed and is anticipated to contribute to the vision of an empowered knowledge economy in India.

This paper is an effort to present various aspects of the KMS by NeGD based on their journey taken so far with the effort of providing insights into the benefits that can be reaped with a simple initiative of adoption of KMS in any public organization.

CONCEPTUAL BACKGROUND OF KMS FOR E-GOVERNANCE

Ecosystem of KMS for e-Governance

An initiative under the CB- II scheme under Digital India, KMS for e-Governance is expected to help in managing the skill, scale and speed of e-Governance projects. The ecosystem of KMS encompasses the following:

- **NeGD:** Preparing vision & strategic objectives, defining functionality & scope, conducting reviews etc.
- **KM Team:** Coordinating with stakeholders, incorporating feedback, managing project, reporting etc.
- **KMS Governance:** Overseeing the KM initiative, approving budget etc.

- **KMS Advisory Committee:** Providing guidance and expertise to the KM initiative, suggesting roadmap for KMS implementation, providing leads for collaboration with international Governments/ multilateral institutions towards inculcating best practices on KM.
- **KMS Implementation Committee**: Monitoring the execution of KMS initiative, creating policy for KMS usage and making regulations to protect the integrity of knowledge assets.
- **System Developer for KMS:** Designing the KM solution, providing technical support during operations & maintenance.
- **Knowledge Managers/ Champions:** Uploading, reviewing & enhancing knowledge objects, highlighting the best practices nationally/ internationally with respect to KM processes and work flows.
- **People & Culture:** Collaboration, change management, replication and recognition.
- **Other Systems:** Integration with Learning Management System (LMS), Project Management System (PMS), Human Resource Management System (HRMS) etc.
- **Beneficiaries:** NeGD, SeMTs, MeitY, MMPs.

The ecosystem of KMS for e-Governance has been depicted in Figure 1.

Figure 1. Ecosystem of KMS for e-Governance

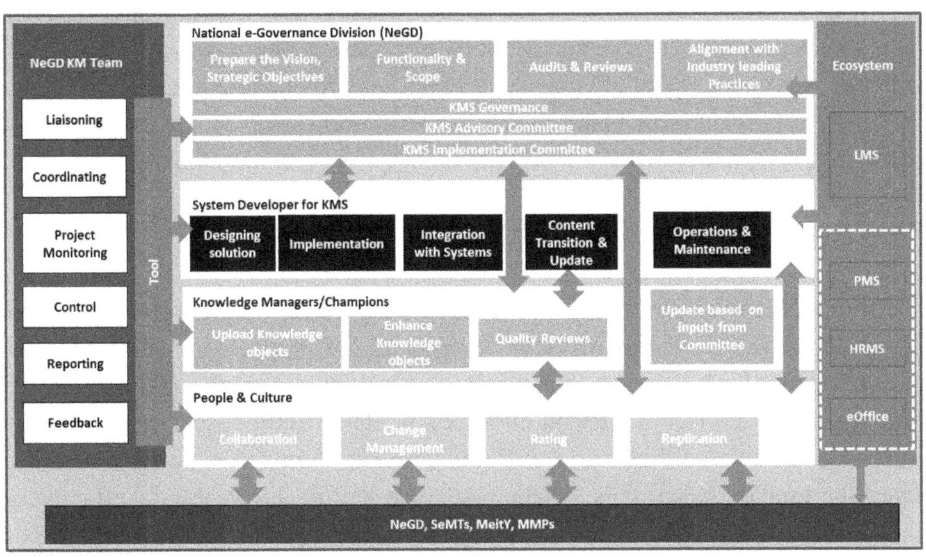

KMS has been envisioned to provide impetus in enabling and sustaining a collaborative ecosystem for knowledge sharing across all levels of Government, thus transforming the e-Governance workforce into smart contributors and learners in a 'knowledge sharing culture'.

Need for KMS

Timely execution of Government projects has been crucial. It necessitates dissemination of good practices so that the same could be replicated judiciously elsewhere towards managing projects effectively. A need was realized for documenting the scattered knowledge accumulated over time that can be utilized to enhance the skills of man-power. Further, the danger of losing knowledge due to retirement/ transfers of Government officials was a major concern. These factors together prepared the ground for development of KMS by NeGD.

The Digital India vision provides impetus for momentum and progress on e-Governance initiatives to promote inclusive growth that comprises electronic services, products, devices, manufacturing and job opportunities. India in the 21st century must strive to meet the aspirations of its citizens where Government and its services reach their doorsteps and contribute towards sustained development. There is a requirement to build adequate and relevant capacities at all levels thriving on the large knowledge base that already exists in tacit, explicit and embedded form in the Government sector in India. The experience of the project implementation and workforce of the Government needs to be captured as lessons learnt – this will help in providing insights to the Government personnel, executing projects under Digital India. Since time is of essence and delivery in services is of utmost importance, it is imperative to create a pool of knowledge which can provide references and insights into the decisions and work being undertaken at different levels for executing various projects.

Key Objectives/ Functions of KMS

Collaboration and creation of a knowledge culture are the broad objectives, based on which the foundation of KMS has been built. It is expected to meet multiple objectives. Firstly, enhance organizational value by enabling employees to intuitively find, share and connect to relevant information related to the Government policies and processes by providing a congenial environment through the portal. Secondly, equip the employees to work together to solve day to day problems effectively and quickly. And finally, share and create knowledge as a product for governance, progress from the data to knowledge by systematic reasoning, achieving the critical attainment of Governmental goal and strategy to acquire core knowledge.

Key Features of KMS

While conceptualizing the features of KMS in line with the requirement of the stakeholders, Digital India vision, objectives of CB-II scheme and various dimensions for implementation of KMS were analyzed to identify features that create a suitable impact. The various dimensions of KMS are presented in Figure 2.

The following functionalities are incorporated into the KMS.

- **Quick Content Creation and Document Management:** Provides an option to the user to add content to organizational document. While adding the content, the user needs to feed certain information e.g. 'Title of the document', 'Domain/ Department', 'Tags' etc. before the page can be submitted to reviewers who can approve, reject or correct the content.
- **Taxonomy, Process and Workflows:** The documents uploaded by the users are published under suitable categories e.g. business process, manuals, policies, procedure, norms, guidelines, case studies, lessons learned, project reports, technical reports, white papers, knowledge stories and alike.

Figure 2. Dimensions of KMS

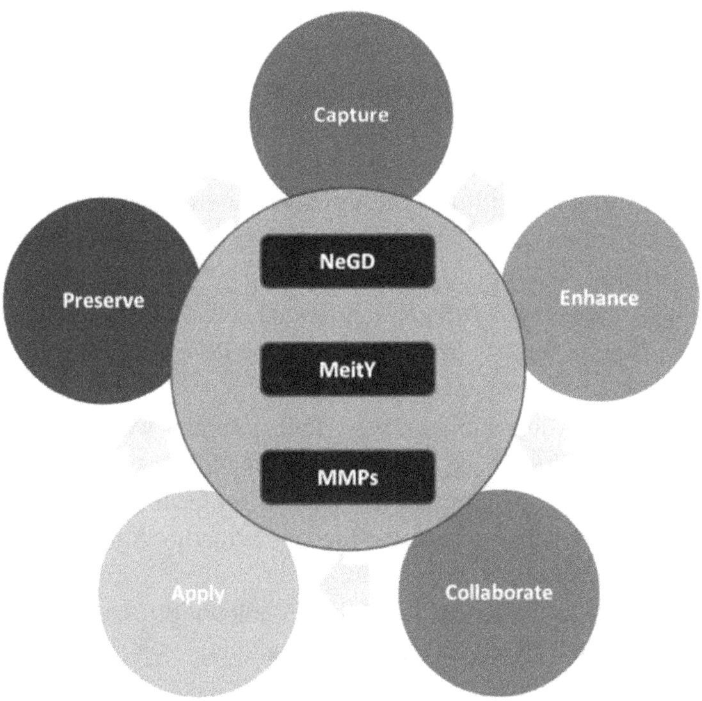

- **Guided Questions for Knowledge Capture:** Successful process and reasons for failure: Provides an option to the user to add lessons gained from their experiences. While adding the lesson learned, user needs to fill the fields on 'Lesson Title', 'Tags', 'Problem Statement', 'How did you solve it', 'Root Cause Analysis', 'Lesson Learned from success, as well as Failure'.
- **Collaboration:** Generation, evaluation and approval of innovative ideas: Provides the workspace collaboration embodied with various features e.g. Blogs, Forum, Bookmarks, Action Tracker, and Event Calendar etc.
- **Documentation:** System-captured meta-data, Date, Tag, Automatic versioning: Provides an option to users to upload new version of the documents uploaded and also to restore any versions of the same.
- **Integrated Search and Retrieval:** Provides a powerful, out of the box search capability to KMS, supported by search methods like wildcard search.
- **Gamification:** Badges, likes/rating and comments: Provides a way of enhancing KMS usage with game design elements to increase user engagement, content creation and user acceptance.
- **Expert Locator:** Provides an option to users to search experts by the keywords and ask their queries to them. Also, the answered queries can be listed and sorted, for users' reference.
- **Flexible, Heuristic, Suggestive Platform:** KMS is capable to suggest and assist users based the keywords searched earlier on the system. It is enabled with 'Type ahead' search, 'Boolean' search, 'Wild card' search, 'Quoted' (or phrase) search, search based on 'Morphology' etc.
- **Integration With Other Systems and Mobile Based Access:** Facilitates integration with Learning Management System (LMS) application wherein the users will be able to access their registered courses through KMS.
- **Cognitive Computing:** It is a cutting-edge feature which combines machine learning algorithms and advance data mining capabilities in KM (O'Dell & Trees, 2016).
- The salient features of KMS are highlighted below.
- **Profiles:** Help to quickly find the people one needs by searching across the organization using keywords.
- **Communities:** Allow one to create, find, join and work with people who share a common interest, responsibility or area of expertise.
- **Blog:** Uses a web log to present an idea and get feedback from others.
- **Wikis:** Are a convenient, online way for teams to author content collaboratively, edit it and publish it.
- **Forums:** Provide increased flexibility by allowing discussion and sharing experience to take place outside of Communities.

- **Bookmarks:** Help to save, organize and share already visited knowledge objects.
- **Activities:** Help to organize work, plan next steps and easily tap expanding professional network.
- **Files:** Are used to store and share content with other people.
- **Knowledge Repository:** Assists in storing required knowledge for easy retrieval and reuse.
- **Ask an Expert:** Provides a platform to ask specific topic related queries to the identified Domain Expert.

KMS Implementation Plan and Structure

Based on the past experience in implementation of such large project with involvement of varied stakeholders, a phased approach has been adopted, thus infusing learning from each phase into the implementation plan, supported with the governance structure defining roles and responsibilities of the various stakeholders including the knowledge champions, domain experts and leadership.

The overall implementation has thus been divided into three phases; with the first phase covering the knowledge management within the NeGD including State e-Mission Teams (SeMTs), the second phase covering MeitY and the third phase reaching the stakeholders handling MMPs under e-Kranti. Figure 3 broadly depicts the overall stakeholder implementation framework for NeGD's KMS.

Towards implementation of KMS phase I, the project plan was developed along with organization chart, escalation matrix and Standard Operating Procedure (SOP). The System/ Functional Requirement Specifications (SRS/ FRS) were created and user interface was designed. On personalization front of the web system, System Design Document (SDD) was developed, personalization themes were applied, chat engine and gamification were also developed and Quality Assurance (QA) testing was conducted. On customization and integration part, the web portal has been customized as per the SDD and the KMS portal has been integrated with Learning Management System.

In line with the standard methodology for execution of User Acceptance Testing (UAT), the UAT was executed post finalization of FRS and completion of development/customization of application based on agreed FRS. Subsequent to this, Requirement Traceability Matrix (RTM) was developed for the UAT with respect to agreed FRS. Once the UAT execution started, no changes were allowed in the application till the end of UAT exercise and any further amendment was deployed with proper versioning and in the form of patches only.

Figure 3. Implementation phases of KMS for e-Governance

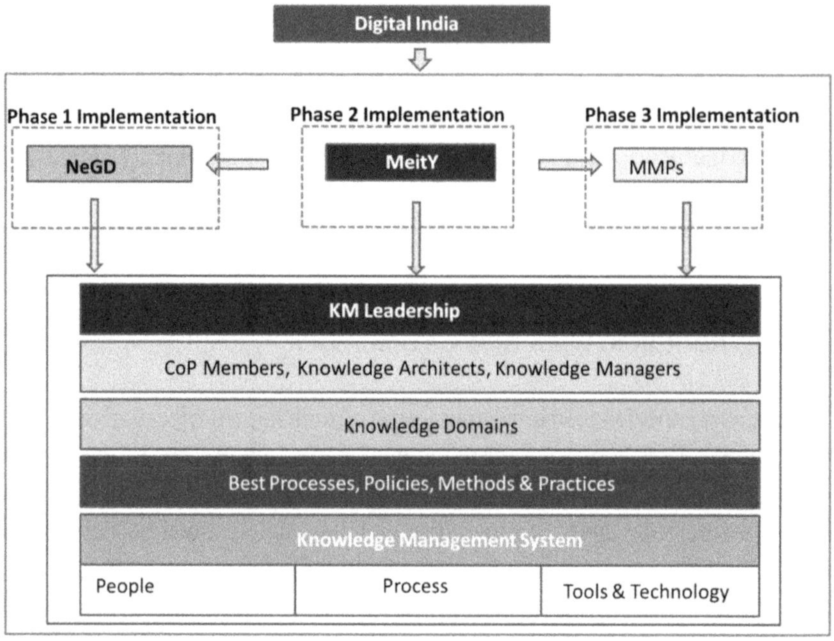

For requirement gathering towards enhancing the KMS, national level workshops are planned with stakeholders including leaders from NeGD, SeMTs, MeitY and MMPs.

METHODOLOGY

In the first step, value proposition was identified leading to visioning exercise for framing the objectives and goals of KMS implementation in NeGD, aligned with their strategic objectives. Detailed discussions were conducted with key stakeholders to capture their broad requirements for KMS. Further, the implementation strategy/ roadmap was formulated which adopts a phase wise implementation of KMS. Based on the strategy formulation, broad level requirements and work flows were drafted based on which an implementation partner was selected through an open tendering process. The requirements were further elaborated based on good practices, scanning across various organizations (national as well as international). The Phase I implementation has been achieved and the impact assessment framework has been created which would provide the feedback on the content as well as other aspects of the KMS.

FRAMEWORK FOR KMS

Implementation of a structured KM is a major decision with respect to organizational working/ procedures and requires significant (multi-year) organizational commitment including budget allocation and a comprehensive change management in the organization. Hence, there was a need to establish a strong business case/ value proposition that must have the concurrence of the organizational top leadership.

In this backdrop, a need was felt for capturing views of the diverse stakeholders of the organization in the following areas:

- Current issues and challenges related to knowledge.
- Suitability/ sufficiency of currently available organized knowledge for effective working of the stakeholders in performing its designated mandate for the next 5-10 years.
- Requirements of knowledge for facilitating innovation towards meeting the longer-term needs of the citizens who are of direct concern to the organization/ programme.
- The possible differentiator(s) for the organization/ programme when knowledge and expertise are better shared and transferred.
- The suitable scenario/ ideal case for the organization with respect to KM.

KM necessarily requires cultural change in the organization, as cultural changes emerge from the leadership. It was agreed that the KM agenda needs to be driven top down, especially in its initial stages of formation and implementation.

The framework for KMS has been designed, taking into consideration the work experience and learning drawn from the best practices in the field of Knowledge Management. Figure 4 depicts the 5 distinct phases of the KM framework implemented by NeGD viz. Initiate, Assess, Plan, Design, Implement & evolve, along with the key activities and outputs pertaining to each of these phases.

The framework is spread across five distinct phases: (i) Initiate – where the need for KM in the organization is established and a vision for the same is developed in line with the organizational objectives; (ii) Assess – where a detailed assessment of the organization is carried out in the context of Policy, People, Process, Content, and Technology with respect to KM; (iii) Plan – where the Strategy, Governance Structure, Policy and Roadmap/ Budgetary Estimates are drawn for KM, (iv) Design – where the KM flows, roles & responsibilities are defined/ standardized, the ICT design is prepared and operational plans are laid out; (v) Implement & Evolve – where the KM system is implemented in accordance with the plan and design, adequate Monitoring and Evaluation activities are commissioned and the KM evolves toward maturing in the organization (Tucker, 2013).

Figure 4. Framework for KMS

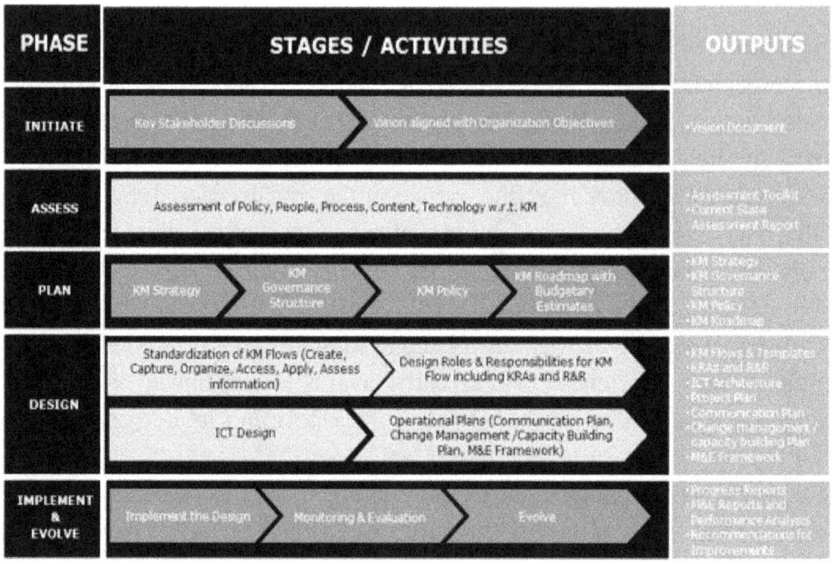

KEY OUTCOMES EXPECTED THROUGH KMS

NeGD is working on the deployment of KMS in the targeted Government departments – with activities such as conducting internal requirement gathering, taking feedback and reviews from stakeholders, intelligentsia, academia, and private agencies at multiple levels. The following outcomes are expected out of the implementation and commissioning of KMS for e-Governance across different phases:

- Knowledge creation and capture at NeGD, MeitY and MMPs will become a part of the employee's work flow and process. Knowledge storage/ repository will be readily available to all, to access useful knowledge related to e-Governance domain such as best practices, risk factors, subject matter, lessons learnt etc.
- Knowledge sharing and enrichment will include knowledge submission, evaluation and publishing. Knowledge dissemination/ replication (use of shared knowledge by others) about any issues related to e-Governance, Digital India, Government departments will take place by:
- Publishing the results and lessons learnt from each projects.
- Capturing any new knowledge that might have been obtained during reuse of the knowledge objects.
- Sharing of new ideas, methods and best practices adopted and replicated.

- Rating of contents and comments by users of the KMS.
- Rewarding and recognizing the contributors of best knowledge objects as "knowledge champions."

Reach of KMS will be potentially increased to cover most Government stakeholders related to e-Governance spread across the country; this will facilitate sharing and replication of knowledge without the need for physical movement from one location to other. Scalability of initiatives on e-Governance in departments spread across India is also expected to enhance, since the knowledge assets of all e-Governance related subjects are expected to be easily accessible.

LAUNCH OF KMS PHASE I

The continued efforts, dedication and perseverance of the team at NeGD enabled it towards successful launch of KMS Phase I on 27th March 2017. Since then, NeGD has been monitoring the usage of KMS on a daily basis to identify and reward the early adopters of the system. Dashboard on usage of KMS are being prepared by NeGD on a daily basis which facilitates the analysis and identification of trends and development of action plan for accelerating the adoption rate for the system across a diversified set of stakeholders (Table 1).

Every knowledge object is reviewed by an identified set of people before getting published over KMS. The validity of some of the knowledge objects may be for a limited timeframe, after which they get expired/ archived by KMS (Table 2).

One of the key attributes of KMS is the differential access to the knowledge objects being published. Based on the type of access, the knowledge objects published over KMS can be classified under 3 categories viz. 'Department Private' i.e. accessible to a particular department/ function, 'Department Public' i.e. accessible to everyone in the organization, 'Digital India' i.e. accessible to everyone in the organization as well as to citizens. The publisher of a knowledge object assigns a particular type of access to it, based on the nature, confidentiality and applicability of the knowledge object (Table 3).

The KMS users are recognised for their active participation and valued contribution to KMS. Users earn points for their various kinds of activities performed over KMS such as uploading/ sharing knowledge objects over 'Knowledge Repositories', uploading 'Lessons Learned', raising queries/ responding to queries under 'Ask an Expert', writing 'Blogs', posting 'Wikis', putting discussions or liking/ disliking posts over 'Communities' etc. Based on the points accumulated by users over the time, their 'level' progresses from 'Newbie' to 'Beginner', 'Self-Pacer', 'Expert', 'Champion' and finally to 'Master'. Moreover, 'badges' are awarded to users for

Table 1. User registration over KMS (Function wise)

Department/ Function	No. of Users Registered
Administration	16
Awareness & Communication	14
Capacity Building	13
DigiSevak	1
Digital Locker	30
Finance	10
Government e-Market	4
Human Resource	6
National Centre of Geo-informatics	4
Open forge & collaboration platform	1
Programme Management	10
Project Management Information System	3
Rapid Assessment System	9
SeMTs	205
Strategic Unit	156
Technology Management	7
UMANG	5

Table 2. Status of knowledge objects over KMS

Status of Knowledge Objects	No. of Knowledge Objects
Published	515
Draft	4
Expired	8

Table 3. Access type of knowledge objects published over KMS (Category wise)

Access Type of Knowledge Objects Published	No. of Knowledge Objects
Digital India	401
Department Public	98
Department Private	24

earning a threshold score in a particular timeframe. Any registered user of KMS can view the 'level' or 'badge' pertaining to all the users by accessing their respective profiles over KMS. Further, performance of a particular department/ function is estimated as the aggregate of points earned by all their respective members (Table 4).

Identification of critical knowledge and selection of suitable tools (such as webinars) towards dissemination of knowledge among stakeholders have been the key guiding factors for Digital India knowledge sharing initiative (see Appendix).

CHALLENGES FACED IN IMPLEMENTATION OF KMS

NeGD has faced a few challenges in implementing the phase I of KMS and is anticipating some of the following challenges towards implementing the subsequent phases of KMS as well.

Table 4. Function wise performance over KMS

Department/ Function	Points Earned
SeMTs	1847
Capacity Building	554
Administration	400
Digital Locker	382
Strategic Unit	225
Programme Management	162
Finance	160
Rapid Assessment System	74
UMANG	70
Technology Management	67
Awareness & Communication	57
National Centre of Geo-informatics	45
Human Resource	43
Awareness	30
DigiSevak	30
Project Management Information System	30
UMANG	15
Open forge & collaboration platform	14
Government eMarket	12

- Lack of KM standards in public sector
- Difficulty in finding and getting the right knowledge experts
- Content is mostly unorganized
- Information pertaining to governance is not updated regularly
- Knowledge sharing is not encouraged by the organization
- All requisite information are not readily available
- Available knowledge objects are not known, resulting in duplication of efforts
- Lack of a proper storage mechanism
- States, Ministries and Departments are at different stages of KM readiness

Towards overcoming these challenges, the key strategies formulated by NeGD include its top down approach of KM implementation with extensive involvement of the leadership in conjunction with a structured rewards and recognition mechanism for KMS adoption. Following are some of the recognitions planned by NeGD towards encouraging and sustaining the adoption of KMS.

- Top 3 contributors of the week/ month/ quarter
- Top 3 knowledge managers of the week/ month/ quarter
- Top 3 departments/ functions of the week/ month/ quarter

CONCLUSION

KMS for e-Governance is a pioneering initiative. KMS has been applied across different disciplines but this is a fresh approach to knowledge management for the Government departments and the e-Governance subject. As any organization moves and grows through different stages of maturity before formally adopting a KM solution, where KM maturity enhances from being Aware to Develop, Practice, Optimize and finally Lead. NeGD is also following a similar maturity cycle while implementing KMS, see Figure 5.

NeGD is currently transitioning from “Developing” stage to “Practicing” stage of KM maturity wherein the system has been developed with KM capabilities to best utilize them for expected outcomes. The implemented KM capabilities and the realization of initial benefits which will form a base for implementation of further phases. During the course of implementing KMS in two subsequent phases, it will further evolve and optimize, ultimately reaching to “Leading” stage, wherein the entire MeitY would have differentiated itself based on its KM capabilities. The KMS initiative by NeGD intends to be a transformational approach towards revolutionising the delivery of citizen services across India, by leveraging the accumulated learnings through conversion of tacit knowledge of Government officials into explicit knowledge.

Figure 5. KM Maturity

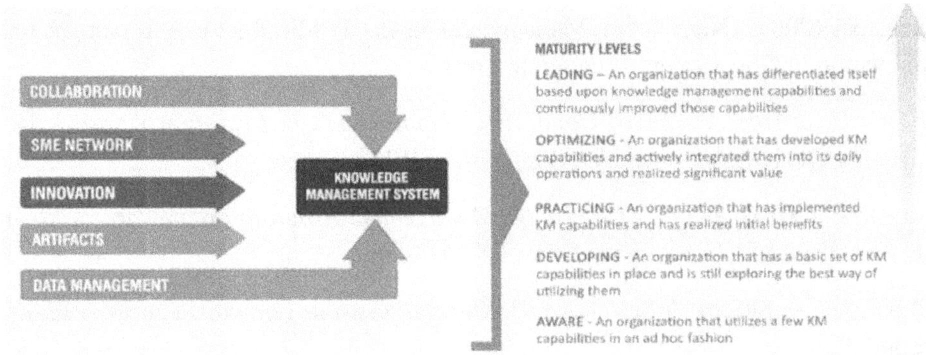

ACKNOWLEDGMENT

This experience paper is a record of KMS deployment project at NeGD for which the Capacity Building team is working diligently to successfully deploy a KMS for e-Governance in the Government arena. The paper has been the result of immense efforts and cooperation of various people and organizations.

We are thankful to Capacity Building team and Project Management Unit handling the role of project management and providing extremely valuable insights and precious time they have devoted in providing support for the development of the paper. We also thank the private agencies for their presentations and resources which formed our reference material.

REFERENCES

Afgan, N. H., & Carvalho, M. G. (2010). The Knowledge Society: A Sustainability Paradigme. *The CADMUS Journal*, *1*(1), 28–41.

Baguma, R. (2016). *Knowledge Societies Policy Handbook: United Nations University- Operating Unit on Policy Driven Electronic Governance*. UNU-EGOV.

Davenport, T. H. (1994). Saving IT's Soul: Human-Centered Information Management. *Harvard Business Review*, *72*(2).

Duhon, B. (1998). It's all in our Heads. *Inform (Silver Spring, Md.)*, *12*(8), 8–13.

Engida, G. (2016). *How can Digital Government Support the Development of Knowledge Societies?* Keynote Lecture, 9th International Conference on Theory and Practice of Electronic Governance (ICEGOV2016), Montevideo, Uruguay.

GESCI. (2012). *Global e-Schools and Communities Initiative*. GESCI.

McNabb. (2007). Knowledge Management in the Public Sector-A Blueprint for Innovation in Government. Academic Press.

O'Dell, C., & Trees, L. (2016). *Cognitive Computing and the Evolution of Knowledge Work*. APQC KM Advanced Working Group White Paper.

Tucker, E. (2013). *APQC's Knowledge Management Program Framework: A Road Map for Your KM Journey*. Houston, TX: Academic Press.

Uriarte, F. A. (2008). *Introduction to Knowledge Management*. Jakarta: ASEAN Foundation.

APPENDIX

Table 5. Webinars organised by Digital India Portal towards dissemination of critical knowledge

Webinar Topic	Date	Live Participation in Digital India Portal (NeGD)
Performance Management System-Training: HRIS Tool	26 April 2017	124
Legal Aspects of RFP/RFE	05 May 2017	99
Tax Deducted at Source (TDS) in Goods & Services Tax (GST)	09 May 2017	400
Wanna Cry Ransomware Threat	19 May 2017	293
Case Study Writing	26 May 2017	51
Digi Locker	02 June 2017	83
My Gov	09 June 2017	125
Implementation of Cloud in the Government Ministries	15 June 2017	353
Transitional Provisions in GST Law	21 June 2017	3,284
Buyer registration and buying through GeM	07 July 2017	120
Registration of normal taxpayer and composite dealer in GST portal (Webinar will be conducted in Hindi language)	12 July 2017	628
Composition Levy Scheme in GST	19 July 2017	630
Payment Processes in GST	26 July 2017	1,653
GSTR-1 and its preparation with return offline tool	02 August 2017	1,902
GSTR-1 and its preparation with Return offline tool (In Marathi Language)	02 August 2017	816
Filing of GSTR-3B Return (in English/Hindi language)	09 August 2017	2,086
GSTR 1 and its preparation through offline tool in Tamil Language	09 August 2017	1,251
Filing of GSTR 3B Return (In Hindi Language)	16 August 2017	1,889
Filing of GSTR 3B Return (In Marathi Language)	16 August 2017	1,358
Filing of GSTR 3B Return In Telugu	18 August 2017	1,440
Filing of GSTR 3B Return " In Tamil Language"	23 August 2017	1,265
GSTR 1 and its preparation through offline tool " in Malayalam Language "	23 August 2017	927
Filing of GSTR 3B Return "In Bengali Language" by GSTN in Association with Digital India LMS	24 August 2017	438

continued on following page

Table 5. Continued

Webinar Topic	Date	Live Participation in Digital India Portal (NeGD)
Filing of Form GST TRAN-1 In Telugu Language by Telangana State Tax Dept in association with Digital India & GST	24 August 2017	150
Webinar on Filing of GSTR 1	30 August 2017	1,789
Webinar on Filing of GSTR 1(in Marathi Language)	30 August 2017	989
Webinar on Filing of GSTR-1 (in Telugu Language)	04 September 2017	505
Preparation and Filing of GSTR 2 (in English Language)	06 September 2017	1,561
Preparation and Filing of Form GST TRAN 1 (in English Language)	06 September 2017	1,695
Filing of GSTR 2 on GST portal (in Hindi Language)	13 September 2017	1,793
Filing of GSTR 2 on GST portal (in Tamil Language)	13 September 2017	826
GSTR 1 and its preparation through offline tool (In Kannada Language)	20 September 2017	243
GSTR 1 and its preparation through offline tool (In Bengali Language)	20 September 2017	91
Registering and using Digital Signature Certificate (DSC) at GST portal(in English Language) by GSTN on 27-09-2017 at 2.30 PM IST	27 September 2017	984
Resolution of key issues in filing of GSTR 3B GSTR 1 and TRAN 1 at GST portal (in English Language)	04 October 2017	1,651
Filing of GSTR 2 at GST portal (in Marathi language)I 11th October I 1430 hrs IST	11 October 2017	1,105
GSTR 2 filing online & using Offline tool (in English Language)	17 October 2017	746
Using offline tool for filing GSTR 2 and GSTR 3B (in Tamil language)	25 October 2017	726
Using offline tool for filing GSTR 2 (in Hindi Language)	30 October 2017	1,635
“”GCCS Pre-event Webinar on Cyber4Growth”” (in English Language)	01 November 2017	221

Chapter 3
Knowledge Management in the Non-Governmental Organizations Context

Mansour Esmaeil Zaei
Panjab University, India

ABSTRACT

NGOs are recognized as knowledge-intensive organizations in nature. This is because of the employees' and volunteers' professionalism and knowledgeable experiences and the area in which NGOs work. However, like other organizations, NGOs have fewer financial and personal resources but huge and greater demand for their services. Consequently, leading NGOs started to reengineer their core processes and organizational paradigms to minimize the cost and time spent on internal functions in order to apply the greater part of their energies externally. To meet these targets, NGOs develop and formalize systems and mechanisms for converting and retaining their tacit knowledge to explicit knowledge over time successfully. This strategic and systematic process and mechanism for data capture, storage, classification, and retrieval is knowledge management. Hence, this chapter will attempt to fill the absence of KM study in NGOs. It will help to understand KM from the perspective of NGOs.

DOI: 10.4018/978-1-5225-4200-1.ch003

INTRODUCTION

Information and knowledge are critical for perceiving all the human aspirations. As knowledge society, acquisition of information and knowledge and its utilization have intense and pervasive impact on improvement the quality of citizens' lives and empower them. People who have access to information and who understand how to use the acquired information by making informed choices in the processes of exercising their political, social, economic and legal rights become empowered, which, in turn, enable them to build their strengths and assets (M., 2012).

Based on the right to information to remove information asymmetry, the societies have made endeavors for democratizing knowledge resources by way of putting in place the mechanisms for free flow of information and ideas (M., 2012). However, the exchange and sharing information in society is professional work, which requiring expert organizations like non-governmental organizations (hereinafter-NGOs). NGOs are non-profit oriented organizations in nature. They are more cost-effective and have a better ability to effectively access masses as compared to the public sector. Moreover, NGOs act as democratization vehicles can play a fundamental humanitarian role to accomplish themselves as "a counterbalance to the state power, protecting human rights, opening up communication channels and participation, and promoting activism and pluralism." (Edwards & Hulme, 1996). However, NGOs have limited resources and time to meet stakeholders' and citizen's needs, develop their strengths, and maintain operational capacity. Thus, "The restructuring of the NGOs has made it essential for NGO leaders to develop new systems of management and governance that build organizational capacity to develop and manage a diverse funding base, respond to the accountability requirements of multiple funders, manage employees and volunteers, market the organization and oversee inter-organizational relationships and partnerships, manage daily operations, and monitor service delivery " (Schwartz & Austin, 2008). To meet these changes, NGOs should design, develop and formalize systems or mechanisms for converting and retaining their tacit knowledge to explicit knowledge over time successfully (Ragsdell, 2013). This strategic and systematic process and mechanism for data capture, storage, classification and retrieval is knowledge management (hereinafter-KM).

BACKGROUND

The Non-Governmental Organizations

In last few decades, developing countries have witnessed dramatic growth in the number, nature, reach, influence and diversity of NGOs (Voluntary Action

Network India, 2012). This fast-growing rate still continues in partnership with the governments which is a steering engine in nations building. This is done to constitute a progressive society and to decrease the suffering of people (Rai, 2014). However, like other organizations, the NGOs have limited financial and personal resources, but huge and increasing demand for their services. Moreover, most of governments in developing countries have failed to deliver products and services to the grassroots level because of faulty mechanisms, which are highly bureaucratic, rule bound and confusing. Limited budget and human capital in government, vested political interests, inappetence of government employees, corruption, and procedural red-tapism are prime factors for the failure of successive governments to provide facilities at the lowest levels in the society (Tek, 2002). Because of this discontent and criticism of governments performance, NGOs became a more attractive, alternative option for delivering services to the poor, disadvantaged and landless people. Hence, the transfer of resources at the grassroot level became more direct and efficient (Tek, 2002; Ahmed, 2004).

The term NGO includes a wide range starting from large national NGOs, branches of international NGOs and small grassroots to local organizations. They range from rural to urban, with various, different aims, capacities, functions, and responsibilities (Tek, 2002). There are many terminologies which are interchangeable as well as overlapping to one another. Based on their diversity in formation, orientation, operation, dissolution, etc. Thus, due to NGOs' various roles, structure, orientation, and form of interaction with the client, it makes it difficult to draw an obvious definition about NGOs. Accordingly, the NGOs have been defined upon the basis of some fundamental and well-known characteristics namely voluntariness, participation (democratic in nature), independent of the government (private), personal relevance (self-governing), non-formalization, non-political, non-profit making, and development oriented (Matschke *et al.,* 2012; Salamon & Anheier, 1992; Tek, 2002). Depending on the general functional characteristics, NGOs can be defined as "formal (professionalized) independent societal organizations whose primary aim is to promote common goals at the national or the international level" (Martens, 2002). The World Bank also defines NGOs as "private organizations that pursue activities to relieve the suffering, promote the interests of the poor, protect the environment, provide basic social services, or undertake community development" (World Bank and Civil Society Collaboration, 2002).

NGOs as knowledge-intensive (Greenaway & Vuong, 2010) and professionally-staffed organizations (Streeten, 1997) aiming to contribute to charity and philanthropist activities, relief and rehabilitation activities, art and cultural activities, protection services, services and delivery, education preparation, development (socio-economic, human capitals, and development of human) (United Nation Volunteers, 2012; Atack, 1999). Apart from these, NGOs also provide financial, technical and manpower assistance, mobilization of assets from the internal and external sources, networking and alliance-building, research and innovation activities, assessment and monitoring activities, capacity building (Baccaro, 2001; Langran, 2002), information diffusion and documentation (United Nation Volunteers, 2012), awareness raising (Desai, 2005; Baccaro, 2001), decentralization of the central government (Hibbard & Tang, 2004), rights and entitlement (Voluntary Action Network India, 2012), and political and public policy advocacy (Atack, 1999) among poor, marginalized and needy people. They also positively encourage and engage people to participate in activities, and act as a network among community and systems, in collaboration with the government.

Defining and Classifying of Knowledge

NGOs today are faced with different challenges in the competitive and dynamic social and economic environment to be at par or even better than their counterparts (Zaei & Kapil, 2016). Accordingly, knowledge as most strategically-important resource and its management can play a vital role in long-term sustainability and organizational survival (Singh *et al.*, 2006). The knowledge should be used in NGOs as a value addition to redesign and improve products, programs or services (Rathi *et al.*, 2014), and to increase positive organizational learning for the betterment of the community and its welfare and development. In the words of de Vasconcelos *et al.* (2005), "Knowledge in an NGO is the collection of expertise, experience and information that individuals and workgroups use during the execution of their tasks. It is produced and stored by individual minds, or implicitly encoded and documented in organizational processes, services and systems".

Like other organizations, in NGOs, knowledge is embedded and flows through several entities including routines, policies, processes, systems, practices, norms, organization culture and identity, documents and individual brain (Mvungi & Jay, 2009; Kulkarni *et al.*, 2006). Knowledge provides a base for an individual to understand data and information at a shared level (Alavi & Leidner, 2001). NGOs should understand how this knowledge is created, shared, and used within the organization and individual to make them able to perceive the value and importance of knowledge and to avoid wasteful cycles of re-learning and significant failures. For instance, most of the voluntarily acquired knowledge is not encoded and documented through meaningful way and usually held tacitly in their mind for reuse when the demand arises.

Knowledge is classified into four domains namely individual, group, organization and inter-organizational (Haslinda & Sarinah, 2009). Moreover, knowledge is reused and shared by four cycles including the individual to the NGOs, and respectively to the broader society (Ragsdell *et al.*, 2014). For NGOs, the knowledge that their members frequently possess is a treasure of personal experience which consists of situational knowledge, factual knowledge, procedural knowledge, and knowledge-in-use (Rathi *et al.,* 2016). Rathi *et al.* (2016) identified five broad categories and their sub-categories of knowledge in NGOs which are summarized in Figure 1.

Conceptual Analysis on Knowledge Management

KM, as an emerging discipline, has been defined and discussed in different ways due to its complexity and elasticity of the meaning .For instance, KM is defined as a *process* (creating, capturing, developing, sharing, and effectively using organizational knowledge) (Davenport & Prusak, 1998; Kinney, 1998); as a *method* (exploration and transformation of knowledge into asset) (Sharp, 2006; Erickson, 2015); as an *approach* (to improve organization's learning and performance, and achieving organizational objectives) (Walczak, 2008; Fong & Choi, 2009; Luxmi, 2014;

Figure 1. Five major categories and their sub-categories of knowledge for NGOs

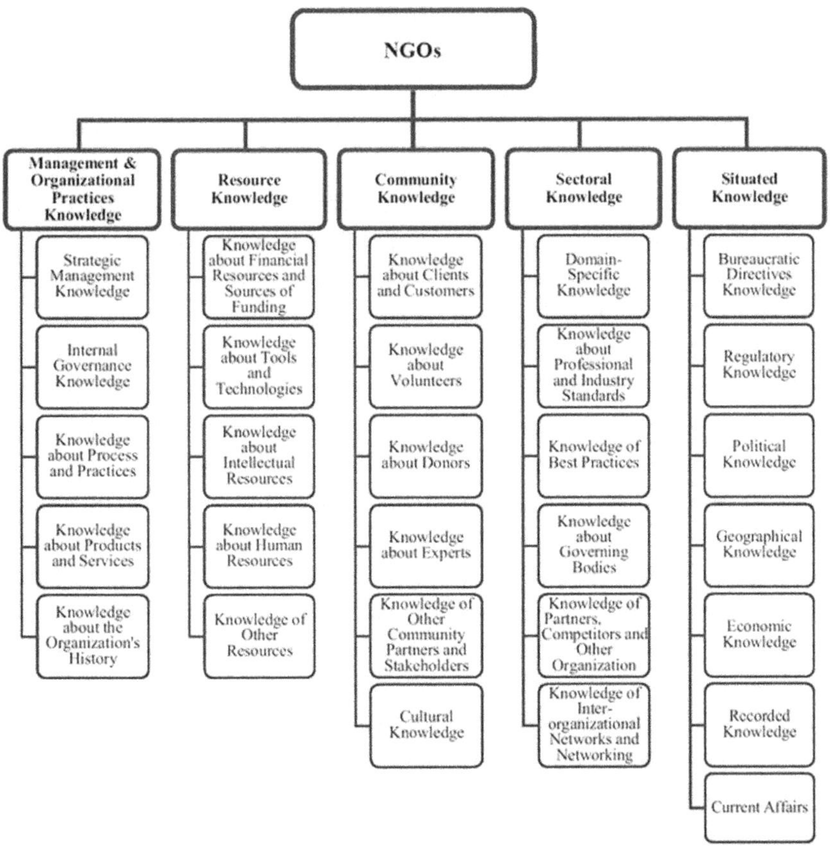

Jain & Moreno, 2015); as a *system* (composed of human and technological tools/components) (Edwards *et al.,* 2005; Maier, 2007; Jain, 2009; Becerra-Fernandez & Sabherwal, 2010); and as a *mechanism* (external knowledge search and acquisition (Holsapple & Joshi, 2004), capture, codification and storage (Hoegl & Schulze, 2005), diffusion (Brockman & Morgan, 2003), interpretation (Herder *et al.,* 2003), generation, recombination, mobilization (Alavi & Tiwana, 2002), reflection and learning from outcomes (Davenport & Prusak, 1998). Moreover, while some authors describe KM as a process (Bassi, 1997; Bhatt, 2001; Choy & Suk, 2005), the others provide purpose-based (Wiig, 1997; Martin, 2000; Jennex, 2005) definitions.

Despite the lack of a universally accepted concise definition of KM, two definitions are adopted and developed to better achieve chapter objectives: The first definition which follows is derived from the above views which include both the purpose and processes of KM. It states that "KM is an integrated range of strategies, practices, systems, tools and techniques designed and developed in an organization which is adopted by individuals, groups, NGOs, and respectively the broader society through a broad range of functions. These functions include knowledge identification and creation, knowledge collection and capture, storage and organization, sharing and dissemination, and application and use from variety of social contexts for social problem solving, increasing the body of knowledge in society, betterment of the community, welfare and development, avoiding wasteful cycles of re-learning and significant failures in an NGOs, and building an institutional memory for volunteers knowledge and skills to make NGOs more efficient and effective. It is done in order to maximize positive visibility, transparency, accountability (to multiple funders), responsiveness, cost-effectiveness and organizational learning in the society through outstanding collaboration and partnership with government to build a nation consequently". KM can broadly be defined as: "systematic approach to ensure that the right knowledge is available to the right processors at the right time in the right representations for the right cost in order to foster right relationships, decisions, and actions with respect to an entity's mission (Holsapple, 2008) through knowledge externalization, sharing, innovation, and socialization" (Tseng et al., 2015). Thus, the objective of KM is to leverage on the organizational knowledge processes and resources in order to improve knowledge rehearsals, work-flows, organizational behaviors to settle on better decisions and enhance organizational performance (Razmerita *et al.,* 2016).

KNOWLEDGE MANAGEMENT IN NGOs

KM became popular in the NGOs since the 1990s as a part of the modern management paradigm (Corfield *et al.,* 2013). But, in comparison to the government bodies, business units, research institutes, and financial institutions, implementation of KM initiatives in NGOs is still in its infancy (Kebede, 2010). For example, in India, as of now, only Chennai has active NGOs which produce knowledge and combine it with advocacy towards the local government (Goìmez & Knorringa, 2016).

Today NGOs are recognized as knowledge-intensive organizations in nature. This is because of the employees' and volunteers' professionalism and knowledgeable experiences and the area in which NGOs work (Greenaway & Vuong, 2010). However, like other organizations, NGOs have fewer financial and personal resources, but huge and greater demand for their services (Matschke *et al.*, 2012). Consequently, leading NGOs started to reengineer their core processes and organizational paradigms to minimize the cost and time spent on internal functions in order to apply the greater part of their energies externally (Downes & Marchant, 2016). For meet these targets, KM as a process of knowledge identification and creation, knowledge collection and capture, storage and organization, sharing and dissemination, and application and use (Maier & Moseley, 2003), should be used to support and improve the human capital knowledge and skills, and NGOs performance and capability. KM practices can assist to provides strengthen communications among the NGOs and its stakeholders to raising social awareness, allowing transparency in their operations, volunteers' development, cost reduction, creating new knowledge, improved efficiency, productivity, delivery, flexibility and innovation (Singh *et al.,* 2006).

The effective KM solutions may be employed within the NGOs themselves, between different NGOs that work together and, ultimately, between NGOs and society as a whole (de Vasconcelos *et al.,* 2005). This will help to tackle problems and achieve internal efficiencies and compete externally (Renshaw & Krishnaswamy, 2009). Indeed, many socio-economic development challenges are too complex and costly to resolve unilaterally, and call for collaboration between a diverse and often dispersed range of partners, such as local and international NGOs, policymakers, donors and knowledge institutes (Puri, 2007). All this requires NGOs with high quality internal learning and information processing systems and positive interaction with external KM and learning systems, external information flows, and policy trends (Chittoo *et al.,* 2010).

However, due to uniqueness of the NGO sector in its operation and orientation (Anantatmula & Stankosky, 2008), some literature emphasized on the lack of key processes and knowledge needed to assist them to develop, evaluate, document, and share successful KM programs (Hurley & Green, 2005). Compared to other organizations there are some special characteristics of NGOs such as voluntariness, participation, personal relevance, and non-formalization that effect KM (Matschke *et al.,* 2012). NGOs could more effectively manage their knowledge through a balance between technology, people, task and structure with a coordinated sharing of knowledge across the sector (Greenaway & Vuong, 2010). In addition, the review of previous studies demonstrated two directions about KM in NGOs. Some studies deal with effectiveness of KM practices in NGOs (Smith & Lumba, 2008; Matzkin, 2008; Cantu & Mondragon, 2016), because of limited obscurity and consensus about how to implement KM. In contrast, the other studies discussed about ineffectiveness of KM practices due to inappropriate KM strategies, "dynamics of power, opportunism, suspicion, and asymmetric learning strategies" (Larsson et al., 1998) in NGOs, and some special characteristics of NGOs that influence KM practices (Smith & Lumba, 2008; Hume & Hume, 2008).

It is important to differentiate NGOs on the basis of size, operation and orientation so that effective and appropriate KM practices for NGOs can be identified and failures can be avoided. The KM planning framework proposed by Hume and Hume (2008) addresses three categories of NGOs: small, medium and large-sized, where the size of an organization will influence the extent of their KM implementation and development. Knowledge in small NGOs can be very unstructured and informal, but their inherent processes, structural immaturity and size constraints offer opportunities for implementing socialization strategies to enhance knowledge sharing. Medium-sized NGOs possess skills, experience and processes that allow them more agility than small and larger NGOs in developing their KM capability. They are able to approach KM incrementally, balancing their strategic and day-to-day operational demands, even though being constrained by limited financial and human resources. Large NGOs, with their inherent cultural and environmental differences, place greater emphasis on leadership capabilities. This is done to overcome cultural and operational gaps, across managerial and operational levels, to drive a consistent KM program. However, the strategically and operationally more mature staff of large NGOs will grasp opportunities to share and develop best practices and business processes directed in support of their particular service mission.

KM INITIATIVES AND NGOS: ENABLERS AND BARRIERS

The success and growth of NGOs in today's knowledge society depends on how well they manage the knowledge of their employees and volunteers (Fink & Ploder, 2007) in order to maximize positive visibility, transparency, accountability, responsiveness, cost-effectiveness, and organizational learning to deliver human services, provide solutions and develop ideas and innovations for sustainable socio-economic development (Denner & Blackman, 2013). Therefore, implementation and application of KM initiatives can assist NGOs for the purpose of achieving better organizational efficiency, effectiveness, and performance (Earl, 2001). Spending resources on developing KM programs without an organized plan (Gunasekaran, Khalil & Rahman, 2002) is of limited use to NGOs. Through these plans the NGOs should be able to understand and identify which types of KM initiatives have more possibility and suitability to the context of the NGOs (Earl, 2001). Indeed, each NGOs should deploy KM practices in its own unique way. Till date no one KM strategy has been universally adopted or accepted due to the broad and multi-dimensionality of KM practices which covers most aspects of the organization's activities. The broad priorities of KM initiatives in NGOs depends on NGOs environment, operations and motivation. Based on these factors, NGOs may have focused on all or part of the dimensions of KM to meet their specific organizational requirements and goals. Moreover, managers' view about knowledge also has a significant impact on the type of KM initiatives. If managers view knowledge as an object, then KM initiatives emphasize on building knowledge stocks in the organizations. Similarly, if managers viewed knowledge as a process, then KM initiatives should highlight the flow of knowledge in the processes of knowledge creation, knowledge sharing and knowledge distribution (Haslinda & Sarinah, 2009).

Generally, NGOs start KM initiatives as part of their communication efforts, planning, monitoring and evaluation, and lesser from extent their documentation centers (UNCF and Regional Office for South Asia, 2008). NGOs should give priorities to capturing employees/voluntaries knowledge, exploitation of existing knowledge resources or assets, and improving access to NGOs. Then, emphasizing on "capturing and re-using past experience, after-action reviews to capture learning, and building and mining knowledge stores". Finally, focuses on generic KM initiatives that enhance better communication, learning and knowledge sharing. Through KM initiatives in NGOs, employees and volunteers will be able to harness best practices and lessons learned from across the organization's contractual portfolio and apply these proven solutions quickly to address their specific community's technical and programmatic requirements.

Prior studies reveal that several critical factors have positive contribution to organizations' KM initiative's success. A critical issue in adoption of KM initiatives is the primary readiness of the organization to accept, adopt, and employ new KM processes by changing or adapting the organizational culture to facilitate, support, and encourage the sharing, application, and creation of knowledge (Kanagasabapathy *et al.,* 2006). Franco and Mariano (2007) in a qualitative analysis expressed that ICT have been closely associated with the development of a great majority of KM initiatives. Leibowitz and Megbolugbe (2003) stated that the success of KM initiatives depends on *knowledge sharing*. They identified five broad dimensions of knowledge sharing research: "organizational context, interpersonal and team characteristics, cultural characteristics, individual characteristics, and motivational factors". In the study of 31 KM projects, Davenport *et al.* (1998) explored some critical factors for KM practices success such as culture and processes, developing a common goal and language for knowledge identification and selection. Human factors such as fear, cultural change, capturing of tacit knowledge, ease of use, stakeholder involvement, and benefits acknowledgment also affected the implementation of KM initiatives (Horak, 2001). Magnier-Watanabe and Senoo (2008) recognized organizational characteristics (structure, membership, relationship, and strategy) that affects different KM practices (knowledge acquisition, storage, diffusion, and application) in organizations. It focuses on competence building, culture change, setting up appropriate rewards and incentives structure (Arntzen *et al.,* 2009). Stankosky (2005) recommend that successful implementation of KM requires the mergence and equilibrium of four KM dimensions, i.e. leadership, learning, organization structure, and technology in an organizational-wide setting. Cardoso *et al.* (2012) assessed "organizational commitment, knowledge-centered culture, and training" and their effect on KM initiatives in a non-profit organization. They found that knowledge-centered culture and training played crucial roles in the successful implementation of KM initiatives. For the success of formal and informal KM practices in NGOs, organizational commitment, knowledge-centered culture, incentive and rewards, trust, organizational structure, training, organizational knowledge, local/indigenous knowledge, democratic knowledge flow and communication, empowerment of the local people, stimulation of double loop learning, and sustainable development have vital role.

In contrast, some major reasons and barriers exist behind failure of KM initiatives. A study in 1997 pointed that more than 84% of all KM initiatives fail (Lucier & Torsilieri, 1997). Bach *et al.* (2009) highlighted accepting and sustaining a KM culture remains the key challenges for NPOs. ICT also negatively associated with failure of various KM initiatives especially when the KM system was not perceived relevant, useful, and easy to use (Razmerita *et al.,* 2016). O'Connor (2000) explained that compensation, individuality, billing and tradition are some of the most important barriers to KM initiatives in today's organization. According to Schönström (2005), barriers to KM initiatives include: familiarity, coordination, incentives, authority, system, and culture. Frost (2014) discovered several causal failure factors for implementing KM initiatives which include lack of performance indicators and measurable benefits; inadequate management support; inappropriate planning, design, coordination, and assessment; inadequate skill and knowledge of managers and workers; problems with organizational culture and improper organizational structure. The main barriers to successful implementation of KM in the NGOs, most notably, individual barriers, organizational barriers, and technical barriers. These barriers may be sectorially and potentially dependent on specific contexts (Bloice & Burnett, 2016). Moreover, difficulty in integrating volunteers and complex funding arrangements, and acceptance of change and ability of leaders to develop a friendly knowledge culture are key challenges that needs to be overcome.

FUTURE TRENDS

The main issue for future work is: how can we discover and handle effective KM for NGOs? There is a need to research the attributes affecting the implementation of KM processes/practices, in the particular context of NGOs. Future works also can focus on identifying numerous areas where practical recommendations can be implemented to improve KM initiatives in NGOs.

CONCLUSION

NGOs, just like public/private organizations, need effective KM initiatives to succeed. However, NGOs face challenges and barriers distinct from those in for-profit corporations: organizational strategies and missions are different, the nature of the cash flow is different, and the nature of the employees is different (Greenaway & Vuong, 2012). Thus, NGOs should be selective and realistic in implementing particular KM processes/practices and customize them to meet particular organizational needs. They should consider a longer tenure for gaining benefits from KM. To develop KM strategies in NGOs, a multi-partisan approach and support mechanisms from government, businesses and the NGOs is needed. For now, what is currently known about KM, in general, can help benefit NGOs now.

REFERENCES

Ahmed, Z. U. (2004). Accountability and Control in Non-Governmental Organisations (NGOs) – A Case of Bangladesh. *Proceeding Fourth Asia Pacific Interdisciplinary Research in Accounting Conference.*

Jain, A. K., & Moreno, A. (2015). Organizational Learning, Knowledge Management Practices and Firm's Performance: An Empirical Study of a Heavy Engineering Firm in India. *The Learning Organization, 22*(1), 14–39. doi:10.1108/TLO-05-2013-0024

Alavi, M., & Leidner, D. E. (2001). Review: Knowledge Management and Knowledge Management Systems: Conceptual Foundations and Research Issues. *Management Information Systems Quarterly, 25*(1), 107–136. doi:10.2307/3250961

Alavi, M., & Tiwana, A. (2002). Knowledge Integration in Virtual Teams: The Potential Role of KMS. *Journal of the American Society for Information Science and Technology, 53*(12), 1029–1037. doi:10.1002/asi.10107

Anantatmula, V. S., & Stankosky, M. (2008). KM Criteria for Different Types of Organisations. *International Journal of Knowledge and Learning*, *4*(1), 18–35. doi:10.1504/IJKL.2008.019735

Arntzen, A. A. B., Worasinchai, L., & Ribière, V. M. (2009). An Insight into Knowledge Management Practices at Bangkok University. *Journal of Knowledge Management*, *13*(2), 127–144. doi:10.1108/13673270910942745

Atack, I. (1999). Four Criteria of Development NGO Legitimacy. *World Development*, *27*(5), 855–864. doi:10.1016/S0305-750X(99)00033-9

Baccaro, L. (2001). Civil Society, NGOs, and Decent Work Policies: Sorting Out the Issues. ILO/International Institute for Labour Studies.

Bach, P. M., Lee, R. L., & Carroll, M. J. (2009). *Knowledge Management Challenges in the Non-Profit Sector*. Retrieved from http://mfile.narotama.ac.id/files/Information%20System/Encyclopedia%20of%20Information%20Science%20and%20Technology%20(2nd%20Edition)/Knowledge%20Management%20Challenges%20in%20the%20Non-Proft%20Sector.pdf

Bassi, L. J. (1997). Harnessing the Power of Intellectual Capital. *Training & Development*, *51*(12), 25–31.

Baud, I. (2016). Digitisation and Participation in Urban Governance: The Contribution of ICT-Based Spatial Knowledge Management in Indian Cities. In Local Governance, Economic Development and Institutions (pp. 86-97). Palgrave Macmillan UK.

Becerra-Fernandez, I., & Sabherwal, R. (2010). *Knowledge Management: Systems and Processes*. London: M.E. Sharpe.

Bhatt, G. D. (2001). Knowledge Management in Organizations: Examining the Interaction Between Technologies, Techniques, And People. *Journal of Knowledge Management*, *5*(1), 68–75. doi:10.1108/13673270110384419

Blackman, D., & Kennedy, M. (2009). Knowledge Management and Effective University Governance. *Journal of Knowledge Management*, *13*(6), 547–563. doi:10.1108/13673270910997187

Bloice, L., & Burnett, S. (2016). Barriers to Knowledge Sharing in Third Sector Social Care: A Case Study. *Journal of Knowledge Management*, *20*(1), 125–145. doi:10.1108/JKM-12-2014-0495

Brockman, B. K., & Morgan, R. M. (2003). The Role of Existing Knowledge in New Product Innovativeness and Performance. *Decision Sciences*, *34*(2), 385–419. doi:10.1111/1540-5915.02326

Cardoso, L., Meireles, A., & Peralta, C. F. (2012). Knowledge Management and Its Critical Factors in Social Economy Organizations. *Journal of Knowledge Management, 16*(2), 267–284. doi:10.1108/13673271211218861

Chittoo, H., Nowbutsing, B. M., & Ramchurn, R. (2010). Knowledge Management: Promises and Premises. *Global Journal of Management and Business Research, 10*(1), 123–131.

Choy, C. S., & Suk, C. Y. (2005). Critical Factors in the Successful Implementation of Knowledge Management. *Journal of Knowledge Management Practice*, *6*(1), 234–258.

Corfield, A., Paton, R., & Little, S. (2013). Does Knowledge Management Work in NGOs?: A Longitudinal Study. *International Journal of Public Administration, 36*(3), 179–188. doi:10.1080/01900692.2012.749281

Davenport, T. H., & Prusak, L. (1998). *Working Knowledge: How Organizations Manage What They Know*. Boston: Harvard Business Press.

Davenport, T. H., De Long, D. W., & Beers, M. C. (1998). Successful Knowledge Management Projects. *Sloan Management Review*, *39*(2), 43–57.

de Vasconcelos, J., Seixas, P. C., Lemos, P. G., & Kimble, C. (2005). Knowledge Management in Non-Governmental Organisations: A Partnership for the Future. *Proceedings of the 7th International Conference, Enterprise Information Systems (ICEIS)*.

Desai, V. (2005). NGOs, Gender Mainstreaming, and Urban Poor Communities in Mumbai. *Gender and Development*, *13*(2), 90–98. doi:10.1080/13552070512331332290

Downes, T., & Marchant, T. (2016). The Extent and Effectiveness of Knowledge Management in Australian Community Service Organisations. *Journal of Knowledge Management, 20*(1), 49–68. doi:10.1108/JKM-11-2014-0483

Earl, M. (2001). Knowledge Management Strategies: Toward a Taxonomy. *Journal of Management Information Systems*, *18*(1), 215–233. doi:10.1080/07421222.2001.11045670

Edwards, J. S., Collier, P. M., & Shaw, D. (2005). *Knowledge Management and Its Impact on the Management Accountant*. London: The Chartered Institute of Management Accountants (CIMA). Retrieved from http://www.cimaglobal.com/Documents/Thought_leadership_docs/MigratedDocsMarch2010/Resouces%20(pdfs)/Research%20full%20reports/Knowledge%20management%20and%20its%20impact%20on%20the%20management%20accountant.pdf

Edwards, M., & Hulme, D. (1996). Too Close for Comfort? The Impact of Official Aid on Nongovernmental Organizations. *World Development*, *24*(6), 961–973. doi:10.1016/0305-750X(96)00019-8

Erickson, G. S., & Rothberg, H. N. (2014). Data, Information, and Knowledge: Developing an Intangible Assets Strategy. In *Handbook of Research on Organizational Transformations through Big Data Analytics* (pp. 85–96). Hershey, PA: IGI Global.

Fink, K., & Ploder, C. (2007). A Comparative Study of Knowledge Processes and Methods in Austrian and Swiss SMEs. *Proceeding of 13th European Conference on Information Systems*, 704-715.

Fong, P. S. W., & Choi, S. K. Y. (2009). The Processes of Knowledge Management in Professional Services Firms in the Construction Industry: A Critical Assessment of Both Theory and Practice. *Journal of Knowledge Management*, *13*(2), 110–126. doi:10.1108/13673270910942736

Franco, M., & Mariano, S. (2007). Information Technology Repositories and Knowledge Management Processes: A Qualitative Analysis. *Vine*, *37*(4), 440–451. doi:10.1108/03055720710838515

Frost, A. (2014). *A Synthesis of Knowledge Management Failure Factors*. Retrieved from http://www.academia.edu/download/35998692/A_Synthesis_of_Knowledge_Management_Failure_Factors.pdf

Greenaway, K. E., & Vuong, D. C. (2010). Taking Charities Seriously: A Call for Focused Knowledge Management Research. *International Journal of Knowledge Management*, *6*(4), 87–97. doi:10.4018/jkm.2010100105

Greenaway, K. E., & Vuong, D. C. (2012). Knowledge Management in Charities. In *Organizational Learning and Knowledge: Concepts, Methodologies, Tools and Applications* (pp. 1381–1389). Hershey, PA: IGI Global. doi:10.4018/978-1-60960-783-8.ch409

Gunasekaran, A., Khalil, O., & Rahman, S. R. (Eds.). (2002). *Knowledge and Information Technology Management: Human and Social Perspectives*. Hershey, PA: IGI Global.

Haslinda, A., & Sarinah, A. (2009). A Review of Knowledge Management Models. *Journal of International Social Research*, *2*(9), 187–198.

Herder, P. M., Veeneman, W. W., Buitenhuis, M. D. J., & Schaller, A. (2003). Follow the Rainbow: A Knowledge Management Framework for new Product Introduction. *Journal of Knowledge Management*, *7*(3), 105–115. doi:10.1108/13673270310485668

Hibbard, M., & Chun Tang, C. (2004). Sustainable Community Development: A Social Approach from Vietnam. *Community Development (Columbus, Ohio)*, *35*(2), 87–104.

Hoegl, M., & Schulze, A. (2005). How to Support Knowledge Creation in New Product Development: An Investigation of Knowledge Management Methods. *European Management Journal*, *23*(3), 263–273. doi:10.1016/j.emj.2005.04.004

Holsapple, C. W., & Joshi, K. D. (2004). A Formal Knowledge Management Ontology: Conduct, Activities, Resources, and Influences. *Journal of the American Society for Information Science and Technology*, *55*(7), 593–612. doi:10.1002/asi.20007

Horak, B. J. (2001). Dealing with Human Factors and Managing Change in Knowledge Management: A Phased Approach. *Topics in Health Information Management*, *21*(3), 8–17. PMID:11234733

Hume, C., & Hume, M. (2008). The Strategic Role of Knowledge Management in Nonprofit Organisations. *International Journal of Nonprofit and Voluntary Sector Marketing*, *13*(2), 129–140. doi:10.1002/nvsm.316

Hurley, T. A., & Green, C. W. (2005). Knowledge Management and the Nonprofit Industry: A Within and Between Approach. *Journal of Knowledge Management Practice*, *6*(1), 1–10.

Jain, S. (2009). Modern Knowledge Management and Computer-based Technology the Inseparable Phenomenon. *Global Business Review*, *10*(2), 159–171. doi:10.1177/097215090901000202

Jennex, M. (2005). What is Knowledge Management? *International Journal of Knowledge Management*, *1*(4), 1–4.

Kanagasabapathy, K. A., Radhakrishnan, R., & Balasubramanian, S. (2006). *Empirical Investigation of Critical Success Factor and Knowledge Management Structure for Successful Implementation of Knowledge Management System: A Case Study in Process Industry*. Retrieved from http://hosteddocs.ittoolbox.com/KKRR41106.pdf

Kebede, G. (2010). Knowledge Management: An Information Science Perspective. *International Journal of Information Management, 30*(5), 416–424. doi:10.1016/j.ijinfomgt.2010.02.004

Kinney, T. (1998). Knowledge Management, Intellectual Capital and Adult Learning. *Adult Learning, 10*(2), 2–5. doi:10.1177/104515959901000201

Kulkarni, U. R., Ravindran, S., & Freeze, R. (2006). A Knowledge Management Success Model: Theoretical Development and Empirical Validation. *Journal of Management Information Systems, 23*(3), 309–347. doi:10.2753/MIS0742-1222230311

Langran, L. V. (2002). *Empowerment and the Limits of Change: NGOs and Health Decentralization in the Philippine* (Doctoral dissertation). Toronto: University of Toronto.

Larsson, R., Bengtsson, L., Henriksson, K., & Sparks, J. (1998). The Inter-Organizational Learning Dilemma: Collective Knowledge Development in Strategic Alliances. *Organization Science, 9*(3), 285–305. doi:10.1287/orsc.9.3.285

Liebowitz, J., & Megbolugbe, I. (2003). A Set of Frameworks to Aid the Project Manager in Conceptualizing and Implementing Knowledge Management Initiatives. *International Journal of Project Management, 21*(3), 189–198. doi:10.1016/S0263-7863(02)00093-5

Lucier, C. E., & Torsilieri, J. D. (1997). Why Knowledge Programs Fail: A CEO's Guide to Managing Learning. *Strategy & Business, 9*(4), 14–28.

Luxmi. (2014). Organizational Learning Act as a Mediator between the Relationship of Knowledge Management and Organizational Performance. *Management and Labour Studies, 39*(2), 31–41.

Nirmala, M. (2012). Right to Information and NGO's – A Study. *International Journal of Social Science & Interdisciplinary Research, 1*(12), 119–130.

Magnier-Watanabe, R., & Senoo, D. (2008). Organizational Characteristics as Prescriptive Factors of Knowledge Management Initiatives. *Journal of Knowledge Management, 12*(1), 21–36. doi:10.1108/13673270810852368

Maier, D. J., & Moseley, J. L. (2003). The Knowledge Management Assessment Tool (KMAT). *Annual-San Diego-Pfeiffer and Company, 1*, 169–184.

Maier, R. (2007). *Knowledge Management Systems: Information and Communication Technologies for Knowledge Management*. New York: Springer Science & Business Media.

Martens, K. (2002). Mission Impossible? Defining Nongovernmental Organizations. *Voluntas, 13*(3), 271–285. doi:10.1023/A:1020341526691

Martin, B. (2000). Knowledge Management Within the Context of Management: An Evolving Relationship. *Singapore Management Review, 22*(2), 17.

Matschke, C., Moskaliuk, J., & Cress, U. (2012). Knowledge Exchange Using Web 2.0 Technologies in NGOs. *Journal of Knowledge Management, 16*(1), 159–176. doi:10.1108/13673271211199007

Matzkin, D. S. (2008). Knowledge Management in the Peruvian Non-Profit Sector. *Journal of Knowledge Management, 12*(4), 147–159. doi:10.1108/13673270810884318

Mvungi, M., & Jay, I. (2009). Knowledge Management Model for Information Technology Support Service. *Electronic Journal of Knowledge Management, 7*(3), 353–366.

O'Connor, K. (2000). How to Overcome the Cultural Barriers That Can Blockade Knowledge Management. *Law Technology News.* Retrieved from http://www.legaltechnews.com

Puri, S. K. (2007). Integrating Scientific with Indigenous Knowledge: Constructing Knowledge Alliances for Land Management in India. *Management Information Systems Quarterly, 31*(2), 355–379. doi:10.2307/25148795

Ragsdell, G. (2013). Voluntary Sector Organisations: Untapped Sources of Lessons for Knowledge Management. *Proceedings of the 10th International Conference on Intellectual Capital, Knowledge Management and Organizational Learning*, 349-355.

Ragsdell, G., Espinet, E. O., & Norris, M. (2014). Knowledge Management in the Voluntary Sector: A Focus on Sharing Project Know-How and Expertise. *Knowledge Management Research and Practice, 12*(4), 351–361. doi:10.1057/kmrp.2013.21

Rai, M. (2014). *Corruption and Governance in India — Current Status and Way Forward.* New Delhi: Voluntary Action Network India (VANI). Retrieved from http://www.vaniindia.org/publicationpdf/pub6jan15.pdf

Rathi, D., Given, L. M., & Forcier, E. (2016). Knowledge Needs in the Non-Profit Sector: An Evidence-Based Model of Organizational Practices. *Journal of Knowledge Management, 20*(1), 23–48. doi:10.1108/JKM-12-2014-0512

Rathi, D. M., Given, L., & Forcier, E. (2014). Interorganisational Partnerships and Knowledge Sharing: The Perspective of Non-Profit Organisations (NPOs). *Journal of Knowledge Management, 18*(5), 867–885. doi:10.1108/JKM-06-2014-0256

Razmerita, L., Phillips-Wren, G., & Jain, L. C. (Eds.). (2016). Advances in Knowledge Management: An Overview. In Innovations in Knowledge Management. Springer-Verlag Berlin Heidelberg.

Renshaw, S., & Krishnaswamy, G. (2009). Critiquing the Knowledge Management Strategies of Non-Profit Organizations in Australia. *Proceedings of the World Academy of Science, Engineering and Technology (WASET), 37*, 456-464. Retrieved from http://citeseerx.ist.psu.edu/viewdoc/download?doi=10.1.1.192.8007&rep=rep1&type=pdf

Salamon, L. M., & Anheier, H. K. (1992). In Search of the Non-Profit Sector. I: The question Of Definitions. *Voluntas, 3*(2), 125–151. doi:10.1007/BF01397770

Schönström, M. (2005). Creating Knowledge Networks: Lessons from Practice. *Journal of Knowledge Management, 9*(6), 17–29. doi:10.1108/13673270510629936

Schwartz, S. L., & Austin, M. J. (2008). Leading and Managing Nonprofit Organizations: Mapping the Knowledge Base of Nonprofit Management in the Human Services. *Nonprofit Management in the Human Services*, 1-94. Retrieved from http://mackcenter.berkeley.edu/assets/files/articles/Leading%20and%20Managing%20Nonprofit%20Organizations%20Mapping%20the%20Knowledge%20Base.pdf

Sharp, P. (2006). MaKE: A Knowledge Management Method. *Journal of Knowledge Management, 10*(6), 100–109. doi:10.1108/13673270610709242

Singh, M. D., Shankar, R., Narain, R., & Kumar, A. (2006). Survey of Knowledge Management Practices in Indian Manufacturing Industries. *Journal of Knowledge Management, 10*(6), 110–128. doi:10.1108/13673270610709251

Smith, J. G., & Lumba, P. M. (2008). Knowledge Management Practices and Challenges in International Networked NGOs: The Case of One World International. *Electronic Journal of Knowledge Management, 6*(2), 167–176.

Stankowsky, M. A. (2005). Advances in Knowledge Management: University Research Toward an Academic Discipline. In *Creating the Discipline of Knowledge Management: The Latest in University Research*. Burlington: Elsevier Butterworth-Heinemann. doi:10.1016/B978-0-7506-7878-0.50005-3

Streeten, P. (1997). Nongovernmental Organizations and Development. *The Annals of the American Academy of Political and Social Science, 554*(1), 193–210. doi:10.1177/0002716297554001012

Tek, N. D. (2002). *The role of Non-Governmental Organisations in the improvement of livelihood in Nepal*. Tampere University Press.

Tseng, T. L., Huang, C. C., Fan, Y. N., & Lee, C. H. (2015). Quality Control Using Agent Based Framework. In *Encyclopedia of Information Science and Technology* (3rd ed., pp. 5211–5223). Hershey, PA: IGI Global.

UNCF and Regional Office for South Asia. (2008). *Learning from KM Experiences: Case studies on KM initiatives in UNICEF South Asia.* UN Regional Offices and Selected Agencies Possible. Retrieved from http://www.unicef.org/rosa/Learning_from_KM_Experiences.pdf

United Nation Volunteers (UNV). (2012). *Volunteering in India: Contexts, Perspectives and Discourses*. New Delhi: United Nations Development Programme. Retrieved from http://www.in.undp.org/content/dam/india/docs/UNV/volunteering-in-india-contexts-perspectives-and-discourses.pdf?download

Voluntary Action Network India. (2012). *Status of the Voluntary Sector in India: A Study Report*. New Delhi: Voluntary Action Network India (VANI). Retrieved from http://www.vaniindia.org/update/Inside%20Pages%20-Status%20Voluntary%20Sector%20dt%2022-6-13.pdf

Walczak, S. (2008). Knowledge Management and Organizational Learning: An International Research Perspective. *The Learning Organization, 15*(6), 486–494. doi:10.1108/09696470810907392

Wiig, K. M. (1997). Knowledge Management: An Introduction and Perspective. *Journal of Knowledge Management, 1*(1), 6–14. doi:10.1108/13673279710800682

World Bank and Civil Society Collaboration. (2002). *Non-Governmental Organizations and Civil Society Engagement in World Bank Supported Projects: Lessons from OED Evaluations*. Retrieved from http://lnweb90.worldbank.org/oed/oeddoclib.nsf/DocUNIDViewForJavaSearch/851D373F39609C0B85256C230057A3E3/$file/LP18.pdf

Zaei, M. E., & Kapil, P. (2016). The Role of Intellectual Capital in Promoting Knowledge Management Initiatives. *Knowledge Management & E-Learning: An International Journal, 8*(2), 317-333.

Zapata Cantu, L. E., & Mondragon, C. E. (2016). Knowledge Management in Mexican NPOs: A Comparative Study in Organizations with a Local and National Presence. *Journal of Knowledge Management, 20*(1), 69–87. doi:10.1108/JKM-12-2014-0494

Chapter 4
Crowdsourcing in Innovation Activity of Enterprises on an Example of Pharmaceutical Industry

Elżbieta Pohulak-Żołędowska
Wrocław University of Economics, Poland

ABSTRACT

The chapter considers issues connected with innovation creation in open innovation model. The knowledge flow in open innovation has been presented. The main "product" of knowledge economy—innovations (as a concept)—are symbolic goods, founded in symbols – not in atoms. This notion causes some consequences typical for information goods, like ease of replication or exchange, zero-marginal replication costs, and cheap storage. On the other hand, there are growing innovation production costs, and uncertainty and risk of innovation activity that discourage companies from being innovative. The idea of open innovation is being used in pharmaceutical industry more and more often in order to cut innovation costs and shorten the new drugs pipelines. One of the most "open" dimensions of innovation activity in pharmaceutical industry is crowdsourcing: a specific sourcing model, an internet-enabled business model that harnesses the creative ability of agents external to organization.

DOI: 10.4018/978-1-5225-4200-1.ch004

INTRODUCTION

Contemporary economies and industries have become more and more dependent on knowledge and information. It is noteworthy that modern economies are the knowledge-based economies. Modern industries, often being the result of laboratory discovery, are the vital evidence of the pure knowledge influence on economy. This new knowledge phenomenon broadens the definition of traditional economy – based on the physical goods exchange - with symbolic goods, embodying the knowledge itself. Basing the economy on a foundation of knowledge had to have consequences for the goods' production process. The symbolic character of knowledge, the ease of its exchange, replication and flow are features differing this resource from physical ones.

The term Open Innovation was coined by Professor Henry Chesbrough, referring to the need for firms to adapt to a fast-changing environment, increasing competition and specialization of firms. Open Innovation is defined as "a paradigm that assumes that firms can and should use external ideas as well as internal ideas, and internal and external paths to market, as the firms look to advance their technology" (Chesbrough, 2003). Crowdsourcing is one of the most "open" dimensions of sourcing for appropriate knowledge used in open innovation model.

Innovative pharmaceutical industry is an example of the industry strongly depending on new knowledge. New drugs serving unmet medical needs are one of the key value drivers of research-based pharmaceutical companies. Companies made diverse steps to increase their innovation potential by opening innovation with the use of open source, innovation centres, or crowdsourcing.

The goal of the article is to analyse the knowledge flow in open innovation platform with respect to the use of crowdsourcing.

Open Innovation Paradigm

The open innovation paradigm consists of four elements (1) the knowledge cloud, (2) marketable innovations, (3) undeveloped innovations, and (4) open knowledge platform (Chesbrough et al., 2006, pp. 1-14; Bianchi, 2011, pp.23-24).

The first one - the knowledge cloud, is determined by the rule of importance of both internally and externally established knowledge. Internally established knowledge is similar to the public domain scientific output (e.g. publications). Externally originated one comes from companies' failed or stuck projects – unfinished, of undisclosed market potential, unmarketable according to present conditions.

The second element of this paradigm are innovations (successfully commercialized scientific research results). Such an attitude to the innovation process does cause its discontinuity. Opposite to the closed (traditional) model of innovation, open innovation model implies interruption of the innovation process. Discovery does not necessarily have to be done within the same firm that introduces product to the market.

The third of the examined components - undeveloped innovations, consists of all projects that stuck in the laboratory without the possibility of market entry. It is a common practice to free the firm's temporarily redundant knowledge in order to broaden the common pool resources (knowledge cloud) that could benefit further discoveries (in-licensing example).

The fourth element of open innovation paradigm - open knowledge platform, combines all previews rules into the institutional order, without which the commercial dimension of open innovation model could not be achieved.

Figure 1. Knowledge flow in open innovation
Source: author's composition

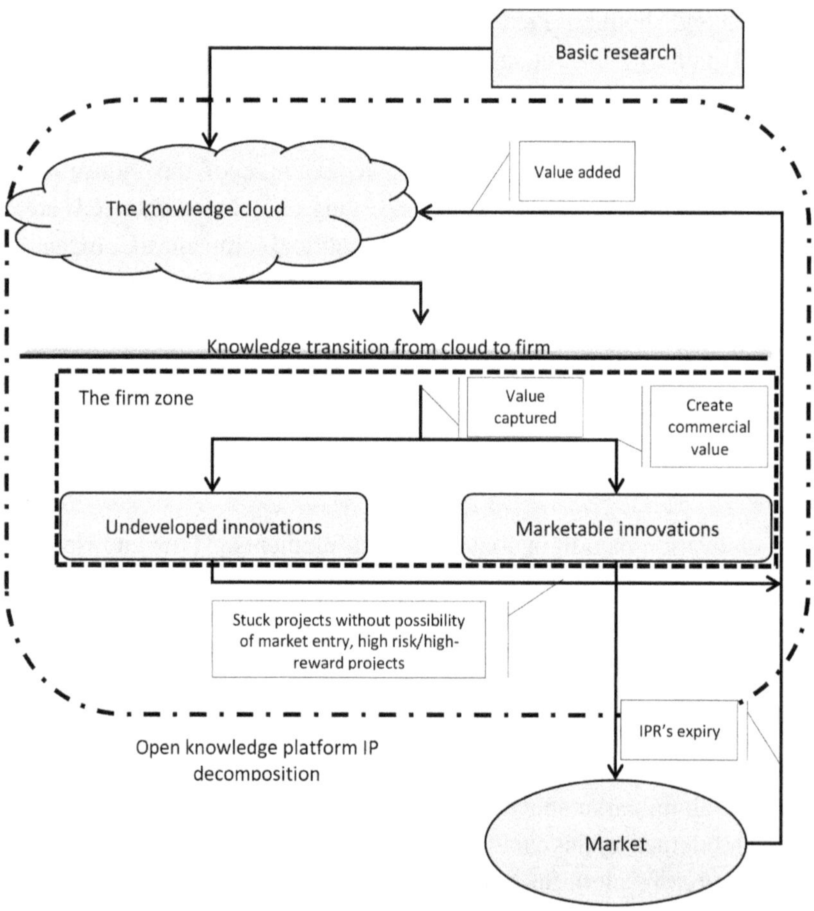

The Knowledge Cloud as an Open Source for the Pharmaceuticals Industry

The first element of the open innovation paradigm is the knowledge flow platform (knowledge cloud). This is the first step of the opening process in each area of interest. The open platform of transferring information, ideas and opinions is one of key factors influencing scientific progress. Only the dialog between various actors can provide a new, sometimes extraordinary or even surprising discovery. The advantage of 'openness' over 'closeness' is the fresh, outsider look on the problem, often breaking stereotypes, accelerating the positive change.

The openness is in the contemporary economics often identified to the network. As a matter of fact open protocol of communication is necessary to establish network. According to Kelly, decentralization is the driving force of dynamic development of today's society.

Interdependence characterizes all aspects of human activity. This feature is the basis of the logic of networks (formulated by Kelly) where open communication between the nodes is the process of superior value (Kelly, 2010, pp. 1-10). Manuel Castells describes the same phenomena as crucial factors of Internet development and success. Castells claims also that 'the openness' is a culture-determined phenomenon, and that it is a base of key technological feature of global communication - a common use (Castells, 2001, pp.36-38). Castells' insights on the culture-determined aspects of 'openness' imply the great change in the existing way of thinking about all areas where exclusiveness (closeness) were considered to be an effective action scheme. It is noteworthy that it was the scientists' society that influenced today's image of the openness. This new approach differs in every aspect from industrial-era principles applied by industrial-era entrepreneurs. It is worth to notice that in the age of globally distributed information dominance the openness culture is the valid foundation for modern society.

In production and development, open source as a philosophy promotes a universal access via free license to a product's design or blueprint, and universal redistribution of that design or blueprint, including subsequent improvements to it by anyone. Open source code is typically created as a collaborative effort in which programmers improve upon the code and share the changes within the community. In the pharmaceutical industry the 'open source' idea has to be reconsidered. Unlike the software creation – in the pharmaceutical industry 'the source' or none modification of it can be regarded as a final product.

The basis for the distinction between ICT and pharmaceutical industry in this issue is the fact that they produce products based on different foundations. The foundation for software is not material – those are bits of information that construct the virtual product, e.g. the digital information good. In the pharmaceutical industry the product is a physical drug, produced in a traditional production process. The foundation of it are the laws of nature because it is based on scarce atoms of real matter. In this context it is noteworthy that 'open source' idea in the pharmaceutical industry can be implemented only on the pre-initiatory stage of product conceptualization, when the study focuses on the properties of a natural phenomenon. It means that 'openness' occurs only on the level of pure science based basic research.

Building the common base of knowledge is not an easy process, because the most critical information is often protected by privacy concerns. It's all locked up in insurance companies, academic and research centres, and government health agencies, and it is very difficult to get because there is no conduit by which this information consistently reaches the research community (Waldron, 2012). What research scientists wants is information on health outcomes, mortality, health conditions of patients, and their behaviour in the context of the disease. Scientists also want information from gene banks or tissue banks from those patients for whom a history is known. At present even a wider scope of information is more and more often the subject of the collaborative 'openness" in the pharmaceutical industry research sector. For the purpose of this article it will be called 'the knowledge cloud'.

Knowledge Sources in the Knowledge Cloud

The substance of knowledge cloud inflows and outflows is information. The information inflow to the knowledge cloud can be of three types. First type of info comes from Academia. Information of this type is embodied in publications which represent the university research results. This type of research is mainly the basic research. It is connected with a traditional profile of university's activity. The 'knowledge cloud' benefits here form the new, unchecked, unverified data.

The second information stream comes from collaborative projects. In those partnerships public actors (universities, research institutes) meet private ones (pharmaceutical companies) in order to discover new areas of knowledge, solve problems of 'stuck', potentially innovative projects, and stimulate new growth areas by public finance support (Allarakhia, 2011, p.6). This sort of information is a result of private (company) knowledge "release" and forwarding it to public institutions.

The third knowledge inflow source is a result of different agreements between specific business players. This last type constitutes the body between open and close concept. It is noteworthy that results of such relations is more in the type of a "club good" than of a public domain. Still the openness in this issue appears in diffusion of knowledge between competing firms. Example of these are: licensing, joint R&D agreements, corporate venture capital, joint ventures and acquisitions· The first source of knowledge inflow is the most open one, strongly connected to the science ethos emphasized by Castells. As he claims, scientists, as science producers have created their own values, where "sharing" is the value of the highest range. Sharing of thoughts, sharing of research output etc (Castells, 2001, p.40). On the other hand good opinion in the professional environment can make a scientist an expert who, thanks to his scientific reliability, can benefit on the labour market. This mechanism works similarly on the software market where young programmers get involved in an open project in order to create themselves a brand. Yet it is noteworthy that this 'basic science research' knowledge inflow is an example of different dimensions of academic science (Pohulak-Żołędowska, 2011, pp. 289-308). First of all - pure academic science – in the shape of educated staff and basic research -as the mission of Academia has always been advancement of science through teaching and research. Therefore publicly funded, unintentional, widening the scope of useful knowledge research is often found as the attractive target. Post-academic science – when the Academia begins to play a vital role in the economic system. The core strength of universities in strengthening the biotech and pharma capabilities lies in its pursuit of all known and rare aspects of biology and systems biology. This gives an edge to the academic scientists in identifying and validating novel molecular targets for various diseases, developing assays and to some extent, in probe discovery. In general, the mission of the industrial sector is not set up to do comprehensive basic research on biological targets, which warrants active collaboration between industry and academia (Roy, McDonald, & Chaguturu, 2011, pp. 130-136).

The second source of knowledge cloud inflow can be understood as an extension of basic research output inflow to the knowledge cloud. The difference here lies in the company's attitude to the problem. The 'undeveloped innovations' are understood as failed company's projects or company's projects that stuck in the conceptual phase of company's R&D department, or they can be understood as joint, multidimensional research on high-risk/high-reward life science areas. The knowledge that inflows to the knowledge cloud is very often a fruit of different forms of cooperation between private and public entities. The common feature of all mentioned partnerships is the fact that they function in the high risk environment, because of the type of projects they are formed for. The 'undeveloped innovations' part of the chart, concerns the projects for which the innovation process got the 'openness' attribute. It is noteworthy that the opening of innovation process breaks the rule of innovation process continuity (within one firm, using one firm's capabilities) (Pohulak-Żołędowska, 2013, pp. 43-56). Opening innovation process empowers the knowledge cloud with the institutional support, because many public or semi-public institutes and organizations are being formed in order to meet the challenges of multithreaded research on tool molecules (like small molecules), new chemistries, antibodies or biomarkers. An example here can be the Novartis Institutes for Biomedical Research (NIBR) an associate of about 300 members form different academic disciplines. Creating by NIBR 'research home' gives opportunity to solve still undeveloped technologies. This initiative is supported by private enterprises, universities and public sector. It also provides on-line platform with working papers, articles, and post docs (Novartis Repository). Another form of such a collaboration in research is NIH Roadmap Initiative in USA and its European counterpart – EU-OPENSCREEN (Roy et al. 2011, pp.131-133) which resulted in emergence of probe discovery in Academia, as well as high throughput screening (HTS) centers harbored in universities all over USA and compound libraries[1] like PubChem (Roy et al., 2010, pp.764–778). It is worth to notice here that described 'openness' concept in the sphere of pharmaceutical industry is not the openness in the meaning of public good. As it refers to specialized organizations and institutes chosen thanks to their intellectual and technical potential and, of course, fundraising capabilities (mainly public), the notion of openness is restricted to the 'involved' club, which makes this sort of knowledge inflow more a club good than a purely public one. It means that in some aspects of knowledge creation in the "undeveloped innovations" part of the chart 'open' does not mean 'free'.

The last portion of knowledge inflow to the knowledge cloud is the result of company's successful innovation activity – a product know-how. This is the most exclusive method of knowledge creation, and for a wide range of potential users, available only after intellectual property rights expiry. The knowledge inflow concerns the complete data on developed products after they lose their law protection that gives their owners the right to monopoly profits. The private knowledge passes to the public domain and increases the public knowledge available in the 'knowledge cloud'.

So, those three types of knowledge inflows augment the 'knowledge cloud' in three different ways. As brand new information that can be a source of market-potential idea– those are the scientific publication of basic research output. As unsolved problems free to the general public in hope to find a collaborative solution which can be used in the future to gain profits. And finally, as a part of the public domain knowledge that is automatically added to the knowledge cloud after intellectual property rights expiry. Of course this value inflow mechanism proposition isn't a perfect image of economic reality. It is still an abstract model that explains main relations between actors creating the knowledge cloud. In practice, for sure, the knowledge inflows are not that simply constructed.

Really Free Knowledge Flow??

Developments of information and communication technology make it easier to collaborate or jointly innovate, that is why the open innovation becomes increasingly attractive business solution in some industries[2]. It is noteworthy that literature shows different shades of openness in innovation process. An open innovation in these literature seem to have two crucial characteristics in that openness is relative and that it is defined by the 'willingness to cross the boundary of a firm either to source or diffuse innovation'. In other words, there are varying degrees of openness in the definition of open innovation and that as long as the firms are utilizing resources outside the firm, this is viewed as open.

The hereby presented model tries to generalize the processes of knowledge flow in open innovation. There are some interactions between actors taking part in the discussed paradigm that cause knowledge flow and increase of the knowledge value. The model can be divided into some parts – the knowledge cloud, that undoubtedly represents the open knowledge- the most open part of the open innovation process. Knowledge collected in the knowledge cloud can be regarded as the commons. It is created not for profit but it does not exclude it. Contains described in the hereby article sorts of knowledge delivered by public, private (like crowdsourcing) and PPP institutions. Not for profit types of innovative conducts are done when the firms want to explore a certain business model or market, or to jointly create knowledge that does not exist. In inbound exchanges, they take what are disclosed or published (public domain knowledge), participate in "open source" type community to jointly create codes or participate in open innovation platforms to unilaterally pose innovation tasks / problems and assignment. (i.e. "crowd sourcing") (Lee et al., n.d., p. 6). In outbound exchange, open innovation can be practiced by firms freely reveal or disclose what they know or their innovation "tasks", contribute back to the community where they took the knowledge from or by providing a kit for the users to participate in the innovation process. Even in this context, modalities of exchange are controlled through mandatory IP law, or contracts, or norms of the community, or rules of participation (terms of uses, and association). Literature shows numerous examples of new R&D structures within pharmaceutical companies, that aim in fostering open innovation dialogue with academia. It is noteworthy that they represent mainly the 'knowledge cloud' suppliers with the very basic research needed on the pre-discovery or early discovery stage (Roy et al., 2010, pp.764–778). There may be mentioned Eli Lilly-PD2 Initiative, Merck-Sage Bionetworks, GSK-caBIG Collaboration, Structural Genomic Consortium and many others (Lilly, n.d.; Sage Bionetworks, n.d.).

Open Source and Crowdsourcing in Pharma

The costs for pharmaceutical R&D increased in the past decades significantly. Munos (2009, 959-968) reported an annual inflation-adjusted increase of R&D costs of 8.6% for the period of 1950–2009. Other studies support this view: while the costs per NME were published to be USD 250 million before the 1990s, the average out-of-the-pocket costs per NME have been calculated to be USD 403 million (2000s) and USD 873 million (2010), respectively (Paul, 2010, pp. 203-2014). The actual

Table 1. R&D efficiencies of multinational pharmaceutical companies (2006–2014)

Company	Total R&D Expenditures (USD million) (2006–2014)	Number of FDA Approved NMEs (2006– 2014)	R&D Efficiency (USD million/ NME) (2006–2014)
Abbott/Abbvie	31,292	1	31,292
Eli Lilly	40,232	4	10,058
Roche	78,340	9	8704
Sanofi	42,948	6	7158
Merck& Co.	62,745	9	6972
Pfizer	72,125	11	6557
AstraZeneca	45,081	7	6440
Novartis	72,100	13	5546
Amgen	30,437	6	5073
GSK	47,109	12	3926
Takeda	23,361	6	3893
Bristol-Myers Squibb	33,006	9	3667
BoehringerIngelheim	22,920	7	327

Merck & Co including Schering Plough (starting 2009), Pfizer including Wyeth (starting 2009), Roche including Genentech (starting 2010), Novartis including Alcon (starting 2010), Sanofi including Genzyme (starting 2011)

Source: (Annual company reports, FDA, n.d.)

challenge for the industry comes from putting the costs of pharmaceutical R&D in context to the output, namely the number of NMEs launched to the market.

In the last years, more and more pharmaceutical companies realized that their low R&D efficiencies necessitate changes to their R&D ecosystems. In an analysis of major research-based pharmaceutical companies it was shown that 73% of the investigated companies were making process changes in R&D (Kruse et al., 2014, pp.11-20).

The open source philosophy is based on transparency, freedom-to-operate, access to results and products for everybody, collaborative improvements, no financial reward for contributors, but recognition in providing a better solution to a challenge. Although these principles do not fit in the context of the IP-driven pharmaceutical sector, some pharmaceutical companies entered the arena of open source innovation. For example, GSK together with Alnylam Pharmaceuticals and the MIT have formed the Pool for Open Innovation against neglected tropical diseases (NTDs) providing open access to 2300 patents in respect to the treatment of tropical diseases (Alnylam, n.d.). GSK also collaborates with Bayer and Novartis (n.d.) in the Global TB Alliance. Although GSK's has been focusing on neglected diseases so far, it also started to apply this open innovation model to other therapeutic areas, such as to infectious and rare diseases or to its clinical trial data (Harrison, 2011, pp. 3-4). Other examples of open source models in the pharmaceutical industry are the Open Source Drug Discovery initiative (OSDD, n.d.) that aims at providing affordable healthcare for neglected diseases and the African Network for Drugs and Diagnostics Innovation (ANDI) (n.d.) that was launched in 2008 (Schuhmacher et al., 2016, p.9). Crowdsourcing Eli Lilly (Lilly, n.d.) is a pioneer and leader in the crowdsourcing field in the pharmaceutical industry. It initiated several crowdsourcing initiatives such as Innocentive® or YourEncore- both are now operated independently. YourEncore (n.d.) is an expert network working in technology industry, such as life science, consumer and food industries, that support companies to access expert know-how to help to solve the companies' problems. Fields of expertise in the pharmaceutical industry are preclinical and clinical development, clinical operations, manufacturing, regulatory affairs, organizational effectiveness, safety, pharmacovigilance, and quality management. Innocentive® (n.d.) is a global network of more than 365,000 registered problem solvers coming from about 200 countries and problem-posting companies, such as AstraZeneca, Eli Lilly, NASA, Procter & Gamble, Syngenta, have partnered with InnoCentive® to get innovative ideas provided. More than 2000 external challenges and more than 40,000 solutions were posted since the start of Innocentive® in 2001, and more than 1500 rewards have been given so far (Innocentive, n.d.). Alternatively, the crowd can bring in new ideas, such as target proposals, that are sourced to the R&D pipeline if evaluated positively. In 2009, Bayer Healthcare has started its crowd-sourcing platform Grants4Targets where it offers two types of grants of EUR 5000–10,000 and EUR 10,000–125,000 for anyone who, for example, submits a target structure that is interesting for research (Schuhmacher et al., 2016, p.9). The crowdsourcing platform receives noticeable global recognition, as around 2000 interested experts click the website per month. So far, most of the proposals came from Germany (21%), Europe (except Germany, 39%) and the US (23%) in the fields of oncology (64%), cardiology (26%) and gynecology (8%). Most of the target approaches were small molecules (63%). Until today, more than 1110 applications were filed, 13% of which were accepted and rewarded with a total sum of EUR 3.2 million resulting in 6 lead generation, one lead optimization and two preclinical development projects (Dorsch et al., 2015, pp. 74-76).

CONCLUSION

As described in the hereby article the open innovation idea presented on pharmaceutical industry's example contains all features of openness. It is open source in the preliminary phase. Later, as the knowledge cloud – it is constructed of both open source and – open innovation – the collaborative form of it.

The current state of the R&D-based pharmaceutical industry has developed business models that are highly reliant on the capture of intellectual property (IP) and exclusivity as a means for generating funding across the process. This is especially important given the high costs of the regulatory process and clinical trials. The current business model of the pharmaceutical industry is unable to meet all medical needs, especially in the areas of neglected and rare diseases. In response, a variety of open source models have been implemented by a variety of organizations.

The reduced R&D efficiency makes it necessary for pharmaceutical companies to realign their R&D concepts. Certainly, open innovation has proven to be a concept of significant attention for the pharmaceutical industry. Either it can be used to complement the traditional R&D model to increase the reach of the internal R&D organization, to access external innovation more easily and to reduce R&D costs. Research alliance concepts such as the CTI and crowdsourcing can be ranked as most valuable examples to improve the R&D efficiencies

REFERENCES

Allarakhia, M. (2011). *Novartis Institutes for Biomedical Research*. CanBiotech Inc.

Alnylam. (n.d.). Investors. *Alnylam*. Retrieved from: http://investors.alnylam.com/releasedetail. cfm?ReleaseID=466757

ANDi. (n.d.). *ANDi: Health innovation for development*. Retrieved from: http://www.andi-africa.org

Bianchi, M., Cavaliere, A., Chiaroni, D., Frattini, F., & Chiesa, V. (2011). Organisational modes for Open Innovation in the bio-pharmaceutical industry: An exploratory analysis. *Technovation*, *31*(1), 22–33. doi:10.1016/j.technovation.2010.03.002

Castells, M. (2001). *The Internet Galaxy: Reflections on the Internet, Business, and Society*. Oxford, UK: Oxford University Press. doi:10.1007/978-3-322-89613-1

Chesbrough, H. (2003). *Open Innovation. The New Imperative for Creating and Profiting from Technology*. Boston: Harvard Business School Press.

Chesbrough, H. (2006), Open Innovation: A New Paradigm for Understanding Industrial Innovation. In Open Innovation Researching a New Paradigm. Oxford University Press.

Dorsch, H., Jurock, A. E., Schoepe, S., Lessl, M., & Asadullah, K. (2015). Grants4Targets—an open innovation initiative to foster drug discovery collaborations between academia and the pharmaceutical industry. *Nature Reviews. Drug Discovery*, *14*(1), 74–76. doi:10.1038/nrd3078-c2 PMID:25430867

FDA. (n.d.). Annual company reports. *FDA*. Retrieved from: http:// www.fda.gov/downloads/Drugs/ DevelopmentApprovalProcess/ HowDrugsareDevelopedandApproved/ DrugandBiologicApprovalReports/ UCM081805.pdf

Harrison C., (2011). GlaxoSmithKline opens the door on clinical data sharing. *NatureReview.Drug Discovery*, *11*, 891–892.

IFPMA. (n.d.). Global alliance for TB drug development (TB alliance). *IFPMA Health Partnerships Directory*. Retrieved from: http:// partnerships.ifpma.org/ partnership/global-alliance-fortb-drug-development-tb-alliance

Innocentive. (n.d.). Innovate with innocentive. *Innocentive*. Retrieved from: www. innocentive.com

Kelly, K. (2001). *Nowe reguły nowej gospodarki. Dziesięć nowych strategii biznesowych dla świata połączonego siecią*. Warszawa: WIG Press.

Kruse, S. (2014). Pharmaceutical RandD productivity: The role of alliances. *Journal of Commercial Biotechnology*, (20): 11–20.

Lee, N. (n.d.). *Interfacing Intellectual Property Rights and Open Innovation*. Retrieved from http://www.wipo.int/edocs/mdocs/mdocs/en/wipo_ipr_ge_11/ wipo_ipr_ge_11_topic6.pdf

Lilly. (n.d.). *Lilly: Open innovation drug discovery*. Retrieved from: https:// openinnovation.lilly.com/dd/

Munos, B. (2009). Lessons from 60 years of pharmaceutical innovation. *Nature Reviews. Drug Discovery*, *8*(8), 959–968. doi:10.1038/nrd2961 PMID:19949401

Novartis. (n.d.). The Novartis Repository. *Novartis*. Retrieved from: http://oak. novartis.com

OSDD. (n.d.). *Open source drug discovery*. Retrieved from: http://www.osdd.net/ home

Paul, S. M., Mytelka, D. S., Dunwiddie, C. T., Persinger, C. C., Munos, B. H., Lindborg, S. R., & Schacht, A. L. (2010). How to improve R&D productivity: The pharmaceutical industry's grand challenge. *Nature Reviews. Drug Discovery*, *9*(9), 203–214. doi:10.1038/nrd3078 PMID:20168317

Pohulak-Żołędowska, E. (2011). Knowledge Production: Industrial Science as a Source of Economies Innovations, Wrocław University of Economics. Argumenta Oeconomica, 19(26).

Pohulak-Żołędowska, E. (2013). Industrial Meaning of University Basic Research in Modern Economies. *Managerial Economics, 14*. 10.7494/manage.2013.14.137

Roy, A. (2011). Recent Trends in Collaborative, Open Source Drug Discovery. *The Open Conference Proceedings Journal*. Retrieved from http://benthamscience.com/open/toprocj/articles/V002/130TOPROCJ.pdf

Roy, A., McDonald, P.R., Sittampalam, S., & Chaguturu, R. (2010). Open access high throughput drug discovery in the public domain: a Mount Everest in the making. *Curr Pharm Biotechnol., 11*(7).

Sage Bionetworks. (n.d.). Retrieved from: http://sagebase.org/

Schuhmacher, Gassmann, O., & Hinder, M. (2016). Chasnging R&D Models in research-based pharmaceutical companies. *Journal of Translational Medicine*, *14*(1), 105. doi:10.118612967-016-0838-4 PMID:27118048

Waldron, R. F. (2012). *Open Innovation in Pharma – Defining Dialogue*. Retrieved from http://www.pharmexec.com/pharmexec/article/articleDetail.jsp?id=788391&pageID=1&sk=&date=

Your Encore. (n.d.). We are a talent community of experts united in our pursuit to make an impact. *Your Encore*. Retrieved from: www.yourencore.com

ENDNOTES

1. For example NIH through its Roadmap initiative set up a Molecular Libraries Program (MLP) to help mine human genome and to explore new ways to study the functions of genes and signaling pathways. MLPCN, Molecular Libraries Probe Production Centers Network, as part of the MLP, provides academic researchers with an opportunity to perform large scale compound screening for identification of small molecules that can be optimized as probes.
2. Best examples are software and biotechnology so far.

Chapter 5
Knowledge Sharing and Innovative Work Behavior:
An Extension of Social Cognitive Theory

Van Dong Phung
The University of Technology, Australia

Igor Hawryszkiewycz
The University of Technology, Australia

ABSTRACT

The growing importance of knowledge sharing is promoting individual innovative work behavior (IWB) to create new products or services for innovative business systems. Also, the key challenges faced by individuals in their knowledge sharing behavior (KSB) are personal perceptions and environmental influences. Thus, this chapter provides a research model using an extension of social cognitive theory that comprises environmental factors (subjective norms, trust), personal factors (knowledge self-efficacy, enjoyment in helping others, organizational rewards, reciprocal benefits, and psychological ownership of knowledge), KSB, and IWB. The authors advance to implement mixed-methods approaches to evaluate the proposed model. The authors believe that this research will contribute to deeper understanding of the effects of personal and environmental factors and KSB on IBW within organizations. The model is also expected to be tested in any organizations in which future researchers or practitioners wish to test this model.

DOI: 10.4018/978-1-5225-4200-1.ch005

INTRODUCTION

Knowledge has been recognized as critical key to creativity and innovation in any organizations. An organization successfully develops knowledge sharing (KS) culture that would help to promote its employee's attitudes and behaviors in general, and innovative work behavior (IWB) in particular. Integrating KS in business plan is promising approach to build the KS culture and bridge the gap between the KS and performing business practices lead to innovation (Lin, 2007a; Law & Ngai, 2008). However, KS has not met many organizations' expectation. Accordingly, research on KS has attracted the interest many researchers, scholars and practitioners for decades. They have embarked on filling one of the following gaps in the literature. Firstly, the inconsistent findings on factors influence KSB. For example, some authors found that organizational rewards has positively impact on KSB (Hsu et al., 2007; Liou et al., 2016), while others revealed no significant relationship between organizational rewards and knowledge sharing (Lin, 2007a; Phung et al., 2017). Secondly, there has been little research on the relationship between KSB and IWB to build an organization that is innovative to the requests of knowledge-based development. Finally, KS has only focused on the technology perspectives in many organizations, in particular technology infrastructures (Hsu et al., 2007; Pfeffer & Sutton, 1999). Yet, explicit studies specifically oriented to the problems of KS in term of environmental and personal factors are rare (Hsu et al., 2007).

Thus, the interest of this chapter is to formulate an extension of social cognitive theory (SCT) in order to deeper understand the relationships between environmental and personal factors and KSB to promote IWB in organizations. In addition, the chapter also explores the moderating roles of transformational leadership on environment-personal factors and KSB, and transactive memory systems on KSB and IWB.

SCT was developed by Bandura (1986), and it was used to investigate the effects of environmental and personal factor on KSB in virtual communities (Hsu et al., 2007; Lin et al., 2009; Chang et al., 2015; Liou et al., 2016; Moon et al., 2016; Rahman et al., 2016). This theory indicates that an individual behavior is affected by social influences and personal perceptions. As applied to this study, this theory holds that the authors would expect environment and personal factors to influence or explain KSB because the theory states that a behavior that has personal perception in environmental influences would be taken by a person. This chapter will contribute to the literature of KS by investigating and answering the main research question as follows:

- **RQ.1:** What factors influence KSB?
- **RQ.2:** How does KSB influence IWB?

- **RQ.3:** What are the joint effects of transformational leadership and environment-personal factors on KSB?
- **RQ.4:** What are the joint effects of transactive memory systems quality and KSB on IWB?

The organization of the chapter is as follows. The background is presented in the next section, followed by describing the theory perspectives towards a theoretical research model. Then, the research framework for the application of the proposed research model is described in the model implementation section. The next section is to outline the future trends. Finally, the conclusion with the remarks is given.

BACKGROUND

This section provides broad definitions and discussions of knowledge sharing behavior (KSB) and innovative work behavior (IWB). It also reviews empirical studies on KSB based on social cognitive theory (SCT) that is main focus of this chapter.

Innovative Work Behavior

According to Janssen (2000), IWB involves three components considering as consecutive steps in personal innovation: idea creation, idea promotion, and idea implementation. The first step of the individual innovation is to create idea that is generation of new and valuable ideas in any field (Amabile et al., 1996). Second, potential colleagues or partners will be promoted the idea which occurs when an individual has created an idea and engages in social activities to get supporter surrounding an idea (Janssen, 2000). Finally, the innovation process involves idea application by developing a model or innovative prototype that is likely to be tried and utilized in teams or the whole organization (Kanter, 1998). Basic innovations are accomplished by individuals, whilst the completion of more complicated innovations often needs teamwork relies upon a diversity of knowledge, ability, and work roles (Janssen, 2000; Kanter, 1998). With the belief that individual IWB have positively effects on work outcomes, several researchers have dedicated increasing attention to factors that potentially foster IWB such as KS and IWB (Radaelli et al., 2014) and KS determinants, behaviors, and IWB (Akhavan et al., 2015). First, Radaelli et al. (2014) conducted a study which investigated the new insights into how employees' KS impacts their IWB. This study proposed three mechanisms linking an individual's KS behaviors to his or her own IWB: (1) a direct impact whereby the act of sharing derives a recombination and translation of knowledge that promotes innovation; (2) an indirect impact by which KS creates social conditions (i.e., reciprocation with new knowledge) for innovation; (3) a distal influence whereby the antecedents of KS also facilitates innovation. The results indicated that individuals who share knowledge also engage more in generating, promoting and implementing innovations. It also recommended that it is the act of knowledge recombination and translation embedded in KS that utilizes the most positive impact on IWB. Second, Yu et al. (2013) examined individual-level KS and innovative behavior of employees and interactions between the individual level of KS and the climate of innovation within the organization. The findings showed that KS and interactive behavior among staff in the finance and insurance industry in Taiwan enhanced innovative behavior and the ability to innovate and there is a positive association between KS and innovative behavior. Finally, Akhavan et al. (2015) examined the influence of socio-psychological factors from different theoretical perspectives, whether it leads to superior employees' IWB. The results supported the influences of three motivational factors (perceived loss of knowledge power, perceived reputation enhancement, and perceived enjoyment in helping others) and two social capital factors (social interaction ties and trust) on employees' attitude toward KS. The study also specified that individuals' KS behaviors improve their IWB.

Knowledge Sharing Behavior

Knowledge is a significant organizational resource. KS contributes to developing competitive advantages for organizations in complex environments, such as the improvement of intellectual capital, by encouraging the exchange and creation of knowledge within an organization. This is because knowledge is the key factor for achieving continuous innovation at both individual and organizational levels. It is also examined a closely related factor for the progress of any individual or organization, hence it is an essential indicator to be studied in the KS on individual IWB. Davenport and Prusak (1998) defined KSB as the process involving the social exchange of knowledge between individuals and groups of people. The authors advanced the measurement of KSB by the frequency of knowledge dissemination that can also be beneficial for an organization. In turn, KS is relied upon knowledge management, which is a necessary activity in all businesses. Any KS activities occurring within an organization between its employees often rely on both knowledge-giving and knowledge-receiving. Knowledge management is a broader term that caters to a wide range of topics, while KS is a specific focus area of KM (Hendriks, 1999). KS, when performed in conjunction with other aspects of the step-by-step process of KM (creation, storage, sharing, and application) can fulfil a strategic necessity for organizations that wish to improve their capabilities and performance (Lee & Hong, 2002).

Empirical Studies on KSB Based on SCT

This section reviews the key empirical KSB studies based on SCT. A comprehensive understanding of the literature available on KSB is examined that could yield a theoretical foundation for the research. In consistent with the aim of the chapter, the focus, thus, can be prevented by existing research models based on SCT.

Most of the key empirical KSB studies based on SCT have focused on virtual communities. The first study adopted SCT based model to examine the determinants of KSB was conducted by Hsu et al. (2007). These authors are as the pioneers who first utilized SCT on the field of KSB in virtual communities. This study examined the one environmental factor (trust) and two personal factors consisting of KS self-efficacy and outcome expectations. Respondents were 274 individual members of virtual communities via the discussion forum of Yahoo!. The study found that KS self-efficacy, personal outcome expectations, and trust significantly influence KSB in virtual communities. The result indicated that KS self-efficacy was deemed an important role in guiding personal behavior. The study suggested that managers/leaders should provide some strategies such as online training or support programs to improve individual self-efficacy to encourage members believe on themselves and share their knowledge with other members in virtual communities. Moreover, the findings also revealed that member would be more positive attitude on KS when they believe that they could strengthen the relationships with others by sharing their knowledge. The study also recommended that having high level of trust with others would help members mitigate barriers that facilitate self-regulating policies, source disclosure and establish brands of virtual communities. Hsu et al. (2007) recommended that the future research should explore the most environmental factors such as subjective norms.

Based on Hsu et al. (2007), many other studies have continuously applied SCT to examine KSB in virtual communities (Lin et al., 2009; Chang et al., 2015; Liou et al., 2016; Moon et al., 2016; Rahman et al., 2016). These studies examined the different the environmental and personal factors as shown in Table 1. The findings from these studies are quite consistent implied that virtual member KSB is affected by social influences and personal perceptions. These two major of determinants of KSB, environmental and personal factors, promote the choice of behavior indicates that KSBs are active agents rather than passive receivers of environmental pressures to share knowledge on them. However, there has still been a lack of studies about KSB that apply SCT in organizations. Unlike virtual communities, an organization has formal policies and procedures to guide the individual's KSB with the common interests or needs reach to organizational goals. Hence, studying KBS based on SCT is imperative to contribute to deeper understanding of KSB leads to creativity and innovation in organizations.

Table 1. Dimensions of environmental and personal factors, and KSB across studies

Factors	Related Literature					
	Hsu et al. (2007)	Lin et. al (2009)	Chang et al. (2015)	Liou et al. (2016)	Moon et al. (2016)	Rahman et al. (2016)
Subjective norm						✓
Norm of reciprocity		✓		✓		
Trust	✓	✓	✓			
Commitment			✓			
Knowledge self-efficacy	✓	✓	✓	✓	✓	
Outcome expectations	✓				✓	
Perceived relative advantage		✓				
Perceived compatibility						
Rewards				✓		
Reciprocity				✓		
Community loyalty		✓				
Community participation				✓		
Sharing goal orientation					✓	
Organizational climate					✓	
Attitudes towards KS						✓
Behavioral intention						✓

TOWARDS A THEORETICAL RESEARCH MODEL

This section presents the development of the proposed theoretical research model which is developed based on social cognitive theory with a set of critical variables based on the literature review. Also, this section presented the process of developing the measurement scales will be used to measure the model constructs. Finally, this section explains the relationships between the model constructs and proposes the research hypotheses. This model is expected to be tested by future researchers or practitioners who wish to study the KSB and IWB.

Social Cognitive Theory (SCT)

SCT was first introduced by Bandura (1986) as a broader framework for understanding human motivation, thought and behavior to predict and explain individual behavior and behavior changes. In this chapter, SCT is served as the theoretical foundation for developing the theoretical research model to examine the relationship between environment influences, personal factors and KSB.

In SCT's model, environmental influences, personal factors, and behaviors act as interactive relationships (Wood & Bandura, 1989). Bandura (2002) explains the main concepts of SCT by the "triadic reciprocal causation" as follows (Figure 1):

- Environmental influences that impact the individual capacity to successfully fulfil the behavior;
- Personal factors determine whether a person has low or high knowledge self-efficacy leads to his/her behavior and;
- Behavior is the response which a person gains after his/her performing a certain behavior.

Towards a Knowledge Sharing Behavior Model

SCT declares that a certain action that involves personal perception in a social environment would be taken by a person. A personal perception to behave in a certain way consists of cognitive factors. One is self-efficacy or the belief is a potential significant factor impacting the decision of sharing knowledge (Bock & Kim, 2002). Engaging in KS may require the sense of the self-confidence and ability of individuals (Lin, 2007a). Lin (2007a) indicates that people who find enjoyment in KS and consequently helping other people is more like to be motivated in sharing their knowledge with others. Other important factor has significant influence on individual KS decisions is outcome expectations associated with organizational rewards and reciprocal benefits (Hsu et al., 2007; Wang & Noe, 2010). Wang and Noe (2010) found that person's beliefs with regards to psychological ownership of knowledge is very important as when people perceived they owned knowledge instead of the organization they would engage in KS. Moreover, subjective norm

Figure 1. The interactions between environment, person and behavior (Bandura, 1986)

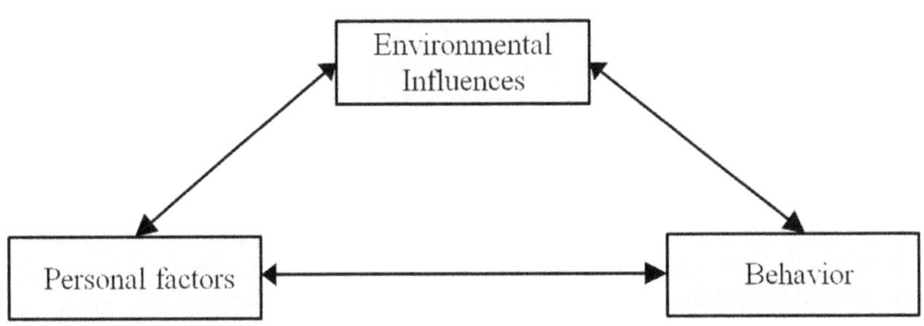

shows employee's feeling regarding the social pressure which they perceive a given behavior surrounding them. Employees with positive subjective norms lead to given behaviors than the concerned behavior intentions would be more positive in KS. Finally, trust has also been recognized as an essential determinant influencing KS (Hsu et al., 2007; Wang & Noe, 2010).

Model Development

Prior studies have emphasized several factors that influence individual KSB including subjective norm, trust, psychological ownership, and motivation (extrinsic and intrinsic motivation) (e.g., Hsu et al., 2007; Lin, 2007b). Therefore, the authors could rationally believe that a personal KSB would be guided by personal perceptions and social influences. The model is an extension of Bandura's SCT (1986) that aims at providing a way to examine the effects of environmental and personal factors on KSB leads to IWB. It also considers the two moderators, transformational leadership and transactive memory systems, on the relationships between constructs of the model.

The model is conceptualized by eleven main constructs: two environmental factors, five personal factors, KSB, IWB, transformational leadership, and transactive memory systems quality (Figure 2). The definitions of these constructs are explained as follows.

- **Subjective Norms:** "The extent to which an individual perceives whether social pressure will influence the performance of KS behavior" (Ajzen, 1991).
- **Trust:** "The extent of belief in good behaviors, competence, and reliability of members with respect to sharing knowledge in the organization" (Lee & Choi, 2003).
- **Knowledge Self-Efficacy:** "The extent of confidence in employees' ability to sharing knowledge that is important to the organization" (Lin et al., 2009).
- **Enjoyment in Helping Others:** "Knowledge workers who derive enjoyment from helping others may be more favorable oriented toward KS and more inclined to share knowledge" (Lin, 2007a).
- **Organizational Rewards:** "The degree to which a reward system to share any new and creative ideas and effectiveness KS" (Lin, 2007a).
- **Reciprocal Benefits:** "Reciprocal benefit is a form of conditional benefit; that is, individual expect future benefits from his or her present actions" (Hung et al., 2011).
- **Psychological Ownership of Knowledge:** "The extent to which individuals believe on the possession and are responsible towards the knowledge they possess" (Han et al., 2010).

- **Knowledge Sharing Behavior:** The extent to which a person performs KS activities in the organization (Davenport & Prusak, 1998; Lin et al., 2009).
- **Innovative Work Behavior:** "The extent to which employees behave to create, promote, and implement new ideas in an group or organization" (Janssen, 2000).
- **Transformational Leadership:** "The extent to which leader motivates followers to work for transcendental goals (big improvements) and for higher level self-actualizing needs instead of immediate self-interest" (Bass & Avolio, 1997).
- **The Quality of Transactive Memory System (TMS):** The extent to which team members are able to recognize and utilize the knowledge and expertise of other team members (Ariff, 2013; Brandon & Hollingshead, 2004).

Hypotheses Development

Environmental Factors

Subjective Norms (SN)

According to Ajzen (1991), the subjective norm is a social factor which can be described as the extent to which a person perceives social pressure to perform or

Figure 2. The proposed research model showing factors based on SCT

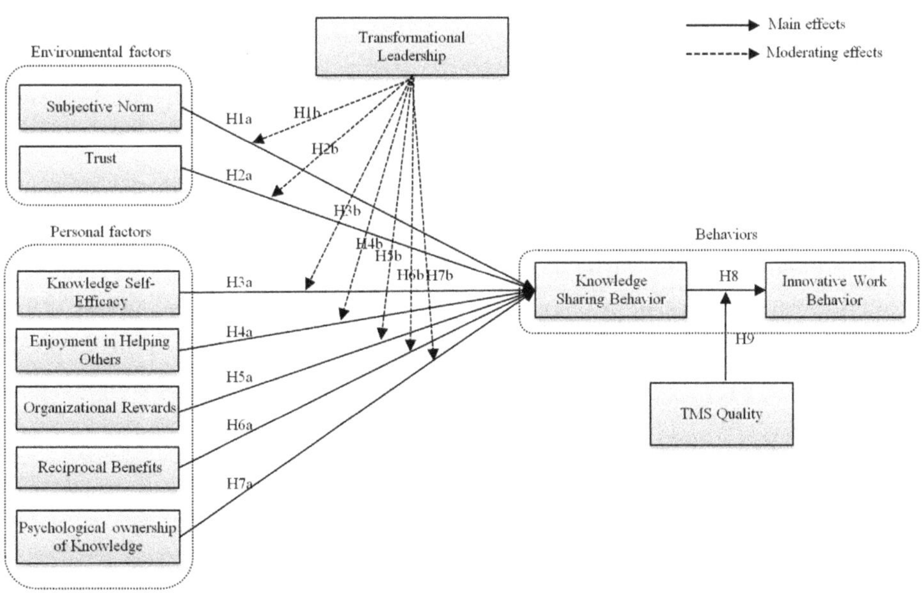

not to perform certain behavior. Subjective norm has acquired significant practical support as an import antecedent to behavioral (Bock et al., 2005). Hee (2000) emphasized the impact of others who are important to the employee such as "close friends, relatives, colleagues, or business partners". Subjective norm shows personal emotion regarding the social pressure they perceive about given behaviors surrounding them. Also, employees with positive subjective norms lead to given behaviors than the concerned behavior intentions would be more positive in KS. Therefore, it can be hypothesized that.

- **Hypothesis One A:** SN has a positive impact on KSB.

Trust (TRU)

Lee and Choi (2003) defined trust as maintaining reciprocal faith in each other in terms of intention and behaviors. It may encourage the exchange of knowledge to be substantive, influential, and open (Lee & Choi, 2003). Trust affects KS decisions and with trust, a person becomes less willing to share knowledge with others (Davenport & Prusak, 1998). According to Nonaka (1994) interpersonal trust is a key factor in teams, groups and organizations to establishing an environment for KS. Employees are more willing to engage into KS when they have a high level of trust in their relationships (Lee & Choi, 2003). Thus, interpersonal trust increases individuals' tendency to participate in KS practices (Fukuyama, 1995). Therefore, it can be hypothesized that:

- **Hypothesis Two A:** TRU has a positive impact on KSB.

Personal Factors

Knowledge Self-Efficacy (KSE)

According to Lin (2007a), "Knowledge self-efficacy is an individual's judgment of his or her ability to organize and execute successful performance in everyday tasks". The individual's sense of self-efficacy is affected by the tendency of individuals to take actions such as level of problems, expressed interest, persistence and task effort (Hsu et al., 2007). Lin's study shows that knowledge sharing contributions improve an organization's performance if staff increase their willingness to give and receive knowledge (Lin, 2007a). Therefore, it can be hypothesized that:

- **Hypothesis Three A:** KSE has a positive impact on KSB.

Enjoyment in Helping Others (EHO)

Prior research shows that employees are inherently interested in giving knowledge because of the enjoyment acquired from helping others (Wasko & Faraj, 2005). Thus, employees is likely more favorably oriented toward sharing their knowledge in terms of both giving and receiving (Lin, 2007a). Therefore, it can be hypothesized that:

- **Hypothesis Four A:** EHO has a positive impact on KSB.

Expected Organizational Rewards (REW)

Providing incentives and rewards to motivate staff to contribute in knowledge sharing adoption are recommended (Wong, 1989). Employees who share their knowledge may improve team performance and consecutively increase the personal rewards received. Incentives and rewards encourage staff to share knowledge (Bock et al., 2005). Expected organizational rewards point out what the organizational values form individual behaviors (Lin, 2007a). Expected organizational rewards can vary according to the organization policies from monetary incentives to non-monetary awards (Davenport & Prusak, 1998). Therefore, it can be hypothesized that:

- **Hypothesis Five A:** REW has a positive impact on KSB.

Reciprocal Benefit (RB)

Reciprocal benefit is a form of conditional benefit; that is, the individual expects future benefits from his or her present actions. It means that an action is done in response to prior friendly behaviors (Hung et al., 2011). Many researchers have conducted detailed analyses of reciprocity and indicated that it can be valuable to knowledge contributors as they anticipate future help from others (Hung et al., 2011). Also, studies have investigated that reciprocity can yield an effective motivation to encourage KS and consequently establish long-term mutual cooperation (Lin, 2007b). Thus, people who expect reciprocity from other members through sharing their knowledge will share more useful and creative ideas and their satisfaction with the meeting will be higher KS intentions (Hung et al., 2011; Lin, 2007b). Therefore, it can be hypothesized that:

- **Hypothesis Six A:** RB has a positive impact on KSB.

Psychological Ownership of Knowledge (POK)

POK can be described as the degree to which people believe on the possession and are responsible towards the knowledge they possess (Pierce et al., 2001). That is,

POK explains the feeling of possession linking to knowledge in a psychological sense that makes persons regard intangible/tangible objectives as an addition of themselves (Han et al., 2010). Van Dyne and Pierce (2004) found that the POK can stimulate an altruistic spirit, supporting to extra-role behavior such as KSB and individuals who have a sense of POK may display a sense of belonging which impacts altruistic spirit and which influences KSB. Thereby, POK is conductive to KSB on the part of individuals. Therefore, it can be hypothesized that:

- **Hypothesis Seven A:** POK has a positive impact on KSB.

Knowledge Sharing Behavior and Innovative Work Behavior

It is undoubtedly that one's capability of transferring and utilizing knowledge may encourage his or her level of individual innovation, for example, quick problem-solving capacity and improved faster reaction to novel challenges. Several academics highlighted the essential of KS to improve individual IWB (Akhavan et al., 2015; Yu et al., 2013). Effective knowledge processes can create important organizational intellectual capital and intangible resources to improve performance (Nold, 2012). For example, when an employee transfers tacit knowledge into explicit knowledge, the entire organization will benefit from it (Han et al., 2010). This shows that when organizations manage their knowledge assets better, they will then have a greater chance of better performance in both organizational and individual levels (Han et al., 2010; Kowal & Fortier, 1999). This research expects that individual willingness of sharing knowledge with others is likely to sustain IWB. Therefore, it can be hypothesized that.

- **Hypothesis Eight A:** KSB positively impacts IWB.

Moderating Effects

Transformational leadership (TL)

TL is defined as "a process by which leaders inspire their followers to perform at a higher level than expected and to potentially exceed the followers' own self-interests for a high-level of shared vision" (Bass, 1999; Han et al., 2016). It motivates individuals to feel empowered, which enhances individuals' engagement (Han et al., 2016). Such leadership behaviors include four distinct aspects: inspiration, intellectual stimulation, individualized consideration and idealized influence (Bass, 1999; Han et al., 2016). Based on transformational leadership, many modern organizations have taken an active interest in knowledge management to increased creativity and innovation through more effective KS (Han et al., 2016). KS among employees has been considered as one of the vital "success factors" in knowledge management (Han et al., 2016). Furthermore, several studies have been conducted to examine the influence of transformational leadership on KSB and found that social environmental influences and personal factors can be used as an indicator for their KSB. In this study, thus, we believe that transformation leadership can have positive effect on the relationship between environmental and personal factors and KSB. Therefore, it can be hypothesized that.

- **Hypothesis One B:** TL moderates the relationship between subjective norm and KSB.
- **Hypothesis Two B:** TL moderates the relationship between trust and KSB.
- **Hypothesis Three B:** TL moderates the relationship between knowledge self-efficacy and KSB.
- **Hypothesis Four B:** TL moderates the relationship between enjoyment in helping others and KSB.
- **Hypothesis Five B:** TL moderates the relationship between expected organizational rewards and KSB.
- **Hypothesis Six B:** TL moderates the relationship between reciprocity and KSB.
- **Hypothesis Seven B:** TL moderates the relationship between psychological ownership of knowledge and KSB.

The Quality of Transactive Memory Systems (TMS)

The definition of TMS is that it is a team's shared understanding of and "who does what" (Ariff et al., 2011; Brandon & Hollingshead, 2004) and "who knows what" (Ariff et al., 2011; Wegner & Raymond, 1991) in the team. TMS quality is the extent to which team members are able to recognize and utilize the expertise and knowledge of other team members (Brandon & Hollingshead, 2004). In teams with high TMS quality, members actively share with and acquire their knowledge, information and resources from others (Ariff, 2013). However, in teams where TMS quality is low, tasks can be easily divided and members can complete their tasks independently which impede individuals share their knowledge with each other. Therefore, it can be hypothesized that:

- **Hypothesis Nine:** TMS quality moderates the relationship between KSB and IWB.

The Development for Measurement Scales for Measuring the Constructs

In order to develop and validate the measurement scales that can be used to measure the constructs, and test the proposed research model in the future, the researchers developed a survey questionnaire. The questionnaire, with a total of 66 items, is divided into two main parts. The first part has 62 items which aimed to identify the relationships between constructs by asking participants to rate the statements (questions) using a five-point Likert-like scale. Each of questions is designed to represent an indicator or observed variable to measure the corresponding conceptual constructs. The second part, with 4 questions, seeks the demographic information of the survey sample: gender, age, qualification, and working experience. The following sections provide the process to generate, operationalize and validate measurement items.

Survey Design Workshop Series

Once the initial questionnaire has been prepared by the authors with support from experts, the researchers held the 5-week workshop series to strengthen the content and face validity of the instruments for this study. The workshop series took place in the School of Systems, Management and Leadership (SML) at the University of Technology Sydney (UTS) during a consecutive 5-week period. The workshop series was held one per week. The profiles of nine experts participated in these workshops presented in Table 5 in the Appendix. In the first workshop, the research presented the research questions, research model, initial questionnaire version and data analysis techniques. These relevant documents were sent to all participants before each of all workshops. The experts discussed and gave their comments on each part of the questionnaire. The expert 6, 7 and 8 were participated online because of time and distance limit. Based on that, the questionnaire was weekly improved. After the fifth week of the workshop series, the questionnaire was finalized from all aspects of content and format, and ready for the pilot study.

Operationalization of Constructs

All constructs of the conceptual model are the latent constructs, including Subjective norms (SN), Trust (TRU), Knowledge self-efficacy (KSE), Enjoyment in helping others (EHO), Expected organizational rewards (REW), Reciprocal benefits (RB), Psychological ownership of knowledge (POK), Transformational leadership (TL), Knowledge sharing behavior (KSB), the quality of transactive memory systems (TMS) and Innovative work behavior (IWB). Three of these constructs, TL, TMS and

IWB are considered to be second-order constructs, extracted from sub-dimensions. As Hair et al. (2010) suggested, each of these constructs should be measured by at least three items (indicators/observed variables). With this rule of thumb, all eleven constructs are measured by multi-items in order to better the validity and reliability of the measurement scales.

Scaling and Measurement

In this research, the existing measures from prior studies were used for the questionnaire. All items were adapted for use in the KS context in organizations. All indicator variables were measured using a five-point Likert-type scale with two types of anchors, behaviorally and perceptually anchors. Behavioral anchors were ranging from 1=Never to 5=Always, while perceptual anchors ranged from 1=Strongly Disagree (SD) to 5=Strongly Agree (SA). The study employed the Likert-type scales as the recommendation for research involving behavioral and perceptional measurement (Sharma, 2009). Another reason is the implementation of Structural Equation Modeling (SEM) as a data-calculated method (Hair et al., 2010). The rationale that the researcher used these types of anchors for the measurement scale was based on the suggestions of Sharma (2009). He recommended that researchers utilize the behavioral anchors when items refer to specific actions that individuals have taken, such as "Never–Always". Moreover, his research also revealed that perceptual anchors are employed when items that capture responses generally on "Agree–Disagree" Likert scales or on semantic different scales. Therefore, the scales and anchors were used provide the advantage of standardizing and quantifying relative effects.

Item Development

The total of 62 items has been developed as present in Table 6 in the Appendix. The alignment of research questions, hypotheses, survey items, and scale types are provided in Table 2.

Piloting the Measurement Scales

The objective of pilot study is to avoid potential biases and improve the accuracy and validity of the data in the field at the individual level. The pilot study was conducted with a total of 115 lecturers (volunteers with English speaking backgrounds) from two public universities in Vietnam. The participants were given the questionnaire and asked to examine it for relevance, meaningfulness and clarity, and give their onions for all the questions. Next, the research evaluated the reliability for all measurement

Table 2. Alignment of research questions, hypotheses, survey items, and scale types

Research Question	Latent variable	Hypothesis	Item code	Scale Type
Research question 1	Subjective norms (SN)	H1a	SN1, SN2, SN3	1. SD → 5. SA
	Trust (TRU)	H2a	TRU1 to TRU6	1. SD → 5. SA
	Knowledge self-efficacy (KSE)	H3a	KSE1 to KSE4	1. SD → 5. SA
	Enjoyment in helping others (EHO)	H4a	EHO1 to EHO4	1. SD → 5. SA
	Organization rewards (REW)	H5a	REW1 to REW4	1. SD → 5. SA
	Reciprocal benefits (RB)	H6a	RB1, RB2, RB3	1. SD → 5. SA
	Psychological ownership of knowledge (POK)	H7a	POK1 to POK5	1. SD → 5. SA
Research question 3	Transformational leadership (TL) • *Charisma* • *Intellectual stimulation* • *Individualized consideration*	H1a-H7b	CHA1 to CHA7 IS1, IS2, IS3 IC1, IC2, IC3	1. Never → 5. Always
Research question 1, 2, 3, 4	Knowledge sharing behavior (KSB)	All hypothesis	KSB1 to KSB5	1. Never → 5. Always
Research question 4	Quality of Transactive Memory Systems (TMS) • *Who knows what* • *Who does what*	H9	WKW1, WKW2, WKW3 WDK1, WDK2, WDK3	1. Never → 5. Always
Research question 2 & 4	Innovative work behavior (IWB) • *Idea generation* • *Idea promotion* • *Idea implementation*	H8, H9	IGE1, IGE2, IGE3 IPR1, IPR2, IPR3 IIM1, IIM2, IIM3	1. Never → 5. Always

Note: SD: Strongly Disagree; SA: Strongly Agree.

scales through Cronbach's alpha which is most widely used to estimate internal consistency reliability. The higher value of Cronbach's alpha coefficient indicates a higher degree of reliability or internal consistency between the items being tested (Kimberlin & Winterstein, 2008). This value ranges from 0 to 1, with values of 0.6 to 0.7 considered acceptable limit (Kline, 2015). Table 3 shows the value of Cronbach's alpha for each scale used in the current research. All scales have Cronbach's alpha values ranging between 0.711 and 0.858. Therefore, the measurement scales are well above the acceptable limit of 0.70 suggested by Hair et al. (2010), except for EHO3 with the item-total correlation value less than the cutoff value of 0.3. The results, thus, confirms an acceptable internal consistency reliability and evidence of content and construct validity. The scales are good measures of the concept under study (Hair et al., 2010).

Table 3. The Cronbach's alphas of the measurement scales

Measurement Scale	N of items	Cronbach's alpha (α)	Original value of (α)	Deleted items
Subjective norms (SN)	3	0.772		
Trust (TRU)	6	0.845		
Knowledge self-efficacy (KSE)	4	0.838		
Enjoyment in helping others (EHO)	3=4-1	0.832	0.683	EHO3
Expected organizational rewards (REW)	4	0.848		
Reciprocal benefits (RB)	3	0.824		
Psychological ownership of knowledge (POK)	5	0.760		
Transformational leadership (TL) *Charisma (CHA)* *Intellectual stimulation (IS)* *Individualized consideration (IC)*	7 3 3	0.802 0.748 0.781		-
Transactive memory system quality (TMS) *Who know who (WKW)* *Who does what (WDW)*	2 3	0.766 0.845		
Knowledge sharing behavior (KSB)	5	0.858		
Innovative work behavior (IWB) *Ideal generation (IGE)* *Ideal promotion (IPR)* *Ideal implementation (IIM)*	3 3 3	0.739 0.815 0.711		

Note: The original value of Cronbach's alpha for the scales before deleting the items if needed.

MODEL IMPLEMENTATION: RECOMMENDATIONS AND GUIDELINES

The chapter's goal is to implement the model to support for examining the relationships between environmental and personal factors on KSB to promote IWB in any organizations. The previous section describes the development towards a theoretical research model. Thus, this section presents the research framework as the recommendations and guidelines for future researchers or practitioners who wish to empirically test the model. This section begins with the framework for research including the explanation and justification of the selection of the research design, followed by the research design process with more details of steps to apply the model in practice. Finally, this section briefly discusses the data analysis techniques such as factor analysis (explanatory factor analysis - EFA, confirmatory factor analysis - CFA) and structural equation modeling (SEM) that should be used to analyze data for testing the model.

Framework for Research

The Selection of a Research Design

The sequential mixed-methods, including quantitative and qualitative methods, will be used to accomplish the research goal. The questionnaire survey will be conducted in phase one to collect the data from the study sample about their influencing factors that will then be used in the research framework. Based on that phase two will be undertaken by interviews to validate the quantitative results.

This combination is used in a complementary manner (Neuman, 2006) which applies the quantitative approach as the main approach, followed by qualitative approach as a complementary need. It helps to gain the highest level of understanding and investigating the research problem (Neuman, 2005).

Research Design Process

The process for exploring the influences of environmental and personal factors on KSB towards IWB using the proposed research model is described in Figure 3.

Step 1: Questionnaire development

A survey design workshop is conducted to adapt and validate the survey instrument. This is necessary because the items developed in this research should be adapted into a certain context of study where researchers or practitioners wish to test the research model. Once the initial questionnaire has been prepared based on the constructs and items from this research, then, the researchers setup the workshop(s) to strengthen the content and face validity of the instruments into the context of study. Previous section reports how to hold the workshop(s) for questionnaire survey design.

Step 2: Pilot study

A pilot study is carried out to validate the survey questionnaire which benefits the research as discussed above. The draft questionnaire based on the results from Step 1 should be pre-tested because it is adapted to the different research context. As presented in previous section, the pilot study brings the many benefits to the research. It is widely recognized as a vital part of the development of research instruments (Bourque & Fielder 2003).

Step 3: Questionnaire survey

Figure 3. The process for the implementation of testing the research model

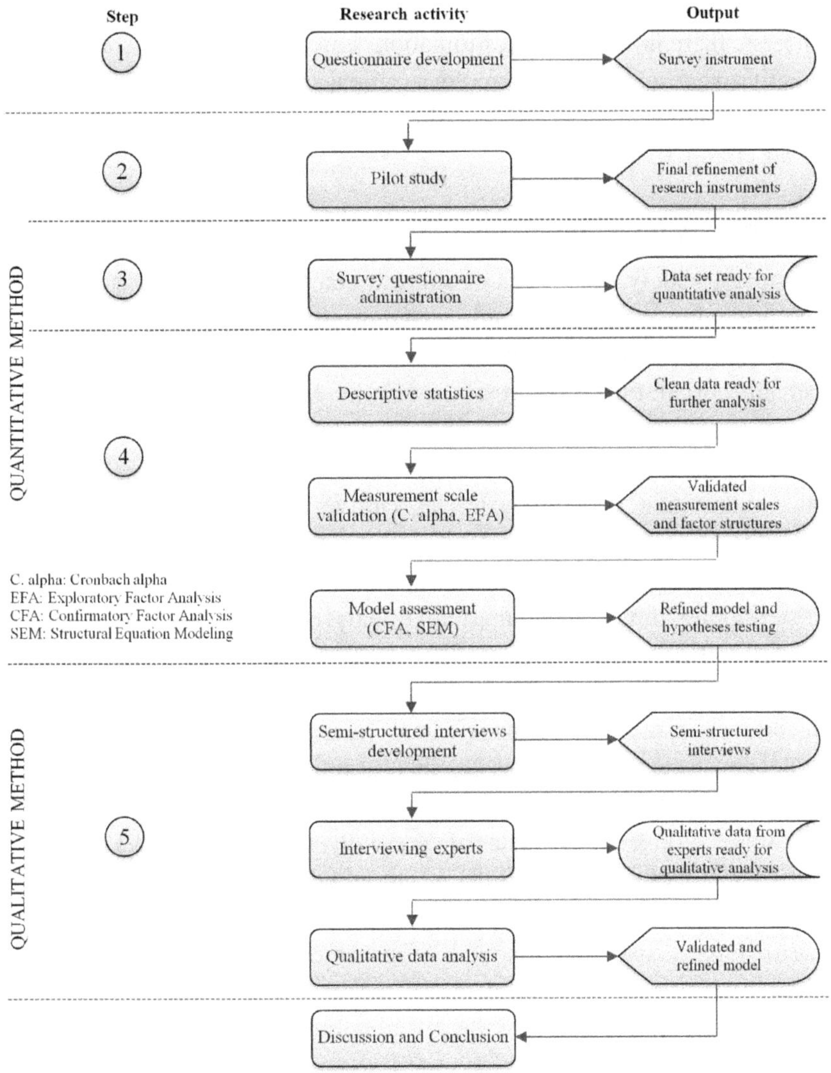

Impacts Owning to Sample Size

It is important to consider the impact of sample size as it has the effect of improving statistical power by minimizing the sampling error (Hair et al., 2010). For sample sizes of 50 or less, remarkable departures from normality are likely to have a considerable effect on the results. However, in large samples sizes of 200 or above, the effects may be insignificant. Furthermore, In SEM, a much larger sample size is required to maintain power and acquire stable parameter estimates and standard errors (Schumacker & Lomax, 2010). It is also due in part to the program preconditions and the multi-observed variables applied to define latent variables. Nevertheless, there has been a question about how large a sample should be taken for a quantitative research. For example, a critical sample size in the 200-400 range (for 10-15 indicators) offered as a benchmark is widely utilized by researchers in SEM (Hair et al., 2010).

Survey Implementation Procedure

The three most widely used types of surveys categorized by Neuman (2006) are mail questionnaire, web survey and self-administered survey. Each of them has its own advantages and disadvantages as present in Table 4. The researchers will select an appropriate type of survey based on the balance of various features such as cost, response rate, etc.

Step 4: Quantitative data analysis-Descriptive statistics, Measurement scale validation, and Model assessment.

This step applies three sets of quantitative analysis. (i) Firstly, descriptive statistics is conducted to find out if the data was ready to continue to the multivariate data analyses step (participants' profiles, missing value, standard deviations, and standard error of the mean); measurement scale analysis is used to capture the meaning of each model construct through an assessment of reliability and validity (Cronbach's alpha). In addition, item-total correlations are used to assess the extent to which a particular item belonged to its scale. (ii) Secondly, the validity of the measurement using an explanatory factor analysis (EFA) is applied to uncover underlying factors of latent constructs as well as to eliminate items with poor contribution over associative factors. (iii) Finally, two-step approach of structural equation modeling (SEM) is implemented to confirm and validate the results of EFA through confirmatory factor analysis (CFA) and examine the causal relationships of the model. The IBM Statistical Package for the Social Sciences (SPSS) and Analysis of Moment Structure

Table 4. Types of surveys and their administrative features

Features	Mail Questionnaire	Web Survey	Self-Administered Survey
Cost	Cheap	Cheapest	Expensive
Speed	Slowest	Fastest	Slow to moderate
Length (No. of questions)	Moderate	Moderate	Longest
Response rate	Lowest	Moderate	Highest

Adapted from Neuman (2006)

(AMOS) are suggested to perform Cronbach's alpha, EFA, CFA and SEM as they are widely used for many quantitative research approach. Factor analysis (EFA, CFA) and SEM will be presented in the next section.

Step 5: Qualitative method

Finally, the qualitative approach (Phase two) is conducted to validate the quantitative results through the semi-structured interviews. This stage helps researchers to also gain experts' suggestions to refine the model and propose the future works.

Factor Analysis Techniques

Factor Analysis

Factor analysis primarily aims to investigate relations between sets of observed and latent variables. In using this technique to analyze data, the researcher ascertains which sets of indicators share common variance–covariance characteristics that define covariance characteristics that define underlying latent variables (i.e. factors) (Schumacker & Lomax, 2010; Byrne, 2016). There are two basic kinds of factor analyses: explanatory factor analysis (EFA) and confirmatory factor analysis (CFA). EFA is used to discover the underlying structure of a relatively large set of variables. On the other hand, CFA confirms and validates the results of EFA (that structure). Consequently, these two factor analyses (EFA and CFA) to SEM, then, are thought of as a complementary choice for a quantitative approach. This combination of EFA and CFA is effective in testing a better measurement scale (Anderson & Gerbing, 1988).

Structural Equation Modeling (SEM)

SEM is suggested to use for testing the proposed research model and hypotheses. This is because SEM, as a second generation approach of regression analysis, is a family of statistical models that attempt to account for the relationships among multi-variables. In the regression approach, researchers can only analyze the relationship of one or more independent constructs with one dependent construct. By contrast, SEM enables researchers to simultaneously estimate the interrelation among multiple dependent and independent constructs (Haenlein & Kaplan, 2004). This research highly recommends using SEM because of its powerful advantages as follows:

1. Its ability to deal with multiple observed variables to better understand their field of research enquiry which is impossible to tackle with the basic statistical

methods that only utilize a limited number of variables (Schumacker & Lomax 2010).

2. Its ability to define a model to explain the entire set of relationships (Hair et al., 2010).
3. The greater recognition given to the validity and reliability of observed scores from measurement instruments (Schumacker & Lomax, 2010).
4. It provides researchers with an increased capability to simultaneously estimate the interrelation between multiple independent (exogenous) and dependent (endogenous) variables in one operation (Schumacker & Lomax, 2010; Kline, 2015).
5. SEM performs multi-group analysis to compare the different models from transformational leadership level of this study (Kline, 2015).
6. It provides a number of indices to evaluate the model fit (Kline, 2015; Schumacker & Lomax, 2010).

FUTURE RESEARCH DIRECTIONS

The research presented in this chapter can be extended and applied in several directions in the future. Firstly, the model can be implemented in two ways including quantitative cross-sectional and longitudinal studies on KSB and IWB at individual level in organizations. However, the researchers may not obtain the perceive KSB across time by cross-sectional studies (Rahman et al., 2016). Hence, the authors suggest that future researchers or practitioners should pay more attention and efforts on conducting the longitudinal studies to investigate the interactive relationship between environmental and personal factors on KSB. Secondly, future research efforts focus on the exploration of how environmental and personal factors influence KSB in organizations in general, in higher education institutions, in particular. This is because these studies are still largely unexamined, especially in non-Western countries in higher education institutions.

CONCLUSION

This chapter has proposed the theoretical model based on social cognitive theory (SCT) for KSB research and practice in organization context. The model has been incorporated the contributions of prior research. Moreover, the research framework can be easily applied for future researchers and practitioners. It also permits quantitative evaluation of KSB towards IWB research and practice. To the authors' best knowledge, there have not been any research model on KSB and IWB based on SCT defined and applied in the organizations so far. Hsu et al. (2007), Lin et al. (2009), Chang et al. (2015), Liou et al. (2016), Moon et al. (2016), and Rahman et al. (2016) adopted a SCT based model to assess the KSB in virtual communities. However, these models had few concerns on the context of organizations that have significant different features compare to virtual communities. Overall, there has been a lack of SCT based models on KSB and IWB in organizations. The authors do not contend that this proposed model is a perfect for the research in the field of KSB. However, the model and its implementation guidelines make it easily to apply and update in the future. It is expected that this research will encourage more studies on KSB and IWB, and on their applications to KSB-research and empirical quantitative evaluation approach.

REFERENCES

Ajzen, I. (1991). The Theory of Planned Behavior. *Organizational Behavior and Human Decision Processes*, *50*(2), 179–211. doi:10.1016/0749-5978(91)90020-T

Akhavan, P., Hosseini, S. M., Abbasi, M., & Manteghi, M. (2015). Knowledge-sharing determinants, behaviors, and innovative work behaviors: An integrated theoretical view and empirical examination. *Aslib Journal of Information Management*, *67*(5), 562–591. doi:10.1108/AJIM-02-2015-0018

Amabile, T. M., Conti, R., Coon, H., Lazenby, J., & Herron, M. (1996). Assessing the work environment for creativity. *Academy of Management Journal*, *39*(5), 1154–1184. doi:10.2307/256995

Ariff, M. I. M. (2013). *Exploring the role of Transactive Memory Systems in Virtual Teams*. Victoria, Australia: The University of Melbourne.

Ariff, M. I. M., Milton, S. K., Bosua, R., & Sharma, R. (2011). Exploring the role of ICT in the formation of transactive memory systems in virtual teams. In *Proceedings of the 15th Pacific Asia Conference on Information Systems: Quality Research in Pacific, PACIS 2011* (pp. 1-12). Queensland: Queensland University of Technology.

Bandura, A. (1986). *Social foundations of thought and action: A social cognitive theory*. Englewood Cliffs, NJ: Prentice-Hall.

Bandura, A. (2002). Social cognitive theory of mass communication. In J. Bryant & M. B. Oliver (Eds.), *Media Effects: Advances in Theory and Research* (pp. 122–138). New York, NY: Routledge.

Bass, B. M. (1999). On the taming of charisma: A reply to Janice Beyer. *The Leadership Quarterly*, *10*(4), 541–553. doi:10.1016/S1048-9843(99)00030-2

Bass, B. M., & Avolio, B. J. (1997). *Full range of leadership: Manual for the Multi-factor Leadership Questionnaire*. Palo Alto, CA: Mind Garden.

Bock, G. W., & Kim, Y. G. (2002). Breaking the myths of rewards: An exploratory study of attitudes about knowledge sharing. *Information Resources Management Journal*, *15*(2), 14–21. doi:10.4018/irmj.2002040102

Bock, G. W., Zmud, R. W., Kim, Y., & Lee, J. (2005). Behavioral intention formation in knowledge sharing: Examining the roles of extrinsic motivators, social psychological forces, and organizational climate. *Management Information Systems Quarterly*, *29*(1), 87–111. doi:10.2307/25148669

Bourque, L. B., & Fielder, E. P. (2003). *How to Conduct Self-Administered and Mail Survey* (2nd ed.). Thousand Oaks, CA: Sage Publications. doi:10.4135/9781412984430

Brandon, D. P., & Hollingshead, A. B. (2004). Transactive Memory Systems in Organisations: Matching Tasks, Expertise, and People. *Organization Science*, *15*(6), 633–644. doi:10.1287/orsc.1040.0069

Byrne, B. M. (2016). *Structural Equation Modeling With AMOS: Basic Concepts, Applications, and Programming* (3rd ed.). Taylor and Francis.

Chang, C. M., Hsu, M. H., & Lee, Y. J. (2015). Factors Influencing Knowledge-Sharing Behavior in Virtual Communities: A Longitudinal Investigation. *Information Systems Management*, *32*(4), 331–340. doi:10.1080/10580530.2015.1080002

Davenport, T. H., & Prusak, L. (1998). *Working Knowledge: How Organizations Manage What They Know*. Boston: Harvard Business School Press.

Fukuyama, F. (1995). *Trust:The Social Virtues and the Creation of Prosperity*. New York: The Free Press.

Gefen, D., Straub, D. W., & Boudreau, M.-C. (2000). *Structural Equation Modeling and Regression: Guidelines for research practice. Communications of the Association for Information Systems*. Citeseer.

Gerbing, D. W., & Anderson, J. C. (1988). An updated paradigm for scale development incorporating unidimensionality and its assessment. *JMR, Journal of Marketing Research*, *25*(2), 186–192. doi:10.2307/3172650

Haenlein, M., & Kaplan, A. M. (2004). A Beginner's Guide to Partial Least Squares Analysis. *Understanding Statistics*, *3*(3), 283–297. doi:10.120715328031us0304_4

Hair, J. F., Black, W. C., Babin, B. J., Anderson, R. E., & Tatham, R. L. (2010). *Multivariate Data Analysis* (7th ed.). Upper Saddle River, NJ: Prentice Hall.

Han, S. H., Seo, G., Yoon, S. W., & Yoon, D. Y. (2016). Transformational leadership and knowledge sharing: Mediating roles of employee's empowerment, commitment, and citizenship behaviors. *Journal of Workplace Learning, 28*(3), 130–149. doi:10.1108/JWL-09-2015-0066

Han, T. S., Chiang, H. H., & Chang, A. (2010). Employee participation in decision making, psychological ownership and KS: Mediating role of organizational commitment in Taiwanese high-tech organizations. *International Journal of Human Resource Management, 21*(12), 2218–2233. doi:10.1080/09585192.2010.509625

Hee, S. P. (2000). Relationships among attitudes and subjective norm: Testing the theory of reasoned action across cultures. *Communication Studies, 51*(2), 162–175. doi:10.1080/10510970009388516

Hendriks, P. (1999). Why share knowledge? The influence of ICT on the motivation for knowledge sharing. *Knowledge and Process Management, 6*(2), 91–100. doi:10.1002/(SICI)1099-1441(199906)6:2<91::AID-KPM54>3.0.CO;2-M

Hsu, M., Ju, L., Yen, C. H., & Chang, M. (2007). Knowledge sharing behaviour in virtual communities: The relationship between trust, self-efficacy, and outcome expectations. *International Journal of Human-Computer Studies, 65*(2), 153–169. doi:10.1016/j.ijhcs.2006.09.003

Hung, S. Y., Durcikova, A., Lai, H. M., & Lin, W. M. (2011). The influence of intrinsic and extrinsic motivation on individuals' knowledge sharing behaviour. *The International Journal of Human Computer Studies, 69*(6), 415-427.

Janssen, O. (2000). Job demands, perceptions of effort-reward fairness and innovative work behaviour. *Journal of Occupational and Organizational Psychology, 73*(3), 287–302. doi:10.1348/096317900167038

Kanter, R. (1988). When a thousand owners bloom: Structural, collective, and social conditions for innovation in organisations. In B. M. Staw & L. L. Cummings (Eds.), *Research in organisational behavior (10)* (pp. 169–211). Greenwich, CT: JAI Press.

Kimberlin, C. L., & Winterstein, A. G. (2008). Validity and reliability of measurement instruments used in research. *American Journal of Health-System Pharmacy, 65*(23), 2276–2284. doi:10.2146/ajhp070364 PMID:19020196

Kline, R. B. (2015). *Principles and Practice of Structural Equation Modeling* (4th ed.). Guilford Publications.

Kowal, J., & Fortier, M. S. (1999). Motivational determinants of flow: Contributions from self-determination theory. *The Journal of Social Psychology*, *139*(3), 355–368. doi:10.1080/00224549909598391

Law, C. C. H., & Ngai, E. W. T. (2008). An empirical study of the effects of knowledge sharing and learning behaviours on firm performance. *Expert Systems with Applications*, *34*(4), 2342–2349. doi:10.1016/j.eswa.2007.03.004

Lee, H., & Choi, B. (2003). Knowledge Management Enablers, Processes, and Organizational Performance: An Integrative View and Empirical Examination. *JMIS*, *20*(1), 179–228.

Lee, S. M., & Hong, S. (2002). An enterprise-wide knowledge management system infrastructure. *Industrial Management & Data Systems*, *102*(1), 17–25. doi:10.1108/02635570210414622

Lin, H. F. (2007a). Knowledge sharing and firm innovation capability: An empirical study. *International Journal of Manpower*, *28*(3/4), 315–332. doi:10.1108/01437720710755272

Lin, H. F. (2007b). Effects of extrinsic and intrinsic motivation on employee knowledge sharing intentions. *Journal of Information Science*, *33*(2), 135–149. doi:10.1177/0165551506068174

Lin, M. J., Hung, S. W., & Chen, C. J. (2009). Fostering the determinants of knowledge sharing in professional virtual communities. *Computers in Human Behavior*, *25*(4), 929–939. doi:10.1016/j.chb.2009.03.008

Liou, D. K., Chih, W. H., Yuan, C. Y., & Lin, C. Y. (2016). The study of the antecedents of knowledge sharing behavior: The empirical study of Yambol online test community. *Internet Research*, *26*(4), 845–868. doi:10.1108/IntR-10-2014-0256

Moon, M. K., Jahng, S. G., Park, S. Y., & Lee, J. E. (2016). The perceptions of knowledge sharing behavior in virtual community: Using an extended social cognitive theory approach. *International Journal of Applied Engineering Research*, *11*(8), 5430–5439.

Neuman, W. L. (2005). *Social research methods: Quantitative and qualitative approaches*. Allyn and Bacon Boston.

Neuman, W. L. (2006). *Social research methods: Qualitative and quantitative approaches* (6th ed.). Boston: Pearson.

Nold, H. A. III. (2012). Linking knowledge processes with firm performance: Organizational culture. *Journal of Intellectual Capital, 13*(1), 16–38. doi:10.1108/14691931211196196

Nonaka, I. (1994). A dynamic theory of organizational knowledge creation. *Organization Science, 5*(5), 14–37. doi:10.1287/orsc.5.1.14

Pfeffer, J., & Sutton, R. (1999). Knowledge "What" to do is not enough: Turning knowledge into action. *California Management Review, 42*(1), 83–108. doi:10.2307/41166020

Phung, V. D., Hawryszkiewycz, I., Chandran, D., & Ha, B. M. (2017). Knowledge Sharing and Innovative Work Behaviour: A Case Study from Vietnam. In *Proceedings of the 28th Australasian Conference on Information Systems (ACIS 2017)*. University of Tasmania.

Pierce, J. L., Kostova, T., & Dirks, K. T. (2001). Toward a Theory of Psychological Ownership in Organizations. *Academy of Management Review*, (26): 298–310.

Radaelli, G., Lettieri, E., Mura, M., & Spiller, N. (2014). Knowledge Sharing and Innovative Work Behaviour in Healthcare: A Micro-Level Investigation of Direct and Indirect Effects. *Creativity and Innovation Management, 23*(4), 400–414. doi:10.1111/caim.12084

Rahman, M. S., Osmangani, A. M., Daud, N. M., & AbdelFattah, F. A. M. (2016). Knowledge sharing behaviors among non academic staff of higher learning institutions. *Library Review, 65*(1/2), 65–83. doi:10.1108/LR-02-2015-0017

Schumacker, R. E., & Lomax, R. G. (2010). *A Beginner's Guide to Structural Equation Modeling* (3rd ed.). New York: Routledge, Taylor & Francis.

Sharma, R., Yetton, P., & Crawford, J. (2009). Estimating the Effect of Common Method Variance: The Method - Method Pair Technique with an Illustration from TAM Research. *Management Information Systems Quarterly, 33*(3), 473–490. doi:10.2307/20650305

Van Dyne, L., & Pierce, J. L. (2004). Psychological ownership and feelings of possession: Three field studies predicting employee attitudes and organizational citizenship behaviour. *Journal of Organizational Behavior, 25*(4), 439–459. doi:10.1002/job.249

Wang, S., & Noe, R. A. (2010). Knowledge sharing: A review and directions for future research. *Human Resource Management Review, 20*(2), 115–131. doi:10.1016/j.hrmr.2009.10.001

Wasko, M. M., & Faraj, S. (2005). Why should I share? Examining social capital and knowledge contribution in electronic networks of practices. *Management Information Systems Quarterly*, *29*(1), 35. doi:10.2307/25148667

Wegner, D. M., Erber, R., & Raymond, P. (1991). Transactive Memory in Close Relationships. *Journal of Personality and Social Psychology*, *61*(6), 923–929. doi:10.1037/0022-3514.61.6.923 PMID:1774630

Wong, K. Y. (1989). Critical success factors for implementing knowledge management in small and medium enterprises. *Industrial Management & Data Systems*, *105*(3/4), 261–279.

Wood, R., & Bandura, A. (1989). Social cognitive theory of organizational management. Academy of management. *Academy of Management Review*, *14*(3), 361–384.

Yu, C., Yu, T., & Yu, C. (2013). KS, organizational climate, and innovative behavior: A cross-level analysis of effects. *Social Behavior and Personality*, *41*(1), 143–156. doi:10.2224bp.2013.41.1.143

ADDITIONAL READING

Hawryszkiewycz, I.T. (2005). A Framework for Integrating Learning into Business Processes. *Information Age*, 26-31.

Hawryszkiewycz, I. T. (2010). *Knowledge Management: Organising Knowledge Based Enterprises. First.* Basingstoke, England: Palgrave Macmillan. doi:10.1007/978-0-230-31355-2

Hawryszkiewycz, I. T. (2010). Perspectives for Integrating Knowledge and Business Process through Collaboration. In I. Bider, T. Halpin, J. Krogstie, S. Nurcan, E. Proper, R. Schmidt, & R. Ukor (Eds.), *Lecture Notes in Business Information Processing 50 - Enterprise, Business-Process and Information* (pp. 82–93). Germany: Springer.

Hawryszkiewycz, I. T. (2014). Cloud Requirements for Facilitating Business Collaboration: A Modeling Perspective. *Journal of Organizational Computing and Electronic Commerce*, *24*(2-3), 174–185. doi:10.1080/10919392.2014.896726

Hawryszkiewycz, I. T. (2017). *Designing Creative Organizations: Tools, Processes and Practice*. Bingley, UK: First, Emerald Books.

Phung, V. D., Hawryszkiewycz, I., & Binsawad, M. H. (2016). Classifying knowledge-sharing barriers by organisational structure in order to find ways to remove these barriers. *In Proceedings - The 8th International Conference on Knowledge and Systems Engineering (KSE 2016)* (pp. 73-78), IEEE, Hanoi, Vietnam.

Phung, V. D., & Hawryszkiewycz, I. T. (2017). Exploring Factors Influencing Knowledge Sharing Behaviour: The Moderating Effect of Transformational Leadership. *In Proceedings of the 18th European Conference on Knowledge Management (ECKM 2017)*, Barcelona.

Phung, V. D., Hawryszkiewycz, I. T., & Binsawad, M. (2017). Exploring How Environmental and Personal Factors Influence Knowledge Sharing Behaviour Leads to Innovative Work Behaviour in Vietnamese Higher Education Institutions. *In Proceedings of the 26th Information Systems Development: Advances in Methods, Tools and Management (ISD2017)*, Larnaca, Cyprus.

Phung, V. D., Hawryszkiewycz, I. T., & Ha, B. M. (2017). The Influence of Knowledge Sharing Behavior and Transactive Memory Systems on Innovative Work Behavior: A Conceptual Model. *In Proceedings – the 9th International Conference on Knowledge and Systems Engineering (KSE 2017),* Hue, Vietnam.

KEY TERMS AND DEFINITIONS

Environmental Factor: The factor from the social environment dimension.

Factor Analysis: The quantitative data analysis technique that aims to investigate relations between sets of observed and latent variables in the research model.

Innovative Work Behavior: An action which a person behaves to create, promote, and implement new ideas in a team, a group or the whole organization.

Knowledge Sharing: A social interaction through which individuals exchange their knowledge, skills, and experiences with each other.

Knowledge Sharing Behavior: An action which a person behaves in knowledge sharing activities in the organization.

Personal Factor: The factors from the individual dimension.

Structural Equation Modeling: The quantitative data analysis technique that aims to examine the casual relationships between variables in the conceptual model and how much the model fit with the practical data.

APPENDIX

Table 5. The profiles of the experts at the survey design workshop series

No.	Expertise	Location	Experience and Strength
1	Professor	SML-UTS	Qualitative method in information systems and knowledge management
2	PhD - Senior lecturer	SML-UTS	Quantitative method in information systems and knowledge management
3	Professor	SML-UTS	Qualitative methods in information systems; Statistical expert
4	PhD-Senior lecturer	SML-UTS	Quantitative method in information systems and knowledge management
5	PhD	SML-UTS	Quantitative method in information systems
6	PhD	University of New South Wales	Qualitative and quantitative method in education; higher education expert; Vietnamese and English language expert
7	PhD	Deakin University	Qualitative and quantitative method in education; higher education expert; Vietnamese and English language expert
8	PhD	School of Education, UTS	Qualitative and quantitative method in education; Vietnamese and English language expert
9	PhD	University of Vienna	Qualitative method in information systems; Expert in developing research models

Note: SML-UTS: School of Systems, Management and Leadership - The University of Technology Sydney

Table 6. The summarization of the measurement scales for each construct

Construct/Code-Item	Related Literature
Subjective norm • SN1: My president thinks that I should share my knowledge with other members in the organization. • SN2: My department's leader thinks that I should share my knowledge with other members in the organization. • SN3: My colleagues think that I should share my knowledge with other members in the organization.	Bock et al. (2005); Ajzen (1991)
Trust Our organization members … • TRU1: are generally trustworthy. • TRU2: have reciprocal faith in other members' behaviors. • TRU3: have reciprocal faith in others' ability. • TRU4: have reciprocal faith in others' behaviors to work toward organizational goals. • TRU5: have reciprocal faith in others' decision toward organizational interests than individual interests. • TRU6: have relationships based on reciprocal faith.	Lee and Choi (2003)

continued on following page

Table 6. Continued

Construct/Code-Item	Related Literature
Knowledge self-efficacy • KSE1: I am confident that I possess knowledge that others in my organization would consider valuable. • KSE2: I have the expertise required to provide valuable knowledge for my organization. • KSE3: Most other employees can provide more valuable knowledge than I can. (Reverse coded). • KSE4: It does not really make any difference whether I share my knowledge with colleagues.	Lin (2007b)
Enjoyment in helping others • EHO1: I enjoy sharing my knowledge with colleagues. • EHO2: I enjoy helping colleagues by sharing my knowledge. • EHO3: It makes me feel good by helping someone by sharing my knowledge. • EHO4: Sharing my knowledge with colleagues is pleasurable.	Lin (2007b)
Rewards • REW1: I will receive a higher salary in return for my KS. • REW2: I will receive a higher bonus in return for my KS. • REW3: I will receive increased promotion opportunities in return for my KS. • REW4: I will receive increased job security in return for my KS.	Lin (2007b)
Reciprocal benefits When I share my knowledge with colleagues ... • RB1: I strengthen ties between existing members of the organization and myself. • RB2: I expand the scope of my association with other organization members. • EB3: I expect to receive knowledge in return when necessary.	Lin (2007b)
Psychological ownership of knowledge • POK1: I feel that the knowledge I have is mine. • POK2: I am willing to treat my own knowledge as if it belongs to everybody in the organization. • POK3: I feel a very high degree of personal ownership for the knowledge that I possess. • POK4: I believe that the knowledge I have acquired during the course of my job is my personal intellectual property. • POK5: Most of the people that work for this organization feel as though they own the organization.	Han (2010); Dyne and Pierce (2004)
Transformational leadership *Charisma* • CHA1: My supervisor instills pride in me for being associated with him/her. • CHA2: My supervisor acts in ways that build other's respect for him/her. • CHA3: My supervisor talks about his/her most important values and beliefs. • CHA4: My supervisor considers the moral and ethical consequences of decisions. • CHA5: My supervisor emphasizes the importance of having a collective sense of mission. • CHA6: My supervisor talks optimistically about the future. • CHA7: My supervisor expresses confidence that goals will be achieved. *Intellectual stimulation* • IS1: My supervisor seeks differing perspectives when solving problems. • IS2: My supervisor suggests new ways of looking at how to complete assignments. • IS3: My supervisor gets me to look at problems from many different angles. *Individualized consideration* • IC1: My supervisor considers me as having different needs from others. • IC2: My supervisor helps me to develop my strengths. • IC3: My supervisor spends time coaching me.	Bass (1999); Han et al. (2016)
Knowledge sharing behavior • KSB1: I frequently participate in KS activities in my department or/and the organization. • KSB2: I usually spend a lot of time conducting KS activities in my department or/and the organization. • KSB3: When participating in my department or/and the university, I usually actively share my knowledge with others. • KSB4: When discussing a complicated issue, I am usually involved in the subsequent interactions. • KSB5: I usually involve myself in discussions of various topics rather than specific topics.	Davenport and Prusak (1998); Hsu et al. (2007)

continued on following page

Table 6. Continued

Construct/Code-Item	Related Literature
Transactive memory systems quality Who knows what (WKW) • WKW1: I have a good understanding of the skills that my colleagues possess. • WKW2: I know the specific expertise that my colleagues possess. • WKW3: I have a good understanding of the knowledge that my colleagues possess. Who does what (WDK) • WDW1: I know the task responsibilities of my colleagues. • WDW2: I know my task responsibilities. • WDW3: When I need some tasks to be performed, I know which colleague to ask for help/ guidance	Ariff et al. (2011); Brandon and Hollingshead (2004)
Innovative work behavior *Idea generation: 3 items* • IGE1: I create new ideas for difficult issues. • IGE2: I search out new working methods, techniques, or instruments. • IEG3: I generate original solutions for problems. *Idea promotion: 3 items* • IPR1: I mobilize support for my new ideas. • IPR2: I make important organizational members enthusiastic for my new ideas. • IPR3: I acquire approval for my new ideas. *Idea implementation: 3 items* • IIM1: I transform my new ideas into useful applications. • IIM2: I introduce my new ideas into the work environment in a systematic way. • IIM3: I evaluate the utility of my new ideas.	Janssen (2000)

Chapter 6
What Motivates the Crowd?
A Literature Review on Motivations for Crowdsourcing

Alireza Amrollahi
Griffith University, Australia

Mohammad Hasan Ahmadi
Shahid Beheshti University, Iran

ABSTRACT

The main objective of the chapter is to provide an insight into the motivation mechanisms for the crowd to participate in crowdsourcing projects. For this to happen, the authors investigate the factors which have been suggested in the literature as influencing the motivation of the crowd and the task type in each study in the related literature and contrasted the motivation factors in various contexts. The systematic literature review method has been used for the purpose of this study. This involved a comprehensive search in five scientific databases which resulted in 575 papers. This initial pool of studies has been refined in various rounds and ended in identification of 37 studies which directly targeted the topic of motivation in crowdsourcing. The study introduces various categories of motivations and investigates the factors which have been utilized in each context. Finally, possible implications for practice and potential research gaps are discussed.

DOI: 10.4018/978-1-5225-4200-1.ch006

INTRODUCTION

Crowdsourcing is the new model for performing organizational tasks which have been introduced in 2006 by Howe (2006). Prior this date, crowdsourcing model had been used by various businesses to attract creative ideas from large numbers of people. The introduction of the term, however, resulted in much more attention to its potential benefits from businesses. A review of 24 crowdsourcing platforms indicated various applications of the model in various contexts including business, city planning, policy development, and event outreach (Seltzer & Mahmoudi, 2013). In January 2015, almost 2,900 websites in 45 languages have been indexed in Crowdsourcing.org and more than 225,000 tasks have been posted on The Amazon Mechanical Turk which is one of the most famous sites in the world. Another successful platform is iStock which is dedicated to photography industry which has been purchased by Getty Images for $50 million in 2006 (Howe, 2006) and its revenue in 2008 was approximately $163 million (Pickerell, 2012). This model has been utilized by other businesses to attract new ideas for improvement in products and services (Alireza Amrollahi, Amir Ghapanchi, & Amir Talaei-Khoei, 2014; Amrollahi & Ghapnchi, 2016; Poetz & Schreier, 2012) and in academia for solving scientific problems (Cooper et al., 2010; Graber & Graber, 2013; Stieger, Matzler, Chatterjee, & Ladstaetter-Fussenegger, 2012) and data collection (Ranard et al., 2014).

The crowdsourcing model has also attracted the attention of researchers after 2006. Tarrell et al. (2013) for instance have reviewed the related research papers in the 15 top IS journals and conferences which resulted in 135 articles which paid attention to different aspects of this model. Various theories from different areas have been used in this area of research to study topics like crowdsourcing process, technology, and governance (Pedersen et al., 2013).

Previous literature had investigated many different aspects of the crowdsourcing phenomena. This includes the concept of crowdsourcing (Doan, Ramakrishnan, & Halevy, 2011; Estellés-Arolas & González-Ladrón-De-Guevara, 2012; Kittur, Chi, & Suh, 2008; Lukyanenko, Parsons, & Wiersma, 2014), crowdsourcing process (Amrollahi, 2015; Lukyanenko & Parsons, 2012; Thuan, Antunes, & Johnstone, 2017), technology (Davis & Lin, 2011; DiGiammarino & Trudeau, 2008; Goldman et al., 2009), and various applications of crowdsourcing (Amrollahi & Ghapnchi, 2016; Gao, Barbier, & Goolsby, 2011; Sharifi, Fink, & Carbonell, 2011).

Furthermore, along with these studies, the behavior of crowd in crowdsourcing projects have been explored by scholars (Haythornthwaite, 2009; Rodriguez et al., 2007; Whelan, 2007). One of the questions in this area which is studied by many researchers is *why people participate in crowdsourcing projects?* As it is described in the literature review section, studies in this category have led to identification of many motivation factors for participation in such projects. However, no study could be found in the literature which reviews crowd motivation factors.

The importance of research on motivating crowd can be highlighted when we refer to the literature confirming the impact of motivated crowd on the effectiveness of crowdsourcing projects and the quality of contributions (Goncalves, Hosio, Rogstadius, Karapanos, & Kostakos, 2015). For this reason, the current study seeks to tackle this shortcoming by a comprehensive and systematic review of the research studies and develops a framework of motivation factors. The main research questions for the current study are:

- **RQ1:** Which factors have been mentioned in the literature as motivator for participation in crowdsourcing projects?
- **RQ2:** Various categories of motivation factors have been used in which type of crowdsourcing projects?

The developed framework will provide a basis for future studies and illustrates potential gaps in the literature. Moreover, it can help practitioners to better plan and manage their crowdsourcing projects. The rest of the paper is structured as follows: background to research on crowdsourcing and related concepts are explained in the next section which is followed by an introduction to the research method used in the current study. The study continues with explaining the results with respect to extracted motivation factors and task types and concludes with a discussion of implications for both practitioners and researchers, and limitations of the study.

LITERATURE REVIEW

Crowdsourcing

The term crowdsourcing was first introduced by Howe (2006) as: "the act of taking a job traditionally performed by a designated agent (usually an employee) and outsourcing it to an undefined generally large group of people in an open call." This definition however, was altered in the subsequent literature in a way that covered involvement of organizational stakeholders and employees and giving the right to organizations to select the participating crowd.

The most recent definition of crowdsourcing is provided by Pedersen et al. (2013, p. 585) after reviewing the related research areas which is: "A collaboration model enabled by people-centric web technologies to solve individual, organizational, and societal problems using a dynamically formed crowd of interested people who respond to an open call for participation."

Although a number of research studies could be found in the literature which investigated the similar topics in contexts like Wikipedia articles (Brändle, 2005; Lin, 2004), it was more highlighted after the development of the term in 2006. The study of elite publications by Tarrell et al. (2013) indicates that number of publications in the area in 2012 has been 5 times more than this number in 2007 which indicates growing attention to this area from academia and this number is still growing (Ghezzi, Gabelloni, Martini, & Natalicchio, 2017; Kaghazgaran, Caverlee, & Alfifi, 2017).

Crowdsourcing has been named in the literature as an instant of openness through IT that is performed through an open process but using the resources that are not openly accessible (Schlagwein, Conboy, Feller, Leimeister, & Morgan, 2017). The crowdsourcing model has been employed by calls for participants both inside and outside organizations for various purposes. The attention to the topic by both practitioners and scholars has resulted in a growth in the studies focusing on this topic. Following these growth, a number of literature review studies have been formed. Table 1 introduces some of the previous reviews.

As can be inferred from the above table, various perspectives of crowdsourcing research have been explored in the previous reviews. However, these reviews have been less focused on behavioral dynamics of individuals who participate in crowdsourcing projects and in particular, no previous review has been addressed the studies on factors motivating the crowd (inside and outside organizations) to take part in a crowdsourcing project. This gap in the literature motivated the current study to focus on the literature on motivational factors in crowdsourcing projects and using a systematic literature review approach, categorize them in a framework.

Table 1. Previous literature review works

Reference	Scope of Review	Results
Tripathi, Tahmasbi, Khazanchi, & Najjar (2014)	Crowdsourcing papers in the top 11 Information Systems (IS) journals.	Typology of the types of crowdsourcing practiced and researched, and the types of problems crowdsourced by organizations.
Ranard et al. (2014)	Peer reviewed literature that used crowdsourcing for health research.	Four distinct types of crowdsourcing tasks.
Hetmank (2013)	Papers on crowdsourcing systems published in peer-reviewed conference proceedings and journals after 2006.	Different 17 definitions of crowdsourcing systems were found and categorized into four perspectives.
Tarrell et al. (2013)	Crowdsourcing papers in the top 11 IS journals.	Analysis of keywords
Pedersen et al. (2013)	Crowdsourcing papers in the top 11 IS journals.	A conceptual model of crowdsourcing.
Ghezzi et al. (2017)	121 scientific articles published between January 2006 and January 2015.	The review recognizes two mainstream disciplines and a general framework for applications of crowdsourcing.

Motivating the Crowd

Crowd is defined in the literature as "the dynamically formed group of individuals who participate in the crowdsourcing problem" (Pedersen et al., 2013, p. 5). Along with progress of crowdsourcing research, the dynamics of crowd and different characteristics of them attracted researchers' attention. This topic was recognized as one of the eight main areas of crowdsourcing according to Pedersen et al. (2013). The same study considered a variety of topics were subject of attention in this area. This ranges from collaboration between people (Haythornthwaite, 2009) to aligning team members (Pennington, 2011; Söldner, Haller, Bullinger, & Möslein, 2009), privacy (Jarvenpaa & Majchrzak, 2010), and building trust among crowd (Farooq, Ganoe, Carroll, & Giles, 2009) in crowdsourcing projects. This study however considered two categories of *individual* and *crowd* as people who can potentially contribute and those who are engaged in the project (Pedersen et al., 2013).

The main question regarding individuals who can potentially participate in a crowdsourcing project is how to attract and motivate them to participate in these project (i.e. how to change them to actual crowd). Various factors have been suggested in the literature in this category which are explained in the following sections. The first study which addressed motivating the crowd to participate in the crowdsourcing projects was work of Brabham (2008) which studied demographics of and motivators for crowd to participate in iStock. Through a survey of 651 participants, making money, developing individual skills, and having fun were recognized as the main motivators for participation in iStock.

Leimeister, Huber, Bretschneider, and Krcmar (2009) also developed a model for motivating participants in idea competitions. The model proposes incentives as a moderator in the relationship between motives of users and activation which consequently leads to participation behavior.

As will be explained in the results section of this study, the literature on crowdsourcing motivation is mainly focused on intrinsic and extrinsic motives of participation. Intrinsic motives of participation have been studied as a motive of participation in similar areas such as open source software (Amrollahi, Khansari, & Manian, 2014, 2015). However, these motives are not always effective in attracting participants to crowdsourcing projects. Gloor and Cooper (2007) identified three principles of "(i) gain power of giving it away; (ii) share with swarm; and (iii) concentrate on swarm, not on making money" as the main principles which can help businesses to leverage the open model of generating innovation.

Regarding extrinsic motives of participation, Kaufmann, Schulze, and Veit (2011) found a strong impact of factors such as immediate payoffs and delayed payoffs on the time crowd workers spent on projects. Also, Yu and Nickerson (2011) in their study of 540 participants in idea generation platforms explain the dark side of extrinsic motives and caution about the impacts they may have on the effectiveness and quality of crowdsourcing projects.

Our review of the current literature indicates an increasing number of studies on crowdsourcing motivation after 2009. Despite the grate attention of academia to the topic of motivation in crowdsourcing literature, except a theoretical classification of motivations which is provided by Kaufmann et al. (2011), no review or categorization could be found in the related literature. This lack of literature review work, motivated us to review the current literature and develop a general framework of motives for participation in crowdsourcing projects in the current study.

Research Method

This study uses systematic literature review approach for the purpose of answering the research questions. A systematic literature review is a methodical way to identify, evaluate, and interpret the available empirical studies conducted on a topic, research question, or a phenomenon of interest (Kitchenham, 2004). This method has been leveraged for many studies to the present day in the information systems area and brought great insight to the field by researchers. Systematic literature review can be beneficial in summarizing evidence about a particular technology, understanding the development of research on a specific area, understanding research gaps in the current literature and areas for future research, providing general frameworks to posit new research activities, and developing guidelines or models based on the available literature (Amrollahi, Ghapanchi, & Talaei-Khoei, 2013; Kitchenham, 2004).

Kitchenham and Charters (2007) suggested five steps for conducting a review: (1) identify resources; (2) study selection; (3) data extraction; (4) data synthesis; and (5) write-up study as a report. Based on these general guidelines, in this study we searched four scientific databases which have been cited as the major sources of research papers in the area of management and information systems (Amrollahi, Ghapanchi, & Talaei-Khoei, 2014; Falagas, Pitsouni, Malietzis, & Pappas, 2008). These databases are: Scopus, ProQuest, Association for Information Systems Electronic Library, and Business Source Premier. These databases were searched with the following set of keywords:

(crowdsourcing OR "crowd sourcing" OR crowdfunding OR crowdsearching OR crowdfunding OR crowdsource OR crowd-based OR "Collective Intelligence" OR "Participatory sensing" OR "citizen science") AND (motivation OR incentive OR pricing OR reward OR motivator OR stimulant)

The initial search for these keywords in the databases resulted in 575 paper. Then irrelevant papers were excluded by reviewing titles, abstracts and full-text papers. After in-depth study of the papers we arrived to the final list of 37 papers and performed our analysis and classification based on those papers. Table 2 shows the number of remaining papers from each database in each stage.

During the exclusion process the relevance of each paper to the crowdsourcing area (and related areas) was verified in reviewing titles and abstracts. Then in study of papers in full-text it was verified if the paper addressed the motivation factors for crowdsourcing or not. As the aim of this study was to study the factors which led to higher levels of motivation for crowd, other studies such as those which suggested incentive mechanisms for crowdsourcing projects, were removed from the final pool of research in this stage. Finally seven papers which were duplicated in various databases were removed and the remaining 37 papers were used for the purpose of analysis. Figure 1 illustrates the exclusion process.

Among the 37 retrieved research papers, 62% used quantitative approach and 22% used qualitative research approach. The remaining 16% used other or mixed approaches. Moreover as depicted in Figure 2 the number of research papers have been grown significantly after 2010 which indicates that the motivation of crowd has been an interesting research topic in recent years.

RESULTS

The final research pool comprised of 37 papers which were studied in depth to find out the factors they suggested for motivation of the crowd. A total number of 220 factors were retrieved from those papers. Moreover, the type of task which has been mentioned in each paper is studied and categorized. The following subsection contains more information about these classifications.

Table 2. Number of papers from each database

	Database	Remaining Papers After			
		Initial Search	**Title Review**	**Abstract Review**	**Full-Text Review**
1	Scopus	450	248	50	13
2	Proquest	72	34	21	8
3	Association for Information Systems electronic library	21	18	12	10
4	Business source premier	32	19	10	6
Total		575	319	93	37

Figure 1. Exclusion process

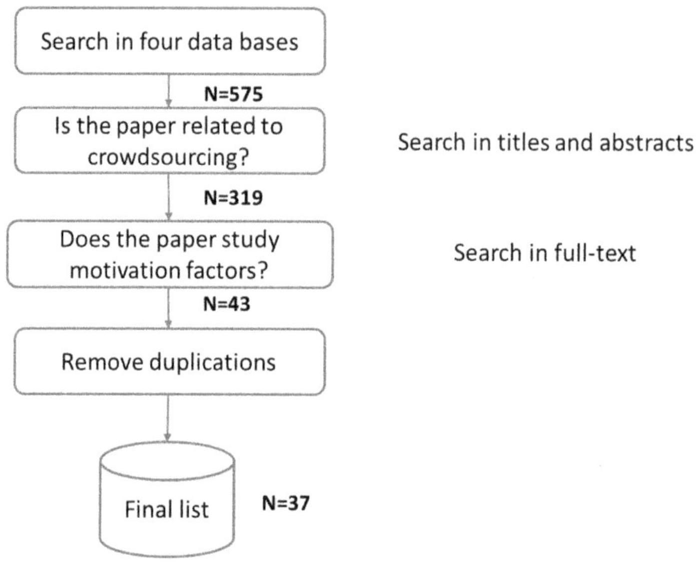

Figure 2. Number of research papers in each year

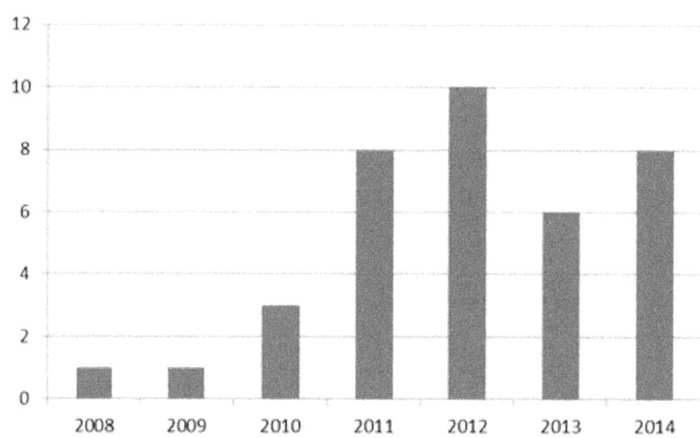

Motivation Factor

In order to classify the motivation factors in the final pool of research, each of the 220 found factors was studied separately and given a tag. Then in a number of iterative studies, the developed tags were studied and some of them were broken down to more than one category and some others were merged to one. Eventually this ended in 12 groups of motivation factors and those categories were again classified in four general categories which are described below.

Monetary

This category of motivation factors includes those projects which pay the crowd for their contribution. This payment could be in form of money, rewards (like free service and final products), or giving the crowd a chance to enter a prize draw.

For instance Brabham (2008) in a study of incentives in iStock found that “the chance to make serious money through one of the t-shirt design contests was a strong motivator (p.1130)”. In the study of 651 responses “the opportunity of making money” was ranked as the highest motive for participants with 89.8 percent of them agreeing that this attracted them to take part in crowdsourcing projects. The role of context (as will be discussed later in this review study) is however very important. As the authors of the above paper in their future study of a governmental platform (Next Stop Design) refer to non-monetary values such as transparency, democratic deliberation, and lack of censorship as their main motives for participation in a crowdsourcing project (Brabham, 2012a).

Work of Füller, Hutter, & Fries (2012) is another example which found the wish to win a cash prize as the most important motive for the crowd. Direct compensation, extrinsic desire for monetary rewards, reward agreement, punishment agreement, betting on result, monetary return, opportunity to get a monetary reward, opportunity for extra income, and monetary return are the other terms which have been used for this category of incentives. Another study on 885 participants on Amazon Mechanical Turk confirmed a relationship between *payment* (monetary extrinsic motive) with demonstrate skills (non-monetary extrinsic motive). In other words, the study confirms that ”Individuals motivated by job-market signaling focus more on choosing structured tasks (i.e., low in unstructuredness) than high-commitment tasks or interdependent tasks because they seek to demonstrate competence” (Pee, Koh, & Goh, 2018, p. 34).

It should be noted that with there is a shift in the literature from monetary based platforms such as iStock (Battistella & Nonino, 2012; Brabham, 2008) and Amazon Mechanical Turk (Antin & Shaw, 2012; Ipeirotis, 2010) to non-monetary websites like Wikipedia (Amrollahi, Tahaei, & Khansari, 2016; Lee & Seo, 2016; Yang & Lai, 2010; Zhang & Zhu, 2006), monetary motives are less discussed in the recent literature.

Extrinsic and Non-Monetary

This category is consisted of motivation factors which will result in short-term and long-term benefits for the crowd but this benefit is not tangible or monetary. Satisfaction of professional needs for the crowd (such as: improvement in ideas and reciprocity action from other projects), recognition, and personal development (in terms of learning and attaining new skills) in professional societies are factors which could be classified in this category.

Füller et al. (2012) has mentioned idea improvement as a motive for crowd which could be an example for *professional needs* subcategory of non-monetary extrinsic motives. Collaboration, reciprocity, use value participation, and meeting own need are other terms which have been used for the motives in professional needs subcategory.

Sending signs that allow conclusions on existing abilities of the sender (Kaufmann et al., 2011) is another subcategory of motives for crowdsourcing which has been identified as *recognition* in the current study. Some other terms which have been used in the literature for this subcategory are: community identification, signalling, public acknowledgement, self-marketing, fame, self-expression, and self-image. In this category, Pee et al. (2018) refers to job-market signaling and "distinguishing among participation in (i.e., choice of) unstructured tasks" as one of the main motives for participation in crowdsourcing projects.

Another study of 244 users in IdeasProject, an open innovation and brainstorming community confirms "recognition from the host company" as the main extrinisc motive for participants and share their knowledge in a crowdsourcing project. The study also verifies that the feedback participants received from others in the crowdsourcing platform helped them to improve their learning and creativity when they submitted their ideas about technological advances and dimensions of the current tasks (Kosonen, Gan, Vanhala, & Blomqvist, 2014; Zhao & Zhu, 2014). Bretschneider and Leimeister (2016) also highlighted the importance of self-marketing-motive or demonstration of personal skills and capabilities and recognition of third parties through crowd ideas as the main motives of participants and idea contributors in the context of Dell's Ideastorm platform.

Finally, acquiring knowledge and skills in the field forms the *development* subcategory of motives in this review which have been mentioned in many studies with various terms such as: skill variety, human capital advancement, professional experience, improving creative skills, empowerment, and benefit for work experience or for professional development. The importance of this category of factors is different among various studies and contexts. Väätäjä (2012) for example found little attention (4% and 21% of responding crowd) in uncreative photo reading context but it has attracted relatively great attention in the context of software development according to the study of Budhathoki and Haythornthwaite (2013).

Intrinsic

This is the last category of crowdsourcing personal motives which is consisted of personal values (such as: altruism and contribute to a scientific improvement), challenge and curiosity, and fun. As the title indicates no long-term or short-term external benefit is achievable through the motives in this category.

The first subcategory in this area is crowds' *values* which have been studied in the literature with various terms such as: altruism, the love of community, commitment, norm-oriented motives, help others, ideology, unique ethos, and socio-political motives. Rotman et al. (2012) studied the effect of values such as educate the society and providing public access to knowledge as factors which can increase the motivation in citizen-science projects. Values have even been cited in studies in uncreative contexts. For example Shaw, Horton, and Chen (2011) mentioned values such as humanization, trust, and solidarity to be effective in motivating crowd in inexpert human raters projects.

With respect to platforms such as Wikipedia which are mainly based on values of helping others and sharing knowledge and wisdom, altruistic motives are more highlighted in the literature. For example, Lee and Seo (2016) based on the analysis of 342 Wikipedia articles concluded that Wikipedia articles are mainly developed through a dominant few people who have strong intrinisc motivations for sharing their knowledge. Another similar study on Wikipedia is the work of Yang and Lai (2010) who studied the impact of contributors' motivation on their willingness to take part in developing Wikipedia articles.

Another subcategory of motives which could be found is related to those workers who do this job as their hobby. This paper categorizes this subcategory of intrinsic motives as *fun*. Bretschneider, Knaub, and Wieck (2014) for example found that enjoyment has a significant effect on the number of submitted soulutions in idea contests. Other than fun (and similar terms such as: enjoyment and recreation) terms like pass time, addiction, and relatxation are also categorised here. The study concludes that internal self-concept-based motivation is the main motivations for users to contribute in Wikipedia. The paper also claims that there is no significant relationship between external self-concept motivation and contributors' intention to share their knowledge on Wikipedia. The authors believe that this is "due to the difficulty establishing strong links with reference groups in the real world as well as the lack of social interaction in Wikipedia" (Yang & Lai, 2010, p. 1382).

Finally a number of research studies have cited people's curiosity or their desire to challenge their own knowledge and skills as a factor which can motive them to participate in the crowdsourcing projects. This challenge is particularly highlighted in the context of creative projects (Naparat & Finnegan, 2013; Paulini, Maher, & Murty, 2014). Kaufman, Flanagan, & Punjasthitkul (2016) studied the impact of social loafing (the tendency to exert less effort in collective tasks in which contributions are anonymous and pooled) and concluded that the scarcity of contributors increases the amount of contribution in gamified crowdsourcing projects.

Morschheuser, Hamari, and Koivisto (2016) in their review of 28 papers focused on gamification for crowdsourcing identified eleven types of gamification in these studies. This shows the importance of gamification and creating fun for participants in crowdsourcing projects. The study also strongly confirms the impact of gamification on the effectiveness of crowdsourcing projects and cites many studies which compared gamified and non-gamified approach of crowdsourcing reporting benefits of the former approach (Goncalves, Hosio, Ferreira, & Kostakos, 2014; Kawajiri, Shimosaka, & Kashima, 2014; Vasilescu, Serebrenik, Devanbu, & Filkov, 2014; Zeng, Tang, & Wang, 2017). The study of Antin and Shaw (2012) also contrasts demographic and origin of contributors in mentioning factors such as having "fun" "killing time" for their participation in crowdsourcing projects. The study reports that contributors from India report these factors less compared to participants in the USA.

Non-Personal

Other than the stated personal factors which increase the motivation of crowd for participation, the study found a number of non-personal factors which are categorized in three categories of organizational motivation (for example: *cost reduction*, *project characteristics* (for instant: social environment or knowledge diversity), and *demographic* (ethnicity of crowd).

An example of the research papers in this category is the comparative study of 2500 workers on MTurk from USA and India and their motivation for participation (Chandler & Kapelner, 2013) or the study of the crowd ethnicity and social class and their motivation (Brabham, 2008). As explained above, the work of Antin and Shaw (2012) is another attempt to study potential differences between participants in crowdsourcing projects from different parts of the world. Based on an study of MTurk the study compares two main origin of workers in the platform (India and USA) and finds "social desirability effects" a more strong motivation for participants in the USA compared to India. Figure 3 illustrates the final classification of motivation factors.

Extrinsic and non-monetary factors form 38% of the factors which have cited in the found literature, while intrinsic factors form 36%, monetary factors form 16%, and non-personal factors form the remaining 10% of factors. Figure 4 also shows the frequency of each subcategory of factors in the studied pool of research. As illustrated in the figure the intrinsic values of the crowd are the factors which have been cited most in the literature as a motivation for crowdsourcing and development

Figure 3. Classification of motivation factors

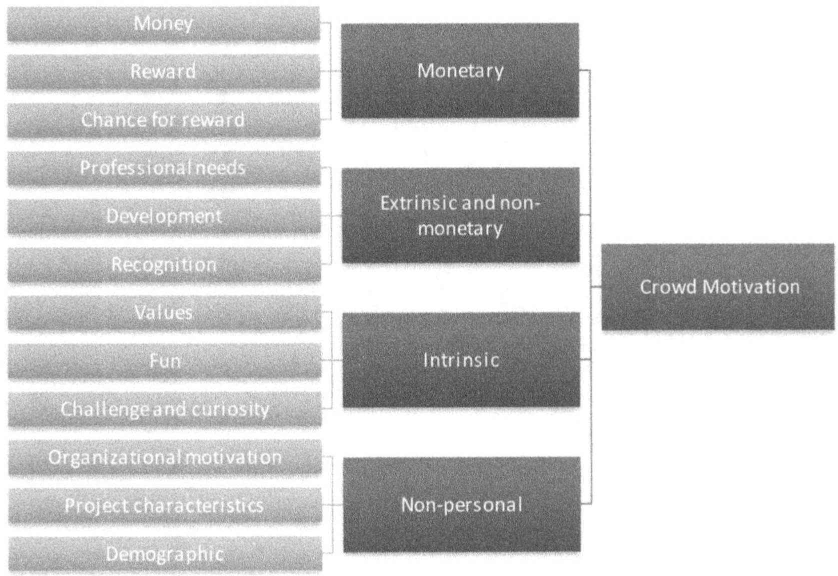

and recognition in the workplace are the other values which have been highly cited in the reviewed papers.

Task Type

More than study the factors which increase the motivation of the crowd for participation, this study reviews the task type which is performed by using crowdsourcing model in each study. Based on this, the reviewed studies have been categorized in four group of creative, uncreative, funding (crowdfunding), and papers which studied unknown or mixed tasks.

Among the reviewed research papers, 43% studied activities such as software development, knowledge sharing, and submitting innovative ideas which require knowledgeable crowd to perform them. Moreover, 36% studied the motivation factors for uncreative tasks (like reading or tagging photos) which require less knowledge and creativity. Finally 14% of papers studied the motivation in the context of crowdfunding projects. Figure 5 illustrates frequency of task types in the found literature.

This study finally investigates various categories of motivation factors which have been used for each type of crowdsourcing task in the literature. Here the number of motivation factors which have been used in each category of crowdsourcing task is investigated. Table 3 shows the result of this investigation.

Figure 4. Frequency of each factor in the found literature

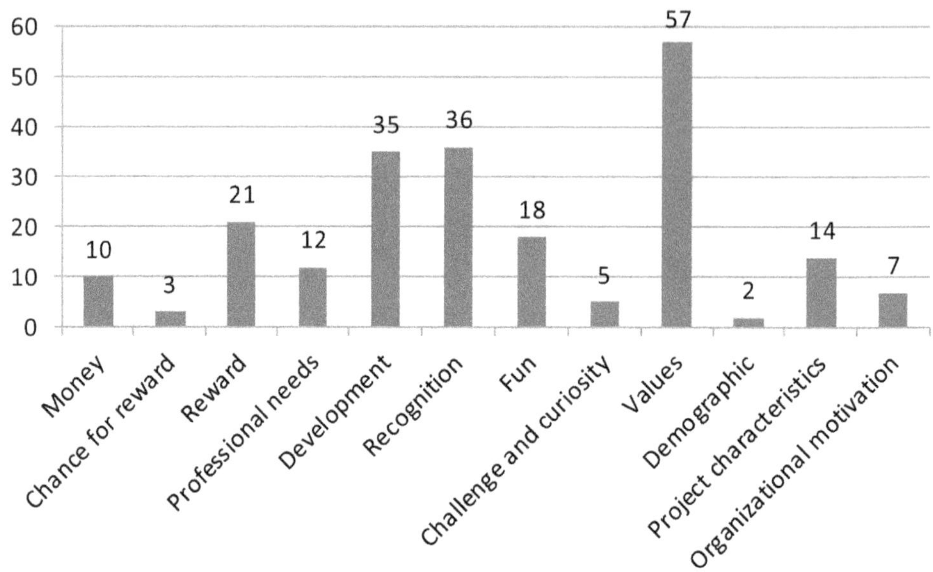

Figure 5. Frequency of each task type in the reviewed studies

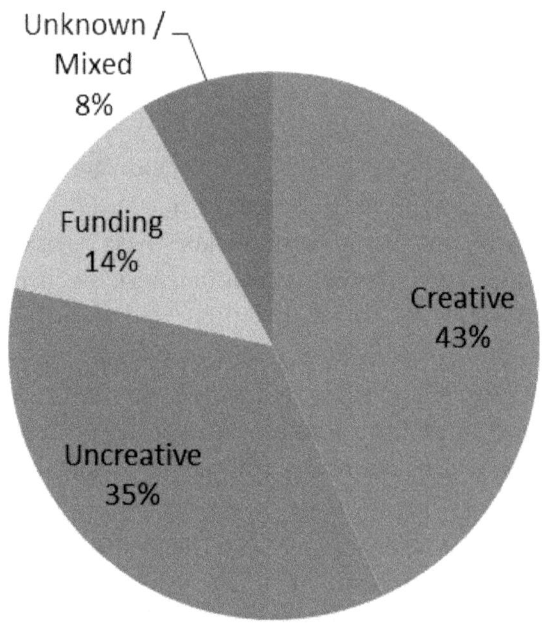

Table 3. Frequency of each motivation category in each type of crowdsourcing task

	Monetary	Extrinsic and Non-Monetary	Intrinsic	Non-Personal
Creative	14	29	27	7
Uncreative	11	41	43	12
Funding	5	7	6	4
Unknown / Mixed	4	6	4	0

DISCUSSION AND CONCLUSION

Crowdsourcing is recognized as an effective approach of performing organizational tasks (Literat, 2017; Litman, Robinson, & Abberbock, 2017; Nguyen et al., 2017) which is highly relied on inputs from diverse crowd (M. J. Pedersen, Stritch, & Taggart, 2017) and requires attention to the dynamics of human behavior who participate in the projects. This study was an attempt to study the motivation of crowds by reviewing the related literature in the crowdsourcing area. The study of 37 papers ended in identification of 220 factors in them which were classified into four categories and 12 subcategories. Moreover, the study reviewed the type of task which was studied in each research and categorized them in four groups.

The result of this study indicates that intrinsic and non-monetary extrinsic factors are the most frequent motivation factors which have been studied in the literature. Even in study of specific task types, significant difference cannot be observed among these two categories of motivation factors. In study of both creative and uncreative tasks, intrinsic and non-monetary factors were the most frequent factors. The relationship between task type and motives for crowdsourcing has been studied in the literature (Pee et al., 2018). The results of the current study confirms that intrinsic motives are the main factors for both creative and uncreative type of tasks. This is aligned with the literature on the impact of different types of motives on structured and un-structured tasks.

Non-personal factors are also more cited in study of uncreative tasks comparing to creative tasks and these factors are even highlighted more than monetary factors of motivation. An interesting founding of this study is the relatively high number of monetary incentives for crowdfunding projects. Although participation in these projects involves donation of money, our review indicates that still monetary rewards have been studied for the motivation of crowd in these projects. Possible implications of this study for practice and research are explained in turn below.

Implication for Practice

This review can benefit practitioners who intend to utilize the crowdsourcing model in their business by creating a framework of possible incentives for them. Moreover, it has been highlighted in the literature that there is usually a barrier between theory and practice in the area of information systems which could be removed by review papers (Amrollahi et al., 2013). This review can provide the practitioners with a guide for selecting appropriate studies in the field and adapt them with their business context (See Appendix).

The developed framework also classifies research papers based on the context (task type) in which the research has been conducted. This classification can give an idea to the practitioners for the best category of incentive according to the context of their business. Based on the result of this study non-monetary extrinsic motivation factors are most studied in the context of creative tasks and crowdfunding, and intrinsic motivation factors are most studied in the context of uncreative tasks. It should be also noted that the amount of research studies in each category is not a proper indicator for appropriateness of the factor for task types. However, this can help the future research and practitioners in the field to compare the result of previous studies and see the body of research in a big picture.

Implication for Research

Although many research studies have studied the motivation process for crowdsourcing project, no review of current factors could be found in the literature. As such, this study fills this gap by providing a comprehensive review of factors which have been mentioned in the literature to this date.This study create a basis for new researchers who want to initiate a research on the factors which affect the motivation of crowd and can illustrates possible research gaps for them. Four main gaps have been found by this study.

The first gap is lack of multi-context research in the area of crowdsourcing motivation. As explained above, 92% of the research studies which were found in the final pool of research papers were based on a specific crowdsourcing platform or task type. Although this will help the audience to have a better understanding of the motivation model in a specific context, it does not provide an insight about the effect of the context and task type in the findings of the study. For this reason, this study encourages future researchers to conduct more multi-context studies and mention the task type as a control factor which can affect the results of the study.

Although some of the research studies in the final pool of research have used theories such as: self-determination theory (Deci & Ryan, 2000; Y. Zhao & Zhu, 2012a), motivation crowding theory (Frey & Jegen, 2001; Liu, Liang, Rajagopalan,

& Sambamurthy, 2011), Motive-Incentive-Activation-Behavior model (MIAB) (Briggs, 2006; Leimeister et al., 2009), protection motivation theory (Tsai et al., 2016), affordance theory and motivation theory (Choy & Schlagwein, 2016), and behavior change theory (de Vries, Truong, Kwint, Drossaert, & Evers, 2016), and the theory of job design (Deci & Ryan, 1985; Zheng, Li, & Hou, 2011), most of the research studies in the final pool do not have a rigorous theoretical background. While the crowdsourcing literature is in general informed by theories (Amrollahi, Amir Ghapanchi, & Talaei-Khoei, 2014), this can be observed as a serious disadvantage in the current literature.

For this reason, future research papers may also consider theories from various areas such as: psychology, sociology, and organization studies to create a better theoretical basis for their research. In particular, theories such as accountability theory (Vance, Lowry, & Eggett, 2015), belief action outcome model (Melville, 2010), social cognitive theory (Bandura, 1977), and the theory of planned behavior (Bobbitt & Dabholkar, 2001) can be utilized in future studies in the area of motivating crowd. Also, studies in the related areas such as motivation factors for open source software development (Hertel, Niedner, & Herrmann, 2003; Lakhani & Von Hippel, 2003; Lakhani & Wolf, 2005) may help the researchers in findings suitable theory base for their studies.

The third observed gap is identification of dependent factor which will be affected by motivation factors. Many different factors such as motivation, contribution level, participation, and quality of contribution have been mentioned in the literature for measuring the effect of crowd motivation. This study recommends future studies to evaluate the effect of motivation on general effectiveness or success of the project to provide a better evaluation. The theoretical background in areas such as information systems success (Delone & Mclean, 2004) and adoption (Venkatesh & Bala, 2008) may help the researchers in this regard. Moreover, the relationship between participation and success has been ignored in most of the research papers which could be considered as an important hypothesis in future studies.

The results of our study indicates that despite few studied which focused on the geographical location of crowd workers (for example Antin and Shaw (2012) and Chandler and Kapelner (2013)) and project type (for example Alam and Campbell (2017)), the context of crowdsourcing project is usually absent in the study of motives for participation. Future research can focus on contextual factors such as status of project, platform type, communication with and between crowd, and the history of crowdsourcing projects on the effectiveness of a factor.

The crowdsourcing model have been extended to many different areas of information systems and management research this includes open strategy (Amrollahi & Rowlands, 2017; Tavakoli, Schlagwein, & Schoder, 2017), group decision making (Morente-Molinera, Pérez, Ureña, & Herrera-Viedma, 2015), organizational collaboration (Mladenow, Bauer, Strauss, & Gregus, 2015), open source software development (Steinmacher, Conte, Gerosa, & Redmiles, 2015), and openness phenomena in general (Schlagwein et al., 2017; Smith & Seward, 2017). Therefore, the results of this study can be extended to these areas in future research.

Finally, most of the research studies in this review used the quantitative survey method for testing hypotheses about the motivation. Future studies may consider qualitative approach and methods such as case study for further investigations of motivation factors.

RESEARCH LIMITATIONS

The first and most important limitation in this study and any other review is the dependency of the founding on the reviewed literature. In this study also motivations for *Open Source Software* (OSS) development have not been considered. Although the process of OSS development is to somehow equivalent to the crowdsourcing model, however, according to some differences which can be found in the nature of these projects and huge amount of research papers in this topic, this paper was dedicated only to those studies which used the term crowdsourcing or one of its synonyms.

Moreover, and in spite of the attempts in the current study to investigate the task type as an important contextual factor, in reviewing the studies the context of research was most of the time missed. For this reason the authors invite interested readers to investigate more about their desired category of factors in the original research. Finally, the review in this study was based on a set of specific keywords and in specific databases and there is always a risk to miss some important studies as a result of this.

REFERENCES

Alam, S., & Campbell, J. (2013). *Dynamic Changes in Organizational Motivations to Crowdsourcing for GLAMs*. Paper presented at the International Conference on Information Systems, Milan.

Alam, S. L., & Campbell, J. (2017). Temporal Motivations of Volunteers to Participate in Cultural Crowdsourcing Work. *Information Systems Research*, *28*(4), 744–759. doi:10.1287/isre.2017.0719

Amrollahi, A. (2015). *A process model for crowdsourcing: insights from the literature on implementation*. Paper presented at the 26th Australasian Conference on Information Systems, Adelaide, Australia.

Amrollahi, A., Ghapanchi, A., & Talaei-Khoei, A. (2014). *A systematic review of the current theory base in the crowdsourcing literature.* Paper presented at the 28th Australian and New Zealand Academy of Management Conference.

Amrollahi, A., Ghapanchi, A., & Talaei-Khoei, A. (2014). *Using Crowdsourcing Tools for Implementing Open Strategy: A Case Study in Education.* Paper presented at the Twentieth Americas Conference on Information System (AMCIS 2014), Savannah, GA.

Amrollahi, A., Ghapanchi, A. H., & Talaei-Khoei, A. (2013). A Systematic Literature Review on Strategic Information Systems Planning: Insights from the Past Decade. *Pacific Asia Journal of the Association for Information Systems*, *5*(2), 39–66.

Amrollahi, A., Ghapanchi, A. H., & Talaei-Khoei, A. (2014). Three Decades of Research on Strategic Information System Plan Development. *Communications of the Association for Information Systems*, *34*(1), 1440–1467.

Amrollahi, A., & Ghapnchi, A. H. (2016). *Open strategic planning in universities: a case study.* Paper presented at the System Sciences (HICSS), 2016 49th Hawaii International Conference on. 10.1109/HICSS.2016.54

Amrollahi, A., Khansari, M., & Manian, A. (2014). *How Open Source Software Succeeds? A Review of Research on Success of Open Source Software.* Academic Press.

Amrollahi, A., Khansari, M., & Manian, A. (2015). *Success of Open Source in Developing Countries: The Case of Iran. In Open Source Technology: Concepts, Methodologies, Tools, and Applications* (pp. 1126–1142). IGI Global. doi:10.4018/978-1-4666-7230-7.ch055

Amrollahi, A., & Rowlands, B. (2017). Collaborative open strategic planning: A method and case study. *Information Technology & People*, *30*(4), 832–852. doi:10.1108/ITP-12-2015-0310

Amrollahi, A., Tahaei, M., & Khansari, M. (2016). *Measuring the Effectiveness of Wikipedia Articles: How Does Open Content Succeed? In Handbook of Research on Innovations in Information Retrieval, Analysis, and Management* (pp. 41–61). IGI Global. doi:10.4018/978-1-4666-8833-9.ch002

Antin, J., & Shaw, A. (2012). Social desirability bias and self-reports of motivation: a study of amazon mechanical turk in the US and India. *Proceedings of the SIGCHI Conference on Human Factors in Computing Systems.* 10.1145/2207676.2208699

Bandura, A. (1977). Self-efficacy: Toward a unifying theory of behavioral change. *Psychological Review*, *84*(2), 191–215. doi:10.1037/0033-295X.84.2.191 PMID:847061

Basiouka, S., & Potsiou, C. (2014). The volunteered geographic information in cadastre: Perspectives and citizens' motivations over potential participation in mapping. *GeoJournal*, *79*(3), 343–355. doi:10.100710708-013-9497-7

Battistella, C., & Nonino, F. (2012). Open innovation web-based platforms: The impact of different forms of motivation on collaboration. *Innovation*, *14*(4), 557–575. doi:10.5172/impp.2012.14.4.557

Battistella, C., & Nonino, F. (2013). Exploring the impact of motivations on the attraction of innovation roles in open innovation web-based platforms. *Production Planning and Control*, *24*(2-3), 226–245. doi:10.1080/09537287.2011.647876

Bobbitt, L. M., & Dabholkar, P. A. (2001). Integrating attitudinal theories to understand and predict use of technology-based self-service: The internet as an illustration. *International Journal of Service Industry Management*, *12*(5), 423–450. doi:10.1108/EUM0000000006092

Brabham, D. C. (2008). Moving the crowd at iStockphoto: The composition of the crowd and motivations for participation in a crowdsourcing application. *First Monday*, *13*(6). doi:10.5210/fm.v13i6.2159

Brabham, D. C. (2012a). The effectiveness of crowdsourcing public participation in a planning context. *First Monday*, *17*(12). doi:10.5210/fm.v17i12.4225

Brabham, D. C. (2012b). Motivations for participation in a crowdsourcing application to improve public engagement in transit planning. *Journal of Applied Communication Research*, *40*(3), 307–328. doi:10.1080/00909882.2012.693940

Brändle, A. (2005). *Too Many Cooks Don't Spoil the Broth*. Paper presented at the The First International Wikimedia Conference, Frankfurt, Germany.

Bretschneider, U., Knaub, K., & Wieck, E. (2014). *Motivations for Crowdfunding: What Drives the Crowd to Invest in Start-Ups?* Academic Press.

Bretschneider, U., & Leimeister, J. M. (2016). Motivation for Open Innovation and Crowdsourcing: Why Does the Crowd Engage in Virtual Ideas Communities? In Open Tourism (pp. 109–120). Springer.

Briggs, R. O. (2006). On theory-driven design and deployment of collaboration systems. *International Journal of Human-Computer Studies*, *64*(7), 573–582. doi:10.1016/j.ijhcs.2006.02.003

Budhathoki, N. R., & Haythornthwaite, C. (2013). Motivation for Open Collaboration Crowd and Community Models and the Case of OpenStreetMap. *The American Behavioral Scientist*, *57*(5), 548–575. doi:10.1177/0002764212469364

Chandler, D., & Kapelner, A. (2013). Breaking monotony with meaning: Motivation in crowdsourcing markets. *Journal of Economic Behavior & Organization*, *90*, 123–133. doi:10.1016/j.jebo.2013.03.003

Choy, K., & Schlagwein, D. (2016). Crowdsourcing for a better world: On the relation between IT affordances and donor motivations in charitable crowdfunding. *Information Technology & People*, *29*(1), 221–247. doi:10.1108/ITP-09-2014-0215

Cooper, S., Khatib, F., Treuille, A., Barbero, J., Lee, J., Beenen, M., ... players, F. (2010). Predicting protein structures with a multiplayer online game. *Nature*, *466*(7307), 756–760. doi:10.1038/nature09304 PMID:20686574

Davis, J. G., & Lin, H. (2011). *Web 3.0 and Crowdservicing*. Paper presented at the AMCIS.

de Vries, R. A., Truong, K. P., Kwint, S., Drossaert, C. H., & Evers, V. (2016). Crowd-Designed Motivation: Motivational messages for exercise adherence based on behavior change theory. *Proceedings of the 2016 CHI Conference on Human Factors in Computing Systems*. 10.1145/2858036.2858229

Deci, E. L., & Ryan, R. M. (1985). *Intrinsic motivation and self-determination in human behavior*. New York: Plenum. doi:10.1007/978-1-4899-2271-7

Deci, E. L., & Ryan, R. M. (2000). The" what" and" why" of goal pursuits: Human needs and the self-determination of behavior. *Psychological Inquiry*, *11*(4), 227–268. doi:10.1207/S15327965PLI1104_01

Delone, W. H., & Mclean, E. R. (2004). Measuring e-commerce success: Applying the DeLone & McLean information systems success model. *International Journal of Electronic Commerce*, *9*(1), 31–47.

DiGiammarino, F., & Trudeau, L. (2008). Virtual networks: An opportunity for government. *Public Management*, *37*(1), 5.

Doan, A., Ramakrishnan, R., & Halevy, A. Y. (2011). Crowdsourcing systems on the world-wide web. *Communications of the ACM*, *54*(4), 86–96. doi:10.1145/1924421.1924442

Estellés-Arolas, E., & González-Ladrón-De-Guevara, F. (2012). Towards an integrated crowdsourcing definition. *Journal of Information Science*, *38*(2), 189–200. doi:10.1177/0165551512437638

Falagas, M. E., Pitsouni, E. I., Malietzis, G. A., & Pappas, G. (2008). Comparison of PubMed, Scopus, web of science, and Google scholar: Strengths and weaknesses. *The FASEB Journal, 22*(2), 338–342. doi:10.1096/fj.07-9492LSF PMID:17884971

Farooq, U., Ganoe, C. H., Carroll, J. M., & Giles, C. L. (2009). Designing for e-science: Requirements gathering for collaboration in CiteSeer. *International Journal of Human-Computer Studies, 67*(4), 297–312. doi:10.1016/j.ijhcs.2007.10.005

Frey, B. S., & Jegen, R. (2001). Motivation crowding theory. *Journal of Economic Surveys, 15*(5), 589–611. doi:10.1111/1467-6419.00150

Frey, K., Haag, S., & Schneider, V. (2011). *The role of interests, abilities, and motivation in online idea contests.* Paper presented at the 10th International Conference on Wirtschaftsinformatik.

Frey, K., Lüthje, C., & Haag, S. (2011). Whom should firms attract to open innovation platforms? The role of knowledge diversity and motivation. *Long Range Planning, 44*(5), 397–420. doi:10.1016/j.lrp.2011.09.006

Frydrych, D., Bock, A. J., Kinder, T., & Koeck, B. (2014). Exploring entrepreneurial legitimacy in reward-based crowdfunding. *Venture Capital, 16*(3), 247–269. doi:10.1080/13691066.2014.916512

Füller, J., Hutter, K., & Fries, M. (2012). Crowdsourcing for Goodness Sake: Impact of Incentive Preference on Contribution Behavior for Social Innovation. *Adv Int Market, 23*, 137–159.

Gao, H., Barbier, G., & Goolsby, R. (2011). Harnessing the crowdsourcing power of social media for disaster relief. *IEEE Intelligent Systems, 26*(3), 10–14. doi:10.1109/MIS.2011.52

Gerber, E. M., & Hui, J. (2013). Crowdfunding: Motivations and deterrents for participation. *ACM Transactions on Computer-Human Interaction, 20*(6), 34. doi:10.1145/2530540

Ghezzi, A., Gabelloni, D., Martini, A., & Natalicchio, A. (2017). Crowdsourcing: A review and suggestions for future research. *International Journal of Management Reviews.* doi:10.1111/ijmr.12135

Gloor, P., & Cooper, S. (2007). The new principles of a swarm business. *MIT Sloan Management Review, 48*(3), 81.

Goldman, J., Shilton, K., Burke, J., Estrin, D., Hansen, M., & Ramanathan, N. (2009). *Participatory Sensing: A citizen-powered approach to illuminating the patterns that shape our world.* Foresight & Governance Project, White Paper, 1-15.

Goncalves, J., Hosio, S., Ferreira, D., & Kostakos, V. (2014). Game of words: tagging places through crowdsourcing on public displays. *Proceedings of the 2014 conference on Designing interactive systems*. 10.1145/2598510.2598514

Goncalves, J., Hosio, S., Rogstadius, J., Karapanos, E., & Kostakos, V. (2015). Motivating participation and improving quality of contribution in ubiquitous crowdsourcing. *Computer Networks*, *90*, 34–48. doi:10.1016/j.comnet.2015.07.002

Graber, M. A., & Graber, A. (2013). Internet-based crowdsourcing and research ethics: The case for IRB review. *Journal of Medical Ethics*, *39*(2), 115–118. doi:10.1136/medethics-2012-100798 PMID:23204319

Haythornthwaite, C. (2009). *Crowds and communities: Light and heavyweight models of peer production*. Paper presented at the System Sciences, 2009. HICSS'09. 42nd Hawaii International Conference on.

Hertel, G., Niedner, S., & Herrmann, S. (2003). Motivation of software developers in Open Source projects: An Internet-based survey of contributors to the Linux kernel. *Research Policy*, *32*(7), 1159–1177. doi:10.1016/S0048-7333(03)00047-7

Hetmank, L. (2013). Components and Functions of Crowdsourcing Systems-A Systematic Literature Review. *Wirtschaftsinformatik*, *4*, 2013.

Howe, J. (2006). *Crowdsourcing: A definition*. Retrieved from http://www.crowdsourcing.com/cs/2006/06/crowdsourcing_a.html

Jarvenpaa, S. L., & Majchrzak, A. (2010). Research commentary—vigilant interaction in knowledge collaboration: Challenges of online user participation under ambivalence. *Information Systems Research*, *21*(4), 773–784. doi:10.1287/isre.1100.0320

Kaghazgaran, P., Caverlee, J., & Alfifi, M. (2017). *Behavioral Analysis of Review Fraud: Linking Malicious Crowdsourcing to Amazon and Beyond*. Paper presented at the ICWSM.

Kaufman, G., Flanagan, M., & Punjasthitkul, S. (2016). Investigating the impact of'emphasis frames' and social loafing on player motivation and performance in a crowdsourcing game. *Proceedings of the 2016 CHI conference on human factors in computing systems*. 10.1145/2858036.2858588

Kaufmann, N., Schulze, T., & Veit, D. (2011). *More than fun and money. Worker Motivation in Crowdsourcing-A Study on Mechanical Turk*. Paper presented at the AMCIS.

Kawajiri, R., Shimosaka, M., & Kashima, H. (2014). Steered crowdsensing: Incentive design towards quality-oriented place-centric crowdsensing. *Proceedings of the 2014 ACM International Joint Conference on Pervasive and Ubiquitous Computing*. 10.1145/2632048.2636064

Kawasaki, H., Yamamoto, A., Kurasawa, H., Sato, H., Nakamura, M., & Matsumura, H. (2012). Top of worlds: method for improving motivation to participate in sensing services. *Proceedings of the 2012 ACM Conference on Ubiquitous Computing*. 10.1145/2370216.2370321

Kelley, T. M., & Johnston, E. (2012). Discovering the appropriate role of serious games in the design of open governance platforms. *Public Administration Quarterly*, 504–554.

Kitchenham, B. (2004). Procedures for performing systematic reviews. Keele University.

Kitchenham, B., & Charters, S. (2007). *Guidelines for performing systematic literature reviews in software engineering EBSE Technical Report*. Retrieved from Durham.

Kittur, A., Chi, E. H., & Suh, B. (2008). Crowdsourcing user studies with Mechanical Turk. *Proceedings of the SIGCHI conference on human factors in computing systems*.

Kosonen, M., Gan, C., Vanhala, M., & Blomqvist, K. (2014). User motivation and knowledge sharing in idea crowdsourcing. *International Journal of Innovation Management, 18*(05), 1450031. doi:10.1142/S1363919614500315

Lakhani, K. R., & Von Hippel, E. (2003). How open source software works:"free" user-to-user assistance. *Research Policy, 32*(6), 923–943. doi:10.1016/S0048-7333(02)00095-1

Lakhani, K. R., & Wolf, R. G. (2005). Why hackers do what they do: Understanding motivation and effort in free/open source software projects. *Perspectives on Free and Open Source Software, 1*, 3-22.

Lee, J., & Seo, D. (2016). Crowdsourcing not all sourced by the crowd: An observation on the behavior of Wikipedia participants. *Technovation, 55*, 14–21. doi:10.1016/j.technovation.2016.05.002

Leimeister, J. M., Huber, M., Bretschneider, U., & Krcmar, H. (2009). Leveraging crowdsourcing: Activation-supporting components for IT-based ideas competition. *Journal of Management Information Systems, 26*(1), 197–224. doi:10.2753/MIS0742-1222260108

Lin, A. (2004). *Wikipedia as participatory journalism: Reliable sources.* Paper for the 5th International Symposium on Online Journalism, Austin, TX.

Literat, I. (2017). Tapping into the Collective Creativity of the Crowd: The Effectiveness of Key Incentives in Fostering Creative Crowdsourcing. *Proceedings of the 50th Hawaii International Conference on System Sciences.* 10.24251/HICSS.2017.212

Litman, L., Robinson, J., & Abberbock, T. (2017). TurkPrime. com: A versatile crowdsourcing data acquisition platform for the behavioral sciences. *Behavior Research Methods, 49*(2), 433–442. doi:10.375813428-016-0727-z PMID:27071389

Liu, C.-C., Liang, T.-P., Rajagopalan, B., & Sambamurthy, V. (2011). *The Crowding Effect Of Rewards On Knowledge-Sharing Behavior In Virtual Communities.* Paper presented at the PACIS.

Lukyanenko, R., & Parsons, J. (2012). Conceptual modeling principles for crowdsourcing. *Proceedings of the 1st international workshop on Multimodal crowd sensing.* 10.1145/2390034.2390038

Lukyanenko, R., Parsons, J., & Wiersma, Y. F. (2014). The IQ of the crowd: Understanding and improving information quality in structured user-generated content. *Information Systems Research, 25*(4), 669–689. doi:10.1287/isre.2014.0537

Mankowski, T. A., Slater, S. J., & Slater, T. F. (2011). An interpretive study of meanings citizen scientists make when participating in Galaxy Zoo. *Contemporary Issues in Education Research, 4*(4), 25–42. doi:10.19030/cier.v4i4.4165

Melville, N. P. (2010). Information systems innovation for environmental sustainability. *Management Information Systems Quarterly, 34*(1), 1–21. doi:10.2307/20721412

Mladenow, A., Bauer, C., Strauss, C., & Gregus, M. (2015). *Collaboration and locality in crowdsourcing.* Paper presented at the Intelligent Networking and Collaborative Systems (INCOS), 2015 International Conference on. 10.1109/INCoS.2015.74

Morente-Molinera, J. A., Pérez, I. J., Ureña, M. R., & Herrera-Viedma, E. (2015). On multi-granular fuzzy linguistic modeling in group decision making problems: A systematic review and future trends. *Knowledge-Based Systems, 74,* 49–60. doi:10.1016/j.knosys.2014.11.001

Morschheuser, B., Hamari, J., & Koivisto, J. (2016). *Gamification in crowdsourcing: a review.* Paper presented at the System Sciences (HICSS), 2016 49th Hawaii International Conference on. 10.1109/HICSS.2016.543

Naparat, D., & Finnegan, P. (2013). *Crowdsourcing Software Requirements and Development: A Mechanism-based Exploration of 'Opensourcing'.* Academic Press.

Nguyen, Q. V. H., Duong, C. T., Nguyen, T. T., Weidlich, M., Aberer, K., Yin, H., & Zhou, X. (2017). Argument discovery via crowdsourcing. *The VLDB Journal, 26*(4), 511–535. doi:10.100700778-017-0462-9

Nov, O., Anderson, D., & Arazy, O. (2010). Volunteer computing: a model of the factors determining contribution to community-based scientific research. *Proceedings of the 19th international conference on World wide web*. 10.1145/1772690.1772766

Nov, O., Arazy, O., & Anderson, D. (2014). Scientists@ Home: What drives the quantity and quality of online citizen science participation? *PLoS One, 9*(4), e90375. doi:10.1371/journal.pone.0090375 PMID:24690612

Parvanta, C., Roth, Y., & Keller, H. (2013). Crowdsourcing 101 A Few Basics to Make You the Leader of the Pack. *Health Promotion Practice, 14*(2), 163–167. doi:10.1177/1524839912470654 PMID:23299912

Paulini, M., Maher, M. L., & Murty, P. (2014). Motivating participation in online innovation communities. *International Journal of Web Based Communities, 10*(1), 94–114. doi:10.1504/IJWBC.2014.058388

Pedersen, J., Kocsis, D., Tripathi, A., Tarrell, A., Weerakoon, A., Tahmasbi, N., ... (2013). *Conceptual foundations of crowdsourcing: A review of IS research.* Paper presented at the 2013 46th Hawaii International Conference on System Sciences (HICSS 46). 10.1109/HICSS.2013.143

Pedersen, M. J., Stritch, J. M., & Taggart, G. (2017). Citizen perceptions of procedural fairness and the moderating roles of 'belief in a just world'and 'public service motivation'in public hiring. *Public Administration, 95*(4), 874–894. doi:10.1111/padm.12353

Pee, L., Koh, E., & Goh, M. (2018). Trait motivations of crowdsourcing and task choice: A distal-proximal perspective. *International Journal of Information Management, 40*, 28–41. doi:10.1016/j.ijinfomgt.2018.01.008

Pennington, D. D. (2011). Bridging the disciplinary divide: Co-creating research ideas in escience teams. *Computer Supported Cooperative Work, 20*(3), 165–196. doi:10.100710606-011-9134-2

Pickerell, J. (2012). *iStockphoto 2012: Semi-Annual Analysis*. Retrieved from http://blog.microstockgroup.com/istockphoto-2012-semi-annual-analysis/

Poetz, M. K., & Schreier, M. (2012). The value of crowdsourcing: Can users really compete with professionals in generating new product ideas? *Journal of Product Innovation Management, 29*(2), 245–256. doi:10.1111/j.1540-5885.2011.00893.x

Raddick, M. J., Bracey, G., Gay, P. L., Lintott, C. J., Murray, P., Schawinski, K., ... Vandenberg, J. (2010). Galaxy zoo: Exploring the motivations of citizen science volunteers. *Astronomy Education Review*, *9*(1), 010103. doi:10.3847/AER2009036

Ranard, B. L., Ha, Y. P., Meisel, Z. F., Asch, D. A., Hill, S. S., Becker, L. B., ... Merchant, R. M. (2014). Crowdsourcing—harnessing the masses to advance health and medicine, a systematic review. *Journal of General Internal Medicine*, *29*(1), 187–203. doi:10.100711606-013-2536-8 PMID:23843021

Rodriguez, M. A., Steinbock, D. J., Watkins, J. H., Gershenson, C., Bollen, J., & Grey, V. (2007). *Smartocracy: Social networks for collective decision making.* Paper presented at the System Sciences, 2007. HICSS 2007. 40th Annual Hawaii International Conference on. 10.1109/HICSS.2007.484

Rotman, D., Preece, J., Hammock, J., Procita, K., Hansen, D., & Parr, C. (2012). Dynamic changes in motivation in collaborative citizen-science projects. *Proceedings of the ACM 2012 conference on Computer Supported Cooperative Work.* 10.1145/2145204.2145238

Schlagwein, D., Conboy, K., Feller, J., Leimeister, J. M., & Morgan, L. (2017). *"Openness" with and without Information Technology: a framework and a brief history.* Springer.

Seltzer, E., & Mahmoudi, D. (2013). Citizen Participation, Open Innovation, and Crowdsourcing Challenges and Opportunities for Planning. *Journal of Planning Literature*, *28*(1), 3–18. doi:10.1177/0885412212469112

Sharifi, M., Fink, E., & Carbonell, J. G. (2011). *Smartnotes: Application of crowdsourcing to the detection of web threats.* Paper presented at the Systems, Man, and Cybernetics (SMC), 2011 IEEE International Conference on. 10.1109/ICSMC.2011.6083845

Shaw, A. D., Horton, J. J., & Chen, D. L. (2011). Designing incentives for inexpert human raters. *Proceedings of the ACM 2011 conference on Computer supported cooperative work.*

Smith, M. L., & Seward, R. (2017). Openness as social praxis. *First Monday*, *22*(4). doi:10.5210/fm.v22i4.7073

Söldner, J.-H., Haller, J., Bullinger, A. C., & Möslein, K. M. (2009). *Supporting Research Collaboration-On the Needs of Virtual Research Teams.* Paper presented at the Wirtschaftsinformatik (1).

Steinmacher, I., Conte, T., Gerosa, M. A., & Redmiles, D. (2015). Social barriers faced by newcomers placing their first contribution in open source software projects. *Proceedings of the 18th ACM conference on Computer supported cooperative work & social computing*. 10.1145/2675133.2675215

Stieger, D., Matzler, K., Chatterjee, S., & Ladstaetter-Fussenegger, F. (2012). Democratizing Strategy: How Crowdsourcing Can be Used for Strategy Dialogues. *California Management Review*, *54*(4), 44–68. doi:10.1525/cmr.2012.54.4.44

Tarrell, A., Tahmasbi, N., Kocsis, D., Tripathi, A., Pedersen, J., Xiong, J., ... (2013). *Crowdsourcing: A Snapshot of Published Research*. Paper presented at the Nineteenth Americas Conference on Information Systems, Chicago, IL.

Tavakoli, A., Schlagwein, D., & Schoder, D. (2017). Open strategy: Literature review, re-analysis of cases and conceptualisation as a practice. *The Journal of Strategic Information Systems*, *26*(3), 163–184. doi:10.1016/j.jsis.2017.01.003

Thuan, N. H., Antunes, P., & Johnstone, D. (2017). A process model for establishing business process crowdsourcing. *AJIS. Australasian Journal of Information Systems*, 21.

Tomczak, A., & Brem, A. (2013). A conceptualized investment model of crowdfunding. *Venture Capital*, *15*(4), 335–359. doi:10.1080/13691066.2013.847614

Tripathi, A., Tahmasbi, N., Khazanchi, D., & Najjar, L. (2014). Crowdsourcing typology: a review of is research and organizations. *Proceedings of the Midwest Association for Information Systems (MWAIS)*.

Tsai, H.-S., Jiang, M., Alhabash, S., LaRose, R., Rifon, N. J., & Cotten, S. R. (2016). Understanding online safety behaviors: A protection motivation theory perspective. *Computers & Security*, *59*, 138–150. doi:10.1016/j.cose.2016.02.009

Väätäjä, H. (2012). Readers' motivations to participate in hyperlocal news content creation. *Proceedings of the 17th ACM international conference on Supporting group work*. 10.1145/2389176.2389234

Vance, A., Lowry, P., & Eggett, D. (2015). *Increasing Accountability through the User Interface Design Artifacts: A New Approach to Addressing the Problem of Access-Policy Violations*. Academic Press.

Vasilescu, B., Serebrenik, A., Devanbu, P., & Filkov, V. (2014). How social Q&A sites are changing knowledge sharing in open source software communities. *Proceedings of the 17th ACM conference on Computer supported cooperative work & social computing*. 10.1145/2531602.2531659

Venkatesh, V., & Bala, H. (2008). Technology acceptance model 3 and a research agenda on interventions. *Decision Sciences, 39*(2), 273–315. doi:10.1111/j.1540-5915.2008.00192.x

Whelan, E. (2007). Exploring knowledge exchange in electronic networks of practice. *Journal of Information Technology, 22*(1), 5–12. doi:10.1057/palgrave.jit.2000089

Yan, J., & Wang, X. (2013). *From Open Source to Commercial Software Development-the Community Based Software Development Model.* Academic Press.

Yang, H.-L., & Lai, C.-Y. (2010). Motivations of Wikipedia content contributors. *Computers in Human Behavior, 26*(6), 1377–1383. doi:10.1016/j.chb.2010.04.011

Yu, L. L., & Nickerson, J. V. (2011). *Generating creative ideas through crowds: An experimental study of combination.* Academic Press.

Zeng, Z., Tang, J., & Wang, T. (2017). Motivation mechanism of gamification in crowdsourcing projects. *International Journal of Crowd Science, 1*(1), 71–82. doi:10.1108/IJCS-12-2016-0001

Zhang, X., & Zhu, F. (2006). *Intrinsic motivation of open content contributors: The case of Wikipedia.* Paper presented at the Workshop on Information Systems and Economics.

Zhao, Y., & Zhu, Q. (2012a). *A Conceptual Model for Participant's Motivation in Crowdsourcing Contest.* Academic Press.

Zhao, Y., & Zhu, Q. (2012b). *Exploring the motivation of participants in crowdsourcing contest.* Academic Press.

Zhao, Y. C., & Zhu, Q. (2014). Effects of extrinsic and intrinsic motivation on participation in crowdsourcing contest. *Online Information Review, 38*(7), 896–917. doi:10.1108/OIR-08-2014-0188

Zheng, H., Li, D., & Hou, W. (2011). Task design, motivation, and participation in crowdsourcing contests. *International Journal of Electronic Commerce, 15*(4), 57–88. doi:10.2753/JEC1086-4415150402

Zou, L., Ke, W., Zhang, J., & Wei, K. K. (2014). *User Creativity in Crowdsourcing Community: From Extrinsic Motivation Perspective.* Paper presented at the 18th Pacific Asia Conference on Information Systems (PACIS 2014), Chengdu, China.

APPENDIX

Table 4. Categories and subcategories of motivation factors and research papers which cited them

Category	Sub-Category	References Which Cited This Subcategory Based on Task Type			
		Creative	Uncreative	Funding	Unknown or mixed
Extrinsic and non-monetary	Development	(Battistella & Nonino, 2012; Brabham, 2012b; Frey, Haag, & Schneider, 2011; Füller et al., 2012; Leimeister et al., 2009; Naparat & Finnegan, 2013; Nov, Anderson, & Arazy, 2010; Paulini et al., 2014; Zheng et al., 2011; Zou, Ke, Zhang, & Wei, 2014)	(Basiouka & Potsiou, 2014; Budhathoki & Haythornthwaite, 2013; Kaufmann et al., 2011; Kelley & Johnston, 2012; Raddick et al., 2010; Shaw et al., 2011; Väätäjä, 2012)		(Parvanta, Roth, & Keller, 2013; Zhao & Zhu, 2012b)
	Professional needs	(Battistella & Nonino, 2012; Füller et al., 2012; Zou et al., 2014)	(Alam & Campbell, 2013; Basiouka & Potsiou, 2014; Budhathoki & Haythornthwaite, 2013; Mankowski, Slater, & Slater, 2011)	(Bretschneider et al., 2014)	(Zhao & Zhu, 2012a, 2012b)
	Recognition	(Battistella & Nonino, 2012; Brabham, 2012b; Leimeister et al., 2009; Nov et al., 2010; Paulini et al., 2014; Yan & Wang, 2013; Zheng et al., 2011)	(Alam & Campbell, 2013; Basiouka & Potsiou, 2014; Budhathoki & Haythornthwaite, 2013; Kaufmann et al., 2011; Kawasaki et al., 2012; Kelley & Johnston, 2012; Nov, Arazy, & Anderson, 2014; Shaw et al., 2011; Väätäjä, 2012)	(Bœuf, Darveau, & Legoux, 2014; Bretschneider et al., 2014)	(Parvanta et al., 2013)
Monetary	Money	(Battistella & Nonino, 2012; Brabham, 2008; Frey, Lüthje, & Haag, 2011; Füller et al., 2012; Leimeister et al., 2009; Zheng et al., 2011)	(Budhathoki & Haythornthwaite, 2013; Chandler & Kapelner, 2013)		(Zhao & Zhu, 2012a)
	Chance for reward	-	(Shaw et al., 2011; Väätäjä, 2012)		
	Reward	(Battistella & Nonino, 2012; Füller et al., 2012; Liu et al., 2011; Paulini et al., 2014; Zou et al., 2014)	(Shaw et al., 2011)	(Bretschneider et al., 2014; Frydrych, Bock, Kinder, & Koeck, 2014; Gerber & Hui, 2013; Tomczak & Brem, 2013)	(Zhao & Zhu, 2012a, 2012b)

continued on following page

Table 4. Continued

Category	Sub-Category	References Which Cited This Subcategory Based on Task Type			
		Creative	Uncreative	Funding	Unknown or mixed
Intrinsic	Values	(Brabham, 2008, 2012b; Füller et al., 2012; Liu et al., 2011; Naparat & Finnegan, 2013; Nov et al., 2010; Paulini et al., 2014; Yan & Wang, 2013; Zheng et al., 2011; Zou et al., 2014)	(Basiouka & Potsiou, 2014; Budhathoki & Haythornthwaite, 2013; Chandler & Kapelner, 2013; Kelley & Johnston, 2012; Mankowski et al., 2011; Nov et al., 2014; Raddick et al., 2010; Rotman et al., 2012; Shaw et al., 2011; Väätäjä, 2012)	(Gerber & Hui, 2013)	(Parvanta et al., 2013)
	Fun	(Brabham, 2008, 2012b; Frey, Haag, et al., 2011; Frey, Lüthje, et al., 2011; Füller et al., 2012; Naparat & Finnegan, 2013; Nov et al., 2010; Paulini et al., 2014)	(Basiouka & Potsiou, 2014; Budhathoki & Haythornthwaite, 2013; Kaufmann et al., 2011; Mankowski et al., 2011; Raddick et al., 2010; Shaw et al., 2011; Väätäjä, 2012)	(Bretschneider et al., 2014)	(Parvanta et al., 2013)
	Challenge and curiosity	(Frey, Haag, et al., 2011; Naparat & Finnegan, 2013; Paulini et al., 2014)	(Mankowski et al., 2011)	(Bretschneider et al., 2014)	
Non-personal	Organizational motivation	(Brabham, 2012b)	(Alam & Campbell, 2013; Basiouka & Potsiou, 2014)		
	Project characteristics	(Battistella & Nonino, 2013; Frey, Lüthje, et al., 2011; Füller et al., 2012; Zheng et al., 2011)	(S. Alam & Campbell, 2013; Kawasaki et al., 2012; Raddick et al., 2010)	(Bœuf et al., 2014; Bretschneider et al., 2014)	
	Demographic	(Brabham, 2008)	(Chandler & Kapelner, 2013)		

Chapter 7
Maturity Profiles of Organizations for Social Media

Edyta Abramek
University of Economics in Katowice, Poland

ABSTRACT

The aim of the study is to analyze case studies of selected organizations in terms of their achievements in the use of social media. The profiling method applied in the study facilitated evaluating the model of the selected organization. It is an efficient technique for exploring data. Graphic objects show the individual characteristics of selected organizations. Graphical visualization makes it easy to gauge the trajectory, the direction of your company's social media strategy, and helps to make a decision to change it. Further analysis of the structure of these models may facilitate the discovery of relevant relationships between the analyzed variables.

INTRODUCTION

The paper focuses on how organizations perceive the potential of social media. Thanks to them people can: create (blogs, podcasts), collaborate and exchange knowledge (wiki sites), establish and maintain contact (social network sites), post posts (forums), organize content (tags, bookmarks), find and get information faster (RSS feeds, dashboards, widgets).

Thanks to them the recipient can become a prosumer. The prosumer by means of social media can demonstrate the activity of presenting his or her opinion, testing prototypes, participating in research or participating in competitions products and services. They allow the creation of products and services resulting from social participation.

DOI: 10.4018/978-1-5225-4200-1.ch007

Social media, unlike traditional media, transforms communications into interactive dialogue. Social media allows you to build closer, more lasting relationships between a company and a community. In the literature of the subject you can find various typologies of the maturity of an organization in the context of the use of social media. There are cases of organizations that are not in the social media at all. There are also organizations that are very active in social media. The least ripe in the social media are decentralized organizations, where the degree of coordination of activities in the use of social media is low or there is no coordination at all. The most mature organizations are those that use social media to formulate business strategies.

The subject of the considerations presented in the article is:

- The maturity of organizations in the use of social media (Buyapowa, 2014;Jussila, Kärkkäinen, & Lyytikkä, 2011;Wilson, Guinan, Parise & Weinberg, 2011) in the company's activity on the example of selected organizations from Poland,
- And the ability to use this knowledge in formulating the vision and strategy of the company's development.

This study focuses on addressing the following research questions:

- **RQ1:** *What kind of social media strategy is actually used in the research organizations?*
- **RQ2:** *How do graphs of the maturity profiles looks like?*
    - **RQ2a:** *What strategy did the organization choose?*
    - **RQ2b:** *Did the organization choose one or does it realize actions specific to several strategies?*
    - **RQ2c:** *Do the strategies of selected organizations in the use of social media and the direction they take in this area are synchronized?*

The targets of the study are shown in Table 1.

BACKGROUND

Media is a tool for preserving and transmitting information. With the development of the Internet, social media was born. They have changed the role of the recipient, who became the creator or co-creator (Evans & McKee, 2010; Li & Bernoff, 2011). The recipient was "engaged". Social media has transformed communication with the recipient into an interactive dialogue. Table 2 shows the types and characteristics of the media. It is worth emphasizing the differences between the concepts: social

Table 1. The targets of the study

The Main Subject	Realization of the Subject
Carrying out a comparative analysis of the maturity of selected organizations in terms of how social media is used.	Analysing of case studies of selected organizations in their use of social media.
Detail Goals	**Realization of the Goals**
Identifying the dominant direction of social media usage.	Working out of the maturity profiles of organizations in the context of the use of social media. Evaluating whether the organization has chosen the best strategy for its resources and objectives.
Determining whether the company does not lose the extra energy to carry out activities characteristic of other strategies which are not connected with its main strategy .	Assessing whether the organization's strategy and objectives are convergent.

media and social network. The concept of social network refers to communities centred on social networking sites.

Social media is the medium by which companies can reach their customers directly. Social media allows companies:

- To engage consumers in building a positive brand image and promoting it,
- To get feedback from consumers (due to communication in both directions),
- To engage consumers to improve products or services.

Consumers, through social media, can directly communicate with the company and have a real impact on building their image or co-creating products or services. Consumers who are referred to as prosumers for social media can be active in the company by: presenting their opinions, participating in research, participating in competitions, testing prototypes of products and services and co-creating them.

Most companies' social media strategies focus on promoting products and services and building brand awareness. Many companies are not able to capitalize on the potential that social media has to offer yet. Current reports and research in this area indicate that traditional companies are dominant in the Polish market (Surma, Krzycki, Prokurat, & Kubisiak, 2012) - companies treat social media as an additional marketing channel. And it is worth pointing out that the number of social media users is constantly growing. At the beginning of 2017 it was already 2.789 billion global social media users, of which 2.549 billion are using them by mobile devices. Compared to 2016 this is an increase of 21 percent. All social media users account for a total of 37 percent of the total population (Kemp, 2017; Sotrender, 2017a).

Table 2. Types of social media

	Mass Media/Broadcast Media	Social Media	Automated Media
Characteristics	Content is created by the publisher. Content is controlled by the publisher - central control, restrictions imposed by law, licenses. Communication with the recipient is one-way. Content publishing is the final stage in the publishing process. The scope of the media is limited.	Content is created by the community. Content is subject to social control - control is individual, not limited. Communication with the recipient is interactive and multidirectional. Content publishing is just the beginning of the publishing process - content is spread through social interaction. The scope of the media is unlimited.	The content created (processing, selection, presented) is without human participation. The main role of the media is aggregation of content from different sources. The scope of the media is unlimited.
Types	TV, press, radio, books, journals, magazines, etc.	Social news sites, blogs, microblogs, forums, wikis, social networking sites (Facebook), social sharing sites, social event sites, social bookmarking sites, virtual social worlds (Second Life), collaborative projects (Wikipedia), content communities, virtual game worlds, etc. (Evans, 2010; Kaplan & Haenlein, 2010).	Personalized news reader such as Feedly, Google News/Reader, Fark, Pulse, News 360, Netvibes.

Formulating a company's growth strategy with the use of social media is still a challenge for businesses. Companies must first (Sotrender, 2017b):

- Recognize the demographics of their customers,
- Understand own customers' behaviours and expectations,
- Identify opinion leaders and brand ambassadors.

Developing a company's growth strategy using feedback from social media is possible through:

- Analysing various indicators (Reach, engagement),
- Analysing the needs of consumers and their expectations,
- Studying the subject matter of the statement and their context,
- Studying of speech leaders and discussion sites,
- Use of advanced data analytics.

The relevance and usefulness of the information itself and the current access to it are essential to formulating a company's development strategy.

SOCIAL MEDIA STRATEGY

Social media changes the way organizations and individuals communicate. They open a new dimension of organization's relations with their clients. Communication is possible in both directions. Thanks to them people can: create (blogs and micro-blogs, videos), maintain contact (virtual worlds, social portals), cooperate and exchange knowledge (web-pages of wiki-type), leave responses (discussion forums, comments), order the content (bookmarks/tags), find information faster (widgets, RSS feeds, dashboards for managers). Social media facilitate the development of online social networks by connecting a user's profile with those of other individuals.

Companies using social network sites like: Facebook, YouTube, QZONE, Instagram, Tumblr, Twitter and messengers like Facebook Messenger, WhatsApp, QQ, WeChat (Kemp, 2017) can quickly mobilize the community. Thanks to them people, communities and organizations can discuss, co-create, modify and share user-generated content faster and regardless of place or time. Literature studies allow us to assess how companies in Poland perceive and exploit the potential of social media. According to the report (Sotrender, 2017a), the most active in the social media are companies:

- Related to Internet and telecommunication media,
- FMCG (Fast Moving Consumer Goods) industry offering products that are regularly and bought almost daily by consumers such as groceries, cosmetics, personal cleaners and hygiene products, household chemicals,
- Related to traditional media.

But still, many organizations cannot identify the type of using social media strategy e.g. (Piskorski, 2011) or do not have them at all. The most important goal of formulating a strategy for using social media is primarily the relevance and usefulness of information for policy makers.

The goal of research was to characterize the types of social media strategy in organizations and identify on this basis, what type of social media strategy the tested organizations has on the current stage of development. The inspiration for the current research was the survey/study called "What is your current strategy of applying social media?" (Wilson et al., 2011). The study revealed the existence of four types of social media strategies:

- **Predictive Practitioner:** Involves the use of social media in a particular area, for example customer service, manufacturing, R&D, marketing.
- **Creative Experimenter:** Contains the use of social media for improvement of specific functional areas or practices of the organization.
- **Social Media Champion:** Represented by organizations, which have an inter-department team dealing with social media. This team coordinates and manages projects in the sphere of social media.
- **Social Media Transformer:** Includes organizations, in which there are many centralized teams dealing with social media. Teams can be scattered across different parts of the world, and yet they easily exchange knowledge thanks to modern technologies.

H. J. Wilson, P. J. Guinan, S. Parise and B. D. Weinberg (2011) have developed a questionnaire, on the basis of which, can be identify the type of organization's strategy for using social media.

The Research Process

The study covered three different organizations, located in Silesia (Poland). It was done using the research method used in the management sciences - case study analysis. The purpose of studying selected cases was to test the theory and its development on the basis of observed regularities. Case studies focused on the relationship between the strategy of using social media and the direction companies take in this regard. The test procedure is shown in Figure 1.

Studying the cases allowed us to recognize the phenomenon in real conditions. The sample selection process was random. The survey was based on survey data from three selected organizations. In the Table 3 was presented a summary of the selected participating organizations.

ORGANIZATIONAL MATURITY PROFILES AND STRATEGIES FOR USING SOCIAL MEDIA: EXPERIMENTAL RESULTS

Thanks to the profiling method identified three maturity profiles of organizations in the use of social media (Figure 2). With regard to the fourth type of strategy, only the area of activity characteristic for this type of activity was indicated.

None of the analysed cases, was a social change initiator. Organizations of this type benefit from the social media on a wide scale, and they regularly use the data from these media and communicate through it. Organization B was the closest thing to this model.

Figure 1. The research process

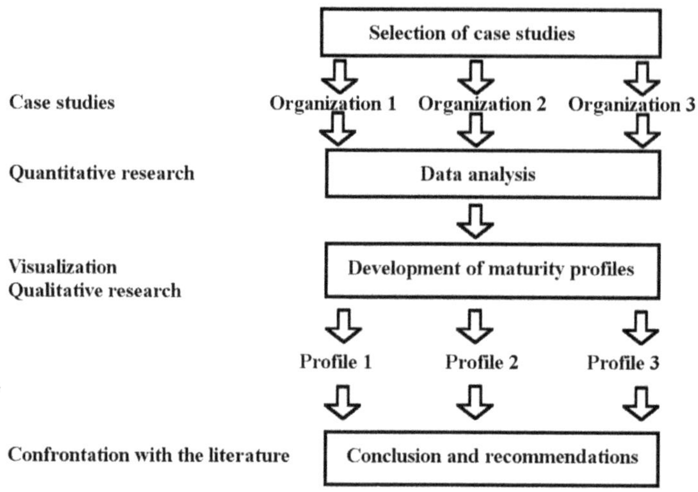

Table 3. Characteristics of the organizations and their area of actions

Organizations	Area of Action and the Nature of the Analysed Organizations	Problems	External Contacts	Target
Organization A	Education / University	Well known problems. Defined sequence of action.	Concentration on activities within the company. External contacts in the development phase, but still limited.	Efficiency Reliability
Organization B	Business / Business accelerator	Problems that require innovative ideas.	Contacts: external, dense and redundant, are basis of action.	Results
Organization C	Medicine / Dental Clinic	Known problems. Unknown sequence of solving of a problem.	External contacts as a source of information for the activities being undertaken.	Coordination of activities

The study revealed the following social media strategies:

- **Organization A - *Creative Experimenter*:** The object of research in this case is a university. Organizations that choose this strategy are looking for ways to improve the areas of their business or the practices that they use. Universities in Poland recognize the potential of social media. They communicate with students via e-mail, they also use Facebook, Instagram and Snapchat. They run programs for representatives (ambassadors) at home and abroad. University projects in Poland in relation to social media are still experimental. They are in the learning phase of projects in the sphere of social media. *In conclusion, we can notice moderate involvement and coordination of the work of university staff in the use of social media.*
- **Organization B - *Social Media Champion*:** The subject of research in this case is the business accelerator, a company that supports the development of startups. The operation of the company is based on the use of social media in daily activities. This company provides jobs (offices, halls), Internet, online tools, business networking. *In conclusion, we can see the great commitment and coordination of employees in the use of social media.*
- **Organization C - *Predictive Practitioner*:** The researcher in this case is a dental clinic. *In conclusion, there is a lack of involvement and coordination of staff practices in the use of social media. Employees are mainly engaged in performing their daily duties.*

Corporate strategies for using social media can be analysed in the context of their innovation and business relevance. These are two main aspects that determine the success of the venture and are responsible for generating competitive advantage as well. Considerations are illustrated in Figure 3.

- *Predictive practitioners* organizations undertake typical projects in social media that are characterized by low innovation and low strategic importance. The risk of this projects to the organization is slight. Projects contribute to reducing operating costs in selected areas.
- *Creative experimenter* organizations are organizations that undertake activities of little or moderate importance to the organization. Actions, however, allow for the breaking of conventional practices, which can contribute to the acquisition of a new consumer segment.
- *Social media champion* organizations are important to the organization's strategy and operations. Changes are being made to well-established areas of business and are designed to increase competitive advantage.

Figure 2. Organizational maturity profiles
Source: Results of the questionnaire (Wilson et al., 2011).
** Lack of example*

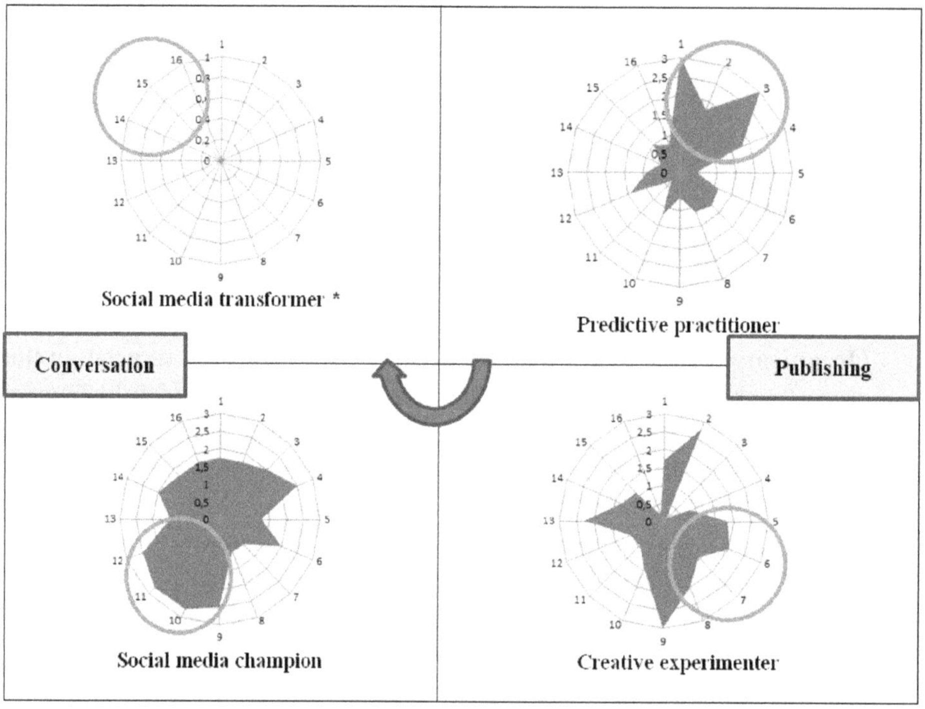

- *Social media transformer* organizations - high innovation, high business value, high risk, failure can be a source of trouble for the organization.
- *Predictive practitioner* (Organization C) and *Social media champion* (Organization B) projects contribute to cost reduction and productivity growth, while *Social media transformer* (Lack of example) and *Creative experimenter* (Organization A) contribute to revenue growth and new value creation.

"Social maturity is not reserved only for massive brands that already have an established customer service machine. Smaller, lesser-known brands can, and should have mature customer service on social as well" (Conversocial, 2017). In addition, the level of maturity of organizations in the social media area was confronted with the Social Media Index. The results are shown in Figure 4.

Observers (Predictive practitioner, Organization C) - the businesses which have not integrated social channels into their customer service strategy. Conservative (Creative experimenter, Organization A) - high investment but low innovation;

Figure 3. The value matrix of social media strategies
Source: Based on (Hartman, Sifonia & Kador, 1999;Wilson et al., 2011).
** Lack of example*

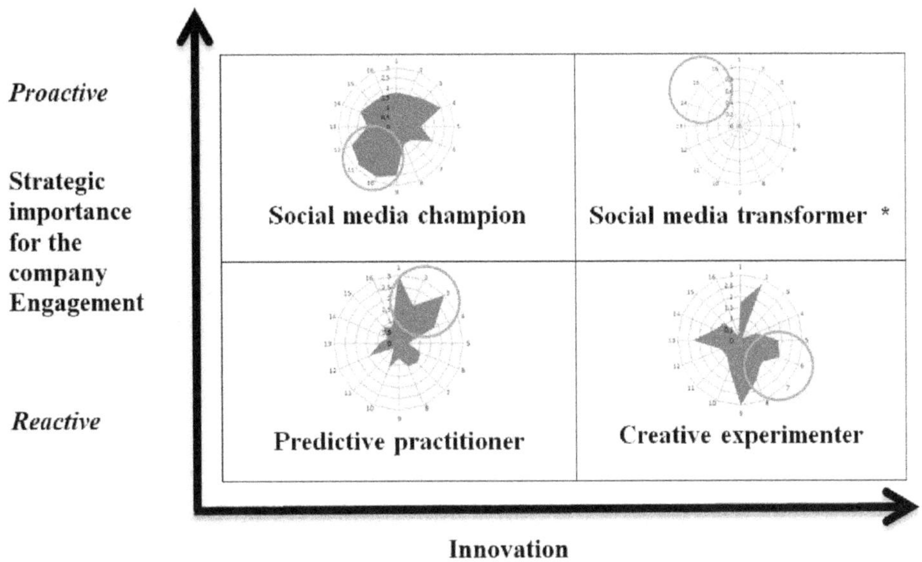

Figure 4. Social Maturity Index
Source: Based on Conversocial (2017) and Wilson et al. (2011)

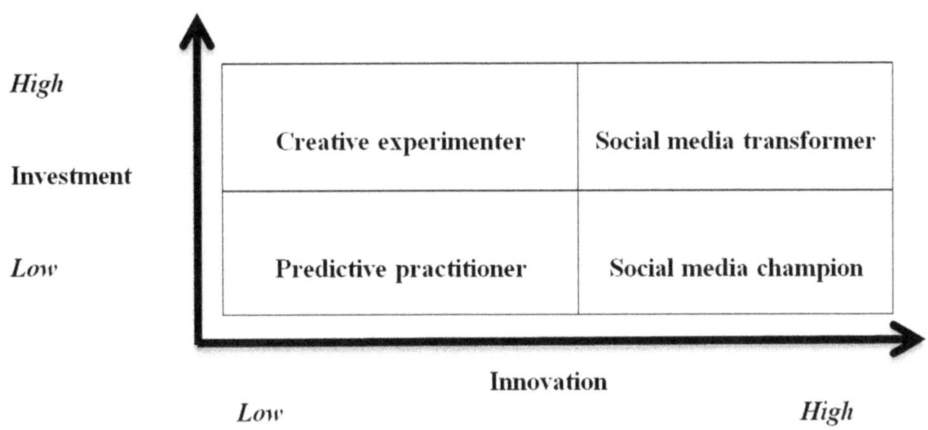

these tend to be larger brands without a solid strategy in social media. Contenders (Social media champion, Organization B) – the organization actively engaging with customers on a variety of social platforms, but without the budget or manpower. Social media transformer– the businesses with strong brand presences across social media.

CONCLUSION AND FUTURE RESEARCH DIRECTIONS

The purpose of the research presented in the article was to analyse selected organizations and to assess the maturity of these organizations using the profiling method. The graphical presentation of the maturity profiles allowed to check if the organization did not waste energy on several strategies at the same time. This method has also allowed us to assess how much the strategies of selected organizations and their respective social media activities are synchronized. There are needed further in-depth research in this area, for example using multi criteria methods in order to assess which organization has the best fit for the chosen strategy.

Due to the growing interest of social media, today's companies need to be open to the usage of social media: dialogue, relationships with consumers building, interactivity.

The strategy in this area should be well known not only to the management but also to its employees. An organization's maturity survey on the use of social media with the profiling method allows for further recommendations for optimizing social media activities. This method is a kind of social media compass.

REFERENCES

Buyapowa. (2014). *The three stages of Social maturity.* Retrieved from http://www.welikecrm.it/wp-content/uploads/2014/06/Social-Maturity.pdf

Conversocial. (2017). *Social Maturity Index.* Retrieved from http://www.conversocial.com/hubfs/socialmaturity.pdf

Evans, D., & McKee, J. (2010). *Social Media Marketing: The Next Generation of Business Engagement.* Wiley Publishing, Inc.

Evans, L. (2010). *Social Media Marketing. Strategies for Engaging in Facebook, Twitter & Other Social Media.* Que Publishing.

Hartman, A., Sifonis, J., & Kador, J. (1999). *Net Ready. Strategies for success in the economy.* McGraw-Hill Companies.

Jussila, J. J., Kärkkäinen, H., & Lyytikkä, J. (2011). *Towards Maturity Modelling Approach for Social Media Adoption in Innovation.* In *Proceedings of the 4th ISPIM Innovation Symposium* (pp. 1-14). Wellington, New Zealand: ISPIM. Retrieved April from https://tutcris.tut.fi/portal/files/6640892/Jussila_2011_Towards_Maturity_Modeling_Approach_for_Social_Media_Adoption_in_Innovation.pdf

Kaplan, A. M., & Haenlein, M. (2010). Users of the World, Unite! The Challenges and Opportunities of Social Media. *Business Horizons*, *53*(1), 59–68. doi:10.1016/j.bushor.2009.09.003

Kemp, S. (2017). *Digital in 2017, Global Overview.* Retrieved April, 2017, from https://wearesocial.com/blog/2017/01/digital-in-2017-global-overview

Li, Ch., & Bernoff, J. (2011). *Groundswell. Winning in a world transformed by social technologies*. Forrester Research.

Piskorski, M. J. (2011). Social Strategies That Work. *Harvard Business Review*, *89*(11), 116–122. PMID:22111430

Sotrender. (2017a). *Facebook Trends Poland.* Retrieved April, from https://www.sotrender.com/trends/facebook/poland/201702/porownanie-branz, DC: Author.

Sotrender. (2017b). *Poznaj swoich odbiorców i zrozum ich zachowanie*. Retrieved from https://www.sotrender.com/pl/audience/, DC: Author.

Surma, K., Krzycki, M., Prokurat, S., & Kubisiak, P. (2012). *Raport z badania Polskie firmy w mediach społecznościowych.* Retrieved from https://www.hbrp.pl/b/raport-z-badania-polskie-firmy-w-mediach-spolecznosciowych/b9PFjezh

Wilson, H. J., Guinan, P. J., Parise, S., & Weinberg, B. D. (2011, July). *What's Your Social Media Strategy? Harvard Business Review.*

Chapter 8
Data Analytics Supporting Knowledge Acquisition

Soraya Sedkaoui
Khemis Miliana University, Algeria & Montpellier University, France & SRY Consulting Montpellier, France

ABSTRACT

This chapter aims to make the case that analytics methods must respond to the significant changes that big data challenges are bringing to operationalizing the production of information and knowledge. More specifically it discusses the analytics dimension of big data challenges and its contribution for value creation. It shows that data analytics tools and methods offer strong support in knowledge acquisition and discovery. This suggests that the effectiveness of an analytics method must be measured based on how it promotes and enhances knowledge, how it improves patterns and understanding of the decision makers, and thereby how it improves their decision making and hence organization performance. This chapter explores the synergies between big data analytics and knowledge discovery by identifying challenges and opportunities in data analytics applications for knowledge acquisition.

INTRODUCTION

Modern information technology, incremental computing power, and online digitalization have opened up new options for utilizing automatically collected and stored data from various sources in multiple formats. According to IBM, the proliferation of web pages, image and video applications, social networks, mobile devices, apps, sensors, and so on, able to generate more than 2.5 quintillion bytes per day, to the extent that 90% of the world's data have been created over the few

DOI: 10.4018/978-1-5225-4200-1.ch008

past years (Cukier & Mayer-Schoenberger, 2013a, 2013b; Dietrich et al., 2014; Foster et al.,2017). The traditional way of formatting information from transactional systems to make them available for 'statistical processing' does not work in a such situation, where data is arriving in huge volumes from diverse sources, and where even the formats could be changing (Sedkaoui, 2017).

Traditional analysis methods have been based largely on the assumption that we can work with data within the confines of their own computing environment. But the growth of the amounts of data is changing that paradigm, especially which ride of the progress in computational data analysis. Faced with this volume and diversification, it is essential to develop analytics tools and techniques to make best use of all of these stocks in order to extract the maximum amount of information and knowledge. The use of big data requires rethinking the process of collecting, processing and the management of data. It's the "analysis" that will be applied to data which will justify big data, not the collection of data itself (Sedkaoui, 2017).

Data Analytics is a rapidly developing field which already shows early promising successes. Nowadays companies are starting to realize the importance of using and analyzing more data to extract knowledge and support their decision strategies. Conceptually, it is easy to comprehend how analytics can be thought of as an integral component of knowledge management (KM) and hence decision making. The key is applying proper analytics and statistics methods to different kind of data. Thus, from this data derive information and then producing knowledge, or which it called the target paradigm of "knowledge discovery", described as a "knowledge pyramid" where data lays at the base (see Ackoff, 1989).

From this, it should be noted that there are considerable synergies between data analytics and KM: both have the goal of improving decision-making, fostering innovation, fueling competitive edge and economic success through the acquisition and application of knowledge. Both operate in a world of increasing deluges of information, with no end in sight (Crane and Self, 2014). These synergies help author to go further to answer this question: *How analytics methods, in the big data context, allow companies to get more value out of the available data and optimize their knowledge acquisition in such a way that it will be more frequently used for better decisions?* In another word: *how knowledge acquisition process can conceptually and operationally use and integrate analytics methods to extract value for better decision-making?*

Exploring the role of big data analytics and its relationship with knowledge discovery process and decision-making is of utmost importance. This paper has the objective of identifying some of the synergies and similarities between the rapidly developing field of big data analytics and the well-established field of KM. The main goal of this study is to show how big data challenges are changing analytics to enhance knowledge acquisition and discovery and support decision-making process.

This study describes a clear relationship between: data analytics and knowledge acquisition, establishing an expanded role for analytics. That is, the role of analysis in knowledge improvement.

DATA ANALYTICS: FROM UNDERSTANDING DATA TO KNOWLEDGE

Understanding big data phenomenon requires exploring the term 'data'. According to the Oxford dictionary (2018), data is defined as: "the quantities, characters, or symbols on which operations are performed by a computer, which may be stored and transmitted in the form of electrical signals and recorded on magnetic, optical, or mechanical recording media". Data is a collection of facts, such as numbers, words, measurements, observations or even just descriptions of things. It existing over the time, it's not new, but what makes it so important is the rapid rate and different types in which it's produced in recent times, or what brings us to turn: "From data to Big data".

Big data have been placed on a pedestal as being something unique and precious (Mayer-Schönberger & Cukier, 2013a). Today's discourse of big data makes it appear to be the solution to all problems of society (Steadman, 2013), and capable of making the world a safer and better place (Olavsrud, 2014). Big data gets global attention and can be best described using the three Vs: volume, variety and velocity. *Volume* denotes the amount of data that is collected which is rapidly increasing (McAfee & Brynjolfsson, 2012). The *variety* marks the types and forms in which data are collected (structured and unstructured with numerous forms: numbers, text, audio, and video). *Velocity* refers to the pace at which data are generated and analyzed.

Big data is a natural crop of the advanced digital artifacts and their applications. Sensors, mobiles and social media networks are examples of modern digital technologies that have permeated our daily lives. A large amount of digital data is being generated every day. Big data have also fundamentally changed the way businesses compete and operate. Boyd and Crawford (2012) claim that big data will fundamentally change the way we view the working world and the production process. This transformed also the relationship between work and society. Big data may contribute to those changes (Davenport, 2014), but predominantly change the way people think.

Big data has changed the perception of knowledge and allow for researchers and practitioners to access data in real-time, and enable them "to collect and analyse that data with an unprecedented breadth and depth and scale" (Lazer et al., 2009, p 722). With growing size typically comes a growing complexity of data structures, of the patterns in the data, and of the models needed to account for the patterns. Its revolutionizing how intelligence is stored and informative analysis can be drawn. Big data has put a great challenge on the current analytics methods.

Data analysis came in in the 20th century when the information age really began. Zhang (2017) have mentioned in his book "data analytics" published in 2017, that the first real data processing machine came during the Second World War. But, the advent of the internet was sparked the true revolution in data analysis. The importance of data analysis started in the late 1960 when we begin to speak about databases as repositories of data. E.F. Codd (Codd, 1970) and his research group at IBM labs applied some mathematical principles and predicate logic to the field of data modelling. Since then, data bases and their evolutions have been used as a source of information to query and manipulate data.

In 1974, still at IBM labs, the first language for database was developed. SEQUEL (Structured English Query Language) (Chamberlin & Boyce, 1974), later called SQL for copyright issues, was the forerunner of all the query languages becoming the standard for relational database. In the 1970s and 1980s, computers could process information, but they were too large and too costly. Only large firms could hope to analyze data with them. Edgar F. Codd was the first to work on data organization by designing database management systems (DBMSs), in particular of relational databases. With the advent of Web 2.0 and the semantic Web era, data analysis has become very important, replacing the traditional storing systems in many applications.

The growth of big data is changing how analyses will be executed. It will also change the scope of analytical questions to be answered, as more data are available. Data volume will continue to grow and in a very real way constitutes a constant source of knowledge. Knowledge is generated by means of big data in various ways and there may be an end to a certain type of theory, but big data calls for entirely new types of theories (Boellstorff, 2015; Tokhi & Rauh, 2015). Illustrating the relationship between big data analytics and knowledge acquisition cannot be clarified without the understanding of KM further.

It's a dazzling, multi-faceted, and controversially discussed concept. Philosophers and representatives of a variety of different disciplines are debating the meaning, definitions, and dimensions of knowledge and KM (Nonaka & Takeuchi, 1995). The field of KM and has always distinguished between data, information, and knowledge, this is represented in the literature as the knowledge hierarchy. This hierarchy is one of the key theoretical frameworks in the field of KM.

It has an important conceptual contribution to make to KM discipline since it attempts to clarify semantics and provides a source of understanding of the term knowledge, which is sought to be 'managed' by using KM. The knowledge hierarchy depicts the conventional concept of knowledge transformations, where data is transformed into information, and information is transformed into knowledge. Several studies claim that the first appearance of knowledge hierarchy is in T.S

Elliot's poem "The Rock" in 1934. In recent literature, many authors refer to the publication "From data to wisdom" of R.L Ackoff published in 1989 as a source of knowledge hierarchy.

An extension to the knowledge hierarchy is expressed by Ackoff (1996), who defines data as symbols, information as data that are processed to be useful, knowledge as application of data and information in order to have the ability to understand ''*how*'' and ''*why*'' (see Figure 1). So, knowledge has a wider and deeper meaning than data or information. It is created from the use, analysis, and productive utilization of data and information. Organizations are very conscious of the importance of knowledge and even more so of the way it is "managed", enriched, and capitalized. They can reap a lot of benefits when this knowledge is managed effectively. KM is a prescribed structured proposal to advance the creation, distribution or use of knowledge in an organization.

This is a formal process of turning knowledge into value. It promotes ongoing business success through the systematic acquisition, synthesis, sharing and use of information insights and experience. Thus, effective KM plays an important role in decision making and correspondingly guiding the strategic plan for knowledge-based organizations in the context of sustainable competitive advantage (Shani & Sena, 2016). Also, KM plays an important role in transforming tacit knowledge (personal ideas and experiences) from individual knowledge to explicit organizational knowledge (documents, products and procedures) and utilizing shared knowledge effectively across an organization (Davenport & Prusak, 1998; Nonaka & Takeuchi, 1995) through various functions by personal, mechanical and electronic means (Hernandez, 2003).

The earlier development of KM was facilitated by the use of the Information and communications technology (ICT) in late 80s. The goal was to manage the increasing amount of data, information and to ensure its usage and flow across the organization. KM is increasingly becoming crucial for enhanced decision making in organizations. Hence, organizations are exploring ways to effectively accumulate and deal with the data, information and knowledge that are accessible today. The challenge in KM using ICT oriented solutions lies in the assimilation of data from different sources and processing the large quantity and types of data to derive valuable information that is delivered through services, consumed by common citizens, governments, and businesses.

The rising challenge for organizations is to process this data to generate useful knowledge to support enhanced decision making. To this end, big data analytics play a significant role in efficient KM that in turns aid in developing business strategic plan and particularly in product development. Data is required to be managed in different steps and most of all analyzed (Kudyba, 2014), for organizations to gain knowledge. In recent past, big data opportunities have gained much momentum to enhance KM in organizations. However, big data due to its various properties like high volume, variety, and velocity can no longer be effectively stored and analyzed with traditional data management techniques to generate values in knowledge acquisition process.

HOW BIG DATA ANALYTICS ARE CHANGING THE KNOWLEDGE EXTRACTION?

In their book "Race Against the Machine" (2011, p.297), Brynjolfsson and Mcaffee referenced the fable of the chess and rice grains (the legend of the wise 'Sissa' in India) to make the point that "exponential increases initially look a lot like linear, but they are not. As time goes by – as we move into the second half of the chessboard – exponential growth confounds our intuition and expectation". With the size of data that are handy today is much more than what we could possibly envisage a decade ago. There is a pressing need to investigate this amount of data and establish its relationship with knowledge acquisition to enhance organizational decision making and acquire competitive advantage.

Organizations are seeking for methods to effectively gather and process the data to create values for improved knowledge discovery. Analytics is a rapidly developing field which already shows early promising successes and considerable synergies with KM. This two fields both improving decision-making through the acquisition of knowledge. The benefits of big data analytics, as well as the challenges associated with it, are known to some extent. Analytics is seen as valuable for organizations, creating new possibilities and opportunities to develop KM. Davenport and Harris (2007, p7) define analytics as: "the extensive use of data, statistical and quantitative analysis, explanatory and predictive models, and fact-based management to drive decisions and actions".

Many researches have been written on about 'big data analytics and knowledge discovery' to find solutions able to help organizations deal with the various challenges while working with knowledge management and big data analytics. Davenport et al. (2013) has outlined a number of potential benefits that organizations can achieve b means of using big data relating to KM. Analytics is the examination, interpretation and discovery of meaningful pattern, trends and knowledge from data and textual information. KM, on the other hand, is concerned with the knowledge processes and practices. The relationship between big data analytics and KM presents the relation of big data and the knowledge hierarchy so that a perspective vision of potential big data stages for knowledge discovery is established.

The main connections between knowledge and big data can be visualized in Figure 1. In order to process the exponential rise of the "Generic awareness", big

Figure 1. [insert caption here].

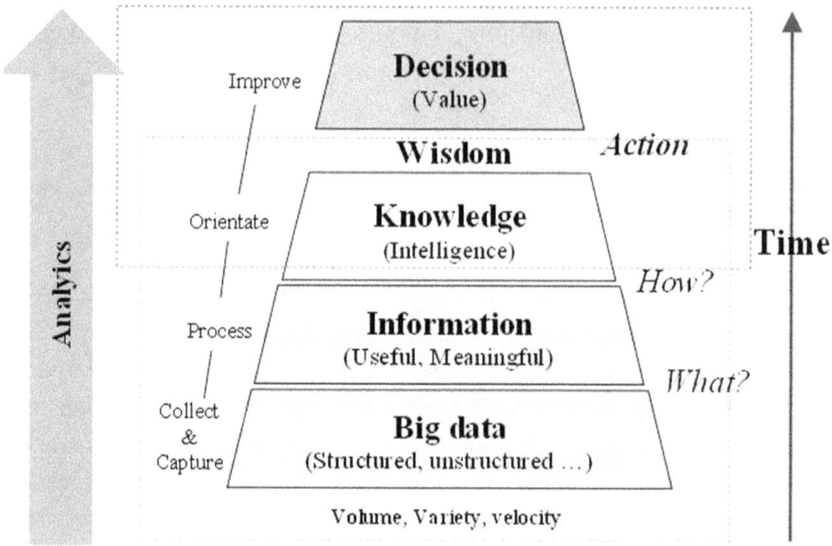

data programs are becoming a mandatory tool for all organizations. The hierarchy is providing an epistemological outlook for the structure of knowledge and has become statutory to the field of organization knowledge (Bernstein, 2011). Data can exist in any form, it simply exists and has no significance beyond its existence. Big data gathering techniques are the first step into encompassing the raw material into a digital form. Information is data that is combined with other information or data and has a meaning, that can be useful or not. In order to structure a large amount of information big data classifying and refining techniques are used.

Knowledge is the compilation of information in a manner that it can be useful and by this being a "deterministic process" (Bellinger, Durval & Mills, 2004); on the other hand, information lacks this quality. At this point, using big data algorithms, an interrogation on the conversation database on how to solve a specific problem will already have a response and become useful with a list of solutions, after second level applied algorithms. So, as a general framework, the knowledge hierarchy remains useful in demarcating analytically fuzzy concepts. This hierarchy is an often used method, with roots in KM, to explain the ways we move from data to information, knowledge and wisdom with a component of actions and decisions (see Figure 1).

One of the main criticisms of the model is that it's a hierarchical one and misses several crucial aspects of knowledge and the new data and information reality in this age of big data. Data available are more unstructured and produced in real-time, so new tools (through big data analytics) are needed to capture them and turn them into actions and decisions. "Actions" and "Decisions", that's what organizations need, because without action there is little sense in gathering, capturing, understanding, leveraging, storing and even talking about data, information and knowledge.

Data is collected from internal sources in addition to external sources. The focus of big data supporting KM will be to do knowledge predictions, knowledge navigation, and knowledge discovery and acquisition to support enhanced operations and decision-making. By focusing on the strategic aspects of developing and protecting knowledge, we can get a better sense of *when* and *how* big data might fit into our conception of how knowledge assets can benefit an organization. By reviewing variables such as the nature of knowledge (tacit and explicit, in particular), we can get a handle of what types of knowledge is suitable to develop in various industries. From this perspective we can start to get an idea of *when* and *where* further contributions from big data may be helpful.

Thus, it can be called as big data based KM that takes full advantage of big data analytics, and which is different from traditional KM regarding a number of factors like it is demonstrated in Table 1. Therefore, the difficulty of transforming big data into value or knowledge is related to its complexity, the essence of which is broadly captured by the three Vs. Each of these dimensions presents both challenges for data management and opportunities to advance decision-making. Three V's provide a challenge associated with working with big data:

- The *volume* put the accent on the storage, memory and computes capacity of a computing system and requires access to a computing cloud.
- *Velocity* stresses the rate at which data can be absorbed and meaningful answers produced.
- The *variety* makes it difficult to develop algorithms and tools that can address that large variety of input data.

The challenges include not just the previous contexts, but also other issues related to scalability, heterogeneity, quality, timeliness, security and privacy which are also a big concern. So, data is very different from data which existed before. In another word, the nature of existing data (greatest dimension, diverse types, mass of data, structured and unstructured ...) does not authorize the use of most conventional statistical methods (tests, regression, classification …). Indeed, these methods are not adapted to these specific conditions of application and in particular suffer from the scourge of dimension. These issues should be seriously considered in big data analytics and in the development of statistical procedures.

UNDERSTANDING DATA TO IMPROVE DECISION-MAKING

Traditionally, the decision-making process is shaped on the model of limited rationality by Herbert Simon (1977): Intelligence, modelling, choice and control. With the exploitation of big data this process is being complicated and has to improve. However, decision-making, business strategy development and the anticipation of change have always been dependent on the quantity and quality of data available. The explosion of a phenomenal amount of data and the need to analyze puts forward the hierarchical model (from data to knowledge).

The knowledge hierarchy is by nature a multidisciplinary endeavor (Piegorsch, 2015): computer scientists construct algorithms to manipulate and organize the data, aided by statisticians and mathematicians who instruct on development and application of quantitative methodology. Then, database expert collect and warehouse the data, software designers write programs that apply the analytics algorithms to the data, engineers build electronics and hardware to implement the programming, and subject-matter/domain experts – that is, biologists, chemists, economists, and social scientists – interpret the finding.

The most important asset of large volumes of data has to do with the fact that they make it possible to apply knowledge and create considerable value. However, in traditional models, key value creation activities can be described using the value chain (Porter, 1985). The value chain concept, which is primarily geared to the physical world, treats data as a supporting element rather than a source of value itself (Rayport & Sviokla, 1995). But, a correct utilization of those enormous of data in the decision- making process is not easy. The main challenge of using data is not in the collect, but in the choice of which data should be sought and how to make sense of it.

So, the process of decision begins when the top manager has to choose which data to look for, even before starting to collect data. Organizations need to use a structured view of data to improve their decision-making process. To achieve this structured view, they have to collect and store data, perform an analysis, and transform the results into useful and valuable information. Big data has the potential to aid in identifying opportunities related to decision in the intelligence phase of Simon's model, where the term of "intelligence" refers to knowledge discovery. The intelligence phase is all about finding the occasions over which a decision should be made (Simon, 1997).

"The major role of the intelligence stage is to identify the problem and collect relevant information" (Turban et al., 2011) which would be used later in the next stages of the decision-making process. Also in this phase, the tools of "Business Intelligence" (see Table 2) may be used to support the organization's discovery of opportunities for decision-making by providing advanced analytics and assuring data integration (Popovič et al, 2012). Predictive modelling and analytics can be of crucial importance for organizations if correctly aligned with their business process and needs and can also lead to significant improvement of their performance and quality of the decisions they make, thus increasing their business value (like: Amazon, eBay, Google, Facebook …) (Davenport & Kim, 2013; Siegel, 2013).

Moreover the type of analysis which is needed to be done on the data depends highly on the results to be obtained through decision-making. This can be done to: (i) incorporate massive data volumes in analysis or (ii) determine upfront which big data is relevant. So, we have two technical entities have come together. First, there is big data for massive amounts of data. Second, there is advanced analytics, which is actually a collection of different tool types, including those based on predictive analytics, data mining, statistics, clustering, data visualization, text analytics, artificial intelligence, and so on (Shroff, 2013; Siegel, 2016).

The general aim of decision-making in the era of big data is to reduce problems to a scale that can be comprehended. Big data brings along with it some huge analytical challenges. The analysis of big data involves multiple distinct phases which include data acquisition and recording, information extraction and cleaning, integration, aggregation and representation, query processing, data modeling and analysis and interpretation. Each of these phases introduces challenges. Heterogeneity, scale, timeliness, complexity, quality, security and privacy are certain challenges of big data analytics. Faced with this challenge companies have sought to go further by automating their strategic decision-making, on the basis of precise indicators from the “big Analytics”.

ANALYTICS APPROACHES IN KNOWLEDGE DISCOVERY PROCESS

Before one attempts to extract and acquire useful knowledge from data, it is important to understand the overall approach or the process that leads to finding new knowledge. The process defines a sequence of steps (with eventual feedback) that should be followed to discover knowledge in data (see the knowledge discovery process ‘KDP’). To advance successfully each step we must apply effective data collection, description, analysis and interpretation (Piegorsch, 2015, Chapter 1). Each step is usually realized with the help of available software tools. Data mining is a particular step in this process – application of specific algorithms for extracting models from data.

The additional steps in the process, such as data preparation, data selection, data cleaning, incorporation of appropriate prior knowledge, and proper interpretation of the results of mining ensure that useful knowledge is derived from the data. Another important point, which represents an often issue in data mining and analytics, is the need for sufficiently high quality in the database. Once the implementation of the first data warehouse in the 1990s the question of the quality of the data was a major issue. In the US, the theorem 'garbage in, garbage out', or the "GIGO" principal, was immediately widespread.

So there is nothing new about this description: only data quality will help produce an event, a forecast or strategic information and define an action lever. Therefore, the volume of data is of little importance, since internal data must be combined with external data in order for a company to obtain the most out of its data. The reconciliation of internal and external data has always been a challenge. There is, however, a serious challenge in making good use of such massive datasets and trying to learn new knowledge of the system or phenomenon that created these data.

Knowledge extraction from data volumes of ever increasing size requires ever more flexible tools to facilitate interactive query. Today's applications are therefore required to extract knowledge from large, often distributed, repositories of text, multimedia or hybrid content. A new generation of computational techniques and tools is required to support the extraction of useful knowledge from the rapidly growing volumes of data. The nature of this quest makes it impossible to use traditional computing techniques. Instead, various soft computing techniques are employed to meet the challenge for more sophisticated solutions in knowledge discovery.

KDP is an automatic, exploratory analysis and modeling of large data for understandable patterns from large and complex datasets. It's focused on the development of methodologies and techniques that 'make sense' out of data, i.e. for extracting relevant and non-trivial information from data. So, data are a set of facts i.e. cases in a database, while a pattern is an expression in some language describing a subset of the data or a model applicable to the subset. This process is thus a sequence of steps that starting from rough data and leads to the discovery of knowledge. This is particularly so where the use of data for decision-making and knowledge discovery is novel.

It may be observed that the KDP is reminiscent of the real beginnings of statistics. However, it's not only using statistics, but also contributing to statistics. The need for effective tools for knowledge discovery and mining is large especially as a crucial component of data-warehouses. Indeed, harnessing data may also require the complete overhaul of the businesses to create structures and processes that can respond to any information gleaned in a short timeframe, potentially even in real-time.

The value of a given piece of data increases in time and depends on the variety of uses it is given (Sedkaoui & Monino, 2016). In this sense, companies must possess the capacity to absorb the entirety of data available, which allows them to assimilate and reproduce knowledge. This capacity requires specific skills familiar with statistical data analytics which becomes a fundamental skill for any scientist dealing with big data. Since statistical methods are applied at the base of the hierarchy (data), the data process guided knowledge discovery will entail an integrated plan of descriptive analysis and predictive modeling.

DISCUSSION

The value of the knowledge to the organization has long been recognized, going back to classic economists such as Schumpeter (1934) and management theorists such as Drucker (1991). The idea that such intangibles might be a key source of competitive advantage also has a deep history, including Nelson & Winter (1982). Sprouting from the resource-based theory of the firm (Wernerfelt, 1984), a more contemporary view has centered squarely on the key role of knowledge in obtaining and sustaining competitive advantage. The most common paradigm in the KM literature is the knowledge hierarchy (Nissen, 2000; Davenport & Prusak, 1998), which is depicted in Figure 1.

This hierarchy cans reveal a number of interesting insights. The first of these concerns the affordances that dictate largely what 'transformations' we are able to do with these concepts. And interestingly, the hierarchy seems to have evolved in parallel as the affordance available has changed when the quantities of both information and data become so large. As the quantity of data increased beyond a manageable size it is seen to have exploded, thus losing its relative structural relationships and its usefulness to us as knowledge.

Data analyzed is no longer necessarily structured in the same way as in previous analysis, but can now be text, images, multimedia content, digital traces, connected objects, etc. the rise of big data reflects the growing awareness of the 'power' behind data, and of the need to enhance gathering, exploitation, sharing and processing. It is not just about the quantity and speed of production of these data, the real revolution lies in what can be created by combining and analyzing these flows.

New analytics approach in big data age combines predictive and prescriptive analytics to predict what will happen and how to make it happen. According to Crane and Self (2014), data analytics can be seen as a threat to the practice of KM because:

- It could relegate the latter to the mists of organizational history in the rush to adopt the latest techniques and technologies.
- It can be approached as an opportunity for KM in that it wrestles with many of the same issues and dilemmas as KM.

Currently, with the progress of Internet of Things (IoT), clouds, big data processing technology, algorithms and so on, it will be possible to turn data into knowledge and then create value for organization. The transformation of big data into knowledge is by no means an easy task. The key lies in the application of more discursive construction of knowledge discovery and a growing trend in knowledge management. Therefore, it is challenging for businesses to analyze and extract knowledge from a universe due to lack of computing resources available.

Embracing innovation and productivity, spur growth, increase safety, and improve operations. To capitalize on its potential, organizations must put data analytics at the center of their strategy. But, they need to establish clear guidelines for data *quality*, *integrity* and *security*, as digital ecosystems can only function efficiently if all parties involved can trust in the security of their data and communication. The analysis of big data is not only a matter of solving computational problems, even if those working on big data in industry primarily come from the natural sciences or computational fields. Rather, expertly analyzing big data also requires thoughtful measurement, careful research design, and the creative deployment of statistical techniques.

In this context, it is necessary to understand the concept of big data analytics, why it exist, how it affects KM, and the benefits it can create and the challenges organizations need to deal with. Connection exists between KM and the burgeoning trend toward the application of big data analytics. All deal with some sort of intangible asset, be it data, information, or knowledge. The relationship between these two fields is clear. Both fields will benefit from initial steps such as this to find ways to arrange a meeting of the minds.

CONCLUSION

The digital revolution is shaking our societies and not only upsetting technology, industry or the economy, but also has profound social consequences. Digital technologies (smartphones, social network, Cloud…) and the advent of the internet are transforming the ICT industry and the way companies across all vertical markets can operate. Nowadays, an increasing number of data silos are created across the world, which means that this growth will never stop. This data is not only voluminous; it is also continuous, streaming, real time, dynamic and volatile (Sedkaoui, 2017). Data has grown exponentially in 'volume', variety' and 'velocity' (Jagadish et al., 2012; Mcaffee & Brynjolfsson, 2012), these '3 Vs' are generally used to describe this phenomenon.

Even with big data, data collection and analysis will become more and more important. The most important asset of large volumes of data has to do with the fact that they make it possible to apply knowledge and create considerable value. Combined with advanced analysis methods, they can provide new explanations for several phenomena. There are two ways to transforms data into a valuable contribution to a company (Sedkaoui & Monino, 2016):

- Transforming data into information is one of the stages of data value production, which is exploited in order to obtain useful information and to successfully carry out company strategies. This automatically involves database information in company decision making processes;
- Transforming data into products or processes adds value to companies. This is produced when data analysis must be implemented in the physical world.

It's then necessary to adapt new approaches, new methods, new knowledge and new ways of working, resulting in new properties and new challenges, as logic referencing must be created and implemented. New analytics methods have to help finding new ways to process that data acquire useful knowledge and make more intelligent decisions.

REFERENCES

Ackoff, R. L. (1989). From data to wisdom. *Journal of Applied Systems Analysis*, *15*, 3–9.

Ackoff, R. L. (1996). On learning and the systems that facilitate it. *Center for Quality of Management Journal.*, *5*(2), 27–35.

Bellinger, G., Durval, C., Mills, A. (2004). *Data, information, knowledge, and wisdom*. Academic Press.

Bernstein, J. (2011). The Data-Information-Knowledge-Wisdom Hierarchy and its Antithesis. *NASKO, 2*(1).

Boellstorff, T. (2015). Making big data, in theory. In T. Boellstorff & B. Maurer (Eds.), *Data, now bigger and better!* (pp. 87–108). Chicago: Prickly Paradigm Press.

Boyd, D., & Crawford, K. (2012). Critical Questions for Big Data. *Information Communication and Society*, *15*(5), 662–679. doi:10.1080/1369118X.2012.678878

Brynjolfsson, E., & McAfee, A. (2011). *Race Against the Machine: How the Digital Revolution is Accelerating Innovation, Driving Productivity, and Irreversibly Transforming Employment and the Economy*. Lexington, MA: Digital Frontier Press.

Brynjolfsson, E., & Mcaffee, A. (2012). Big data: The management revolution. *Harvard Business Review, 90*(10), 60–68. PMID:23074865

Chamberlin, D. D., & Boyce, R. F. (1974, April). SEQUEL: A structured English query language. *Proc. 1974 ACM SIGFIDET Workshop*, 249-264.

Codd, E. F. (1970, June). A relational model of data for large shared data banks. *Communications of the ACM, 13*(6), 377–387. doi:10.1145/362384.362685

Crane, L., & Self, R. J. (2014). Big Data Analytics: A Threat or an Opportunity for Knowledge Management? In L. Uden, D. Fuenzaliza Oshee, I. H. Ting, & D. Liberona (Eds.), *Knowledge Management in Organizations. KMO 2014. Lecture Notes in Business Information Processing* (Vol. 185, pp. 25–34). Cham: Springer. doi:10.1007/978-3-319-08618-7_3

Cukier, K., & Mayer-Schoenberger, V. (2013b). The Rise of Big Data. *Foreign Affairs, 92*(3), 28–40.

Cukier, K., & Mayer-Schonberger, V. (2013a). *Big Data: A Revolution That Will Transform How We Live, Work and Think*. Boston, MA: Houghton Mifflin Harcourt.

Davenport, T., & Prusak, L. (1998). *Working Knowledge*. Boston, MA: Harvard Business School Press.

Davenport, T. H. (2014). *Big data at work: Dispelling the myths, uncovering the opportunities*. Boston: Harvard Business Review Press. doi:10.15358/9783800648153

Davenport, T. H., Barth, P., & Bean, R. (2013). How 'big data' is different. *MIT Sloan Management Review, 54*(1).

Davenport, T. H., & Harris, J. G. (2007). *Computing analytics: the new science of winning*. Boston, MA: Harvard Business School Review Press.

Davenport, T. H., & Kim, J. (2013). *Keeping Up with the Quants: Your Guide to Understanding and Using Analytics*. Harvard Business Review Press.

Dietrich, B. L., Plachy, E. C., & Norton, M. F. (2014). *Analytics across the Enterprise, How IBM realizes Business Value from Big Data and Analytics*. New York: IBM Press.

Drucker, P. F. (1991). 'The new productivity challenge'. *Harvard Business Review, 69*(6), 69–76. PMID:10114929

Eliot, T. S. (1934). *The rock*. Faber & Faber. Available at: http://www.wisdomportal.com/Technology/TSEliot-TheRock.html

Foster, I., Ghani, R., Jarmin, R. S., Kreuer, F., & Lane, J. (2017). *Big Data and Social Science*. Boca Raton, FL: CRC Press.

Hernandez, M. (2003). Asessing tacit knowledge transfer and dimensions of a learning environment in a Colombian business. *Advances in Developing Human Resources*, *5*(2), 215–221. doi:10.1177/1523422303005002009

Jagadish, S. V. K., Septiningsih, E. M., Kohli, A., Thomson, M. J., Ye, C., Redoña, E., ... Singh, R. K. (2012). Genetic advances in adapting rice to a rapidly changing climate. *Journal Agronomy & Crop Science*, *198*(5), 360–373. doi:10.1111/j.1439-037X.2012.00525.x

Kudyba, S. (2014). Information Creation through Analytics. In S. Kudyba (Ed.), *Big Data, Mining, and Analytics. Components of Strategic Decision Making* (pp. 17–48). Boca Raton, FL: CRC Press Taylor and Francis Group. doi:10.1201/b16666-3

Lazer, D, and al. (. (2009). Life in the network: The coming age of computational social science. *Science*, *323*(5915), 721–723. doi:10.1126cience.1167742 PMID:19197046

Nelson, R. R., & Winter, S. G. (1982). *An evolutionary theory of economic change*. Cambridge, MA: Harvard University Press.

Nissen, M. E. (2000). An extended model of knowledge-flow dynamics. *Communications of the Association for Information Systems*, *8*, 251–266.

Nonaka, I., & Takeuchi, H. (1995). *The knowledge creating company: How Japanese companies create the dynamics of innovation*. New York: Oxford University Press.

Olavsrud, T. (2014). *How big data is helping to save the planet*. Available at: http://www.cio.com/article/2683133/big-data/how-big-data-is-helping-to-save-the-planet.html

Oxford English Dictionary. (2018). *Data*. Retrieved from https://en.oxforddictionaries.com/definition/data

Piegorsch, W. W. (2015). *Statistical Data Analytics*. New York: Wiley.

Popovič, A., Hackney, R., Coelho, P. S., & Jaklič, J. (2012). Towards business intelligence systems success: Effects of maturity and culture on analytical decision making. *Decision Support Systems*, *54*(1), 729–739. doi:10.1016/j.dss.2012.08.017

Porter, M. E. (1985). *Competitive Advantage: Creating and Sustaining Superior Performance*. New York: Free Press.

Rayport, J. F., & Sviokla, J. J. (1995). Exploiting the Virtual Value Chain. *Harvard Business Review*, *73*(6), 75–85.

Schumpeter, J. A. (1934). *The theory of economic development*. Cambridge, MA: Harvard University Press.

Sedkaoui, S. (2017). The Internet, Data Analytics and Big Data. In Internet Economics: Models, Mechanisms and Management (pp. 144-166). Gottinger: eBook Bentham Science Publishers.

Sedkaoui, S., & Monino, J. L. (2016). *Big data, Open Data and Data Development*. New York: ISTE-Wiley.

Shani, A.B., & Sena, J. A. (2016). *Knowledge Management and New Product Development: Learning from a Software Development Firm*. Available at: http://ceurws.org/Vol-34/shani_sena.pdf

Shroff, G. (2013). *The Intelligent Web, Search, Smart Algorithms and Big Data*. Oxford, UK: Oxford Univ. Press.

Siegel, E. (2013). *Predictive analytics: The power to predict who will click, buy, lie, or die*. John Wiley & Sons.

Siegel, E. (2016). *Predictive Analytics*. New York: Wiley.

Simon, H. (1977). *The New Science of Management Decision*. Englewood Cliffs, NJ: Prentice Hall.

Simon, H. (1997). *Administrative behavior: A study of decision-making processes in administrative orgnizations*. New York: Free Press.

Steadman, I. (2013). *Big data and the death of the theorist*. Available at: http://www.wired.co.uk/news/archive/2013-01/25/big-data-end-of-theory

Tokhi, A., & Rauh, C. (2015). Die schiere Menge sagt noch nichts. Big Data in den Sozialwissenschaften. *WZB Mitteilungen*, *150*, 6–9.

Turban, E., Liang, T. P., & Wu, S. P. (2011). A framework for adopting collaboration 2.0 tools for virtual group decision making. *Group Decision and Negotiation*, *20*(2), 137–154. doi:10.100710726-010-9215-5

Wernerfelt, B. (1984). 'The resource-based view of the firm'. *Strategic Management Journal*, *5*(2), 171–180. doi:10.1002mj.4250050207

Zhang, A. (2017). *Data analytics: Practical guide to leveraging the power of Algorithms, data science, data mining, statistics, big data, and predictive analysis to improve business, work, and life*. Kindle edition.

KEY TERMS AND DEFINITIONS

Analytics: has emerged as a catch-all term for a variety of different business intelligence (BI)- and application-related initiatives. For some, it is the process of analyzing information from a particular domain, such as website analytics. For others, it is applying the breadth of BI capabilities to a specific content area (for example, sales, service, supply chain and so on). In particular, BI vendors use the "analytics" moniker to differentiate their products from the competition. Increasingly, "analytics" is used to describe statistical and mathematical data analysis that clusters, segments, scores and predicts what scenarios are most likely to happen. Whatever the use cases, "analytics" has moved deeper into the business vernacular. Analytics has garnered a burgeoning interest from business and IT professionals looking to exploit huge mounds of internally generated and externally available data.

Big Data: The term big data is used when the amount of data that an organization has to manage reaches a critical volume that requires new technological approaches in terms of storage, processing, and usage. Volume, velocity, and variety are usually the three criteria used to qualify a database as "big data."

Business Intelligence (BI): Is an umbrella term that includes the applications, infrastructure and tools, and best practices that enable access to and analysis of information to improve and optimize decisions and performance.

Data Analysis: This is a class of statistical methods that makes it possible to process a very large volume of data and identify the most interesting aspects of its structure. Some methods help to extract relations between different sets of data, and thus, draw statistical information that makes it possible describe the most important information contained in the data in the most succinct manner possible. Other techniques make it possible to group data in order to identify its common denominators clearly, and thereby understand them better.

Data Mining: This practice consists of extracting information from data as the objective of drawing knowledge from large quantities of data through automatic or semi-automatic methods. Data mining uses algorithms drawn from disciplines as diverse as statistics, artificial intelligence, and computer science in order to develop models from data; that is, in order to find interesting structures or recurrent themes according to criteria determined beforehand, and to extract the largest possible amount of knowledge useful to companies. It groups together all technologies capable of analyzing database information in order to find useful information and possible significant and useful relationships within the data.

Garbage In, Garbage Out (GIGO): In the field of computer science or information and communications technology refers to the fact that computers, since they operate by logical processes, will unquestioningly process unintended, even nonsensical, input data ("garbage in") and produce undesired, often nonsensical, output ("garbage out"). The principle applies to other fields as well.

Information: It consists of interpreted data, and has discernible meaning. It is lies in descriptions and answers questions like "Who?" "What?" "When?" and "How many?"

Knowledge: It is a type of know-how that makes it possible to transform information into instructions. Knowledge can either be obtained through transmission from those who possess it, or by extraction from experience.

Knowledge Management: Strategies and processes designed to identify, capture, structure, value, leverage, and share an organization's intellectual assets to enhance its performance and competitiveness. It is based on two critical activities: (1) capture and documentation of individual explicit and tacit knowledge, and (2) its dissemination within the organization.

APPENDIX

Table 1. Traditional KM vs big data Based KM

Factors	Traditional KM	BD based KM
Knowledge type	Tacit and codified knowledge	Data is processed in real time to extract useful knowledge
Necessary skills	Apparently not necessary	Analytical skills are highly necessary
Orientation	Highly people oriented	Depends less on people more on machine
Interaction	Face to face interaction with people	Minimal face to face interaction people
Knowledge creation and storage	Tacit knowledge repository is mostly people' brain	Tangible storage of huge size. Cloud storage is mostly used. Knowledge is created through perpetual flow and processing

Table 2. Analytics type

Type	Description	Example
Descriptive	The application of simple statistical techniques that describes what is contained in a data set or database.	An age bar chart is used to depict retail shoppers for a department store that wants to target advertising to customers by age.
Predictive	An application of advanced statistical, information software, or operations research methods to identify predictive variables and build predictive models to identify trends and relationships not readily observed in a descriptive analysis.	Multiple regression is used to show the relationship between age, weight, and exercise on diet food sales. Knowing that relationships exist helps explain why one set of independent variables influences dependent variables such as business performance
Perspective	An application of decision science, management science, and operations research methodologies (applied mathematical techniques) to make best use of allocable resources	A department store has a limited advertising budget to target customers. Linear programming models can be used to optimally allocate the budget to various advertising media

Chapter 9
Crowd Computing:
The Computing Revolution

Pijush Kanti Dutta Pramanik
National Institute of Technology Durgapur, India

Saurabh Pal
Bengal Institute of Technology Kolkata, India

Gaurav Pareek
National Institute of Technology Goa, India

Shubhendu Dutta
Aujas Networks, India

Prasenjit Choudhury
National Institute of Technology Durgapur, India

ABSTRACT

The power of crowd always has brought wonders. The same applies to the computing as well. The accumulated idle CPU cycles of millions of personally owned devices are capable of producing huge computing capacity. We have termed it as crowd computing. Though this very concept has been nurtured in the past through grid computing, in the age of powerful smartphones and tablets, it deserves to have a fresh look. In this chapter, the authors aim to present crowd computing in a modern approach. Readers will be able to gain a fair comprehension of the various aspects of crowd computing and have an insight of the ecosystem of this computing paradigm. The characteristics, benefits, issues, implementational challenges, applications, and examples of crowd computing are portrayed elaborately. To clear the air, crowd computing has been distinguishably compared to other analogous computing systems such as P2P computing, cloud computing, supercomputing, and crowdsourcing. The business values of crowd computing as well as the scope of offering crowd computing as a service have also been explored.

DOI: 10.4018/978-1-5225-4200-1.ch009

1 INTRODUCTION

[I]t may be that a crowd at a particular moment of history creates the object to justify its gathering. - Jennifer Egan (A Visit from the Goon Squad)

On July 14, 1789, a crowd of Parisian revolutionary citizens storm and dismantle the Bastille, a royal fortress that seemed as the symbol of the tyranny of the Bourbon monarchs (French revolutionaries storm Bastille), and marked the first climax of the French Revolution (Encyclopædia Britannica, 2016). History has witnessed many such revolutions instigated and executed by the force of the crowd. Lately, we are experiencing another crowd revolution – the crowd of computers. A crowd of humans is said to be physical if they are all located in a single place and virtual if they connect with each other on some sort of platform to accomplish a task using shared emotions. Whilst Crowd Computing is defined narrowly as being computer-mediated computing using a huge number of computers behaving as a crowd to accomplish one goal of enhancing the computation. Computing-intensive jobs are distributed to multiple computing devices across different geographical and administrative domain, owned by different people. It has been observed that most of the time these public-owned computing devices remain idle thus wasting a great number of CPU cycles. It is quite wondered that even small computers when work together, collaboratively provide huge computation capability that is quite comparable to (or even better than) a supercomputing infrastructure. Buying and maintaining high-performance computing (HPC) systems are exceedingly costly affairs (Pramanik, Choudhury, & Saha, January 2017). Collection of public (user's) computer can give us an economical alternative HPC option (Pramanik, Choudhury, & Saha, January 2017). Volunteer Grid Computing has envisioned this approach and it has been successfully implemented for several projects. Though the concept is not indeed new, in the age of smartphones and tablets, Crowd Computing has touched a new height and become relevant like never before. These mobile devices are getting extremely powerful and fairly resource-intensive. Thanks to their extensive usage, a ubiquitous HPC facility can be availed from anywhere and anytime. With a new wave of digitization across industry and consumer segment, we are experiencing a data deluge in every computing environment which eventually has necessitated the processing of this data to extract the meaningful information at real time. Crowd Computing that offers a ubiquitous and cost-effective HPC facility on demand can effectively abate the ever-increasing demand and supply gap of computing power.

In endeavoring to strengthen the communication and collaboration between machine and human, the term 'Crowd Computing' has been used in quite a few diverse contexts. It has been referred to conceptualize in various ways in the form of Crowdsourcing, human computation, social computing, cloud computing and mobile computing (Parshotam, October 2013). Indeed, it represents different connotation on different perspectives. As a result, people have defined and described Crowd Computing in different aspects in literature. Murray et al. (Murray, Yoneki, Crowcroft, & Hand, August 2010) are probably the first to use the term 'Crowd Computing'. They proposed the idea to spread the computational jobs to a collection of smartphones using an opportunistic network. In this chapter, our reference to Crowd Computing is nearly comparable to the Volunteer Grid Computing. We define Crowd Computing as a distributed computing system where several personally owned computing devices come together offering their free computing cycles to carry out a processing intensive computing task. A broader definition of crowd computing encompasses utilization of a huge number of computers with various capacities distributed geographically, having a different network domain, different governing authorities which willingly collaborate together to accomplish a big computation problem that would otherwise require a huge computation resource to accomplish the tasks. Ideally, the crowd offers their service voluntarily. But, in practical, most often they would like to be rewarded for their service rendering.

The rest of the chapter is organized as follows. In section 2, we discuss the nitty-gritty of Crowd Computing. In section 3, we distinguish Crowd Computing from other similar or quasi-similar computing models. Section 4 enlists some typical characteristics of Crowd Computing while section 5 and 6 mentions the benefits and issues, respectively, of it. Several challenges involved in implementing Crowd Computing are discussed elaborately in Section 7. In section 8, we shall explore the possibility of offering Crowd Computing as a service. In section 9, business values of Crowd Computing are identified. Section 10 identifies some application scenarios of Crowd Computing. In section 11, we shall explore some of the existing Crowd Computing technologies that are in practice. At last, we conclude the chapter in section 12.

2 UNDERSTANDING CROWD COMPUTING

2.1 The Crowd of Computers

The crowd is a definite collection or group of people with shared purpose and emotions (Moraes, & de Souza, 2012). Most people have described crowd in terms of size, as being a large number or group of people. In the context of Crowd Computing, the crowd is being considered as a group of people contributing the idle CPU cycles of the devices they own for various computation job which typically requires substantial computing resource. The crowd, physical or virtual, manifests behavior of a human crowd according to their size, dimensions, and strengths. The crowd can also be classified as open or closed based on the types of membership it supports. Every Crowd Computing activity is performed according to a predetermined purpose defined by an initiator of the activity; typically, an application. The purpose influences the roles of the participants involved.

2.2 How It Works

Crowd Computing is, fundamentally, a distributed computing framework where a big non-trivial task is divided into numerous independent atomic tasks that are distributed over multiple computing devices for processing. These atomic tasks are sometimes referred to as micro-tasks which are kept ready in a job pool. Available crowdworker are being searched for and a set of suitable crowdworkers is selected. Each micro-task from the job pool is assigned to a different crowdworker from that set (though sometimes the same task can be given to different crowdworker to maintain reliability). These micro-tasks are given as simple programs to the crowdworker without any contextual information. After execution of these independent micro-tasks, each crowdworker submits the output to the centralized master where all the micro-results are gathered, checked for errors and assembled to get the final result.

Figure 1. Basic layout of Crowd Computing

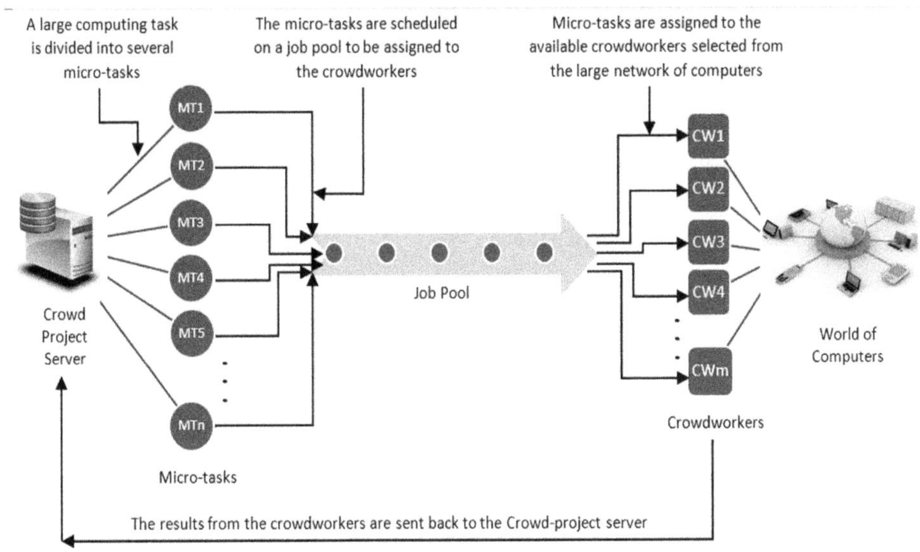

2.3 Basic Components

- **Requester:** Who needs HPC and submit jobs. Typically, it is a server that hosts the crowd project. In large Crowd Computing projects the requester itself maintains the server which hosts the project that intends to leverage Crowd Computing.
- **Crowdworker:** People lend their devices to execute the jobs. These crowd devices are denoted as crowdworkers. The devices may range from smartphone to desktops. When the devices are found idle, the jobs are processed following the (CPU) cycle-stealing scheme.
- **Platform:** Middleware for job management along with the server and client applications. The server application is responsible for job creation, discovering suitable crowdworker, job assigning and job scheduling to the designated crowdworkers. collecting the results from multiple crowdworkers, assemble them, and updating in the server application and for further purposes. It is responsible for implementing failure recovery schemes in case of failures. The client application installed on a crowd device is responsible for getting the job executed, opportunistically, that is assigned to that particular device and sending the result to the server once it is completed.
- **Network:** The computers are connected to the Internet either directly or through Wi-Fi.

2.4 Crowd Computing Approaches

In Crowd Computing, the computing devices may be fixed or mobile. Based on the type of resource, Crowd Computing may be realized through two approaches: Desktop Crowd Computing and Mobile Crowd Computing.

2.4.1 Desktop Crowd Computing

In Desktop Crowd Computing (DCC), computers (desktops and laptops) are usually stationary and connected to the Internet directly.

2.4.2 Mobile Crowd Computing

Mobile Crowd Computing (MCC) comprises the mobile devices such as smartphones and tablets. Nowadays, these devices are getting remarkably powerful and fairly comparable to their non-mobile counterparts like desktops and laptops (Pramanik, Choudhury, & Saha, January 2017). Hence, a sufficient number of connected mobile devices may provide a substantial computation capacity.

Table 1. Difference between desktop crowd computing and mobile crowd computing

	Desktop Crowd Computing	Mobile Crowd Computing
Flexibility	Somewhat rigid due to immobile resources	More flexible as anywhere a computing facility can be set up in ad hoc basis
Reliability	More reliable	Less reliable unless the users do not move for a long period
Availability	Less due to falling popularity of desktops	More due to increased number of smartphone users
Computing capacity	More	Less for the same number of devices
Scalability	Less scalable than MCC	More scalable

Both the approaches have their own advantages as well shortcomings. In terms of hardware configuration, desktop computers certainly are well ahead of the mobile devices. But recent studies (Oh, 2015) suggest that the number of desktop users is decreasing steadily while the number of smartphone users is rising remarkably. In fact, smartphones are going to be the primary computing device for many of the people (Bonnington, 2015). Therefore, the probability of getting a sufficient number of resources is always higher in MCC than in the DCC which negates the advantage of the desktop devices being superior in terms of raw hardware. This also makes MCC more scalable than DCC. The main advantage of MCC over the DCC lies in the context of flexibility. A small-scale Crowd Computing facility can be set up even in the absence of the Internet by connecting the mobile devices through hotspots, Bluetooth or Wi-Fi. But MCC has to deal with the problem with the user's mobility. In MCC, the devices typically use Wi-Fi to connect to the Internet for associating to Crowd Computing. The continuous movement of the user might result in out-of-range and eventually, loss of connection. In that case, failure recovery and job hands-off become the issue of utmost importance. Table 1 summarizes the differences between DCC and MCC.

3 CROWD COMPUTING AND OTHER RELATED COMPUTING PARADIGMS

The term Crowd Computing that has come into being only recently, has often been mistaken for other similar computing models like Grid computing, Cloud computing, Crowdsourcing etc. This section aims to clear the air.

3.1 Crowd Computing vs. P2P Computing

Crowdsourced computing apparently may seem identical to the peer-to-peer (P2P) computing. It is because due to certain similarities such as:

- Both involve multiple (usually large number of) participants.
- In both the cases, the participants are at the same level in the hierarchy.
- In both the cases, all the participants run a common application.
- May expand beyond a single administrative or geographic boundary.
- Both have a dynamic connection.
- Both opt for redundancy to maintain reliability.

But there are some fundamental differences between these two computing paradigms (summarized in Table 2):

- Crowd Computing typically follows client/server model and most often the participants do not communicate to each other.
- Philosophy of P2P computing is to mutually benefit the participants themselves. Crowd Computing is not always mutually beneficial. Here, typically only one party (the crowdsourced project), for whom others contribute their resources, is benefited. Even if the participants get any benefit from the project, the benefit is not reflective in nature i.e. they get compensated in different means whereas, in P2P, everybody gets the exactly similar type of gain.
- P2P computing usually involves storage and retrieval of data and files, not computing.

Table 2. Difference between crowd computing and peer-to-peer computing

	Crowd Computing	**P2P Computing**
Relationship type	Usually many to one	Many to many
Centralized control	Yes	No
Shared resource type	CPU	Data or file
Defining SLA	Complex	Simple
Mutual benefit	Not always	Always

Table 3. Difference between crowd computing and supercomputing

	Crowd Computing	Supercomputing
Centralised controlling	No	Yes
Availability	Not guaranteed	Surely guaranteed
Reliability	Not reliable	Absolutely reliable
Computing Capacity	Depends on the number of devices available	Always high
Cost	Very low	Extremely high
Energy consumption	Negligible	Very high
Security	Unsecured	Highly secured

3.2 Crowd Computing vs. Supercomputing

Crowd Computing offers an economical alternative of Supercomputers. The purpose of both is to provide HPC usually for executing the number crunching batch processing jobs. But the way of delivering the HPC service is totally different. Supercomputers are typically huge non-portable computers stationed at a certain location and usually employed for certain pre-designated jobs. These computers are generally operated by trained people which is a stark contrast to the case of Crowd Computing devices. The differences between these two are summarized in Table 3.

3.3 Crowd Computing vs. Cloud Computing

Crowd Computing is often confused with cloud computing mainly because the two terms appear homophonic. The term 'Crowd Computing' is still unacquainted to people in contrast to the exceedingly hyped 'cloud computing'. The cloud computing is hailed as a disruptive technology platform meant to offer "on demand" centralized computing to both B2B and B2C segments with a well-structured pricing model, while the Crowd Computing is characterized by its voluntary participation by means of distributed computing model. Moreover, a cloud computing service is controlled by a Cloud service provider who determines whom to offer the service and at what price. Therefore, a cloud computing is a well-established utility-based computing model offered by a service provider who owns the entire computing environment and charges the consumer or an enterprise based on the actual usage of computing resources. As a consequence, the consumer doesn't need to invest in procuring the high-cost computing resource, instead, he has to pay for the resources that are actually demanded. This helps in efficient management of computing resources owned by the Cloud provider. Thus, we see a close resemblance of Crowd Computing with cloud computing when it comes to efficient utilization of computing resources, but it is an entirely different computing paradigm in terms of resource ownership and the governing structure which is the hallmark of cloud computing model. A well-defined pricing structure such as on-demand pricing, spot pricing (based on real-time auction) or long-term subscription-based pricing has helped the growth in cloud computing demand. Crowd Computing model is expected to take the economics of computing to the next level by drastically enhancing the efficiency of distributed computing resources. Crowd Computing resembles cloud computing in many aspects, such as:

- Both offers elastic and on-demand computing resource.
- Both are a form of distributed and networked computing.
- In both cases, the computing is carried outside the organizational boundary (not in the case of Private Cloud).
- Both are vulnerable to high risk of privacy and security threats.
- Both aims to save budget on computing infrastructure.

But they differ from each other in several ways, as mentioned below as well in Table 4.

- In cloud computing, the public is the receiver of the service whereas, in Crowd Computing, it is exactly the opposite.
- Cloud resources are centralized but in Crowd Computing, it is highly distributed.
- SLAs (Service Level Agreement) are precisely defined in cloud computing. In volunteer Crowd Computing, SLA may not be of much importance but for non-volunteer Crowd Computing where SLA is a must, there is no standard SLA model.
- Anytime resource availability is guaranteed in cloud computing.
- Crowd Computing facility can be availed without (in case of volunteered service) or with minimal cost. But availing cloud computing always entails money and the cost depends on the type of application and the usage duration.
- Crowd Computing is generally aimed to solve tasks that require huge computing resource. Large projects opt for Crowd Computing. The project initiators maintain the server, the client application, and the middleware as well. While people access cloud computing facility not only for large tasks, but even for small jobs like word processing.

Table 4. Difference between crowd computing and cloud computing

	Crowd Computing	Cloud Computing
Resource location	Highly scattered	Integrated
Availability	Not guaranteed	Guaranteed
Reliability	Not reliable	Highly reliable
Availing cost	Zero or minimal	Considerable to high
Operational and maintenance cost	Very low	Extremely high
Energy efficiency	Highly energy efficient	To run and cool, Cloud resources require enormous energy
Nature of resources	Dynamic	Fixed

3.4 Crowd Computing vs. Crowdsourcing

Crowd Computing is often confused with Crowdsourcing that aspires to tap the human intelligence to be blended with the computer algorithms to make computers even more intelligent and rich in knowledge. How powerful the computers may have become but still there are some jobs that human can do far better and accurately than the computers by applying their cognition and natural instinct. Crowdsourced applications try to tap this human capability to solve the computational problems otherwise difficult for computing infrastructure to accomplish. People directly contribute to a project (e.g. Wikipedia, Yahoo! Answer etc.) by providing human-captured data or knowledge or both. Therefore, Crowdsourcing refers to the involvement of people in computation whereas Crowd Computing refers to the involvement of machines, owned by people, in computation. Crowd Computing aims to harness the processing power of millions of devices whereas Crowdsourcing aims to harness the processing power of millions of human brains. The differences between the two are summarized in Table 5.

Table 5. Difference between crowd computing and crowdsourcing

	Crowd Computing	Crowdsourcing
Resource shared	CPU	Human knowledge and intelligence
Human intervention	Not required	Required
Application type	Computation-intensive	Knowledge-intensive
Importance of QoS	Absolutely important	Comparatively less

4 CHARACTERISTICS OF CROWD COMPUTING

The characteristics mentioned below describes Crowd Computing more precisely (Parshotam, October 2013):

- **Collective Effort:** The beauty of Crowd Computing lies in the collective effort of numerous small, mid-size and big computers in accomplishing a large computing problem. But the interesting point is that these contributors or the crowdworkers typically are oblivion to each other. Nevertheless, this policy of receiving small and fragmented support from the public helps to work out an extensive task purging the requirement of buying large supercomputers.
- **On-Demand Computing:** Who require computing resource do not have to buy or own that permanently. When they require, can avail through Crowd Computing by submitting their jobs to the available crowdworkers.
- **Opportunistic:** One of the most interesting characteristics of Crowd Computing is its opportunistic nature. This opportunism can be experienced in two different contexts. First, the server continuously searches for the available crowdworkers and opportunistically submits a task whenever a suitable one is found. Second, once the job is submitted to the crowdworker, the client application opportunistically pushes the task to the client CPU whenever is sensed as idle.
- **Scalable:** The Crowd Computing paradigm is highly scalable. The infrastructure supporting Crowd Computing could encompass any number of computers. The number of computers participating could range from few computers to millions. The biggest advantage of Crowd Computing is machine could enroll to the system or leave the system willingly without affecting the overall computation.
- **Elastic:** Thanks to high scalability, the requester can involve as many crowdworker, if available, as needed. There is no logical as well as physical (if the server application supports) limitation for that. Note: Elasticity must not be confused with scalability which refers the ability of a system in accommodating expanded features added over the time. Whereas, elasticity refers to a quality of an offered service that can be catered, without limitation, as per the client's requirement.
- **Follows Client/Server Model:** Crowd Computing distinctly follows a client/ server model for data computation. The clients do not interact with other clients for sharing and collaborating work. They communicate with only a remote server from which they take command and return the result after execution. It is the server's responsibility to correspond to the crowdworkers and distribute the micro-tasks among them. The micro-tasks are scheduled

to the clients with their own set of data. Clients asynchronously process the task. The client updates the servers either when the task is completed or when it leaves.

- **Voluntary Participation:** Though this is not an absolute characteristic for the Crowd Computing in general, the majority of the existing Crowd Computing projects rely on the voluntary participation of the people. The term 'voluntary' could be understood as computers share their idle time, without charging any emolument, to process a task sent by some unknown entity. The voluntary contribution of computers enables big computation problems being solved which are otherwise infeasible due to staggering HPC cost.
- **No Human Intervention:** Unlike Crowdsourcing, Crowd Computing has no human intervention in the computation process which is performed at the client-end computer. The server takes the burden to split the big computation problem into small tasks like data crunching etc. which are being delivered to the client for further processing. Client end computer while processing the micro tasks has its own set of data and set of instruction and do not need/require any human intervention of the form like knowledge and intelligence feed. Most of the processing happens in the background without the knowledge of the user. The task processing happens without bothering any application.

5 BENEFITS OF CROWD COMPUTING

- **High Performance:** The accumulated CPU cycles from several computers generates massive processing power that is far more than the yesteryear's supercomputers. This collective processing power even can give the today's sophisticated supercomputers a run for the money.
- **Cost Effective:** Require no upfront investment. One of the brilliant characteristics of Crowd Computing is that it offers better and enhanced computing in contrast to grid and supercomputing facility at very less or reduced cost. The cost of fixed computing resources like supercomputing facility or grid computing is totally eliminated in Crowd Computing. Millions of computing devices provide voluntarily computing service bear no cost to project but to respective participants who willingly donate their CPU resources for the purpose of computing. The computer resource, power, and the network cost are borne fully by the participants. This reduces the overall cost to carry out projects that require big computation power.
- **Maintenance Free:** Since the computing jobs are outsourced to the public owned resources, the organizations which pursue taking advantage of Crowd

Computing are relieved to a great extent from bearing the overhead of infrastructure maintenance and management. They only have to take care of the server and the application software.

- **Leads to Green Computing:** Crowd Computing will ease the power consumption which is a major concern in centralized high-performance clusters. Also, a huge amount of energy is wasted to cool off these centralized systems. Crowd Computing offers a green computing environment by lowering the carbon footprint considerably.

6 ISSUES IN CROWD COMPUTING

Despite some lucrative benefits, Crowd Computing faces some serious issues which need careful attention.

- **Crowdworker Leaves Abruptly:** What happens if a crowdworker leaves the network (either intentionally or due to network failure or low battery) without finishing the job that was assigned to it? This can be taken care of if the crowdworker periodically send the partial results to the server. But the downside of this approach that it will increase the traffic.
- **Crowdworker Intentionally Sends the Incorrect Result:** A crowdworker may ill-intentionally send an unsolicited result to disrupt the crowd project. To avoid this, redundancy has to be adopted. The same job is sent to multiple crowdworkers and the results are compared. If there is any anomaly, they are re-computed. It is important to decide the degree of redundancy to have a balance.
- **Battery Issue in Mobile Crowdworkers:** In the age of growing smartphone users, these devices will contribute most as the crowdworkers. But the major hurdle is the inadequate battery capacity. The battery technologies have not advanced in line with the mobile hardware and computing technologies. People will be timid to offer their smartphones for Crowd Computing in fear of battery drainage. This will badly pull back the potential of MCC.
- **Poor Wireless Connectivity:** Wireless networks are infamous for their low bandwidth and non-reliability. This hampers especially the MCC. Because, people will not be generous enough to use their mobile internet for Crowd Computing. They will participate in Crowd Computing only when their devices are connected to a Wi-Fi connection.

7 CHALLENGES IN CROWD COMPUTING

7.1 Task Farming

The main performance gain for any distributed computing environment is due to decomposition of a big task into several small subtasks followed by their parallel execution. The same is the case with Crowd Computing framework. A lot of research is going on how to decompose complex tasks into simpler ones and without revealing too much about the context. Given the fact that Crowd Computing benefits from mobile and other computing devices, it is important to parallelize the computations by dividing a big non-trivial task into many subtasks. Task farming is one such scheme for achieving task-level parallelism by obtaining a collection of independent atomic tasks that comprise the overall task to be done by the Crowd Computing platform. Task farming is the basis for many distributed systems like Condor (Douglas, Tannenbaum, & Livny, 2005), BOINC (Anderson, 2004), MapReduce (Dean & Ghemawat, 2008) etc. A single master function, in all these systems, has the responsibility of managing a queue of tasks and distributing them among the collection of workers. When a worker completes a task, it asks the master for another one. Each of these subtasks is independent and requires a definite amount of computation time. A task farming algorithm naturally balances the load across its workers and therefore is an obvious choice for distributing work in Crowd Computing systems. For a small-scale crowd computing environment or an MCC, instead of a designated controller, the master device can be chosen from a set of crowd devices. The master must be highly connected with the other crowd devices. As the Crowd Computing network has community structure due to the involvement of humans, it means that there can be groups inside the whole population of crowd devices. So, having many Crowd Computing masters – one for each group from the population, could leads us to a better utility Crowd Computing system, because it is very likely that multiple masters could pool, delegate and distribute tasks more efficiently with high performance. Multiple masters raise the need to intercommunicate among themselves. The best approach for doing this would be opportunistic forwarding to exchange synchronizing messages between the masters.

7.2 Workflow Management

As the computing tasks are outsourced to unknown and not so reliable crowdworkers, workflow management becomes very important. The crowdworkers or crowd devices, as they are usually referred to, perform tasks that are assigned to them by a certain "master". A master can be a crowdworker or any other solicitor of the Crowd Computing platform. No crowdworker knows about the nature and scale of tasks being assigned to any other crowdworker. Outputs of some crowdworkers may be input for some others which means flawed scheduling of tasks may result in serious integrity issues. Another challenge is about the level of expectation from the crowdworker in terms of performance and quality of service. Following considerations await regarding workflow management in Crowd Computing scenario:

- Process design
- Nature of crowd activity
- Workflow patterns

Process design includes initiating a task at the Crowd Computing level, dividing the whole task into atomic subtasks and assigning these subtasks to the contributing systems (crowdworkers). So, while designing a process in Crowd Computing, it is important to develop tools for not only framing the subtasks automatedly but also to reinforce the process design decisions. In Crowd Computing where unidentified crowdworkers from different geographical regions and backgrounds contribute to a common goal, there must be a mechanism to verify the submitted outputs.

Crowd activity can be either standalone or may be incorporated into large-scale processes and require dealing with a rigorous and well-defined methods (Orlowska, 2015).

A periodic examination of the existing *workflow patterns* may unleash possibilities of taking many important rational steps which would otherwise be missing. For example, multiple executions of tasks (redundancy), evaluating the task completion, concurrently performing checks of reputation and reliability of a partner, the credibility of work completed, and generation of potential rewards structure (Kreps & Wilson, 1982).

7.3 Abstraction

In any computing paradigm, abstraction defines hiding unimportant details from the designer and/or end user. In crowd computing, the abstraction challenges lies in defining micro task which could abstract the complexities of the big computation problem. The crowdworker could process the micro task without understanding the complexities of big computational problem. Furthermore, the crowd computing should hide the programming, sub tasking, coordinating, scheduling and managing jobs, data structuring, storage, and processing to the requester and should only give the desired output that is ready to use.

7.4 Maintaining QoS

Quality may have different meanings to different people. It is a non-functional consideration which concerns performance, cost, reliability, security etc. or their combination. Quality is an important consideration in Crowd Computing and is attributed to the Crowd Computing platform in terms of the quality of results of the most substandard crowdworker. Quality concerns arise due to any of the following three reasons:

- Resource contention
- Parallel processing
- Non-centralized control

Resource contention is a result of variability of resource availability. The contention may arise due to hardware/software failure, dynamic system configuration etc. Since these are beyond the control of anyone, ensuring the quality of service in this scenario is difficult. For the systems goes offline/switch off, extra care is to be taken so that the state of the process is saved.

The issue of *parallel processing* arises due to the computing resources being heterogeneous and having varying availability patterns. A big individual task is divided into many subtasks for being processed by the participating crowdworkers. These tasks are allocated to the available and suitable crowdworker. Accuracy and timeliness of the collective delivery by the crowdworkers depend heavily on the availability of computing devices and the scheduling policies of the Crowd Computing platform.

Once the large task is divided into smaller subtasks, it is the local scheduler at each crowdworker's workstation which determines the tasks' local scheduling. Due to non-centralized control over the subtasks, the central workstation has no control over the policies under which the crowdworkers may be executing individual tasks assigned to them. The policies working at the crowdworkers' end may be inefficient and/or malicious in the worst case which may severely affect the quality of the end product.

A *performance modeling* is important because it helps in deciding concrete QoS goals. Once the policy of the system is decided upon, achieving desired QoS becomes an optimization problem with the performance value as the optimization parameter. Computation, communication, interference of crowd tasks is considered for modeling the behavior of a Crowd Computing system.

A concrete assessment is done for all these parameters under each QoS policy discussed earlier. The best policy is chosen based on the values of all these parameters and the same is enforced for resource allocation in the crowd. The overall Crowd

Computing problem which is defined as a comprehensive task is divided into subtasks and assigns each sub-task to an instance of crowdworker based on the pre-determined performance model to optimize the QoS. An algorithm to achieve optimal partition and scheduling of tasks is often costly to realize. Therefore, a heuristic algorithm serves better in this case.

Devising a good QoS solution would require a concrete investigation of the system with respect to the above-mentioned issues. In particular, there are hundreds of results a requester in the Crowd Computing framework may want. So, it is practically infeasible for the requester to verify the quality of each and every result. To monitor the quality of response corresponding to tasks (mainly computational) being distributed among the crowdworkers, following broad categories of techniques are applied one after the other:

- QoS policy
- Performance modeling
- Task scheduling and allocation

The aim of *QoS policy* is to ensure the quality of end-product by bridging the gap between the policies of the Crowd Computing platform and that of the crowdworker. Consider a Crowd Computing platform implementing policies like those in most well-known grid computing platforms like SETI@home. A large non-trivial task is divided into smaller tasks and a crowdworker is assigned a subtask only if crowdworker's machine is found idle. A policy like this ensures that the allocation policy at the Crowd Computing platform does not interfere with the policy at the crowdworkers. These types of policies are sometimes referred to as a *best-effort allocation policy*. This has a serious implication of the QoS of the overall Crowd Computing platform being dependent on the QoS of the crowdworkers. In contrast, allocation policies based on an SLA between each crowdworker and the Crowd Computing platform are more popular for ensuring the quality of subtasks at each crowdworker. Such policies are often called *reservation base policies* and are suitable for real-time Crowd Computing applications. While best-effort policies give equal freedom to the crowdworkers, a reservation-based policy ask for dedication.

7.5 Defining SLA

Since Crowd Computing is based on public resources which do not have a guarantee of resource availability, resource quality, and service quality. Hence, it is essential for both the parties (resource provider and the consumer) to adhere to a predefined Service Level Agreement (SLA). A suitable model is needed for that. The service levels should offer an adequate incentive for each party to attain it, though the penalty or disincentive doesn't seem to be a pragmatic approach. As this is a voluntary participation by the resource owners, a penalty of any form will only discourage the participation whereas a right incentive model will have a positive impact. The incentive could be in form of accumulated points redeemable at a future date through exchange or goods or services in any form. However, a more challenging aspect is measuring and reporting these service level performances.

7.6 Legal Challenges

Crowd Computing concerns about processing workload in a distributed fashion across computing devices connected by internet where the credibility of both the crowdworker and server is neither proved nor known to each other. The resource providers (crowdworker) join the system randomly with no predetermined obligation and reliability; it may raise genuine legal issues in case of any intellectual property right violation of or by any of the participants. To crowdworkers it is not known whether server may or may not jeopardize its personal data. Similarly, as the computing devices are connected to the system through internet in distributed fashion, there is a high possibility of these machines being infected by virus, botnets or affected by any other cyber-attack. It might be possible that the participant itself may have malafide intentions. This may raise the risk of Server data theft, corruption or transmitting false information to server to jeopardize the computational task. Today the legislations across the world have provisions to prosecute the perpetrators found guilty of cybercrime, but the laws concerning to data privacy vary widely across nations. Crowd Computing model should comply with the stringent data privacy laws. The legal issues which must be addressed in crowd computing model in order to safe practice and motivate crowdworkers are:

- Crowdworkers' security and privacy
- Cybercrime inflicting on crowdworkers' device
- Copyright ownership

There must be *security and privacy* guarantee for crowdworkers who collaborate on the Crowd Computing platforms. Information like the amount of time spent by the crowdworker, his or her geo-location, personal data stored in computer, computer resource (software and hardware) and configuration and compensation received in return may be considered sensitive information.

Crowdworkers affected by virus or cyber-attack could breach the security system of the server. The affected machine could also slow down and feed wrong results/data to server and hence affecting the quality of work. Care should be taken to withstand the device which may be having malefic intention. Since mostly crowd computing is voluntary service appropriate steps like honorably removing the crowdworker from the system. For, if the crowdworker is given incentive or other benefits appropriate legal steps should be enforced as per the legal agreement. The other way could be penalizing credit points from crowdworker's account.

Since crowd devices may also be utilized for performing research activities which may potentially lead to an invention, the crowdworker may claim credit as one of the inventors of the product. Also, patent laws require the names of all the inventors to be available at the time of filing the patent. So, if unaddressed, this issue can complicate and considerably delay the patenting process. The Crowd Computing platform must, therefore, resolve this joint inventorship, *copyright and ownership* issues beforehand.

The solutions to the above legal issues including being mindful of all the legal considerations for Crowd Computing and using contracts to clearly define relationships between the Crowd Computing platform and the crowdworkers (Wolfson & Lease, 2011).

7.7 Security, Privacy, and Trust

In Crowd Computing, jobs are sent to unknown computing devices. This exaggerates the trust, privacy and security concerns. A huge amount of processed data/information is gathered from crowed worker over internet possibly from devices like smart mobile devices and collection of standalone computers. There is a high possibility of crowd workers are being infected by virus, botnets or affected by any other cyber-attack. It might be possible that the participant itself may have malafide intentions raising issues like data theft, returning false information etc. Moreover, the credibility of the server system is accountable to crowd workers. As the crowd workers join crowd computing system (server) with no predetermined obligation and reliability, obvious security issue may arise questionable as what if the server infects the client device with virus, malware or jeopardize its personal data? The other risks associated with the information security include hardware risks. The devices (terminals or networking devices) used to report information to the Crowd Computing system may fail, be stolen or suffer security breaches due to malware etc. A lot of information is being submitted by crowd worker as an individual in the public domain network raising question how secure is the data transmission? In each of these cases security of the information may be at great risk. Lacking in security features, the Crowd platform has put down the trustworthiness, thereby affecting the individual's participation.

The sense of security gives a feeling of privacy. The privacy definition says (Westin, 1967), "Information privacy relates to the person's right to determine when, how and to what extent information about him or her is communicated to others". The privacy concern requires the participant not to be disturbed and asked repeatedly or sneaking for any information the individual does not want to share. It is seen that in voluntary distributed computing paradigm like Crowd Computing, most volunteers choose to remain anonymous while sending their inputs (Liezel Cilliers, 2015), thus keeping their information private from others.

It is the sense of security and privacy which generates trust upon a system. Trust is a subjective matter of opinion and does not have a clear definition in any context. Trust is rather considered a complex social phenomenon (Huang & Nicole, 2014). There is no universally acceptable definition for trust is available. Trust in Crowd Computing can be perceived to satisfy three basic characteristics (Mayor, Davis, & Schoorman, 1995) of competence, benevolence, and integrity of the system. Competency relates to the ability of the Crowd Computing system to perform functions (primarily recording information) efficiently and consistently. Benevolence concerns how firmly the fact that the trustee (Crowd Computing system) works in the best interests of the trustor (participant) can be established. Integrity relates to the perception that the information reported by the individuals is available, current and consistent with the originally submitted information.

Crowd Computing leverages the concept of "distributed trust" implying that each participating device should repose trust on others in order to carry out the transaction. Ensuring trustworthiness of Crowd Computing system is important to ensure maximum participation of the users. There are two measures (Liezel Cilliers, 2015) through which trust can be ensured in Crowd Computing namely hard measures and soft measures. *Hard trust* mechanisms are static and preventive in nature. These measures employ standard cryptographic and authentication controls to achieve the required level of trust. Trustworthiness of a system using hard measures is perceived based on the evidence provided by these standard security protocols. *Soft trust* mechanisms take into consideration the human aspect and behavioral analysis based on which a possible security breach is predicted and the recommendations are drawn. While both hard and soft measures work on the basis of standard and recommended controls respectively, the trustworthiness of a system is perceived by the crowd of people on the basis of whether they consider the controls to be adequate or not. Studies like (Liezel Cilliers, 2015) indicate that the trustworthiness of a system increases by employing information security controls - Confidentiality, Integrity, and Availability in the Crowd Computing systems.

The sense of security, privacy and thus privacy could be availed in Crowd Computing system by abiding the parameters like Confidentiality, Integrity and Availability (CIA). Implementing specific control and policies helps to improve the security, privacy and trust levels among the participants and requestor.

- **Confidentiality - Through Access Control Mechanism:** Confidentiality prevents any unauthorized disclosure of information submitted to the Crowd Computing system. This access control allows three services viz. authentication, authorization, and accountability. It ensures that only the genuine participant can avail the Crowd Computing services with access to authorized services along with the auditability of the actions performed. Access control mechanism further helps in ensuring the confidentiality component of the Information security triad.
- **Integrity - Through Encryption:** Integrity refers to the requirement of the information to remain correct until the time it remains in the system. The assurance that the information is not tampered during its transit is possible through an encrypted network channel such as SSL (Secured Socket Layer) protocol. The participants of the Crowd Computing should be using the SSH (Secure Shell) channel (encrypted) to access the remote device instead of Telnet of other remote access protocol.
- **Availability:** The availability of information concerns access of information to all the appropriate stakeholders without undue delay. The devices participating in the Crowd Computing may be rendered unavailable due to various vulnerabilities. Therefore, a periodic vulnerability assessment of these devices should be carried out by a central server which then can prescribe remediation for such vulnerabilities. As a best practice, the participating devices must follow a prescribed security configuration of the devices and ensure that the known vulnerabilities of the systems are plugged before it becomes part of the Crowd network.

7.8 Motivating the Participants

The success of Crowd Computing greatly depends on people's participation. Without enough donated computing resources the whole concept of Crowd Computing becomes futile. People are needed to be motivated to participate in mass computing be it voluntarily or involuntarily. Most of the existing Crowd Computing applications (discussed in section 11) are volunteer based. For voluntary participation, the Crowd Computing projects should be intending to solve some problems for which people usually are concerned of (e.g. social, medical, science etc.). Most of the big computation problem related to medical and health, pharmaceuticals, research in the field of physics, chemistry, mathematic, molecular biology, weather, astrophysics etc. The reason of voluntary participation is a noble cause, which people consider as a responsibility in contributing to the development and wellbeing of human and environment. People generally feel good about contributing to the society for a noble reason (Pramanik, Choudhury, & Saha, January 2017). What's more, if their contribution is acknowledged by making it public, the status-monger people would like to contribute more to have a proudful social status. But in practicality, this type of motivational factor has very little effect. If Crowd Computing needs to be popularized and adopted for a variety of applications, all kind of people from every sector of society is required to be inspired to lend their devices. To engage maximum people in Crowd Computing, they need to be incentivized either monetarily or through other means such as reward points, purchase tokens etc.

An important factor influencing eliciting participation in Crowd Computing is the incentive model followed. It is an imperative open problem to design incentives that can purposefully motivate the participants. Generally speaking, the idea is to use incentives to align the crowd behavior in line with the system goals defined in the previous phase. Due to the scale of Crowd Computing systems, it is important for the system designer to work on a formal model of incentivizing the participation that can be automated to address a maximum number of participants. Such a formal model may also help in systemizing the Crowd Computing framework and make the participants more accountable. A three-dimensional framework for incentive engineering for Crowd Computing (Truong, 2016) has been recently standardized. The three dimensions include the population aspects (P), design objectives (O) and Actions (A).

The *population* aspect of incentive framework unveils the need for improvements in major areas namely activation, contribution, and persistence of crowd. Activation is the extent to which a new user joins the system. Contribution measures the extent of the user contribution in the Crowd Computing aims. Persistence is a measure of the extent of how consistently and continuously a user contributes towards the Crowd Computing functioning. Other important population aspects include quality and compliance of the crowd functioning. While quality tells us how well the tasks are being performed, compliance describes the extent to which the participants adhere to the policy and functional requirements of the system.

As discussed earlier, the *design objectives* work to align the crowd behavior according to the Crowd Computing aims and scope. System characteristics have a significant influence on intensive engineering as it determines the concrete tasks and the amount of effort in terms of computations and intelligence. The design objectives have three aspects namely crowd, task, and system. Crowd aspects consist of aspects like structure, scale, and interaction among crowd. The task and system aspects are related to defining tasks and framework goals respectively.

Finally, the aspects related to Actions include members and tasks assigned to them according to the aim of the Crowd Computing system. It also includes evaluations of tasks based on which various rewards and punishments are decided. The outcome of the analysis is an incentive catalogue which will help crowdworkers in making decision for further involvement.

8 CROWD COMPUTING AS A SERVICE

As we have mentioned earlier, almost all the existing Crowd Computing projects are directed to solve certain specific problems and the required infrastructure (server computer and applications) are maintained by the associated organization or institution. To make Crowd Computing popular, it has to be accessible to the common people. They will not only be crowdworkers but also requesters and be able to avail this facility when they need. For that, there should be some entity or common platform which will do the job as the facilitator between the crowd requesters and the crowdworkers by providing Crowd Computing as a Service (CCaaS), very similar to IaaS (Infrastructure as a Service) in cloud computing. The requester who needed extra computing facility will request to the Crowd Computing service provider. In turn the service provider will arrange the crowdworkers and distribute the job to them. After finishing, the service provider will send the result back to the requester. One legitimate question may arise – why Crowd Computing, when cloud computing is already popular and widely accessible and easily cater the need? The answer is simple – cost effective. Though the purpose of IaaS and CCaaS is alike, accessing the service of the later will be cheaper by a considerably great margin.

9 BUSINESS VALUES

Worldwide there is a growing interest among people in "sharing" model of business such as renting out one's car, apartment, bike or even the Wi-Fi network when we don't need it. In quest of greater efficiency, this sharing economy has now pervaded into the computing world as well. Various reports on data center study have revealed that 80-90% of the capacity of data center servers remain unutilized and therefore, the firms are fast joining the cloud computing bandwagon, which aims to maximize the utilization of computing resources. A similar trend is seen in consumer technology space as well where the high capacity and smart computing devices (desktop, laptop, and mobile phones) are flooded in the market but only a fraction of its capacity is put to real use. These smart devices with high-end processors can be better leveraged through sharing mechanism to create a larger welfare of a community of interest. A closed network of organizations may leverage these distributed devices to solve the complex computational tasks and in turn compensate the owners of these devices for the period of usage. When this network expands to include the larger group of people with converging interest, a much larger computing resource pool is available on tap which reduces the cost of computing significantly. When the cost of creating an information base significantly lowered by utilizing the idle capacities of hundreds and thousands of high-end computing devices, the pricing of the product based on this information base will also be low and which, in turn, increases the demand for the product. Thus, the wider adoption of Crowd Computing will result in the greater welfare of the society.

10 APPLICATIONS

As already discussed, Crowd Computing has great potential in offering cost-effective HPC environment on demand basis. This has open new avenues of applications where the technology suitably meets the demand in less time. In this section, we shall discuss some of the resource-intensive application areas where Crowd Computing would play a significant role in providing computing resources.

10.1 Science

In the field of science and mathematics like physics, astronomy, chemistry, and molecular biology there exists many unsolved theories and concepts. Many assumptions proposed need to be validated for future discovery. Reasoning these demands simulating models and processing huge data and instructions. Some of these tasks are very resource consuming and require supercomputer infrastructures. Lacking in resources is one of the hurdle in futuristic researches. The voluntary participation of computers around the world sharing their CPU cycles and memory gives enormous computing strength to scientist and researcher to sort out the issues. Some of the crowd computing projects that are aimed at solving large scientific problems are ATLAS@Home, Collatz Conjecture, Cosmology@Home, Einstein@ Home, Folding@Home, Ibercivis, Leiden Classical, LHC@Home, Milkyway@ Home, MindModeling@Home, SETI@Home, etc.

10.2 Medical and Health

Medical and health services are data intensive, producing a huge volume of unstructured data which are complicated and changeable. Analysis of these data could benefit in personalized treatment. According to the WHO (World Health Organization) much of the fatal diseases could be cured if detected at the early stage (Wiślicki et al., 2014). In this perspective, the power of Crowd Computing could be exploited to speed up the information output and precision quality. Two of the wide computational based approach for patient diagnosis is simulation modeling and medical imaging (Lee, Tierney, & Johnston, 2006). The simulation modeling allows doctors to have 3D digital representation of patient body geometry and affected region, which enable them to plan future treatment (Cerello). The steps involved in simulation modeling are: i) mathematical representation of an object in a 3D space, and ii) Rendering i.e. conversion of mathematical representation into realistic 3D images (Wiślicki, et al., 2014). These tasks are both computational and data-intensive jobs. Medical imaging (X-ray, MRI, Sonography, PET, SPECT, etc) is another way of diagnosis which offers a different array of visualization of the problem. Analytics of the image in reference to same and other image produces statistical information which could be used for decision making in treatment (Cerello). Besides these, high computation in medical diagnosis is required in cancer treatment for probabilistic modeling of tumor outspread over time and simulation of the effect of the drug on cancer cells. These and other types of diagnostic tasks which require high computation and huge data processing could be really benefited by exploiting Crowd Computing.

Drug discovery and designing for treatment could take more than 15 years of time from the time of its first synthesis in the lab to availability in the market. Designing drug involves selecting the suitable molecular compound and modeling so that it could inhibit the target virus or infectious cell growth. Suitable modeling and rationalizing with computer reduces the development time period. This process is both computational and data intensive task. Each drug design problem includes screening 180,000 compounds. Each analysis of compound on desktop PC takes 3 hours of time. So, a total of 180,000 compounds would take 540,000 hours or roughly 61 years. This job could be reduced by executing parallely in computers in distributed fashion using Crowd Computing technology, improving the efficiency and development time in a span of days or week (Demurjian, 2008).

10.3 Weather Prediction

Weather changes cause heavy financial loss throughout the world. Thunderstorm, hurricanes, rainfall, snowing, flooding, high tides, and temperature change not only take a toll on assets but also on life. Every year billions of dollars are lost because of weather disruptions. Knowing weather condition from previous – weather prediction may help to take precautionary measures and risks aversion. Much of the agriculture business, air traffic, marine business, forestry, and other utility and commercial business depend on weather forecasting. Besides on an everyday life, people can plan beforehand what to wear, their activities and other survival strategies by weather predictions (Weather forecasting). Around the world researcher and scientists are working on weather analysis for accurate prediction. Governments are spending billions on weather forecasting.

Weather prediction involves mathematical modeling of weather and climate governed by the laws of physics, which could predict the behavior of atmosphere over a period of time. Earlier few handful models were used to predict weather forecast, these leads to uncertainties. Presently there exist hundreds of thousand weather forecasting models. To reduce the uncertainties attempts are made to run these big number of models in computers with a permutation of a slight variation of physical parameters like vorticity, divergence, temperature, surface pressure, moisture etc. Crowd Computing armed with the power of huge number of crowdworkers, distributed worldwide can resolve the complex, time-consuming, and computational resource-intensive weather prediction problem in a very short span of time.

10.4 Disaster Management and Communication

Disaster may happen due to natural events like avalanches, floods, fire, hurricanes, thunderstorm, tornadoes, earthquake, landslide, tsunami, volcanos or man-made like construction (building or bridge) collapse, dam failure, nuclear power plant accidents, war, explosions, train accidents etc. Disaster is a global challenge, managing the disaster is a situation which every country faces. Disaster management requires quality of service and information for effective and fast recovery/rescue (Workshop, 2013). Often in the time of disaster communication breaks. Assessment of real-time situation and exchanging information among the victims, the rescuers, and the decision makers is a big problem (Shih, Chen, Lin, & Chung, 2012). Use of satellite and radio phones has its own limitations. Most often satellite phones are unusable due to lack of maintenance, furthermore they are very costly. Radios may be accessible to rescue team but may not to the victims trapped in situation. For fast and targeted rescue, it is important that the actual victim's scenario, the situation, and other constraints be analyzed and evaluated correctly. To assess the situation correctly, it is necessary that the information of the victims and the rescuers captured by UAV in the form of video, images, and other forms of data are analyzed in real-time and distributed properly among rescuers and other authorities. The decision making greatly depends on the quality of information acquired and assessed. Rescue team and stuck out people could use smart mobile devices to capture actual situational video, images and their location. The information could be exchanged among the group of the rescue team and victims through mobile ad-hoc network.

Smart mobile devices of rescuers and victims could be used for the computational job on situational data (video, image, audio, text, and numbers) analysis locally. The information thus assessed could be distributed locally among rescue team or others to have a collective intelligence. Much of the data and information feed is done locally through the mobile devices, the data analysis could be performed by the small-scale crowd of computers formed by volunteer mobile device at the place of situation and in few occasions when data and computation become intensive and goes beyond the scope of local crowd computers, a bigger crowd through middle layer infrastructure could be approached.

10.5 IoT-Based Applications

In IoT-based applications, different electronic devices are connected to share data giving a sense of automation. The application of IoT could be found in home, office, production house, logistics, shopping zone etc. IoT interacts with the user, understands their needs, schedule, working behavior and another pattern. These require continuous data processing and running AI programs to comprehend the situation. This requires good computing power. Small-scale Crowd Computing could be able to distribute the workload among the computing devices available in the house. For example, in smart home based IoT application, the computing workload can be distributed among the smart mobile devices and other tablets and laptop available in the house. Thus, eliminating the need of huge computational resources and associated cost.

10.6 Business Processing

Business processing involves varieties of task including office automation, enterprise resource planning to statistical business data processing for decision making. Office automation jobs involve employee management and other tasks like email/ document searching, sorting, composing and updating etc. For a big enterprise, the various business operations are planned and scheduled by ERP for optimal business output. Other decision-making tasks are based on statistical analysis on financial, market, inventory or other data. Much of these jobs involve human intervention. But use of AI could make it possible to automatized the work structure and workflow management. Crowd Computing along with AI would allow doing micro-task which human perform autonomously with optimized quality. Small offices can apply small scale Crowd Computing whereby the smart mobile devices of the employees can be used to set up MCC to carry out the various office/business jobs without investing on large computation infrastructures.

10.7 Distributed Rendering for 3D Animation

Rendering 3D animation data to convert into full-fledged animation is quite computationally intensive and time taking process. For small animation business enterprises, it is quite difficult to have a high-end computer resources with high computing power, this result in a delay in rendering. The Crowd Computing could be the technology for the application of rendering 3D data. It is very fast in comparison to fixed resources.

11 EXAMPLES

11.1 BOINC

Berkeley Open Infrastructure for Network Computing (BOINC) is a distributed computing infrastructure which presents a middleware to control and coordinate volunteer and grid computing resources. With over millions of active users/clients who are voluntarily sharing their CPU cycles and memory for the various computation intensive programs, BOINC has made possible to outperform grid and supercomputing facilities. As of January 2017, there are about 834,343 active computers throughout the world averaging processing power of 16.912 PetaFlops (Berkeley Open Infrastructure for Network Computing). The BOINC software platform offers the feature like project autonomy, volunteer flexibility to participate in multiple projects, flexible application framework, server scalability, support for large database, and multiple participant platforms (Overview of BOINC). The enormous computing power which BOINC provides has made it a general distributed platform for various work on the diversified field including Physics, mathematics, medicine and health, molecular biology and astrophysics etc. leading to numerous scientific projects running on BOINC.

This distributed computing infrastructure follows client-server architecture. Client machines registered to various projects are controlled and coordinated by BOINC servers. As servers are distributed in multiple machines, practically it can support projects of any size. The server splits a task into micro-tasks and sends them to associated clients. The required processing is performed by the clients and the computational results are uploaded to the server for further validation. The intercommunication between the client and server take place by Remote Procedure Call (RPC). The client can register to multiple projects whereby the computation of each project running on the CPU is independent of each other (BOINC client–server technology). BOINC suitably carry out projects for simulating the physical system, genetic algorithm, and analyzing a large amount of data. There are many projects registered to BOINC. Some of the projects which successfully carried out at BOINC are:

- SETI@Home (SETI@home), an Astrophysics and Astrobiology project initiated by University of California is probably the earliest project of this type which harnesses crowd resources to solve a large scientific problem. The project uses BOINC resources to detect intelligent life outside Earth. In SETI@Home, radio telescopic data are being processed for analysis by distributed volunteer computers.

- Rosetta@Home (Rosetta@home) is a molecular biology project carried out by University of Washington, for developing improved 3D models of proteins to design macromolecular structure. This will ultimately lead scientists to understand protein structure and developing a cure for human diseases.
- RNA world (RNA World project description) uses the BOINC middleware to identify, analyze, structurally predict and design RNA molecules.
- World Community Grid (World Community Grid) an initiative by IBM. BOINC distributed computing facility has been used for multiple projects for the treatment of Cancer, Zika, TB, Ebola, and AIDS.
- Einstein@Home (Einstein@Home) is an astrophysics project taken by University of Wisconsin and Max Plank Institute for Gravitational Physics. The project has taken BOINC resources to search for weak astrophysical signals from the spinning neutron stars or pulsars.
- Climateprediction.net (Climateprediction.net) is a climate study project carried out by Oxford University using BOINC volunteer resources. The project aims to investigate the approximation of climate model. The models are run on volunteer distributed systems thousand times with slight variation. The project studies the future weather for the next century, predicting temperature, rainfall, and extreme weather.
- Leiden Classical (Leiden Classical) project in the field of chemistry carried out by Leiden University. The projects use volunteer computing for surface science calculation using classical dynamics. Volunteers, students, and scientist are welcomed to give their personal calculation. Various simulations on the chemical compound are performed on the grid.
- LHC@Home (LHC@home) project in the field of physics at CERN. BOINC has been used for distributed computing on the simulation to improve the design of LHC and its detector.
- MindModeling@Home (MindModeling@Home) is a project in the field of cognitive science with joint collaboration of University of Dayton and Wright State University. The project uses distributed computing to understand the human brain and the mechanism that enables human performance and learning.

11.2 Non-BOINC

There are several other middleware frameworks which support distributed computing based on voluntary computing mechanism. But unlike BOINC, in non-BOINC project, the client is dedicated to the only kind of project rather running multiple project computation. The easy part is the setup of the environment responsible for the execution of the program at the client side. This type of architecture emphasizes on Windows platform at the client sites. Though very less but crucial projects like Folding@Home (Folding@Home) are using non-BOINC architecture. Folding@ Home is a molecular biology project carried out at Standford University. The project uses volunteer distributed computing to comprehend protein folding, misfolding and related diseases. Emphasis is also given in protein structure prediction.

12 CONCLUSION

Crowd Computing is a wonderful means to achieve HPC economically. Today's extremely powerful mobile devices have taken it to a new height. Crowd Computing can be characterized by different attributes such as collective effort, on-demand computing, scalable and elastic, opportunistic, client/server based etc. Besides being cost effective, it also leads to green computing not forfeiting the performance of supercomputers. For successful exploitation, it has to take care of few issues such as low bandwidth and unreliability of wireless networks, sudden withdrawal of the crowdworkers, intentionally disrupting the system etc. There are also several challenges such as job management, maintaining QoS, security, and privacy etc. are to be addressed. Crowd Computing has potential in solving large problems from several application areas such as science, medical & health, weather prediction, disaster management, business processing etc. It also offers significant business value if properly exercised by the organization. Crowd Computing can cherish the similar success as cloud computing if it is also offered as a service so that anyone who needs HPC can avail the facility whenever required at no or negligible cost.

REFERENCES

Anderson, D. P. (2004). A system for public-resource computing and storage. In *Fifth IEEE/ACM International Workshop on Grid Computing. Berkeley Open Infrastructure for Network Computing*. IEEE.

Berkeley Open Infrastructure for Network Computing. (n.d.). In *Wikipedia*. Retrieved May 29, 2017, from https://en.wikipedia.org/wiki/Berkeley_Open_Infrastructure_for_Network_Computing

BOINC client–server technology. (n.d.). In *Wikipedia*. Retrieved May 29, 2017, from https://en.wikipedia.org/wiki/BOINC_client–server_technology

Bonnington, C. (2015, February 10). *In less than two years, a smartphone could be your only computer.* Retrieved June 27, 2016, from http://www.wired.com/2015/02/smartphone-only-computer/

Cerello, P. (n.d.). *Grid Computing in Medical Applications.* Retrieved from https://indico.cern.ch/event/408139/contributions/979806/attachments/815730/1117739/chep2006-mga.pdf

Climateprediction.net. (n.d.). Retrieved May 29, 2017, from http://www.climateprediction.net/

D, S. E., Moraes, K., & de Souza, J. M. (2012). CSCWD: Five characters in search of crowds. *Proceedings of the 2012 IEEE 16th International Conference on Computer Supported Cooperative Work in Design (CSCWD).*

Dean, J., & Ghemawat, S. (2008). MapReduce: Simplified data processing on large clusters. *Communications of the ACM, 51*(1), 107–113. doi:10.1145/1327452.1327492

Douglas, T., Tannenbaum, T., & Livny, M. (2005). Distributed Computing in practice: The Condor Experience. *Concurrency and Computation: Practice & Experience - Grid Performance, 17*(2), 323 - 356.

Encyclopædia Britannica. (2016, December 23). *French Revolution.* Retrieved 1 12, 2017, from https://www.britannica.com/event/French-Revolution

Einstein@Home. (n.d.). Retrieved May 29, 2017, from https://einsteinathome.org/about

Folding@Home. (n.d.). Retrieved May 29, 2017, from http://folding.stanford.edu/

French revolutionaries storm Bastille. (n.d.). Retrieved from History.com: http://www.history.com/this-day-in-history/french-revolutionaries-storm-bastille

Huang, J., & Nicole, D. (2014). Evidence-based trust reasoning. *HotSoS Symposium.*

Kreps, D. M., & Wilson, R. (1982). Reputation and imperfect information. *Journal of Economic Theory, 27*(2), 253–279. doi:10.1016/0022-0531(82)90030-8

Lee, J., Tierney, B., & Johnston, W. (2006). Data Intensive Distributed Computing: A Medical Application Example. *International Conference on High-Performance Computing and Networking*, 150-158.

Leiden Classical. (n.d.). Retrieved May 29, 2017, from http://boinc.gorlaeus.net/

LHC@home. (n.d.). Retrieved May 29, 2017, from https://lhcathome.cern.ch/lhcathome/index.php

Liezel Cilliers, S. F. (2015). The Relationship Between Privacy, Information Security and the Trustworthiness of a Crowdsourcing System in a Smart City. *Ninth International Symposium on Human Aspects of Information Security & Assurance (HAISA 2015)*, Lesvos, Greece.

Mayor, R., Davis, J., & Schoorman, F. (1995). An integrative model of organizational trust. *Academy of Management Review*, *20*(3), 709–734.

MindModeling@Home. (n.d.). Retrieved May 29, 2017, from https://mindmodeling.org/

Murray, D. G., Yoneki, E., Crowcroft, J., & Hand, S. (2010). *The Case for Crowd Computing*. MobiHeld 2010, New Delhi, India.

Nhat, V. Q., & Truong, S. S.-T. (2016). *Incentive Engineering Framework for Crowdsourcing Systems*. arXiv preprint arXiv:1609.01348

Oh, W. (2015, July 1). *India will overtake US to become world's second largest smartphone market by 2017*. Retrieved March 11, 2016, from https://www.strategyanalytics.com/strategy-analytics/news/strategy-analytics-press-releases/strategy-analytics-press-release/2015/07/01/India-will-overtake-US-to-become-world's-second-largest-smartphone-market-by-2017#.VuHPKPl97IX

Orlowska, M. E. (2015). Challenges for Workflows Technology to Support Crowdsourcing Activities. *Fifth International Conference on Business Intelligence and Technology*.

Overview of BOINC. (n.d.). Retrieved May 29, 2017, from https://boinc.berkeley.edu/trac/wiki/BoincIntro

Parshotam, K. (2013). *Crowd Computing: A Literature Review and Definition*. SAICSIT '13, East London, South Africa.

Pramanik, P. K., Choudhury, P., & Saha, A. (January 2017). Economical Supercomputing thru Smartphone Crowd Computing: An Assessment of Opportunities, Benefits, Deterrents, and Applications from India's Perspective. *International Conference on Advanced Computing and Communication Systems (ICACCS - 2017)*. 10.1109/ICACCS.2017.8014613

RNA World project description. (n.d.). Retrieved May 29, 2017, from https://www.rechenkraft.net/wiki/index.php?title=RNA_World/Projectdescription/en

Rosetta@home. (n.d.). Retrieved May 29, 2017, from http://boinc.bakerlab.org/rosetta/

SETI@home. (n.d.). Retrieved May 29, 2017, from http://setiathome.berkeley.edu/

Shih, C.-S., Chen, L.-J., Lin, C.-J., & Chung, W.-H. (2012). Open Information Gateway for Disaster management. *IEEE International Conference on Communications (ICC).*

Demurjian, S. A. (2008). *Grid Computing and its Applications in the Biomedical Informatics Domain*. Biomedical Informatics.

Weather forecasting. (n.d.). Retrieved June 2, 2017, from https://en.wikipedia.org/wiki/Weather_forecasting

Westin, A. (1967). *Privacy and Freedom*. New York: Atheneum Publishers.

Wiślicki, W., Bednarski, T., Białas, P., Czerwiński, E., Kapłon, Ł., Kochanowski, A., & Silar, M. (2014). *Computing support for advanced medical data analysis and imaging*. Bio-Algorithms and Med-Systems.

Wolfson, S. M., & Lease, M. (2011). Look before you leap: Legal pitfalls of crowdsourcing. *American Society for Information Science and Technology*, *48*(1), 1–10.

Workshop, J. J. (2013). *Big Data and Disaster Management.* NSF & JST Workshop.

World Community Grid. (n.d.). Retrieved May 29, 2017, from https://www.worldcommunitygrid.org/discover.action#curent-projects

Chapter 10
Piloting Crowdsourcing Platform for Monitoring and Evaluation of Projects:
Harnessing Massive Open Online Deliberation (MOOD)

Camilius A. Sanga
Sokoine University of Agriculture, Tanzania

Joseph Philipo Telemala
Sokoine University of Agriculture, Tanzania

Neema Nicodemus Lyimo
Sokoine University of Agriculture, Tanzania

Fredy Kilima
Moshi Co-operative University (MoCU), Tanzania

Kadeghe Fue
Sokoine University of Agriculture, Tanzania

Maulilio John Kipanyula
Sokoine University of Agriculture, Tanzania

ABSTRACT

Crowdsourcing can be viewed as a positive catalyst for effective results in many sectors of the economy including business, governance, agriculture, and health to name a few because it provides unlimited opportunities to people to share information among societies around the world. Despite some considerable efforts to adopt this concept in Tanzania, less has been done on its implementation in monitoring and evaluation of projects. This chapter proposes the development of a crowdsourcing platform as an essential step towards combating corruption, misuse, and embezzlement of funds. The developed crowdsourcing platform for monitoring and evaluation

DOI: 10.4018/978-1-5225-4200-1.ch010

provides an up-to-date status of projects based on key indicators set and from such information, any member in particular organization can monitor and evaluate the progress of a given project. Results of this study show that the platform promotes transparency, collaboration, accountability, and has potential to motivate different actors or stakeholders in monitoring projects funded by government and donors.

INTRODUCTION

This chapter proposes and explores the application of crowdsourcing in monitoring and evaluation (M&E) of projects. It begins by analyzing different ways of involving the crowd in the monitoring process such as through the use of shared spreadsheet, two-way conversation, use of mobile phone and web based systems. It demonstrates how crowdsourcing can be incorporated in a web-based M&E system, followed by a discussion of the preliminary results.

Monitoring and Evaluation (M&E) has been a key component of successful implementation of research and/development projects. Some M&E systems have integrated information and communication technologies (ICTs). However, web applications that allow stakeholders to be effectively involved in monitoring and evaluation have generally been rare. Consequently, stakeholders' have mainly been consulted during periodic M&E leading to limited sharing of knowledge and experiences with the monitoring and evaluation experts and scope for accommodating new ideas and timely adjustments of project activities and implementation schedules. To date there are several participatory web-based ICT monitoring and evaluation systems that can be customized to address these concerns. Web 2.0 applications, in particular, allows prompt sharing of development results and offers new ways for timely measurement of projects' results and outcomes. Web 2.0 applications that have so far been adapted in monitoring and evaluation can be categorized into three forms as detailed in below:

Shared Spreadsheet

Shared spreadsheet allows data to be combined in an online central spreadsheet in which the performance indicators are specified to allow participatory evaluation by various stakeholders through on-line access. Web4forDev article on [1]Monitoring and Evaluation gives an example of Google Doc as a web 2.0 tool used in monitoring and evaluation. The articles hinges on successful cases of blog-based participatory Monitoring and Evaluation systems in South Africa popularized as "I collaborate, e-collaborate and we collaborate[2]". The online document has a worksheet with operational definitions of indicators used; a worksheet where overall target and baseline figures are filled on a monthly basis by project staff in different locations. Note that the 6-monthly totals are automatically calculated and compared with 6-monthly or annual plans and the design allows for graphical representations of key results as a ratio of achievements to targets over time.

Two-Way Conversation

The two-way conversation Monitoring and Evaluation systems are designed for effective assessment of indicators such poverty which tend to be an outcome of multi-dimensional phenomena and hard to quantify using a single quantitative measure. In this context qualitative methods are perceived to be more appropriate to arrive at ideal composite measures (e.g. indices) of a variable of interest. The most recent applications of this method entail social media or user generated content to account for perspectives of different stakeholders on project issues. Through these systems, donors can read directly the success or failure of a respective project. For example, the global crowdsourcing organization called Globalgiving[3] connects nonprofits, donors, and companies from nearly all over the world to mobilize funds for the needy. These entities can potentially gauge the outcomes and impacts of their endeavors from wider applications of Monitoring and Evaluation systems that uphold the two-way conversation approach.

Ordinary Citizen Monitoring Through Mobile Phones

The extent to which ordinary citizens owning cell phones can participate in monitoring and evaluation has been demonstrated through different projects. USHAHIDI[4] software in Kenya, for example, has been instrumental in monitoring many of the real-time issues such political campaigns and election process, response to crisis as well as advocacy and human rights. Ushaurikilimo[5], a mobile phone based extension and advisory system, has also demonstrated its usefulness in linking farmers, extension officers and researchers to deliberate on diverse issues related to agriculture (Sanga et al., 2016b). A free and open-source framework for building robust, highly customized mobile services with web-based dashboards called RAPIDSMS[6] is also available online and it offers a flexible platform and modular components for large-scale data collection, management of complex workflows, and automatic data analysis.

The global prospect for a wider adoption of this participatory Monitoring and Evaluation system is generally considered to be good as the as adoption rate for these ICT based devices among ordinary citizens has been increasing over time (Figure 1).

These three techniques/tools provided by the Web 2.0 involve the community (herein referred to as crowd) in Monitoring and Evaluation. The act of using the crowd from communities to serve as either source or end of service provision is referred to as crowdsourcing. It is important to note that several technologies which enable use of the crowd have emerged as result of recent development in ICT.

CROWDSOURCING

The United States Agency for International Development defines crowdsourcing as the act of sourcing information *...from a group of people in response to an open call, a request for specific information, or for an exchange, organized by a central organizer/organizing body* (USAID, 2013). There are several benefits associated with the use of crowdsourcing in many fields as discussed below.

Rationale of Crowdsourcing

Bott and Young (2012) view crowdsourcing as a core mechanism for effective governance of research and development projects that operate in the highly complex,

Figure 1. Percentage of citizens with mobile phones in selected countries

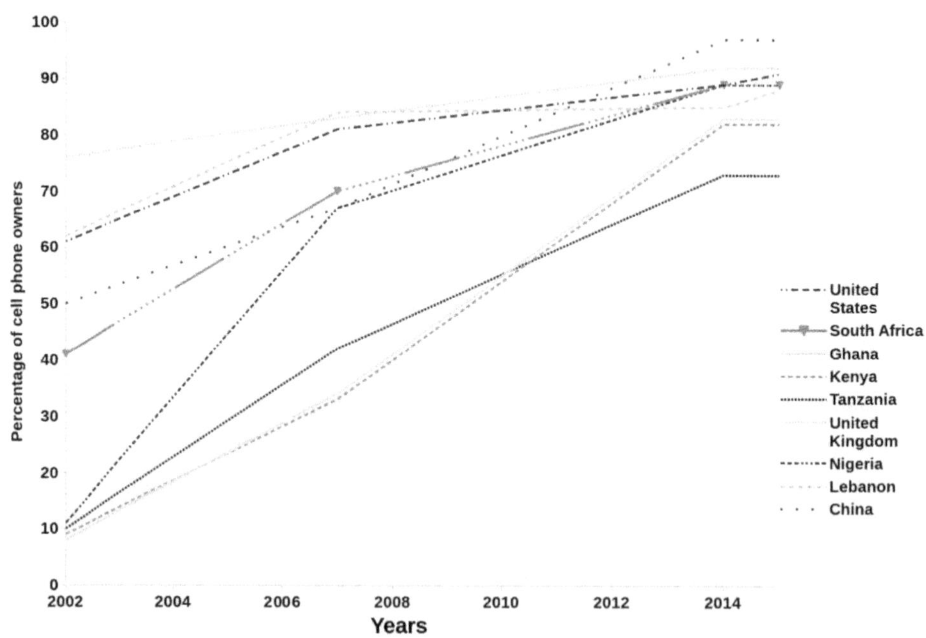

global and dynamic challenges of climate change, poverty, armed conflicts, and other crises. Kittur (2010) reveals that crowdsourcing can be a tool for collaboration and creativity as it allows organization to seek for original thoughts and innovations from workers and stakeholders. Nyaanga (2015) underscores that it is better to solicit every bit of information about different stages of projects' implementation from citizens/stakeholders instead of waiting for officers in charge of Monitoring and Evaluation to visit the sites. Furthermore, a recent study by Sanga *et al.* (2016b) explored the application of crowdsourcing in agricultural extension activities. They proposed a framework that can enable farmers to report problems related to agriculture which can be answered promptly by extension officers and researchers via mobile phones, e-mail or web.

In summary, there is ample evidence from contemporary literature that crowdsourcing can bring about more effective results in many fields of development including governance in international development (Estellés-Arolas& González-Ladrón-De-Guevara, 2012; Bott & Young, 2012), Institutional governance (Kittur, 2010), value chain development (Whitla, 2009; Poetz & Schreier, 2012), dissemination of agricultural information (Sanga *et al.*, 2016a), management of natural resources (McLaren, 2012), health services (Blackwell *et al.*, 2016) and agricultural marketing (Juma *et al.*, 2017) .

Application and Limitations of Crowdsourcing in Tanzania

Mwangungulu *et al.* (2016) present the application of crowdsourcing in surveillance of malaria in Tanzania. The weakness of Mwangungulu's study is that it was only theoretical. Another project titled 'SEMA' focused on promoting the use of mobile phones by citizens to report and/ publish information related to water use problems on the Internet using web based-geographic information systems (WEB-GIS) (Wesselink *et al.*, 2015). Rowley (2013) devised an approach that allowed a crowd from pastoral communities to identify appropriate livestock grazing areas and locate these areas on maps. The weakness of this approach is that user involvement was through a manual process thereby making it difficult to create a dynamic community of practice from pastoralists who are nomadic. Juma *et al.* (2017) present problems, possibilities and opportunities related to the use of crowdsourcing in agricultural marketing. The use of crowdsourcing can be advantageous to rural communities especially the farmers to secure best prices upon selling agricultural products in markets.

Other notable initiatives with respect to crowdsourcing in Tanzania include the use of radio and televisions to source information (views) on a wide range of topical issues such as health and education from the citizens (Georgiadou *et al.*, 2011). These initiatives, which were mainly pioneered by Non-Government Organizations

(NGOs) such as 'TWAWEZA' and 'DARAJA', are increasingly being perfected and adopted by social media and have elicited massive public interest.

Apart from the initiatives by NGOs and private sector to uphold crowdsourcing as means to address common concerns, there have been similar initiatives through E-Government Agency to make the Government more transparent, accountable, and responsive to her citizens (Georgiadou *et al.*, 2011). In respect to this, there are websites that allow citizens to participate in reporting crimes[7], community wide challenges[8] and tracking status of complaints on services that are submitted to relevant authorizes such as providers of energy and transport services[9].

A common weakness with regard to these initiatives in Tanzania is that none has shown how computerized crowdsourcing platform can effectively be deployed in monitoring and evaluation of research and development projects. This deployment is critical in detecting and preventing frauds, misuse of resources and embezzlement of projects' funds (Chezue, 2013).

It is important to note the break-through with respect to citizens' efforts to use social media such as facebook, blogs and twitter for open journalism (Mohamed, 2012) and the freedom it accords to minimize acts related to projects' mismanagement. Also it is important to realize that public concerns raised through social media are not regulated by moderators (Baguma, 2014). Moreover, the freedom to report the acts of projects' mismanagement could be significantly impeded by the Cyber law in Tanzania that was ratified in 2016 (Leverkus, 2016). Thus, the use of crowdsourcing platform in monitoring and evaluation is an ideal approach towards promoting freer and fairer reporting of projects' information.

Monitoring and evaluation information system (MEIS[10]) is one of the earliest applications of crowdsourcing platform for Monitoring and Evaluation systems in Tanzania (Sanga et al., 2013). The system was developed as framework to ease the task of monitoring and evaluation of 17 research projects under Enhancing Pro-poor Innovations in Natural Resources and Agricultural Value-chains (EPINAV) programme at Sokoine University of Agriculture (SUA) (Sanga et al., 2016a). However, this system [11] was not designed to allow different actors and stakeholders of the agricultural and natural resources value chains to submit their monitoring and evaluation report online (Sanga et al., 2016a).

Thus, there is a need to upgrade such system to allow on-line submission of reports by value chain actors and stakeholders. All views from crowds who were jointly working with- or associated to these projects should have been part of the Monitoring and Evaluation report. This chapter demonstrated how crowdsourcing can be integrated in such a web-based Monitoring and Evaluation system and is an important milestone in filling the knowledge gap on this subject because there are only a few applications of this nature in developing countries that mainly focus on sectors others than agricultural and natural resources (Zhao & Zhu, 2014; Jarvis et al., 2015).

SOLUTIONS AND RECOMMENDATIONS

Crowdsourcing Platform for Monitoring and Evaluation

All users of this platform should be members of the Monitoring and Evaluation crowdsourcing community. In order to get access to the system a member has to be registered. The community involved some members who can only read and comment on the reports; and those who can read and write/update any of the project(s) information. The crowd involves a number of actors from SUA including: the Deputy Vice Chancellor Administration and Finance (DVC Administration & Finance), Chief Auditor, Directorate of Research and Publication, EPINAV Coordinator, Monitoring and Evaluation team and project members. Furthermore, this platform connects not only the team within SUA but also stakeholders from outside the University such as staff from the Ministry of Agriculture, Livestock and Fisheries and project partners from Ministry of Agriculture Training Institute (e.g. MATI Uyole, MATI Ilonga), Local Government Authority (e.g. Kilosa District Council) and Universities from Norway (e.g. Norwegian University of Life Sciences (NMBU)).

The following sections give explanations about different parts of the system:

Homepage of the System

The homepage of the crowdsourcing platform is shown in Figure 2. The page provides introduction information about EPINAV program and a list of approved projects. A visitor will have to login into the system in order to view project details. On the right-hand side of the home page is a list of important links to key stakeholders and other relevant information related to the project such as blogs, photo gallery, contacts, EPINAV home page and Tanzania government website.

Upon signing in, an administrator is presented with an interface as shown in Figure 2 that allows him/her to perform a variety of monitoring and evaluation functions such as viewing project details, budget, expenditure, summary for different projects and summary for specific activities associated with a project. Other functions include updating expenditure, registering and updating budget as well as deleting a project.

Figure 2. Log in interface for different project stakeholders

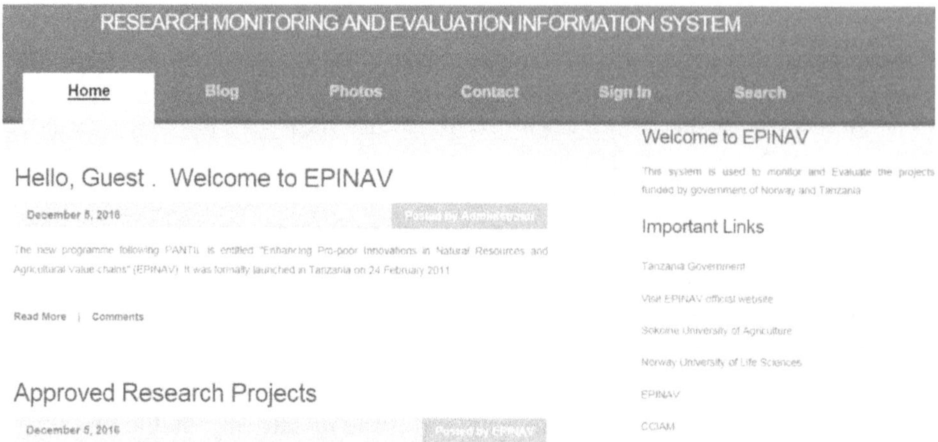

Registration of a New Member

A member has to be registered so as s/he can use the system (Figure 3).

Once a user has successfully logged in, the system will present an interface with different links to enable this user to view budget, expenditure and summary for project activities. Furthermore, depending on his/her privileges, s/he can update project information such as expenditure, budget, delete or register a new project (Figure 4).

Project Registration

On the project registration function, the administrator of the system is presented with a simple form as shown in Figure 5 to enter general information about each project. The form captures information such as sub theme, project name, starting date, ending date and fund allocated.

Once the project details are entered by administration, then a project leader can provide his / her project specific details. In order to add a new project a project leader must register it. Information such as project name, start date, end date and amount of funds allocated must be specified during the registration process.

Project Information

Once a user has chosen to view project details, s/he will be presented with an interface showing details of the project including members, goals, outputs, expenditure and budget as illustrated in Figure 6. Sharing this information among stakeholders of

Figure 3. Form for registering user

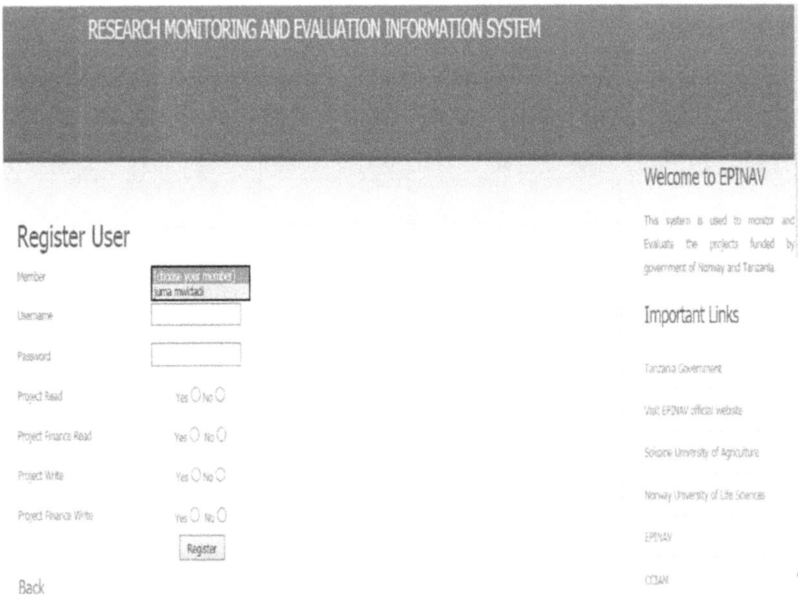

Figure 4. Form for accessing different functions

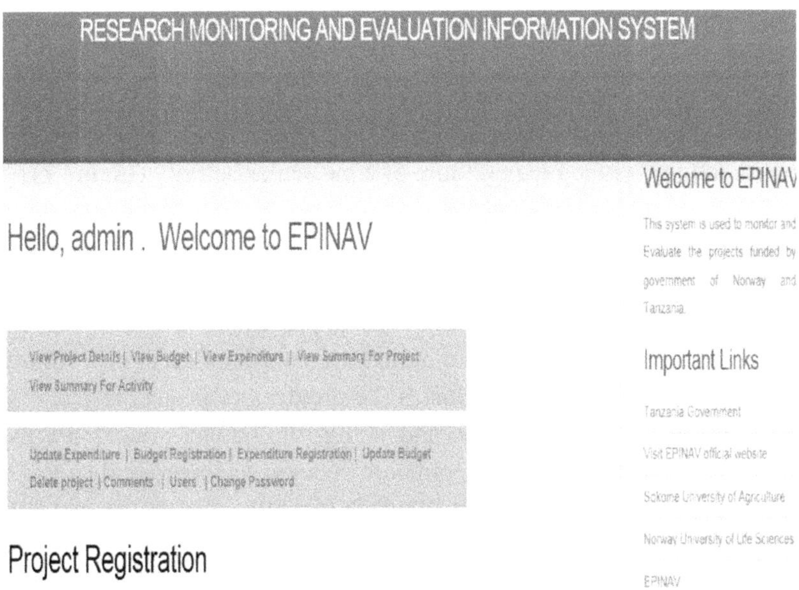

Figure 5. Form for registering a new project by project leader

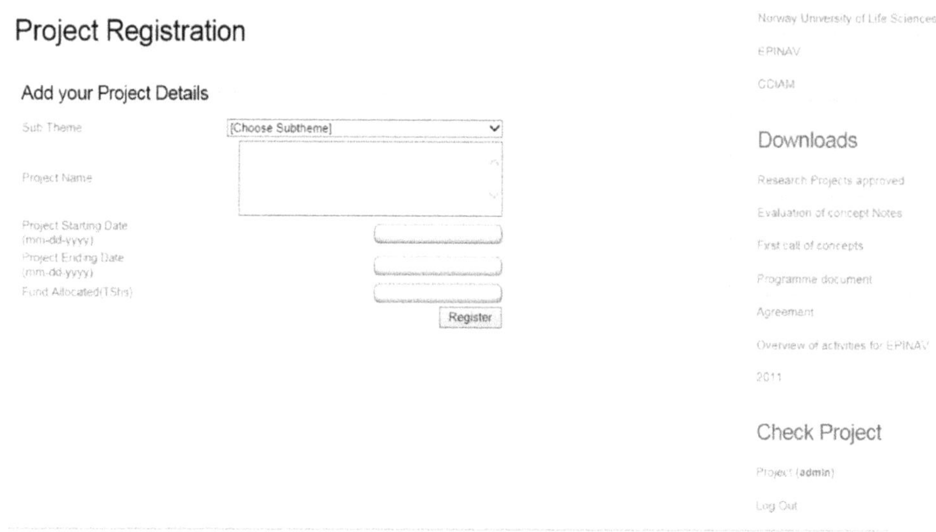

the project, increases transparence and fosters evaluation of project performance by the crowd with vested interest on the project.

Viewing Project Activity Details

A registered member can select a specific activity and view budget and expenditures of that activity. Furthermore, there is also a feature that allows one to select different activities including viewing expenditure of a particular activity (Figure 7).

Evaluating Project Progress

After selecting the first activity, the system will present a view of the expenditure status. The status use indicators like *danger*, *warning* or *success* to represent a state of the project. The system evaluates the progress of project as follows: if an activity has been completed in time and within the budget allocated a message labeled "*success*" will pop-up; if the amount spent exceeds the budget the system displays a "*danger*" message (Figure 8) which indicates that the project has spent more than its budget. When a message labeled "*warning*" pops-up it means the project expenditure is slower than expected. "*Success*" message is displayed when the project's expenditure is in line with the proposed expenditure for that period.

Figure 6. Form for accessing different information of the project which have been entered

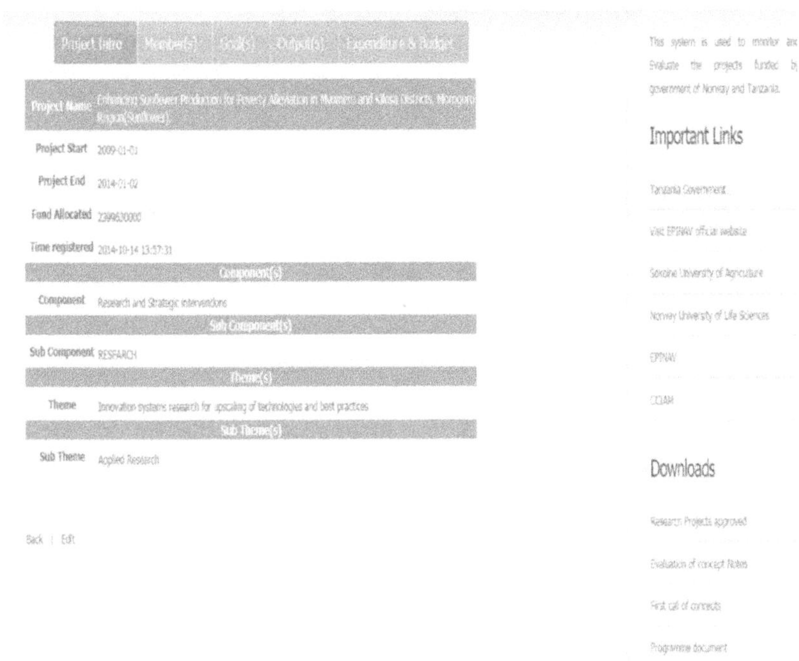

Figure 7. Selection of project, output and activity to view activity details

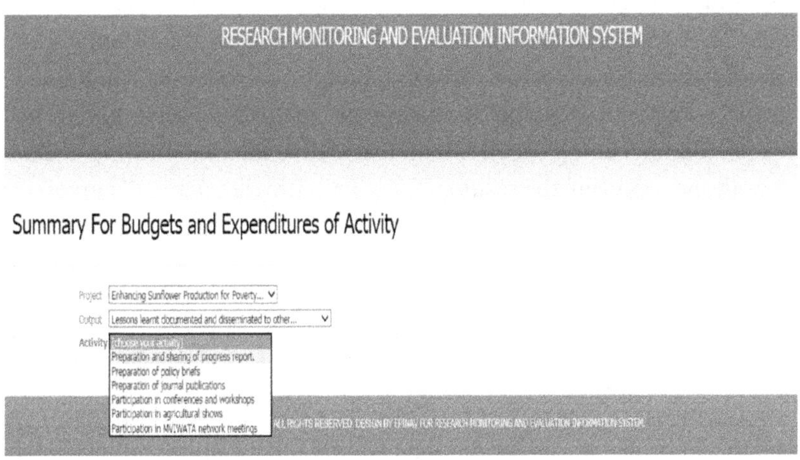

Figure 8. Interface for alert if project is danger, warning or success

DISCUSSION

The steps for developing performance or results based monitoring and evaluation system is similar to that of crowdsourcing platform for monitoring and evaluation of projects. This design has demonstrated how a member of a project or any user with proper credentials and roles as administrator or super user can do any of the following activities: formulation of outcomes and goals, selection of outcome indicators to monitor, setting specific targets and time line, monitoring of the results and analyzing and reporting the results. These activities are part and parcel of a good results based monitoring and evaluation information system (Kusek & Rist, 2001, 2004; Mackay, 2008; Sanga *et al*., 2013) and are consistent with the literature of crowdsourcing platform for monitoring and evaluation of projects. These functions enable policy makers, end user, project owner or project funder to determine whether the project is performing well or is lagging behind its schedule (Figure 8). The design provides immediate feedback for effective management of research and/development projects. Unlike the manual and other traditional monitoring and evaluation systems, the improved design allows for automated feedback as it allows immediate comparisons of achievements and targets not only for project activities but also use of financial resources. However, the system is different from crowdsourcing where users are allowed to participate in all stages of monitoring and evaluation irrespective of whether they are active or passive users (Charalabidis *et al.*, 2014). In this application, electronic participation of user was passive.

The platform enables the project implementers to be accountable for results, transparent, and furthermore, they can provide more efficient and effective services. Lastly, the platform acts as a tool to track the progress of the project without incurring material cost. The chapter has shown successful application of crowdsourcing platform in project monitoring and evaluation. The application responds to fundamental questions that Zhao and Zhu (2014) raise, particularly with respect to (i) Who is the provider of crowdsourcing? (ii) Who is the owner? (iii) What motivates users to participate in crowdsourcing? (iv) How is the mode of participating user defined? In this chapter, the provider of crowdsourcing is a public university (SUA) that owns the system. The users were motivated to participate freely without incentives because of the potential direct benefits they expected from good performance and evaluation of the project (see monitoring and evaluation report[12]). The mode of participating to crowdsourcing was through collaboration (Figure 2 through Figure 8). Thus, the crowdsourcing platform presented in this book chapter has all features needed for the design of a good crowdsourcing project (USAID, 2013; Zhao and Zhu, 2014). These features are:

1. **Matching End-User Demand:** Crowdsourcing platform should allow user to report all information regarding their project including uploading project's logical frame, approved budget for all activities, and milestones. Furthermore, it allows user to upload daily expenditure (Figures 2 to Figure 8).
2. **Creating Desirable Participation Incentives:** Crowdsourcing should allow the project members to report project's performance and get prompt feedback. According to the revised design this feedback is also, forwarded to the coordinating team who are responsible for monitoring of all projects (Figure 8). In broader context, this motivation can also create a positive incentive for governments to allow greater citizen scrutiny and participation in projects' monitoring and evaluation (Bott & Young, 2012).
3. **Ensuring Quick Sign-Up and Usability:** Since different stakeholders were involved in all phases of software development cycle (i.e. participatory development) the developed artifact has good and interactive interface. This allows quick sign-up and use of the system.
4. **Building Local Partnerships:** Since the crowdsourcing platform can aid the decision making of different stakeholders in a project, strong partnership between and across project team members and the coordinating unit is likely to emerge overtime.

5. **Establishing Local Physical Presence:** The project team members can report on the progress of the project anytime and anywhere. This is different from the manual system that requires reporters to fill specific forms and submit hard copies of these forms, which can conveniently be achieved when they are on campus.
6. **Assuring Data Quality:** The revised system has a feature which rejects data that does not conform to the appropriate format in an online form.
7. **Minimizing the Use of Human Resources:** Since the crowdsourcing platform distribute the tasks of reporting to many stakeholders (i.e. crowd), the use of centralized human resources is minimized.

According to Haklay *et al.* (2014), shared interest and benefits between participating stakeholders in a project is necessary for a successful crowdsourcing platform. In this regard, project coordinating officers and project members can voluntarily monitor project from distant locations for shared interests and benefits. The only problem with the revised system is that there is no policy to guide the use of data from the project evaluation and monitoring. This is similar to observation by Bott and Young, (2012) who noted that crowdsourcing project might succumb to problems with respect to how the open data will be used (Sanga *et al.*, 2016b).

CONCLUSION

This chapter has shown how different stakeholders who have common interest in a project can be involved in Monitoring and Evaluation of research and development projects through crowdsourcing platform. This is an empirical contribution in the field of crowdsourcing in monitoring and evaluation which, in many developing countries is still in its infancy stage (Zhao & Zhu, 2014).

Monitoring and evaluation which is based on multiple views of people in the crowd normally fuels efficiency, effectiveness and accountability of the people involved in projects. These factors are critical to ensure sustainability and successful performance of research and development projects. Moreover, the developed system shows that citizens are likely to be more connected and engaged in the Monitoring and Evaluation through crowdsourcing platform. The developed system also demonstrates that these advantages can be achieved at a reduced cost of information search and exchange. Thus, it is suggested that this crowdsourcing platform for Monitoring and Evaluation should be replicated so that the findings can be validated in other contextualized situations.

FUTURE RESEARCH DIRECTIONS

It is important to realize that crowdsourcing requires significant contribution from volunteers with varied perceptions and interests implying that the process is less predictable and controllable. The lesson learnt from the crowdsourcing platform for Monitoring and Evaluation information is that the participatory involvement of varied actors and stakeholders in Monitoring and Evaluation should be accompanied by relevant capacity building programmes to ensure high-level of awareness of the system for effective and consistent use. This opens up a new research agenda on how volunteers can be incentivized to participate in crowdsourcing platform for Monitoring and Evaluation. Motivating people to participate in crowdsourcing platform is a major problem.

To utilize the current advanced technologies like Google docs, Google calendars, Google maps and other cloud based systems on the Internet, the developed platform should be updated to integrate these technologies so as to broaden the source of information and enable more informed and prompt alerts. This will be achieved by using the Application Programming Interfaces (APIs) provided by those systems.

ACKNOWLEDGMENT

The authors gratefully acknowledge funding from EPINAV and support of individual projects under this programme. However, the authors take full responsibility for any errors and other shortcomings of this chapter. Also, we would like to thank Mr. Juma Mwidadi for developing a crowdsourcing platform for monitoring and evaluation projects.

REFERENCES

Baguma, J. (2014, May). Citizens' Advocacy for Public Accountability & Democratic Engagement through ICT Convergence in Eastern Africa. In Conference for E-Democracy and Open Governement (p. 449). Academic Press.

Blackwell, K. A., Travis, M. J., Arbuckle, M. R., & Ross, D. A. (2016). Crowdsourcing medical education. *Medical Education*, *50*(5), 576–576. doi:10.1111/medu.13010 PMID:27072463

Bott, M., & Young, G. (2012). The role of crowdsourcing for better governance in international development. Praxis: *The Fletcher. Journal of Human Security*, *27*(1), 47–70.

Charalabidis, Y. N., Loukis, E., Androutsopoulou, A., Karkaletsis, V., & Triantafillou, A. (2014). Passive crowdsourcing in government using social media. *Transforming Government: People, Process and Policy*, *8*(2), 283–308.

Chezue, B. B. (2013). *Benefits of value for money in public service Projects the case of National Audit Office of Tanzania* (Masters' dissertation). Mzumbe University, Morogoro, Tanzania.

Estellés-Arolas, E., & González-Ladrón-De-Guevara, F. (2012). Towards an integrated crowdsourcing definition. *Journal of Information Science*, *38*(2), 189–200. doi:10.1177/0165551512437638

Georgiadou, Y., Bana, B., Becht, R., Hoppe, R., Ikingura, J., Kraak, M.-J., ... Verplanke, J. (2011). Sensors, empowerment, and accountability: A digital earth view from East Africa. *International Journal of Digital Earth*, *4*(4), 285–304. doi :10.1080/17538947.2011.585184

Haklay, M., Antoniou, V., Basiouka, S., Soden, R., & Mooney, P. (2014). *Crowdsourced geographic information use in government*. World Bank Publications.

Jarvis, A., Eitzinger, A., Koningstein, M., Benjamin, T., Howland, F., Andrieu, N., . . . Corner-Dolloff, C. (2015). *Less is more: the 5Q approach*. Scientific Report. International Center for Tropical Agriculture (CIAT). Available online at: http://dapa.ciat.cgiar.org/

Juma, M. F., Fue, K. G., Barakabitze, A. A., Nicodemus, N., Magesa, M. M., Kilima, F. T. M., & Sanga, C. A. (2017). Understanding Crowdsourcing of Agricultural Market Information in a Pilot Study: Promises, Problems and Possibilities (3Ps). *International Journal of Technology Diffusion*, *8*(4), 1–16. doi:10.4018/IJTD.2017100101

Kittur, A. (2010). Crowdsourcing, collaboration and creativity. *ACM Crossroads*, *17*(2), 22–26. doi:10.1145/1869086.1869096

Kosonen, M., Gan, C., Olander, H., & Blomqvist, K. (2013). My idea is our idea! Supporting user-driven innovation activities in crowdsourcing communities. *International Journal of Innovation Management*, *17*(03), 1–18. doi:10.1142/S1363919613400100

Kusek, Z., & Rist, C. (2001). Building a performance-based monitoring and evaluation system. *Evaluation Journal of Australia*, *1*(2), 14–23. doi:10.1177/1035719X0100100205

Kusek, Z., & Rist, C. (2004). *Ten steps to a Result-based monitoring and evaluation system: A Handbook for Development Practitioner*. Washington, DC: World Bank. doi:10.1596/0-8213-5823-5

Leverkus, P. J. A. (2016). *Catalyzing Governance: Limitations on the Freedom of Expression and its Impact on 'Watch-dogs' in Tanzania's Extractive Industries* (Master's thesis). University of Oslo, Oslo, Norway.

Mackay, K. (2008). *Building Monitoring and Evaluation Systems to Improve Government Performance, Evaluation Capacity Development*. World Bank. Retrieved from http://www.worldbank.org/ieg/ecd/better_government.html

McLaren, R. (2012). *Crowdsourcing Support of Land Administration*. Paper presented at Word Bank Conference on land and Poverty, Washington, DC. Retrieved from http://www.landandpoverty.com/agenda/pdfs/paper/mclaren_robin_paper.pdf

Mohamed, H. (2012). *The Impact of Citizen Journalism on Self Regulation: A Blessing or a Curse?* Retrieved from http://www.academia.edu/download/34292129/Citizen_journalism_and_media_ethics_-_PAPER.pdf

Mwangungulu, S. P., Sumaye, R. D., Limwagu, A. J., Siria, D. J., Kaindoa, E. W., & Okumu, F. O. (2016). Crowdsourcing Vector Surveillance: Using Community Knowledge and Experiences to Predict Densities and Distribution of Outdoor-Biting Mosquitoes in Rural Tanzania. *PLoS One*, *11*(6). doi:10.1371/journal.pone.0156388 PMID:27253869

Nyaanga, P. K. (2015). *Crowdsourcing As A Platform For Monitoring Government Projects* (Master's dissertation). Jomo Kenyatta University of Agriculture and Technology, Kenya.

Poetz, M. K., & Schreier, M. (2012). The value of crowdsourcing: Can users really compete with professionals in generating new product ideas? *Journal of Product Innovation Management*, *29*(2), 245–256. doi:10.1111/j.1540-5885.2011.00893.x

Rowley, T. (2013). Participatory digital map-making in arid areas of Kenya and Tanzania. In: IIED, 2013. Participatory learning and action n.66. Tools for supporting sustainable natural resource management and livelihoods. International Institute for Environment and Development (IIED), London.

Sanga, C., Fue, K., Nicodemus, N., & Kilima, F. (2013). Web-based System for Monitoring and Evaluation of Agricultural Projects. *International Journal of Interdisciplinary Studies on Information Technology and Business*, *1*(1), 17–43.

Sanga, C. A., Masamaki, J. P., Fue, K. G., Mlozi, M. R. S., & Tumbo, S. D. (2016b). Experimenting Open Agricultural Extension Service in Tanzania: A case of Kilosa Open Data Initiative (KODI). *Journal of Scientific and Engineering Research*, *3*(6), 116–124.

Sanga, C. A., Phillipo, J., Mlozi, M. R. S., Haug, R., & Tumbo, S. D. (2016a). Crowdsourcing platform " Ushaurikilimo " enabling questions answering between farmers, extension agents and researchers. *International Journal of Instructional Technology and Distance Learning*, *13*(10), 19–28.

USAID. (2013). *Crowdsourcing Applications For Agricultural Development in Africa*. USAID.

Wesselink, A., Hoppe, R., & Lemmens, R. (2015). Not just a tool. Taking context into account in the development of a mobile app for rural water supply in Tanzania. *Water Alternatives*, *8*(2).

Whitla, P. (2009). Crowdsourcing and its application in marketing activities. *Contemporary Management Research*, *5*(1). doi:10.7903/cmr.1145

Zhao, Y., & Zhu, Q. (2014). Evaluation on crowdsourcing research: Current status and future direction. *Information Systems Frontiers*, *16*(3), 417–434. doi:10.100710796-012-9350-4

KEY TERMS AND DEFINITIONS

Budget: The map that provides how the project funds and expenditure will be done.

Component: A sub part of the EPINAV project.

Crowdsourcing: The act of using internet to get information from large number of people involved in an activity.

Deadline: The time at which the activity or component should be accomplished.

Evaluation: The act of making rational judgement on the progress of project on regard to timeline and budget.

Expenditure: The amount of funds that was used to accomplish a certain activity or component.

Funds: The amount of money available to be used.

Monitoring: The act of checking and observing the project progress over time.

Output: Results expected to be delivered by each activity done in an EPINAV project.

Platform: The standard computer system that provide the directions on how it can run and execute a particular task.

Project: A particular work or research planned and designed to achieve a particular EPINAV theme.

Theme: The directive subject of the particular EPINAV projects.

ENDNOTES

1. http://www.web2fordev.net/en/article/monitoring-and-evaluation-crowdsourcing-project-impact.html
2. http://icollaborate.blogspot.com/2008/06/google-docs-as-online-monitoring-system.html
3. https://www.globalgiving.org
4. https://www.ushahidi.com/
5. http://ushaurikilimo.org/maswalimajibu.php
6. https://www.rapidsms.org/
7. http://www.policeforce.go.tz/index.php/sw/julisha-uhalifu
8. http://www.wananchi.go.tz/
9. http://www.sumatra.go.tz/index.php/submit-enquiries
10. http://meis.ushaurikilimo.org/
11. http://ushaurikilimo.org/slide/
12. https://www.nmbu.no/sites/default/files/pdfattachments/epinav_mid-term_review_final_report.pdf

Compilation of References

Abrahamson, E. (1991). Managerial Fads and Fashions: The diffusion and rejection of innovations. *Academy of Management Review*, *16*, 586–612.

Abrahamson, E. (1996). Management fashion, academic fashion, and enduring truths. *Academy of Management Review*, *21*(3), 616–618.

Abrahamson, E., & Eisenman, M. (2008). Employee-management techniques: Transient fads or trending fashions? *Administrative Science Quarterly*, *53*(4), 719–744. doi:10.2189/asqu.53.4.719

Abrahamson, E., & Fairchild, G. (1999). Management fashion: Lifecycles, triggers, and collective learning processes. *Administrative Science Quarterly*, *44*(4), 708–740. doi:10.2307/2667053

Ackoff, R. L. (1989). From data to wisdom. *Journal of Applied Systems Analysis*, *15*, 3–9.

Ackoff, R. L. (1996). On learning and the systems that facilitate it. *Center for Quality of Management Journal.*, *5*(2), 27–35.

Afgan, N. H., & Carvalho, M. G. (2010). The Knowledge Society: A Sustainability Paradigme. *The CADMUS Journal*, *1*(1), 28–41.

Afuah, A., & Tucci, C. L. (2012). Crowdsourcing as a solution to distant search. *Academy of Management Review*, *37*(3), 355–379. doi:10.5465/amr.2010.0146

Ahmed, Z. U. (2004). Accountability and Control in Non-Governmental Organisations (NGOs) – A Case of Bangladesh. *Proceeding Fourth Asia Pacific Interdisciplinary Research in Accounting Conference.*

Aitamurto, T., Leiponen, A., & Tee, R. (2011). The promise of idea crowdsourcing: Benefits, contexts, limitations. *White Paper June, 2*(30)

Ajzen, I. (1991). The Theory of Planned Behavior. *Organizational Behavior and Human Decision Processes*, *50*(2), 179–211. doi:10.1016/0749-5978(91)90020-T

Akhavan, P., Hosseini, S. M., Abbasi, M., & Manteghi, M. (2015). Knowledge-sharing determinants, behaviors, and innovative work behaviors: An integrated theoretical view and empirical examination. *Aslib Journal of Information Management*, *67*(5), 562–591. doi:10.1108/AJIM-02-2015-0018

Alam, S., & Campbell, J. (2013). *Dynamic Changes in Organizational Motivations to Crowdsourcing for GLAMs*. Paper presented at the International Conference on Information Systems, Milan.

Alam, S. L., & Campbell, J. (2017). Temporal Motivations of Volunteers to Participate in Cultural Crowdsourcing Work. *Information Systems Research*, *28*(4), 744–759. doi:10.1287/isre.2017.0719

Alavi, M., & Leidner, D. E. (2001). Review: Knowledge Management and Knowledge Management Systems: Conceptual Foundations and Research Issues. *Management Information Systems Quarterly*, *25*(1), 107–136. doi:10.2307/3250961

Alavi, M., & Tiwana, A. (2002). Knowledge Integration in Virtual Teams: The Potential Role of KMS. *Journal of the American Society for Information Science and Technology*, *53*(12), 1029–1037. doi:10.1002/asi.10107

Albors, J., Ramos, J. C., & Hervas, J. L. (2008). New learning network paradigms: Communities of objectives, crowdsourcing, wikis and open source. *International Journal of Information Management*, *28*(3), 194–202. doi:10.1016/j.ijinfomgt.2007.09.006

Allarakhia, M. (2011). *Novartis Institutes for Biomedical Research*. CanBiotech Inc.

Alnylam. (n.d.). Investors. *Alnylam*. Retrieved from: http://investors.alnylam.com/releasedetail. cfm?ReleaseID=466757

Amabile, T. M., Conti, R., Coon, H., Lazenby, J., & Herron, M. (1996). Assessing the work environment for creativity. *Academy of Management Journal*, *39*(5), 1154–1184. doi:10.2307/256995

Amrollahi, A. (2015). *A process model for crowdsourcing: insights from the literature on implementation*. Paper presented at the 26th Australasian Conference on Information Systems, Adelaide, Australia.

Amrollahi, A., & Ghapnchi, A. H. (2016). *Open strategic planning in universities: a case study*. Paper presented at the System Sciences (HICSS), 2016 49th Hawaii International Conference on. 10.1109/HICSS.2016.54

Amrollahi, A., Ghapanchi, A., & Talaei-Khoei, A. (2014). *A systematic review of the current theory base in the crowdsourcing literature*. Paper presented at the 28th Australian and New Zealand Academy of Management Conference.

Amrollahi, A., Ghapanchi, A., & Talaei-Khoei, A. (2014). *Using Crowdsourcing Tools for Implementing Open Strategy: A Case Study in Education*. Paper presented at the Twentieth Americas Conference on Information System (AMCIS 2014), Savannah, GA.

Amrollahi, A., Khansari, M., & Manian, A. (2014). *How Open Source Software Succeeds? A Review of Research on Success of Open Source Software*. Academic Press.

Amrollahi, A., Ghapanchi, A. H., & Talaei-Khoei, A. (2013). A Systematic Literature Review on Strategic Information Systems Planning: Insights from the Past Decade. *Pacific Asia Journal of the Association for Information Systems*, *5*(2), 39–66.

Amrollahi, A., Ghapanchi, A. H., & Talaei-Khoei, A. (2014). Three Decades of Research on Strategic Information System Plan Development. *Communications of the Association for Information Systems*, *34*(1), 1440–1467.

Amrollahi, A., Khansari, M., & Manian, A. (2015). *Success of Open Source in Developing Countries: The Case of Iran. In Open Source Technology: Concepts, Methodologies, Tools, and Applications* (pp. 1126–1142). IGI Global. doi:10.4018/978-1-4666-7230-7.ch055

Amrollahi, A., & Rowlands, B. (2017). Collaborative open strategic planning: A method and case study. *Information Technology & People*, *30*(4), 832–852. doi:10.1108/ITP-12-2015-0310

Amrollahi, A., Tahaei, M., & Khansari, M. (2016). *Measuring the Effectiveness of Wikipedia Articles: How Does Open Content Succeed? In Handbook of Research on Innovations in Information Retrieval, Analysis, and Management* (pp. 41–61). IGI Global. doi:10.4018/978-1-4666-8833-9.ch002

Anantatmula, V. S., & Stankosky, M. (2008). KM Criteria for Different Types of Organisations. *International Journal of Knowledge and Learning*, *4*(1), 18–35. doi:10.1504/IJKL.2008.019735

Anderson, D. P. (2004). A system for public-resource computing and storage. In *Fifth IEEE/ACM International Workshop on Grid Computing. Berkeley Open Infrastructure for Network Computing*. IEEE.

ANDi. (n.d.). *ANDi: Health innovation for development*. Retrieved from: http://www.andi-africa.org

Andriole, S. J. (2010). Business impact of Web 2.0 technologies. *Communications of the ACM*, *53*(12), 67. doi:10.1145/1859204.1859225

Ansari, S. M., Fiss, P. C., & Zajac, E. J. (2010). Made to fit: How practices vary as they diffuse. *Academy of Management Review*, *35*(1), 67–92. doi:10.5465/AMR.2010.45577876

Antin, J., & Shaw, A. (2012). Social desirability bias and self-reports of motivation: a study of amazon mechanical turk in the US and India. *Proceedings of the SIGCHI Conference on Human Factors in Computing Systems*. 10.1145/2207676.2208699

Applehans, W., Globe, A., & Laugero, G. (1999). *Managing Knowledge. A Practical Web-Based Approach*. Addison-Wesley.

Archak, N. (2010). *Money, Glory and Cheap Talk: Analyzing Strategic Behavior of Contestants in Simultaneous Crowdsourcing Contests on Topcoder.Com*. Retrieved from http:// pages.stern.nyu.edu/~narchak/wfp0004-archak.pdf

Ariff, M. I. M. (2013). *Exploring the role of Transactive Memory Systems in Virtual Teams*. Victoria, Australia: The University of Melbourne.

Ariff, M. I. M., Milton, S. K., Bosua, R., & Sharma, R. (2011). Exploring the role of ICT in the formation of transactive memory systems in virtual teams. In *Proceedings of the 15th Pacific Asia Conference on Information Systems: Quality Research in Pacific, PACIS 2011* (pp. 1-12). Queensland: Queensland University of Technology.

Arntzen, A. A. B., Worasinchai, L., & Ribière, V. M. (2009). An Insight into Knowledge Management Practices at Bangkok University. *Journal of Knowledge Management*, *13*(2), 127–144. doi:10.1108/13673270910942745

Asrar-ul-haq, M., & Anwar, S. (2016). A systematic review of knowledge management and knowledge sharing: Trends, issues, and challenges. *Cogent Business & Management*, *3*(1), 1–17. doi:10.1080/23311975.2015.1127744

Astley, W. G., & Zammuto, R. F. (1992). Organization Science, Managers and Language Games'. *Organization Science*, *3*(4), 443–460. doi:10.1287/orsc.3.4.443

Atack, I. (1999). Four Criteria of Development NGO Legitimacy. *World Development*, *27*(5), 855–864. doi:10.1016/S0305-750X(99)00033-9

Baccaro, L. (2001). Civil Society, NGOs, and Decent Work Policies: Sorting Out the Issues. ILO/International Institute for Labour Studies.

Bach, P. M., Lee, R. L., & Carroll, M. J. (2009). *Knowledge Management Challenges in the Non-Profit Sector*. Retrieved from http://mfile.narotama.ac.id/files/Information%20System/Encyclopedia%20of%20Information%20Science%20and%20Technology%20(2nd%20Edition)/Knowledge%20Management%20Challenges%20in%20the%20Non-Proft%20Sector.pdf

Baguma, J. (2014, May). Citizens' Advocacy for Public Accountability & Democratic Engagement through ICT Convergence in Eastern Africa. In Conference for E-Democracy and Open Governement (p. 449). Academic Press.

Baguma, R. (2016). *Knowledge Societies Policy Handbook: United Nations University- Operating Unit on Policy Driven Electronic Governance*. UNU-EGOV.

Balamurugan, Ch., & Roy, S. (2013). Human computer interaction paradigm for business process task crowdsourcing. *Proceedings of the 11th Asia Pacific Conference on Computer Human Interaction*, 364-273. 10.1145/2525194.2525294

Bandura, A. (1977). Self-efficacy: Toward a unifying theory of behavioral change. *Psychological Review*, *84*(2), 191–215. doi:10.1037/0033-295X.84.2.191 PMID:847061

Bandura, A. (1986). *Social foundations of thought and action: A social cognitive theory*. Englewood Cliffs, NJ: Prentice-Hall.

Bandura, A. (2002). Social cognitive theory of mass communication. In J. Bryant & M. B. Oliver (Eds.), *Media Effects: Advances in Theory and Research* (pp. 122–138). New York, NY: Routledge.

Barney, J. (1991). Firm resources and sustained competitive advantage. *Journal of Management*, *17*(1), 99–120. doi:10.1177/014920639101700108

Basiouka, S., & Potsiou, C. (2014). The volunteered geographic information in cadastre: Perspectives and citizens' motivations over potential participation in mapping. *GeoJournal*, *79*(3), 343–355. doi:10.100710708-013-9497-7

Bass, B. M. (1999). On the taming of charisma: A reply to Janice Beyer. *The Leadership Quarterly*, *10*(4), 541–553. doi:10.1016/S1048-9843(99)00030-2

Bass, B. M., & Avolio, B. J. (1997). *Full range of leadership: Manual for the Multifactor Leadership Questionnaire*. Palo Alto, CA: Mind Garden.

Bassi, L. J. (1997). Harnessing the Power of Intellectual Capital. *Training & Development*, *51*(12), 25–31.

Basto, D., Flavin, T., & Patino, C. (2010). *Crowdsourcing Public Policy Innovation*. Working Paper, Heinz College Carnegie Mellon University.

Battistella, C., & Nonino, F. (2012). Open innovation web-based platforms: The impact of different forms of motivation on collaboration. *Innovation, 14*(4), 557–575. doi:10.5172/impp.2012.14.4.557

Battistella, C., & Nonino, F. (2013). Exploring the impact of motivations on the attraction of innovation roles in open innovation web-based platforms. *Production Planning and Control, 24*(2-3), 226–245. doi:10.1080/09537287.2011.647876

Baud, I. (2016). Digitisation and Participation in Urban Governance: The Contribution of ICT-Based Spatial Knowledge Management in Indian Cities. In Local Governance, Economic Development and Institutions (pp. 86-97). Palgrave Macmillan UK.

Bayus, B. L. (2012). *Crowdsourcing New Product Ideas Over Time: An Analysis of Dell's Ideastorm Community.* UNC Kenan-Flagler Research Paper 5.

Becerra-Fernandez, I., & Sabherwal, R. (2010). *Knowledge Management: Systems and Processes*. London: M.E. Sharpe.

Bellinger, G., Durval, C., Mills, A. (2004). *Data, information, knowledge, and wisdom*. Academic Press.

Benders, J., & van Veen, K. (2001). What's in a fashion? Interpretative viability and management fashions. *Organization, 8*(1), 48–49. doi:10.1177/135050840181003

Berkeley Open Infrastructure for Network Computing. (n.d.). In *Wikipedia*. Retrieved May 29, 2017, from https://en.wikipedia.org/wiki/Berkeley_Open_Infrastructure_for_Network_Computing

Bernhard, S. (Ed.). (2010). *Leveraging Applications of Formal Methods, Verification, and Validation*. Berlin: Springer.

Bernstein, J. (2011). The Data-Information-Knowledge-Wisdom Hierarchy and its Antithesis. *NASKO, 2*(1).

Bhatt, G. D. (2001). Knowledge Management in Organizations: Examining the Interaction Between Technologies, Techniques, And People. *Journal of Knowledge Management, 5*(1), 68–75. doi:10.1108/13673270110384419

Bianchi, M., Cavaliere, A., Chiaroni, D., Frattini, F., & Chiesa, V. (2011). Organisational modes for Open Innovation in the bio-pharmaceutical industry: An exploratory analysis. *Technovation, 31*(1), 22–33. doi:10.1016/j.technovation.2010.03.002

Blackman, D., & Kennedy, M. (2009). Knowledge Management and Effective University Governance. *Journal of Knowledge Management, 13*(6), 547–563. doi:10.1108/13673270910997187

Blackwell, K. A., Travis, M. J., Arbuckle, M. R., & Ross, D. A. (2016). Crowdsourcing medical education. *Medical Education*, *50*(5), 576–576. doi:10.1111/medu.13010 PMID:27072463

Bloice, L., & Burnett, S. (2016). Barriers to Knowledge Sharing in Third Sector Social Care: A Case Study. *Journal of Knowledge Management*, *20*(1), 125–145. doi:10.1108/JKM-12-2014-0495

Bobbitt, L. M., & Dabholkar, P. A. (2001). Integrating attitudinal theories to understand and predict use of technology-based self-service: The internet as an illustration. *International Journal of Service Industry Management*, *12*(5), 423–450. doi:10.1108/EUM0000000006092

Bock, G. W., & Kim, Y. G. (2002). Breaking the myths of rewards: An exploratory study of attitudes about knowledge sharing. *Information Resources Management Journal*, *15*(2), 14–21. doi:10.4018/irmj.2002040102

Bock, G. W., Zmud, R. W., Kim, Y., & Lee, J. (2005). Behavioral intention formation in knowledge sharing: Examining the roles of extrinsic motivators, social psychological forces, and organizational climate. *Management Information Systems Quarterly*, *29*(1), 87–111. doi:10.2307/25148669

Boellstorff, T. (2015). Making big data, in theory. In T. Boellstorff & B. Maurer (Eds.), *Data, now bigger and better!* (pp. 87–108). Chicago: Prickly Paradigm Press.

BOINC client–server technology. (n.d.). In *Wikipedia*. Retrieved May 29, 2017, from https://en.wikipedia.org/wiki/BOINC_client–server_technology

Bonnington, C. (2015, February 10). *In less than two years, a smartphone could be your only computer.* Retrieved June 27, 2016, from http://www.wired.com/2015/02/smartphone-only-computer/

Bott, M., & Young, G. (2012). The role of crowdsourcing for better governance in international development. Praxis: *The Fletcher. Journal of Human Security*, *27*(1), 47–70.

Boudreau, K. J., & Lakhani, K. R. (2013). Using the crowd as an innovation partner. *Harvard Business Review*, *91*(4), 60–69. PMID:23593768

Bourque, L. B., & Fielder, E. P. (2003). *How to Conduct Self-Administered and Mail Survey* (2nd ed.). Thousand Oaks, CA: Sage Publications. doi:10.4135/9781412984430

Boyd, D., & Crawford, K. (2012). Critical Questions for Big Data. *Information Communication and Society*, *15*(5), 662–679. doi:10.1080/1369118X.2012.678878

Brabham, D. C. (2008). Moving the crowd at iStockphoto: The composition of the crowd and motivations for participation in a crowdsourcing application. *First Monday, 13*(6). doi:10.5210/fm.v13i6.2159

Brabham, D. C. (2012a). The effectiveness of crowdsourcing public participation in a planning context. *First Monday, 17*(12). doi:10.5210/fm.v17i12.4225

Brabham, D. C. (2012b). Motivations for participation in a crowdsourcing application to improve public engagement in transit planning. *Journal of Applied Communication Research, 40*(3), 307–328. doi:10.1080/00909882.2012.693940

Brabham, D. C. (2013). *Using crowdsourcing in government.* Washington, DC: IBM Center for the Business of Government.

Brabham, D. C. (2015). *Crowdsourcing in the Public Sector.* Georgetown University Press.

Brändle, A. (2005). *Too Many Cooks Don't Spoil the Broth.* Paper presented at the The First International Wikimedia Conference, Frankfurt, Germany.

Brandon, D. P., & Hollingshead, A. B. (2004). Transactive Memory Systems in Organisations: Matching Tasks, Expertise, and People. *Organization Science, 15*(6), 633–644. doi:10.1287/orsc.1040.0069

Bretschneider, U., & Leimeister, J. M. (2016). Motivation for Open Innovation and Crowdsourcing: Why Does the Crowd Engage in Virtual Ideas Communities? In Open Tourism (pp. 109–120). Springer.

Bretschneider, U., Knaub, K., & Wieck, E. (2014). *Motivations for Crowdfunding: What Drives the Crowd to Invest in Start-Ups?* Academic Press.

Briggs, R. O. (2006). On theory-driven design and deployment of collaboration systems. *International Journal of Human-Computer Studies, 64*(7), 573–582. doi:10.1016/j.ijhcs.2006.02.003

Brockman, B. K., & Morgan, R. M. (2003). The Role of Existing Knowledge in New Product Innovativeness and Performance. *Decision Sciences, 34*(2), 385–419. doi:10.1111/1540-5915.02326

Brown, G., & Yule, G. (2003). *Discourse Analysis.* Cambridge, UK: Cambridge University Press.

Brynjolfsson, E., & McAfee, A. (2011). *Race Against the Machine: How the Digital Revolution is Accelerating Innovation, Driving Productivity, and Irreversibly Transforming Employment and the Economy.* Lexington, MA: Digital Frontier Press.

Brynjolfsson, E., & Mcaffee, A. (2012). Big data: The management revolution. *Harvard Business Review, 90*(10), 60–68. PMID:23074865

Budhathoki, N. R., & Haythornthwaite, C. (2013). Motivation for Open Collaboration Crowd and Community Models and the Case of OpenStreetMap. *The American Behavioral Scientist, 57*(5), 548–575. doi:10.1177/0002764212469364

Bukowitz, W. R., & Williams, R. L. (2000). *The Knowledge Management Fieldbook, Financial Time*. London: Prentice Hall.

Burger-Helmchen, T., & Pénin, J. (2010). The limits of crowdsourcing inventive activities: What do transaction cost theory and the evolutionary theories of the firm teach us? *Workshop on Open Source Innovation*, France.

Burger-Helmchen, T., & Pénin, J. (2010). The Limits of Crowdsourcing Inventive Activities: What Do Transaction Cost Theory and the Evolutionary Theories of the Firm Teach Us? *Workshop on Open Source Innovation*, Strasbourg, France.

Buyapowa. (2014). *The three stages of Social maturity*. Retrieved from http://www.welikecrm.it/wp-content/uploads/2014/06/Social-Maturity.pdf

Byrne, B. M. (2016). *Structural Equation Modeling With AMOS: Basic Concepts, Applications, and Programming* (3rd ed.). Taylor and Francis.

Cacciattolo, K. (2015). *Understanding Social Phenomenon, An Analysis of the Combination of Qualitative and Quantitative Methods to Understand Social Phenomenon*. Academic Press.

Callaghan, C. W. (2015). Crowdsourced 'R&D' and medical research. *British Medical Bulletin, 115*(1), 1–10. doi:10.1093/bmb/ldv035 PMID:26307550

Cardoso, L., Meireles, A., & Peralta, C. F. (2012). Knowledge Management and Its Critical Factors in Social Economy Organizations. *Journal of Knowledge Management, 16*(2), 267–284. doi:10.1108/13673271211218861

Carson, P. P., Lanier, P. A., Carson, K. D., & Birkenmeier, B. J. (1999). A historical perspective on fad adoption and abandonment. *Journal of Management History, 5*(6), 320–333. doi:10.1108/13552529910288109

Carson, P. P., Lanier, P. A., Carson, K. D., & Guidry, B. N. (2000). Clearing a path through the management fashion jungle: Some preliminary trailblazing. *Academy of Management Journal, 43*(6), 1143–1158. doi:10.2307/1556342

Castells, M. (2001). *The Internet Galaxy: Reflections on the Internet, Business, and Society*. Oxford, UK: Oxford University Press. doi:10.1007/978-3-322-89613-1

Cerello, P. (n.d.). *Grid Computing in Medical Applications*. Retrieved from https://indico.cern.ch/event/408139/contributions/979806/attachments/815730/1117739/chep2006-mga.pdf

Chamberlin, D. D., & Boyce, R. F. (1974, April). SEQUEL: A structured English query language. *Proc. 1974 ACM SIGFIDET Workshop*, 249-264.

Chandler, D., & Kapelner, A. (2013). Breaking monotony with meaning: Motivation in crowdsourcing markets. *Journal of Economic Behavior & Organization*, *90*, 123–133. doi:10.1016/j.jebo.2013.03.003

Chang, C. M., Hsu, M. H., & Lee, Y. J. (2015). Factors Influencing Knowledge-Sharing Behavior in Virtual Communities: A Longitudinal Investigation. *Information Systems Management*, *32*(4), 331–340. doi:10.1080/10580530.2015.1080002

Chan, K., Li, S., & Zhu, J. (2015). Fostering Customer Ideation in Crowdsourcing Communities: The Role of Online Interactions with Peers and Firm. *Journal of Interactive Marketing*, *31*, 42–62. doi:10.1016/j.intmar.2015.05.003

Charalabidis, Y. N., Loukis, E., Androutsopoulou, A., Karkaletsis, V., & Triantafillou, A. (2014). Passive crowdsourcing in government using social media. *Transforming Government: People, Process and Policy*, *8*(2), 283–308.

Chen, L., Marsden, J. R., & Zhang, Z. (2012). Theory and analysis of company-sponsored value cocreation. *Journal of Management Information Systems*, *29*(2), 141–172. doi:10.2753/MIS0742-1222290206

Chesbrough, H. (2006), Open Innovation: A New Paradigm for Understanding Industrial Innovation. In Open Innovation Researching a New Paradigm. Oxford University Press.

Chesbrough, H. (2003). *Open Innovation. The New Imperative for Creating and Profiting from Technology*. Boston: Harvard Business School Press.

Chesbrough, H. W. (2010). Business Model Innovation: Opportunities and Barriers. *Long Range Planning*, 43.

Chesbrough, H. W., & Crowther, A. K. (2006). Beyond High Tech: Early Adopters of Open Innovation in other Industries. *R & D Management*, *36*(3), 229–236. doi:10.1111/j.1467-9310.2006.00428.x

Chezue, B. B. (2013). *Benefits of value for money in public service Projects the case of National Audit Office of Tanzania* (Masters' dissertation). Mzumbe University, Morogoro, Tanzania.

Chi, E. H., & Bernstein, M. S. (2012). Leveraging Online Populations for Crowdsourcing. *IEEE Internet Computing*, *16*(5), 10–12. doi:10.1109/MIC.2012.111

Chittoo, H., Nowbutsing, B. M., & Ramchurn, R. (2010). Knowledge Management: Promises and Premises. *Global Journal of Management and Business Research*, *10*(1), 123–131.

Choy, C. S., & Suk, C. Y. (2005). Critical Factors in the Successful Implementation of Knowledge Management. *Journal of Knowledge Management Practice*, *6*(1), 234–258.

Choy, K., & Schlagwein, D. (2016). Crowdsourcing for a better world: On the relation between IT affordances and donor motivations in charitable crowdfunding. *Information Technology & People*, *29*(1), 221–247. doi:10.1108/ITP-09-2014-0215

Climateprediction.net. (n.d.). Retrieved May 29, 2017, from http://www.climateprediction.net/

Codd, E. F. (1970, June). A relational model of data for large shared data banks. *Communications of the ACM*, *13*(6), 377–387. doi:10.1145/362384.362685

Cole, R. E. (1989). *Strategies for Learning: Small Group Activities in American, Japanese, and Swedish Industry*. Berkeley, CA: University of California Press.

Colquitt, J. A., Scott, B. A., & LePine, J. A. (2007). Trust, trustworthiness, and trust propensity: A meta-analytic test of their unique relationships with risk taking and job performance. *The Journal of Applied Psychology*, *92*(4), 909–927. doi:10.1037/0021-9010.92.4.909 PMID:17638454

Conversocial. (2017). *Social Maturity Index*. Retrieved from http://www.conversocial.com/hubfs/socialmaturity.pdf

Cooper, S., Khatib, F., Treuille, A., Barbero, J., Lee, J., Beenen, M., ... players, F. (2010). Predicting protein structures with a multiplayer online game. *Nature*, *466*(7307), 756–760. doi:10.1038/nature09304 PMID:20686574

Corfield, A., Paton, R., & Little, S. (2013). Does Knowledge Management Work in NGOs?: A Longitudinal Study. *International Journal of Public Administration*, *36*(3), 179–188. doi:10.1080/01900692.2012.749281

Crandall, W. R., Crandall, R. E., & Ashraf, M. (2006). *The perilous world of management fashion: An examination of their life cycles and the problem of scholarly lags*. Atlanta, GA: Academy of Management Proceedings.

Crane, L., & Self, R. J. (2014). Big Data Analytics: A Threat or an Opportunity for Knowledge Management? In L. Uden, D. Fuenzaliza Oshee, I. H. Ting, & D. Liberona (Eds.), *Knowledge Management in Organizations. KMO 2014. Lecture Notes in Business Information Processing* (Vol. 185, pp. 25–34). Cham: Springer. doi:10.1007/978-3-319-08618-7_3

Cukier, K., & Mayer-Schoenberger, V. (2013b). The Rise of Big Data. *Foreign Affairs*, *92*(3), 28–40.

Cukier, K., & Mayer-Schonberger, V. (2013a). *Big Data: A Revolution That Will Transform How We Live, Work and Think.* Boston, MA: Houghton Mifflin Harcourt.

Cummings, J. N. (2004). Work groups, structural diversity, and knowledge sharing in a global organization. *Management Science*, *50*(3), 352–364. doi:10.1287/mnsc.1030.0134

Czarniawska-Joerges, B. (1995). Narration or Science? Collapsing the division in organization studies. *Organization*, *2*(1), 11–33. doi:10.1177/135050849521002

D, S. E., Moraes, K., & de Souza, J. M. (2012). CSCWD: Five characters in search of crowds. *Proceedings of the 2012 IEEE 16th International Conference on Computer Supported Cooperative Work in Design (CSCWD).*

Davenport, T. H. (1994). Saving IT's Soul: Human-Centered Information Management. *Harvard Business Review*, *72*(2).

Davenport, T. H. (2014). *Big data at work: Dispelling the myths, uncovering the opportunities.* Boston: Harvard Business Review Press. doi:10.15358/9783800648153

Davenport, T. H., Barth, P., & Bean, R. (2013). How 'big data' is different. *MIT Sloan Management Review*, *54*(1).

Davenport, T. H., De Long, D. W., & Beers, M. C. (1998). Successful Knowledge Management Projects. *Sloan Management Review*, *39*(2), 43–57.

Davenport, T. H., & Harris, J. G. (2007). *Computing analytics: the new science of winning*. Boston, MA: Harvard Business School Review Press.

Davenport, T. H., & Kim, J. (2013). *Keeping Up with the Quants: Your Guide to Understanding and Using Analytics*. Harvard Business Review Press.

Davenport, T. H., & Prusak, L. (1988). *Working Knowledge - How Organisations Manage What They Know*. Boston: Harvard Business School Press.

Davenport, T. H., & Prusak, L. (1998). *Working Knowledge: How Organizations Manage What They Know*. Boston: Harvard Business Press.

Davenport, T., & Prusak, L. (1998). *Working Knowledge*. Boston, MA: Harvard Business School Press.

Davis, J. G., & Lin, H. (2011). *Web 3.0 and Crowdservicing*. Paper presented at the AMCIS.

de Vasconcelos, J., Seixas, P. C., Lemos, P. G., & Kimble, C. (2005). Knowledge Management in Non-Governmental Organisations: A Partnership for the Future. *Proceedings of the 7th International Conference, Enterprise Information Systems (ICEIS)*.

de Vries, R. A., Truong, K. P., Kwint, S., Drossaert, C. H., & Evers, V. (2016). Crowd-Designed Motivation: Motivational messages for exercise adherence based on behavior change theory. *Proceedings of the 2016 CHI Conference on Human Factors in Computing Systems*. 10.1145/2858036.2858229

Dean, J., & Ghemawat, S. (2008). MapReduce: Simplified data processing on large clusters. *Communications of the ACM*, *51*(1), 107–113. doi:10.1145/1327452.1327492

Deci, E. L., & Ryan, R. M. (1985). *Intrinsic motivation and self-determination in human behavior*. New York: Plenum. doi:10.1007/978-1-4899-2271-7

Deci, E. L., & Ryan, R. M. (2000). The" what" and" why" of goal pursuits: Human needs and the self-determination of behavior. *Psychological Inquiry*, *11*(4), 227–268. doi:10.1207/S15327965PLI1104_01

Delone, W. H., & Mclean, E. R. (2004). Measuring e-commerce success: Applying the DeLone & McLean information systems success model. *International Journal of Electronic Commerce*, *9*(1), 31–47.

Demurjian, S. A. (2008). *Grid Computing and its Applications in the Biomedical Informatics Domain*. Biomedical Informatics.

Desai, V. (2005). NGOs, Gender Mainstreaming, and Urban Poor Communities in Mumbai. *Gender and Development*, *13*(2), 90–98. doi:10.1080/13552070512331332290

Dietrich, B. L., Plachy, E. C., & Norton, M. F. (2014). *Analytics across the Enterprise, How IBM realizes Business Value from Big Data and Analytics*. New York: IBM Press.

DiGiammarino, F., & Trudeau, L. (2008). Virtual networks: An opportunity for government. *Public Management*, *37*(1), 5.

Dimitrova, S. G. (2013). *Implementation of Crowdsourcing into Business and Innovation Strategies: A Case Study at Bombardier Transportation, Germany.* Retrieved December 1, 2017, from https://publications.polymtl.ca/1311/1/2013_Sylvia_GueorguievaDimitrova.pdf

Doan, A., Ramakrishnan, R., & Halevy, A. Y. (2011). Crowdsourcing systems on the world-wide web. *Communications of the ACM*, *54*(4), 86–96. doi:10.1145/1924421.1924442

Dorsch, H., Jurock, A. E., Schoepe, S., Lessl, M., & Asadullah, K. (2015). Grants4Targets—an open innovation initiative to foster drug discovery collaborations between academia and the pharmaceutical industry. *Nature Reviews. Drug Discovery*, *14*(1), 74–76. doi:10.1038/nrd3078-c2 PMID:25430867

Douglas, T., Tannenbaum, T., & Livny, M. (2005). Distributed Computing in practice: The Condor Experience. *Concurrency and Computation: Practice & Experience - Grid Performance, 17*(2), 323 - 356.

Downes, T., & Marchant, T. (2016). The Extent and Effectiveness of Knowledge Management in Australian Community Service Organisations. *Journal of Knowledge Management*, *20*(1), 49–68. doi:10.1108/JKM-11-2014-0483

Drucker, P. F. (1991). 'The new productivity challenge'. *Harvard Business Review*, *69*(6), 69–76. PMID:10114929

Drucker, P. F. (1999). *Społeczeństwo prokapitalistyczne*. Warszawa: PWN.

Duhon, B. (1998). It's all in our Heads. *Inform (Silver Spring, Md.)*, *12*(8), 8–13.

Earl, M. (2001). Knowledge Management Strategies: Toward a Taxonomy. *Journal of Management Information Systems*, *18*(1), 215–233. doi:10.1080/07421222.2001.11045670

Edwards, J. S., Collier, P. M., & Shaw, D. (2005). *Knowledge Management and Its Impact on the Management Accountant.* London: The Chartered Institute of Management Accountants (CIMA). Retrieved from http://www.cimaglobal.com/Documents/Thought_leadership_docs/MigratedDocsMarch2010/Resouces%20(pdfs)/Research%20full%20reports/Knowledge%20management%20and%20its%20impact%20on%20the%20management%20accountant.pdf

Edwards, M., & Hulme, D. (1996). Too Close for Comfort? The Impact of Official Aid on Nongovernmental Organizations. *World Development*, *24*(6), 961–973. doi:10.1016/0305-750X(96)00019-8

Einstein@Home. (n.d.). Retrieved May 29, 2017, from https://einsteinathome.org/about

Eliot, T. S. (1934). *The rock*. Faber & Faber. Available at: http://www.wisdomportal.com/Technology/TSEliot-TheRock.html

Encyclopædia Britannica. (2016, December 23). *French Revolution*. Retrieved 1 12, 2017, from https://www.britannica.com/event/French-Revolution

Engida, G. (2016). *How can Digital Government Support the Development of Knowledge Societies?* Keynote Lecture, 9th International Conference on Theory and Practice of Electronic Governance (ICEGOV2016), Montevideo, Uruguay.

Erickson, G. S., & Rothberg, H. N. (2014). Data, Information, and Knowledge: Developing an Intangible Assets Strategy. In *Handbook of Research on Organizational Transformations through Big Data Analytics* (pp. 85–96). Hershey, PA: IGI Global.

Estellés-Arolas, E., & González-Ladrón-De-Guevara, F. (2012). Towards an integrated crowdsourcing definition. *Journal of Information Science*, *38*(2), 189–200. doi:10.1177/0165551512437638

Evans, D., & McKee, J. (2010). *Social Media Marketing: The Next Generation of Business Engagement*. Wiley Publishing, Inc.

Evans, L. (2010). *Social Media Marketing. Strategies for Engaging in Facebook, Twitter & Other Social Media*. Que Publishing.

Falagas, M. E., Pitsouni, E. I., Malietzis, G. A., & Pappas, G. (2008). Comparison of PubMed, Scopus, web of science, and Google scholar: Strengths and weaknesses. *The FASEB Journal*, *22*(2), 338–342. doi:10.1096/fj.07-9492LSF PMID:17884971

Farooq, U., Ganoe, C. H., Carroll, J. M., & Giles, C. L. (2009). Designing for e-science: Requirements gathering for collaboration in CiteSeer. *International Journal of Human-Computer Studies*, *67*(4), 297–312. doi:10.1016/j.ijhcs.2007.10.005

Faulkner, D., & Bowman, C. (1996). Strategie konkurencji. Gebethner i s-ka, Warszawa.

FDA. (n.d.). Annual company reports. *FDA*. Retrieved from: http://www.fda.gov/downloads/Drugs/ DevelopmentApprovalProcess/ HowDrugsareDevelopedandApproved/ DrugandBiologicApprovalReports/ UCM081805.pdf

Feller, J., Finnegan, P., Hayes, J., & O'Reilly, P. (2012). Orchestrating sustainable crowdsourcing: A Characterisation of Solver Brokerages. *The Journal of Strategic Information Systems*, *21*(3), 216–232. doi:10.1016/j.jsis.2012.03.002

Fink, D., Hochachka, W., Zuckerberg, B., Winkler, D., Shaby, B., Munson, M., ... Kelling, S. (2010). Spatiotemporal Exploratory Models for Broad-Scale Survey Data. *Ecological Applications*, *20*(8), 2131–2147. doi:10.1890/09-1340.1 PMID:21265447

Fink, K., & Ploder, C. (2007). A Comparative Study of Knowledge Processes and Methods in Austrian and Swiss SMEs. *Proceeding of 13th European Conference on Information Systems*, 704-715.

Folding@Home. (n.d.). Retrieved May 29, 2017, from http://folding.stanford.edu/

Fong, P. S. W., & Choi, S. K. Y. (2009). The Processes of Knowledge Management in Professional Services Firms in the Construction Industry: A Critical Assessment of Both Theory and Practice. *Journal of Knowledge Management*, *13*(2), 110–126. doi:10.1108/13673270910942736

Foster, I., Ghani, R., Jarmin, R. S., Kreuer, F., & Lane, J. (2017). *Big Data and Social Science*. Boca Raton, FL: CRC Press.

Franco, M., & Mariano, S. (2007). Information Technology Repositories and Knowledge Management Processes: A Qualitative Analysis. *Vine*, *37*(4), 440–451. doi:10.1108/03055720710838515

French revolutionaries storm Bastille. (n.d.). Retrieved from History.com: http://www.history.com/this-day-in-history/french-revolutionaries-storm-bastille

Frey, K., Haag, S., & Schneider, V. (2011). *The role of interests, abilities, and motivation in online idea contests*. Paper presented at the 10th International Conference on Wirtschaftsinformatik.

Frey, B. S., & Jegen, R. (2001). Motivation crowding theory. *Journal of Economic Surveys*, *15*(5), 589–611. doi:10.1111/1467-6419.00150

Frey, K., Lüthje, C., & Haag, S. (2011). Whom should firms attract to open innovation platforms? The role of knowledge diversity and motivation. *Long Range Planning*, *44*(5), 397–420. doi:10.1016/j.lrp.2011.09.006

Frost, A. (2014). *A Synthesis of Knowledge Management Failure Factors*. Retrieved from http://www.academia.edu/download/35998692/A_Synthesis_of_Knowledge_Management_Failure_Factors.pdf

Frydrych, D., Bock, A. J., Kinder, T., & Koeck, B. (2014). Exploring entrepreneurial legitimacy in reward-based crowdfunding. *Venture Capital*, *16*(3), 247–269. doi:10.1080/13691066.2014.916512

Fukuyama, F. (1995). *Trust: The Social Virtues and the Creation of Prosperity*. New York: The Free Press.

Fuller, A., Unwin, L., Felstead, A., Jewson, N., & Kakavelakis, K. (2007). Creating and using knowledge: An analysis of the differentiated nature of workplace learning environments. *British Educational Research Journal, 33*(5), 743–759. doi:10.1080/01411920701582397

Füller, J., Hutter, K., & Fries, M. (2012). Crowdsourcing for Goodness Sake: Impact of Incentive Preference on Contribution Behavior for Social Innovation. *Adv Int Market, 23*, 137–159.

Galata, S. (2004). *Strategiczne zarządzanie organizacjami. Wiedza intuicja strategie etyka*. Warszawa: Difin.

Gao, H., Barbier, G., & Goolsby, R. (2011). Harnessing the crowdsourcing power of social media for disaster relief. *IEEE Intelligent Systems, 26*(3), 10–14. doi:10.1109/MIS.2011.52

Gao, S., Li, L., Li, W., Janowicz, K., & Zhang, Y. (2014). Constructing gazetteers from volunteered big geo-data based on Hadoop. *Computers, Environment and Urban Systems, 61*, 172–186. doi:10.1016/j.compenvurbsys.2014.02.004

Gassenheimer, J. B., Siguaw, J. A., & Hunter, G. L. (2013). Exploring motivations and the capacity for business crowdsourcing. *Academy of Marketing Science, 3*, 205–216.

Gefen, D., Straub, D. W., & Boudreau, M.-C. (2000). *Structural Equation Modeling and Regression: Guidelines for research practice. Communications of the Association for Information Systems*. Citeseer.

Georgiadou, Y., Bana, B., Becht, R., Hoppe, R., Ikingura, J., Kraak, M.-J., ... Verplanke, J. (2011). Sensors, empowerment, and accountability: A digital earth view from East Africa. *International Journal of Digital Earth, 4*(4), 285–304. doi:10.1080/17538947.2011.585184

Gerber, E. M., & Hui, J. (2013). Crowdfunding: Motivations and deterrents for participation. *ACM Transactions on Computer-Human Interaction, 20*(6), 34. doi:10.1145/2530540

Gerbing, D. W., & Anderson, J. C. (1988). An updated paradigm for scale development incorporating unidimensionality and its assessment. *JMR, Journal of Marketing Research, 25*(2), 186–192. doi:10.2307/3172650

GESCI. (2012). *Global e-Schools and Communities Initiative*. GESCI.

Ghaziani, A., & Ventresca, M. J. (2005). Keywords and Cultural Change: Frame Analysis of Business Model Public Talk, 1975-2000. *Sociological Forum*, *20*(4), 523–559. doi:10.100711206-005-9057-0

Ghezzi, A., Gabelloni, D., Martini, A., & Natalicchio, A. (2017). Crowdsourcing: A review and suggestions for future research. *International Journal of Management Reviews*. doi:10.1111/ijmr.12135

Gill, J., & Whittle, S. (1993). Management by panacea: Accounting for transience. *Journal of Management Studies*, *30*(2), 281–295. doi:10.1111/j.1467-6486.1993.tb00305.x

Giroux, H. (2006). It was such a handy term: Management fashions and pragmatic ambiguity. *Journal of Management Studies*, *43*(6), 1227–1260. doi:10.1111/j.1467-6486.2006.00623.x

Gloor, P., & Cooper, S. (2007). The new principles of a swarm business. *MIT Sloan Management Review*, *48*(3), 81.

Goldman, J., Shilton, K., Burke, J., Estrin, D., Hansen, M., & Ramanathan, N. (2009). *Participatory Sensing: A citizen-powered approach to illuminating the patterns that shape our world.* Foresight & Governance Project, White Paper, 1-15.

Goncalves, J., Hosio, S., Ferreira, D., & Kostakos, V. (2014). Game of words: tagging places through crowdsourcing on public displays. *Proceedings of the 2014 conference on Designing interactive systems*. 10.1145/2598510.2598514

Goncalves, J., Hosio, S., Rogstadius, J., Karapanos, E., & Kostakos, V. (2015). Motivating participation and improving quality of contribution in ubiquitous crowdsourcing. *Computer Networks*, *90*, 34–48. doi:10.1016/j.comnet.2015.07.002

Graber, M. A., & Graber, A. (2013). Internet-based crowdsourcing and research ethics: The case for IRB review. *Journal of Medical Ethics*, *39*(2), 115–118. doi:10.1136/medethics-2012-100798 PMID:23204319

Greenaway, K. E., & Vuong, D. C. (2010). Taking Charities Seriously: A Call for Focused Knowledge Management Research. *International Journal of Knowledge Management*, *6*(4), 87–97. doi:10.4018/jkm.2010100105

Greenaway, K. E., & Vuong, D. C. (2012). Knowledge Management in Charities. In *Organizational Learning and Knowledge: Concepts, Methodologies, Tools and Applications* (pp. 1381–1389). Hershey, PA: IGI Global. doi:10.4018/978-1-60960-783-8.ch409

Gummesson, E. (1993). Quality Management in Service Organisational. International Service Quality Association.

Gunasekaran, A., Khalil, O., & Rahman, S. R. (Eds.). (2002). *Knowledge and Information Technology Management: Human and Social Perspectives*. Hershey, PA: IGI Global.

Haenlein, M., & Kaplan, A. M. (2004). A Beginner's Guide to Partial Least Squares Analysis. *Understanding Statistics*, *3*(3), 283–297. doi:10.120715328031us0304_4

Hair, J. F., Black, W. C., Babin, B. J., Anderson, R. E., & Tatham, R. L. (2010). *Multivariate Data Analysis* (7th ed.). Upper Saddle River, NJ: Prentice Hall.

Haklay, M., Antoniou, V., Basiouka, S., Soden, R., & Mooney, P. (2014). *Crowdsourced geographic information use in government*. World Bank Publications.

Halder, B. (2014). Evolution of crowd sourcing: Potential data protection, privacy and security concerns under the new media age. *Revista Democracia Digital e Governo Eletrônico*, *1*(10), 377–393.

Halder, B. (2014). Evolution of crowdsourcing: Potential data protection, privacy and security concerns under the new Media Age. *Democracia Digital e Governo Eletrônico, Florianópolis*, *10*, 377–393.

Han, S. H., Seo, G., Yoon, S. W., & Yoon, D. Y. (2016). Transformational leadership and knowledge sharing: Mediating roles of employee's empowerment, commitment, and citizenship behaviors. *Journal of Workplace Learning*, *28*(3), 130–149. doi:10.1108/JWL-09-2015-0066

Han, T. S., Chiang, H. H., & Chang, A. (2010). Employee participation in decision making, psychological ownership and KS: Mediating role of organizational commitment in Taiwanese high-tech organizations. *International Journal of Human Resource Management*, *21*(12), 2218–2233. doi:10.1080/09585192.2010.509625

Harrison C., (2011). GlaxoSmithKline opens the door on clinical data sharing. *NatureReview.Drug Discovery*, *11*, 891–892.

Hartman, A., Sifonis, J., & Kador, J. (1999). *Net Ready. Strategies for success in the economy*. McGraw-Hill Companies.

Haslinda, A., & Sarinah, A. (2009). A Review of Knowledge Management Models. *Journal of International Social Research*, *2*(9), 187–198.

Haythornthwaite, C. (2009). *Crowds and communities: Light and heavyweight models of peer production*. Paper presented at the System Sciences, 2009. HICSS'09. 42nd Hawaii International Conference on.

Hee, S. P. (2000). Relationships among attitudes and subjective norm: Testing the theory of reasoned action across cultures. *Communication Studies*, *51*(2), 162–175. doi:10.1080/10510970009388516

Heipke, C. (2010). Crowdsourcing geospatial data. *ISPRS Journal of Photogrammetry and Remote Sensing*, *65*(6), 550–557. doi:10.1016/j.isprsjprs.2010.06.005

Hendriks, P. (1999). Why share knowledge? The influence of ICT on the motivation for knowledge sharing. *Knowledge and Process Management*, *6*(2), 91–100. doi:10.1002/(SICI)1099-1441(199906)6:2<91::AID-KPM54>3.0.CO;2-M

Herder, P. M., Veeneman, W. W., Buitenhuis, M. D. J., & Schaller, A. (2003). Follow the Rainbow: A Knowledge Management Framework for new Product Introduction. *Journal of Knowledge Management*, *7*(3), 105–115. doi:10.1108/13673270310485668

Hernandez, M. (2003). Asessing tacit knowledge transfer and dimensions of a learning environment in a Colombian business. *Advances in Developing Human Resources*, *5*(2), 215–221. doi:10.1177/1523422303005002009

Hertel, G., Niedner, S., & Herrmann, S. (2003). Motivation of software developers in Open Source projects: An Internet-based survey of contributors to the Linux kernel. *Research Policy*, *32*(7), 1159–1177. doi:10.1016/S0048-7333(03)00047-7

Hetmank, L. (2013). Components and Functions of Crowdsourcing Systems-A Systematic Literature Review. *Wirtschaftsinformatik*, *4*, 2013.

Hibbard, M., & Chun Tang, C. (2004). Sustainable Community Development: A Social Approach from Vietnam. *Community Development (Columbus, Ohio)*, *35*(2), 87–104.

Hoegl, M., & Schulze, A. (2005). How to Support Knowledge Creation in New Product Development: An Investigation of Knowledge Management Methods. *European Management Journal*, *23*(3), 263–273. doi:10.1016/j.emj.2005.04.004

Holsapple, C. W., & Joshi, K. D. (2004). A Formal Knowledge Management Ontology: Conduct, Activities, Resources, and Influences. *Journal of the American Society for Information Science and Technology*, *55*(7), 593–612. doi:10.1002/asi.20007

Horak, B. J. (2001). Dealing with Human Factors and Managing Change in Knowledge Management: A Phased Approach. *Topics in Health Information Management*, *21*(3), 8–17. PMID:11234733

Howe, J. (2006). *Crowdsourcing: A definition*. Retrieved from http://www.crowdsourcing.com/cs/2006/06/crowdsourcing_a.html

Howe, J. (2006). The Rise of Crowdsourcing. *Wired Magazine, 14*(6).

Howe, J. (n.d.a). *The Soundbyte Version*. Retrieved December 1, 2017, from http://www.crowdsourcing.com

Howe, J. (n.d.b). *The White Paper Version*. Retrieved December 1, 2017, from http://www.crowdsourcing.com

Howe, J. (2006). The Rise of Crowdsourcing. *Wired Magazine*, *14*(6), 1–4.

Howe, J. (2008). *Crowdsourcing: Why the Power of the Crowd Is Driving the Future of Business*. New York: Crown Publishing Group.

Hsu, M., Ju, L., Yen, C. H., & Chang, M. (2007). Knowledge sharing behaviour in virtual communities: The relationship between trust, self-efficacy, and outcome expectations. *International Journal of Human-Computer Studies*, *65*(2), 153–169. doi:10.1016/j.ijhcs.2006.09.003

Huang, J., & Nicole, D. (2014). Evidence-based trust reasoning. *HotSoS Symposium.*

Hume, C., & Hume, M. (2008). The Strategic Role of Knowledge Management in Nonprofit Organisations. *International Journal of Nonprofit and Voluntary Sector Marketing*, *13*(2), 129–140. doi:10.1002/nvsm.316

Hung, S. Y., Durcikova, A., Lai, H. M., & Lin, W. M. (2011). The influence of intrinsic and extrinsic motivation on individuals' knowledge sharing behaviour. *The International Journal of Human Computer Studies, 69*(6), 415-427.

Hurley, T. A., & Green, C. W. (2005). Knowledge Management and the Nonprofit Industry: A Within and Between Approach. *Journal of Knowledge Management Practice*, *6*(1), 1–10.

Huston, L., Sakkab, N. (2006). Connect and Develop. Inside Procter&Gamble's New Model for Innovation. *Harvard Business Review*.

IFPMA. (n.d.). Global alliance for TB drug development (TB alliance). *IFPMA Health Partnerships Directory.* Retrieved from: http:// partnerships.ifpma.org/partnership/global-alliance-fortb-drug-development-tb-alliance

Innocentive. (n.d.). Innovate with innocentive. *Innocentive.* Retrieved from: www.innocentive.com

Jagadish, S. V. K., Septiningsih, E. M., Kohli, A., Thomson, M. J., Ye, C., Redoña, E., ... Singh, R. K. (2012). Genetic advances in adapting rice to a rapidly changing climate. *Journal Agronomy & Crop Science*, *198*(5), 360–373. doi:10.1111/j.1439-037X.2012.00525.x

Jain, A. K., & Moreno, A. (2015). Organizational Learning, Knowledge Management Practices and Firm's Performance: An Empirical Study of a Heavy Engineering Firm in India. *The Learning Organization*, *22*(1), 14–39. doi:10.1108/TLO-05-2013-0024

Jain, R. (2010). *Investigation of Governance Mechanisms for Crowdsourcing Initiatives*. AMCIS Proceed.

Jain, R. (2010). Investigation of Governance Mechanisms for Crowdsourcing Initiatives. *AMCIS Proceedings*.

Jain, S. (2009). Modern Knowledge Management and Computer-based Technology the Inseparable Phenomenon. *Global Business Review*, *10*(2), 159–171. doi:10.1177/097215090901000202

Janssen, O. (2000). Job demands, perceptions of effort-reward fairness and innovative work behaviour. *Journal of Occupational and Organizational Psychology*, *73*(3), 287–302. doi:10.1348/096317900167038

Jarvenpaa, S. L., & Majchrzak, A. (2010). Research commentary—vigilant interaction in knowledge collaboration: Challenges of online user participation under ambivalence. *Information Systems Research*, *21*(4), 773–784. doi:10.1287/isre.1100.0320

Jarvis, A., Eitzinger, A., Koningstein, M., Benjamin, T., Howland, F., Andrieu, N., . . . Corner-Dolloff, C. (2015). *Less is more: the 5Q approach*. Scientific Report. International Center for Tropical Agriculture (CIAT). Available online at: http://dapa.ciat.cgiar.org/

Jennex, M. (2005). What is Knowledge Management? *International Journal of Knowledge Management*, *1*(4), 1–4.

Jeppesen, L. B., & Lakhani, K. R. (2010). Marginality and Problem-Solving Effectiveness in Broadcast Search. *Organization Science*, *21*(5), 1016–1033. doi:10.1287/orsc.1090.0491

Juma, M. F., Fue, K. G., Barakabitze, A. A., Nicodemus, N., Magesa, M. M., Kilima, F. T. M., & Sanga, C. A. (2017). Understanding Crowdsourcing of Agricultural Market Information in a Pilot Study: Promises, Problems and Possibilities (3Ps). *International Journal of Technology Diffusion*, *8*(4), 1–16. doi:10.4018/IJTD.2017100101

Jussila, J. J., Kärkkäinen, H., & Lyytikkä, J. (2011). *Towards Maturity Modelling Approach for Social Media Adoption in Innovation*. In *Proceedings of the 4th ISPIM Innovation Symposium* (pp. 1-14). Wellington, New Zealand: ISPIM. Retrieved April from https://tutcris.tut.fi/portal/files/6640892/Jussila_2011_Towards_Maturity_Modeling_Approach_for_Social_Media_Adoption_in_Innovation.pdf

Kaghazgaran, P., Caverlee, J., & Alfifi, M. (2017). *Behavioral Analysis of Review Fraud: Linking Malicious Crowdsourcing to Amazon and Beyond.* Paper presented at the ICWSM.

Kanagasabapathy, K. A., Radhakrishnan, R., & Balasubramanian, S. (2006). *Empirical Investigation of Critical Success Factor and Knowledge Management Structure for Successful Implementation of Knowledge Management System: A Case Study in Process Industry.* Retrieved from http://hosteddocs.ittoolbox.com/KKRR41106.pdf

Kanter, R. (1988). When a thousand owners bloom: Structural, collective, and social conditions for innovation in organisations. In B. M. Staw & L. L. Cummings (Eds.), *Research in organisational behavior (10)* (pp. 169–211). Greenwich, CT: JAI Press.

Kaplan, A. M., & Haenlein, M. (2010). Users of the World, Unite! The Challenges and Opportunities of Social Media. *Business Horizons, 53*(1), 59–68. doi:10.1016/j.bushor.2009.09.003

Kapur, M., & Kinzer, C. (2007). Examining the effect of problem type in a synchronous computer-supported collaborative learning (CSCL) environment. *Educational Technology Research and Development, 55*(5), 439–459. doi:10.100711423-007-9045-6

Karger, D. R., Oh, S., Shah, D. (2011). Iterative. Learning for Reliable Crowdsourcing Systems. *Neural Information Processing Systems*, 1953-1961.

Kaufman, G., Flanagan, M., & Punjasthitkul, S. (2016). Investigating the impact of'emphasis frames' and social loafing on player motivation and performance in a crowdsourcing game. *Proceedings of the 2016 CHI conference on human factors in computing systems.* 10.1145/2858036.2858588

Kaufmann, N., Schulze, T., & Veit, D. (2011). *More than fun and money. Worker Motivation in Crowdsourcing-A Study on Mechanical Turk.* Paper presented at the AMCIS.

Kawajiri, R., Shimosaka, M., & Kashima, H. (2014). Steered crowdsensing: Incentive design towards quality-oriented place-centric crowdsensing. *Proceedings of the 2014 ACM International Joint Conference on Pervasive and Ubiquitous Computing.* 10.1145/2632048.2636064

Kawasaki, H., Yamamoto, A., Kurasawa, H., Sato, H., Nakamura, M., & Matsumura, H. (2012). Top of worlds: method for improving motivation to participate in sensing services. *Proceedings of the 2012 ACM Conference on Ubiquitous Computing.* 10.1145/2370216.2370321

Kebede, G. (2010). Knowledge Management: An Information Science Perspective. *International Journal of Information Management*, *30*(5), 416–424. doi:10.1016/j.ijinfomgt.2010.02.004

Kelley, T. M., & Johnston, E. (2012). Discovering the appropriate role of serious games in the design of open governance platforms. *Public Administration Quarterly*, 504–554.

Kelly, K. (2001). *Nowe reguły nowej gospodarki. Dziesięć nowych strategii biznesowych dla świata połączonego siecią*. Warszawa: WIG Press.

Kemp, S. (2017). *Digital in 2017, Global Overview*. Retrieved April, 2017, from https://wearesocial.com/blog/2017/01/digital-in-2017-global-overview

Kieser, A. (1996). Moden und Mythen des Organisierens. *Die Betriebswirtschaft*, *56*, 21–40.

Kieser, A. (1997). Rhetoric and my thin management fashion. *Organization*, *4*(1), 49–74. doi:10.1177/135050849741004

Kimberlin, C. L., & Winterstein, A. G. (2008). Validity and reliability of measurement instruments used in research. *American Journal of Health-System Pharmacy*, *65*(23), 2276–2284. doi:10.2146/ajhp070364 PMID:19020196

Kinney, T. (1998). Knowledge Management, Intellectual Capital and Adult Learning. *Adult Learning*, *10*(2), 2–5. doi:10.1177/104515959901000201

Kitchenham, B. (2004). Procedures for performing systematic reviews. Keele University.

Kitchenham, B., & Charters, S. (2007). *Guidelines for performing systematic literature reviews in software engineering EBSE Technical Report*. Retrieved from Durham.

Kittur, A. (2010). Crowdsourcing, collaboration and creativity. *ACM Crossroads*, *17*(2), 22–26. doi:10.1145/1869086.1869096

Kittur, A., Chi, E. H., & Suh, B. (2008). Crowdsourcing user studies with Mechanical Turk. *Proceedings of the SIGCHI conference on human factors in computing systems*.

Kleeman, F., Voss, G. G., & Rieder, K. (2008). Un(der)paid Innovators: The Commercial Utilization of Consumer Work through crowdsourcing. Science. *Technology and Innovation Studies*, *4*(1), 5–26.

Klincewicz, K. (Ed.). (2016). *Zarządzanie, organizacje i organizowanie – przegląd perspektyw teoretycznych*. Warszawa: Wydawnictwo Naukowe Wydziału Zarządzania Uniwersytetu Warszawskiego. doi:10.7172/978-83-65402-29-5.2016.wwz.9

Kline, R. B. (2015). *Principles and Practice of Structural Equation Modeling* (4th ed.). Guilford Publications.

Klososky, S. (2011). *Enterprise social technology*. Austin, TX: GreenLeaf Book Group Press.

Kogut, B., & Zander, U. (1992). Knowledge of the firm, combinative capabilities and the replication of technology. *Organization Science*, *3*(3), 383–397. doi:10.1287/orsc.3.3.383

Kosonen, M., Gan, C., Olander, H., & Blomqvist, K. (2013). My idea is our idea! Supporting user-driven innovation activities in crowdsourcing communities. *International Journal of Innovation Management*, *17*(03), 1–18. doi:10.1142/S1363919613400100

Kosonen, M., Gan, C., Vanhala, M., & Blomqvist, K. (2014). User motivation and knowledge sharing in idea crowdsourcing. *International Journal of Innovation Management*, *18*(05), 1450031. doi:10.1142/S1363919614500315

Kowalczyk, A., & Nogalski, B. (2007). *Zarządzanie wiedzą. Koncepcja i narzędzia*. Warszawa: Difin.

Kowal, J., & Fortier, M. S. (1999). Motivational determinants of flow: Contributions from self-determination theory. *The Journal of Social Psychology*, *139*(3), 355–368. doi:10.1080/00224549909598391

Kowalska, M. (2015). *Crowdsourcing internetowy – pozytywny wymiar partycypacji społecznej. Konteksty – istota – uwarunkowania*. Warszawa: Wydawnictwo Stowarzyszenie Bibliotekarzy Polskich.

Kreps, D. M., & Wilson, R. (1982). Reputation and imperfect information. *Journal of Economic Theory*, *27*(2), 253–279. doi:10.1016/0022-0531(82)90030-8

Kruse, S. (2014). Pharmaceutical RandD productivity: The role of alliances. *Journal of Commercial Biotechnology*, (20): 11–20.

Kudyba, S. (2014). Information Creation through Analytics. In S. Kudyba (Ed.), *Big Data, Mining, and Analytics. Components of Strategic Decision Making* (pp. 17–48). Boca Raton, FL: CRC Press Taylor and Francis Group. doi:10.1201/b16666-3

Kulkarni, U. R., Ravindran, S., & Freeze, R. (2006). A Knowledge Management Success Model: Theoretical Development and Empirical Validation. *Journal of Management Information Systems*, *23*(3), 309–347. doi:10.2753/MIS0742-1222230311

Kusek, Z., & Rist, C. (2001). Building a performance-based monitoring and evaluation system. *Evaluation Journal of Australia*, *1*(2), 14–23. doi:10.1177/1035719X0100100205

Kusek, Z., & Rist, C. (2004). *Ten steps to a Result-based monitoring and evaluation system: A Handbook for Development Practitioner*. Washington, DC: World Bank. doi:10.1596/0-8213-5823-5

Lakhani, K. R., & Wolf, R. G. (2005). Why hackers do what they do: Understanding motivation and effort in free/open source software projects. *Perspectives on Free and Open Source Software, 1*, 3-22.

Lakhani, K. R., & Von Hippel, E. (2003). How open source software works:"free" user-to-user assistance. *Research Policy*, *32*(6), 923–943. doi:10.1016/S0048-7333(02)00095-1

Lang, G., & Ohana, M. (2012). Are management fashions dangerous for organizations? *International Journal of Business and Management*, *7*(20), 81–89. doi:10.5539/ijbm.v7n20p81

Langran, L. V. (2002). *Empowerment and the Limits of Change: NGOs and Health Decentralization in the Philippine* (Doctoral dissertation). Toronto: University of Toronto.

Larsson, R., Bengtsson, L., Henriksson, K., & Sparks, J. (1998). The Inter-Organizational Learning Dilemma: Collective Knowledge Development in Strategic Alliances. *Organization Science*, *9*(3), 285–305. doi:10.1287/orsc.9.3.285

Law, C. C. H., & Ngai, E. W. T. (2008). An empirical study of the effects of knowledge sharing and learning behaviours on firm performance. *Expert Systems with Applications*, *34*(4), 2342–2349. doi:10.1016/j.eswa.2007.03.004

Lazer, D, and al. (. (2009). Life in the network: The coming age of computational social science. *Science*, *323*(5915), 721–723. doi:10.1126cience.1167742 PMID:19197046

Lee, N. (n.d.). *Interfacing Intellectual Property Rights and Open Innovation*. Retrieved from http://www.wipo.int/edocs/mdocs/mdocs/en/wipo_ipr_ge_11/wipo_ipr_ge_11_topic6.pdf

Lee, H., & Choi, B. (2003). Knowledge Management Enablers, Processes, and Organizational Performance: An Integrative View and Empirical Examination. *JMIS*, *20*(1), 179–228.

Lee, J., & Seo, D. (2016). Crowdsourcing not all sourced by the crowd: An observation on the behavior of Wikipedia participants. *Technovation*, *55*, 14–21. doi:10.1016/j.technovation.2016.05.002

Lee, J., Tierney, B., & Johnston, W. (2006). Data Intensive Distributed Computing: A Medical Application Example. *International Conference on High-Performance Computing and Networking*, 150-158.

Lee, S. M., & Hong, S. (2002). An enterprise-wide knowledge management system infrastructure. *Industrial Management & Data Systems*, *102*(1), 17–25. doi:10.1108/02635570210414622

Leiden Classical. (n.d.). Retrieved May 29, 2017, from http://boinc.gorlaeus.net/

Leimeister, J.M. & Zogaj S. (2013). Neue Arbeitsorganisation durch Crowdsourcing. *Hans-Böckler-Stiftung Arbeitspapier Arbeit und Soziales*, 287.

Leimeister, J.M. (2012). Crowdsourcing: Crowdfunding, Crowdvoting, Crowdcreation. *Zeitschrift für Controlling und Management*, 56.

Leimeister, J. M. (2012). Crowdsourcing, Crowdfunding, Crowdvoting, Crowdcreation. *Zeitschrift für Controlling und Management*, *56*(6), 388–392. doi:10.136512176-012-0662-5

Leimeister, J. M., Huber, M., Bretschneider, U., & Krcmar, H. (2009). Leveraging crowdsourcing: Activation-supporting components for IT-based ideas competition. *Journal of Management Information Systems*, *26*(1), 197–224. doi:10.2753/MIS0742-1222260108

Leverkus, P. J. A. (2016). *Catalyzing Governance: Limitations on the Freedom of Expression and its Impact on 'Watch-dogs' in Tanzania's Extractive Industries* (Master's thesis). University of Oslo, Oslo, Norway.

Levitt, T. (1991). *Marketing Imagination*. New York: The Free Press.

LHC@home. (n.d.). Retrieved May 29, 2017, from https://lhcathome.cern.ch/lhcathome/index.php

Li, Ch., & Bernoff, J. (2011). *Groundswell. Winning in a world transformed by social technologies*. Forrester Research.

Liebowitz, J., & Megbolugbe, I. (2003). A Set of Frameworks to Aid the Project Manager in Conceptualizing and Implementing Knowledge Management Initiatives. *International Journal of Project Management*, *21*(3), 189–198. doi:10.1016/S0263-7863(02)00093-5

Liezel Cilliers, S. F. (2015). The Relationship Between Privacy, Information Security and the Trustworthiness of a Crowdsourcing System in a Smart City. *Ninth International Symposium on Human Aspects of Information Security & Assurance (HAISA 2015)*, Lesvos, Greece.

Lilly. (n.d.). *Lilly: Open innovation drug discovery.* Retrieved from: https:// openinnovation.lilly.com/dd/

Lin, A. (2004). *Wikipedia as participatory journalism: Reliable sources.* Paper for the 5th International Symposium on Online Journalism, Austin, TX.

Lin, H. F. (2007a). Knowledge sharing and firm innovation capability: An empirical study. *International Journal of Manpower*, *28*(3/4), 315–332. doi:10.1108/01437720710755272

Lin, H. F. (2007b). Effects of extrinsic and intrinsic motivation on employee knowledge sharing intentions. *Journal of Information Science*, *33*(2), 135–149. doi:10.1177/0165551506068174

Lin, M. J., Hung, S. W., & Chen, C. J. (2009). Fostering the determinants of knowledge sharing in professional virtual communities. *Computers in Human Behavior*, *25*(4), 929–939. doi:10.1016/j.chb.2009.03.008

Liou, D. K., Chih, W. H., Yuan, C. Y., & Lin, C. Y. (2016). The study of the antecedents of knowledge sharing behavior: The empirical study of Yambol online test community. *Internet Research*, *26*(4), 845–868. doi:10.1108/IntR-10-2014-0256

Literat, I. (2017). Tapping into the Collective Creativity of the Crowd: The Effectiveness of Key Incentives in Fostering Creative Crowdsourcing. *Proceedings of the 50th Hawaii International Conference on System Sciences.* 10.24251/HICSS.2017.212

Litman, L., Robinson, J., & Abberbock, T. (2017). TurkPrime. com: A versatile crowdsourcing data acquisition platform for the behavioral sciences. *Behavior Research Methods*, *49*(2), 433–442. doi:10.375813428-016-0727-z PMID:27071389

Liu, C.-C., Liang, T.-P., Rajagopalan, B., & Sambamurthy, V. (2011). *The Crowding Effect Of Rewards On Knowledge-Sharing Behavior In Virtual Communities.* Paper presented at the PACIS.

Louis, C.A. (2013). Organizational Perspectives of Open Innovation in Government. *iConference Proceedings.*

Lucier, C. E., & Torsilieri, J. D. (1997). Why Knowledge Programs Fail: A CEO's Guide to Managing Learning. *Strategy & Business*, *9*(4), 14–28.

Lukyanenko, R., & Parsons, J. (2012). Conceptual modeling principles for crowdsourcing. *Proceedings of the 1st international workshop on Multimodal crowd sensing*. 10.1145/2390034.2390038

Lukyanenko, R., Parsons, J., & Wiersma, Y. F. (2014). The IQ of the crowd: Understanding and improving information quality in structured user-generated content. *Information Systems Research*, *25*(4), 669–689. doi:10.1287/isre.2014.0537

Luxmi. (2014). Organizational Learning Act as a Mediator between the Relationship of Knowledge Management and Organizational Performance. *Management and Labour Studies, 39*(2), 31–41.

Mackay, K. (2008). *Building Monitoring and Evaluation Systems to Improve Government Performance, Evaluation Capacity Development*. World Bank. Retrieved from http://www.worldbank.org/ieg/ecd/better_government.html

Madsen, D. O., & Stenheim, T. (2014). Perceived benefits of balanced scorecard implementation: Some preliminary evidence. *Problems and Perspectives in Management*, *12*(3), 81–90.

Magnier-Watanabe, R., & Senoo, D. (2008). Organizational Characteristics as Prescriptive Factors of Knowledge Management Initiatives. *Journal of Knowledge Management*, *12*(1), 21–36. doi:10.1108/13673270810852368

Maier, D. J., & Moseley, J. L. (2003). The Knowledge Management Assessment Tool (KMAT). *Annual-San Diego-Pfeiffer and Company*, *1*, 169–184.

Maier, R. (2007). *Knowledge Management Systems: Information and Communication Technologies for Knowledge Management*. New York: Springer Science & Business Media.

Majchrzak, A., & Malhotra, A. (2013). Towards an Information Systems Perspective and Research Agenda for Open Innovation Crowdsourcing. *The Journal of Strategic Information Systems*, 22.

Majchrzak, A., & Malhotra, A. (2013). Towards an Information Systems Perspective and Research Agenda on Crowdsourcing for Innovation. *The Journal of Strategic Information Systems*, *22*(4), 257–268. doi:10.1016/j.jsis.2013.07.004

Malone, T. W., Laubacher, R., & Dellarocas, C. (2010). The collective intelligence genome. *IEEE Engineering Management Review*, *38*(3), 38–52. doi:10.1109/EMR.2010.5559142

Mankowski, T. A., Slater, S. J., & Slater, T. F. (2011). An interpretive study of meanings citizen scientists make when participating in Galaxy Zoo. *Contemporary Issues in Education Research*, *4*(4), 25–42. doi:10.19030/cier.v4i4.4165

Marjanovic, S., Fry, C., & Chataway, J. (2012). Crowdsourcing based business models: In search of evidence for innovation 2.0. *Science & Public Policy*, *39*(3), 318–332. doi:10.1093cipolcs009

Martens, K. (2002). Mission Impossible? Defining Nongovernmental Organizations. *Voluntas*, *13*(3), 271–285. doi:10.1023/A:1020341526691

Martin, B. (2000). Knowledge Management Within the Context of Management: An Evolving Relationship. *Singapore Management Review*, *22*(2), 17.

Matschke, C., Moskaliuk, J., & Cress, U. (2012). Knowledge Exchange Using Web 2.0 Technologies in NGOs. *Journal of Knowledge Management*, *16*(1), 159–176. doi:10.1108/13673271211199007

Matzkin, D. S. (2008). Knowledge Management in the Peruvian Non-Profit Sector. *Journal of Knowledge Management*, *12*(4), 147–159. doi:10.1108/13673270810884318

Mayor, R., Davis, J., & Schoorman, F. (1995). An integrative model of organizational trust. *Academy of Management Review*, *20*(3), 709–734.

Mazzolini, M., & Maddison, S. (2007). When to jump in: The role of the instructor in online discussion forums. *Computers & Education*, *49*(2), 193–213. doi:10.1016/j.compedu.2005.06.011

McDermott, R. (1999). Why information technology inspired but cannot deliver knowledge management. *California Management Review*, *41*(4), 103–117. doi:10.2307/41166012

McLaren, R. (2012). *Crowdsourcing Support of Land Administration*. Paper presented at Word Bank Conference on land and Poverty, Washington, DC. Retrieved from http://www.landandpoverty.com/agenda/pdfs/paper/mclaren_robin_paper.pdf

McNabb. (2007). Knowledge Management in the Public Sector-A Blueprint for Innovation in Government. Academic Press.

Melville, N. P. (2010). Information systems innovation for environmental sustainability. *Management Information Systems Quarterly*, *34*(1), 1–21. doi:10.2307/20721412

Micklethwait, J., & Wooldridge, A. (2000). *Szamani zarządzania*. Poznań: Zysk i S-ka.

MindModeling@Home. (n.d.). Retrieved May 29, 2017, from https://mindmodeling.org/

Mladenow, A., Bauer, C., Strauss, C., & Gregus, M. (2015). *Collaboration and locality in crowdsourcing*. Paper presented at the Intelligent Networking and Collaborative Systems (INCOS), 2015 International Conference on. 10.1109/INCoS.2015.74

Mohamed, H. (2012). *The Impact of Citizen Journalism on Self Regulation: A Blessing or a Curse?* Retrieved from http://www.academia.edu/download/34292129/Citizen_journalism_and_media_ethics_-_PAPER.pdf

Moon, M. K., Jahng, S. G., Park, S. Y., & Lee, J. E. (2016). The perceptions of knowledge sharing behavior in virtual community: Using an extended social cognitive theory approach. *International Journal of Applied Engineering Research*, *11*(8), 5430–5439.

Morente-Molinera, J. A., Pérez, I. J., Ureña, M. R., & Herrera-Viedma, E. (2015). On multi-granular fuzzy linguistic modeling in group decision making problems: A systematic review and future trends. *Knowledge-Based Systems*, *74*, 49–60. doi:10.1016/j.knosys.2014.11.001

Morschheuser, B., Hamari, J., & Koivisto, J. (2016). *Gamification in crowdsourcing: a review*. Paper presented at the System Sciences (HICSS), 2016 49th Hawaii International Conference on. 10.1109/HICSS.2016.543

Muhdi, L., Daiber, M., Friesike, S., & Boutellier, R. (2011). The crowdsourcing process: An intermediary mediated idea generation approach in the early phase of innovation. *International Journal of Entrepreneurship and Innovation Management*, *14*(4), 315–332. doi:10.1504/IJEIM.2011.043052

Munos, B. (2009). Lessons from 60 years of pharmaceutical innovation. *Nature Reviews. Drug Discovery*, *8*(8), 959–968. doi:10.1038/nrd2961 PMID:19949401

Murray, D. G., Yoneki, E., Crowcroft, J., & Hand, S. (2010). *The Case for Crowd Computing*. MobiHeld 2010, New Delhi, India.

Mvungi, M., & Jay, I. (2009). Knowledge Management Model for Information Technology Support Service. *Electronic Journal of Knowledge Management*, *7*(3), 353–366.

Mwangungulu, S. P., Sumaye, R. D., Limwagu, A. J., Siria, D. J., Kaindoa, E. W., & Okumu, F. O. (2016). Crowdsourcing Vector Surveillance: Using Community Knowledge and Experiences to Predict Densities and Distribution of Outdoor-Biting Mosquitoes in Rural Tanzania. *PLoS One*, *11*(6). doi:10.1371/journal.pone.0156388 PMID:27253869

Nahapiet, J., & Ghoshal, S. (1998). Social Capital, Intellectual Capital, and the Organizational Advantage. *Academy of Management Review*, *23*(2), 242–266.

Naparat, D., & Finnegan, P. (2013). *Crowdsourcing Software Requirements and Development: A Mechanism-based Exploration of 'Opensourcing'*. Academic Press.

Nelson, R. R., & Winter, S. G. (1982). *An evolutionary theory of economic change*. Cambridge, MA: Harvard University Press.

Neuman, W. L. (2005). *Social research methods: Quantitative and qualitative approaches*. Allyn and Bacon Boston.

Neuman, W. L. (2006). *Social research methods: Qualitative and quantitative approaches* (6th ed.). Boston: Pearson.

Nguyen, Q. V. H., Duong, C. T., Nguyen, T. T., Weidlich, M., Aberer, K., Yin, H., & Zhou, X. (2017). Argument discovery via crowdsourcing. *The VLDB Journal*, *26*(4), 511–535. doi:10.100700778-017-0462-9

Nhat, V. Q., & Truong, S. S.-T. (2016). *Incentive Engineering Framework for Crowdsourcing Systems*. arXiv preprint arXiv:1609.01348

Nicolai, A. T., & Dautwiz, J. M. (2010). Fuzziness in Action: What Consequences Has the Linguistic Ambiguity of the Core Competence Concept for Organizational Usage? *British Journal of Management*, *21*(4), 874–888. doi:10.1111/j.1467-8551.2009.00662.x

Nirmala, M. (2012). Right to Information and NGO's – A Study. *International Journal of Social Science & Interdisciplinary Research*, *1*(12), 119–130.

Nissen, M. E. (2000). An extended model of knowledge-flow dynamics. *Communications of the Association for Information Systems*, *8*, 251–266.

Nold, H. A. III. (2012). Linking knowledge processes with firm performance: Organizational culture. *Journal of Intellectual Capital*, *13*(1), 16–38. doi:10.1108/14691931211196196

Nonaka, I. (1994). A dynamic theory of organizational knowledge creation. *Organization Science*, *5*(5), 14–37. doi:10.1287/orsc.5.1.14

Nonaka, I., & Takeuchi, H. (1995). *The knowledge creating company: How Japanese companies create the dynamics of innovation*. New York: Oxford University Press.

Novartis. (n.d.). The Novartis Repository. *Novartis*. Retrieved from: http://oak.novartis.com

Nov, O., Anderson, D., & Arazy, O. (2010). Volunteer computing: a model of the factors determining contribution to community-based scientific research. *Proceedings of the 19th international conference on World wide web*. 10.1145/1772690.1772766

Nov, O., Arazy, O., & Anderson, D. (2014). Scientists@ Home: What drives the quantity and quality of online citizen science participation? *PLoS One*, *9*(4), e90375. doi:10.1371/journal.pone.0090375 PMID:24690612

Nyaanga, P. K. (2015). *Crowdsourcing As A Platform For Monitoring Government Projects* (Master's dissertation). Jomo Kenyatta University of Agriculture and Technology, Kenya.

O'Connor, K. (2000). How to Overcome the Cultural Barriers That Can Blockade Knowledge Management. *Law Technology News*. Retrieved from http://www.legaltechnews.com

O'Dell, C., & Trees, L. (2016). *Cognitive Computing and the Evolution of Knowledge Work*. APQC KM Advanced Working Group White Paper.

Oh, W. (2015, July 1). *India will overtake US to become world's second largest smartphone market by 2017*. Retrieved March 11, 2016, from https://www.strategyanalytics.com/strategy-analytics/news/strategy-analytics-press-releases/strategy-analytics-press-release/2015/07/01/India-will-overtake-US-to-become-world's-second-largest-smartphone-market-by-2017#.VuHPKPl97IX

Olavsrud, T. (2014). *How big data is helping to save the planet*. Available at: http://www.cio.com/article/2683133/big-data/how-big-data-is-helping-to-save-the-planet.html

Orlowska, M. E. (2015). Challenges for Workflows Technology to Support Crowdsourcing Activities. *Fifth International Conference on Business Intelligence and Technology*.

OSDD. (n.d.). *Open source drug discovery*. Retrieved from: http://www.osdd.net/home

Overview of BOINC. (n.d.). Retrieved May 29, 2017, from https://boinc.berkeley.edu/trac/wiki/BoincIntro

Oxford English Dictionary. (2018). *Data*. Retrieved from https://en.oxforddictionaries.com/definition/data

Parshotam, K. (2013). *Crowd Computing: A Literature Review and Definition*. SAICSIT '13, East London, South Africa.

Parvanta, C., Roth, Y., & Keller, H. (2013). Crowdsourcing 101 A Few Basics to Make You the Leader of the Pack. *Health Promotion Practice*, *14*(2), 163–167. doi:10.1177/1524839912470654 PMID:23299912

Paulini, M., Maher, M. L., & Murty, P. (2014). Motivating participation in online innovation communities. *International Journal of Web Based Communities*, *10*(1), 94–114. doi:10.1504/IJWBC.2014.058388

Paul, S. M., Mytelka, D. S., Dunwiddie, C. T., Persinger, C. C., Munos, B. H., Lindborg, S. R., & Schacht, A. L. (2010). How to improve R&D productivity: The pharmaceutical industry's grand challenge. *Nature Reviews. Drug Discovery*, *9*(9), 203–214. doi:10.1038/nrd3078 PMID:20168317

Paulus, P. B., & Dzindolet, M. (2008). Social Influence, Creativity and Innovation. *Social Influence*, *3*(4), 228–247. doi:10.1080/15534510802341082

Pedersen, J., Kocsis, D., Tripathi, A., Tarrell, A., Weerakoon, A., Tahmasbi, N., ... (2013). *Conceptual foundations of crowdsourcing: A review of IS research.* Paper presented at the 2013 46th Hawaii International Conference on System Sciences (HICSS 46). 10.1109/HICSS.2013.143

Pedersen, M. J., Stritch, J. M., & Taggart, G. (2017). Citizen perceptions of procedural fairness and the moderating roles of 'belief in a just world'and 'public service motivation'in public hiring. *Public Administration*, *95*(4), 874–894. doi:10.1111/padm.12353

Pee, L., Koh, E., & Goh, M. (2018). Trait motivations of crowdsourcing and task choice: A distal-proximal perspective. *International Journal of Information Management*, *40*, 28–41. doi:10.1016/j.ijinfomgt.2018.01.008

Pennington, D. D. (2011). Bridging the disciplinary divide: Co-creating research ideas in escience teams. *Computer Supported Cooperative Work*, *20*(3), 165–196. doi:10.100710606-011-9134-2

Perkmann, M., & Spicer, A. (2008). How are management fashions institutionalized? The role of institutional work. *Human Relations*, *61*(6), 811–844. doi:10.1177/0018726708092406

Pfeffer, J., & Sutton, R. (1999). Knowledge "What" to do is not enough: Turning knowledge into action. *California Management Review*, *42*(1), 83–108. doi:10.2307/41166020

Phung, V. D., Hawryszkiewycz, I., Chandran, D., & Ha, B. M. (2017). Knowledge Sharing and Innovative Work Behaviour: A Case Study from Vietnam. In *Proceedings of the 28th Australasian Conference on Information Systems (ACIS 2017)*. University of Tasmania.

Pickerell, J. (2012). *iStockphoto 2012: Semi-Annual Analysis*. Retrieved from http://blog.microstockgroup.com/istockphoto-2012-semi-annual-analysis/

Piegorsch, W. W. (2015). *Statistical Data Analytics*. New York: Wiley.

Pierce, J. L., Kostova, T., & Dirks, K. T. (2001). Toward a Theory of Psychological Ownership in Organizations. *Academy of Management Review*, (26): 298–310.

Piskorski, M. J. (2011). Social Strategies That Work. *Harvard Business Review*, *89*(11), 116–122. PMID:22111430

Poetz, M. K., & Schreier, M. (2012). The value of crowdsourcing: Can users really compete with professionals in generating new product ideas? *Journal of Product Innovation Management*, *29*(2), 245–256. doi:10.1111/j.1540-5885.2011.00893.x

Pohulak-Żołędowska, E. (2011). Knowledge Production: Industrial Science as a Source of Economies Innovations, Wrocław University of Economics. Argumenta Oeconomica, 19(26).

Pohulak-Żołędowska, E. (2013). Industrial Meaning of University Basic Research in Modern Economies. *Managerial Economics, 14*. 10.7494/manage.2013.14.137

Popovič, A., Hackney, R., Coelho, P. S., & Jaklič, J. (2012). Towards business intelligence systems success: Effects of maturity and culture on analytical decision making. *Decision Support Systems*, *54*(1), 729–739. doi:10.1016/j.dss.2012.08.017

Porter, M. E. (1985). *Competitive Advantage: Creating and Sustaining Superior Performance*. New York: Free Press.

Pramanik, P. K., Choudhury, P., & Saha, A. (January 2017). Economical Supercomputing thru Smartphone Crowd Computing: An Assessment of Opportunities, Benefits, Deterrents, and Applications from India's Perspective. *International Conference on Advanced Computing and Communication Systems (ICACCS - 2017)*. 10.1109/ICACCS.2017.8014613

Probst, G., Raub, S., & Romhardt, K. (2002). *Zarządzanie wiedzą w organizacji*. Kraków: Oficyna Ekonomiczna.

Puri, S. K. (2007). Integrating Scientific with Indigenous Knowledge: Constructing Knowledge Alliances for Land Management in India. *Management Information Systems Quarterly*, *31*(2), 355–379. doi:10.2307/25148795

Radaelli, G., Lettieri, E., Mura, M., & Spiller, N. (2014). Knowledge Sharing and Innovative Work Behaviour in Healthcare: A Micro-Level Investigation of Direct and Indirect Effects. *Creativity and Innovation Management*, *23*(4), 400–414. doi:10.1111/caim.12084

Raddick, M. J., Bracey, G., Gay, P. L., Lintott, C. J., Murray, P., Schawinski, K., ... Vandenberg, J. (2010). Galaxy zoo: Exploring the motivations of citizen science volunteers. *Astronomy Education Review*, *9*(1), 010103. doi:10.3847/AER2009036

Ragsdell, G. (2013). Voluntary Sector Organisations: Untapped Sources of Lessons for Knowledge Management. *Proceedings of the 10th International Conference on Intellectual Capital, Knowledge Management and Organizational Learning*, 349-355.

Ragsdell, G., Espinet, E. O., & Norris, M. (2014). Knowledge Management in the Voluntary Sector: A Focus on Sharing Project Know-How and Expertise. *Knowledge Management Research and Practice*, *12*(4), 351–361. doi:10.1057/kmrp.2013.21

Rahman, M. S., Osmangani, A. M., Daud, N. M., & AbdelFattah, F. A. M. (2016). Knowledge sharing behaviors among non academic staff of higher learning institutions. *Library Review*, *65*(1/2), 65–83. doi:10.1108/LR-02-2015-0017

Rai, M. (2014). *Corruption and Governance in India — Current Status and Way Forward*. New Delhi: Voluntary Action Network India (VANI). Retrieved from http://www.vaniindia.org/publicationpdf/pub6jan15.pdf

Rajala, R., Westerlund, M., Vuori, M., & Hares, J. P. (2013, December). From Idea Crowdsourcing to Managing User Knowledge, Technology Innovation. *Management Review*.

Ranard, B. L., Ha, Y. P., Meisel, Z. F., Asch, D. A., Hill, S. S., Becker, L. B., ... Merchant, R. M. (2014). Crowdsourcing—harnessing the masses to advance health and medicine, a systematic review. *Journal of General Internal Medicine*, *29*(1), 187–203. doi:10.100711606-013-2536-8 PMID:23843021

Rathi, D. M., Given, L., & Forcier, E. (2014). Interorganisational Partnerships and Knowledge Sharing: The Perspective of Non-Profit Organisations (NPOs). *Journal of Knowledge Management*, *18*(5), 867–885. doi:10.1108/JKM-06-2014-0256

Rathi, D., Given, L. M., & Forcier, E. (2016). Knowledge Needs in the Non-Profit Sector: An Evidence-Based Model of Organizational Practices. *Journal of Knowledge Management*, *20*(1), 23–48. doi:10.1108/JKM-12-2014-0512

Rayport, J. F., & Sviokla, J. J. (1995). Exploiting the Virtual Value Chain. *Harvard Business Review*, *73*(6), 75–85.

Razmerita, L., Phillips-Wren, G., & Jain, L. C. (Eds.). (2016). Advances in Knowledge Management: An Overview. In Innovations in Knowledge Management. Springer-Verlag Berlin Heidelberg.

Renshaw, S., & Krishnaswamy, G. (2009). Critiquing the Knowledge Management Strategies of Non-Profit Organizations in Australia. *Proceedings of the World Academy of Science, Engineering and Technology (WASET), 37*, 456-464. Retrieved from http://citeseerx.ist.psu.edu/viewdoc/download?doi=10.1.1.192.8007&rep=rep1&type=pdf

Rigby, D. & Zook, C. (2002, October). Open-market innovation. *Harvard Business Review*.

RNA World project description. (n.d.). Retrieved May 29, 2017, from https://www.rechenkraft.net/wiki/index.php?title=RNA_World/Projectdescription/en

Roberts, B. W., Walton, K. E., & Viechtbauer, W. (2006). Patterns of mean-level change in personality traits across the life course: A metaanalysis of longitudinal studies. *Psychological Bulletin, 132*(1), 3–27. doi:10.1037/0033-2909.132.1.1

Rodriguez, M. A., Steinbock, D. J., Watkins, J. H., Gershenson, C., Bollen, J., & Grey, V. (2007). *Smartocracy: Social networks for collective decision making*. Paper presented at the System Sciences, 2007. HICSS 2007. 40th Annual Hawaii International Conference on. 10.1109/HICSS.2007.484

Rosetta@home. (n.d.). Retrieved May 29, 2017, from http://boinc.bakerlab.org/rosetta/

Rost, K., & Osterloh, M. (2009). Management Fashion Pay-for-Performance for CEOs. *Schmalenbach Business Review, 61*(2), 119–149. doi:10.1007/BF03396781

Rotman, D., Preece, J., Hammock, J., Procita, K., Hansen, D., & Parr, C. (2012). Dynamic changes in motivation in collaborative citizen-science projects. *Proceedings of the ACM 2012 conference on Computer Supported Cooperative Work*. 10.1145/2145204.2145238

Rouse, A. C. (2010). A preliminary taxonomy of crowdsourcing. *21st Australasian Conference on Information Systems*.

Røvik, K. A. (2011). From fashion to virus: An alternative theory of organizations' handling of management ideas. *Organization Studies, 32*(5), 631–653. doi:10.1177/0170840611405426

Rowley, T. (2013). Participatory digital map-making in arid areas of Kenya and Tanzania. In: IIED, 2013. Participatory learning and action n.66. Tools for supporting sustainable natural resource management and livelihoods. International Institute for Environment and Development (IIED), London.

Roy, A. (2011). Recent Trends in Collaborative, Open Source Drug Discovery. *The Open Conference Proceedings Journal*. Retrieved from http://benthamscience.com/open/toprocj/articles/V002/130TOPROCJ.pdf

Roy, A., McDonald, P.R., Sittampalam, S., & Chaguturu, R. (2010). Open access high throughput drug discovery in the public domain: a Mount Everest in the making. *Curr Pharm Biotechnol.*, *11*(7).

Roy, S., Balamurugan, C., & Gujar, S. (2013). Sustainable employment in India by crowdsourcing enterprise tasks. *Proceedings of the 3rd ACM Symposium on Computing for Development*. 10.1145/2442882.2442904

Ryan, R. M., & Deci, E. L. (2000). Self-determination theory and the facilitation of intrinsic motivation, social development, and well-being. *The American Psychologist*, *55*(1), 68–78. doi:10.1037/0003-066X.55.1.68 PMID:11392867

Sabou, M., Bontcheva, K., Derczynski, L., & Scharl, A. (2014). Corpus Annotation through Crowdsourcing: Towards Best Practice Guidelines. *Proceedings of the Conference on Language Resources and Evaluation (LREC)*.

Sage Bionetworks. (n.d.). Retrieved from: http://sagebase.org/

Salamon, L. M., & Anheier, H. K. (1992). In Search of the Non-Profit Sector. I: The question Of Definitions. *Voluntas*, *3*(2), 125–151. doi:10.1007/BF01397770

Sanga, C. A., Masamaki, J. P., Fue, K. G., Mlozi, M. R. S., & Tumbo, S. D. (2016b). Experimenting Open Agricultural Extension Service in Tanzania: A case of Kilosa Open Data Initiative (KODI). *Journal of Scientific and Engineering Research*, *3*(6), 116–124.

Sanga, C. A., Phillipo, J., Mlozi, M. R. S., Haug, R., & Tumbo, S. D. (2016a). Crowdsourcing platform " Ushaurikilimo " enabling questions answering between farmers, extension agents and researchers. *International Journal of Instructional Technology and Distance Learning*, *13*(10), 19–28.

Sanga, C., Fue, K., Nicodemus, N., & Kilima, F. (2013). Web-based System for Monitoring and Evaluation of Agricultural Projects. *International Journal of Interdisciplinary Studies on Information Technology and Business*, *1*(1), 17–43.

Saxton, G. D., Oh, O., & Kishore, R. (2013). Rules of Crowdsourcing: Models, Issues, and Systems of Control. *Information Systems Management*, *30*(1), 2–20. doi:10.1080/10580530.2013.739883

Schall, D. (2012). *Service-Oriented Crowdsourcing - Architecture, Protocols and Algorithms. Springer Briefs in Computer Science*. Springer.

Schemmann, B., Herrmann, A. M., Chappin, M. M. H., & Heimeriks, G. J. (2016). Crowdsourcing Ideas: Involving Ordinary Users in the Ideation Phase of New Product Development. *Research Policy*, *45*(6), 1145–1154. doi:10.1016/j.respol.2016.02.003

Schlagwein, D. & Bjorn-Andersen, N. (2014). Organizational Learning with Crowdsourcing: The Revelatory Case of LEGO. *Journal of the Association for Information Systems, 15*(11).

Schlagwein, D., Conboy, K., Feller, J., Leimeister, J. M., & Morgan, L. (2017). *"Openness" with and without Information Technology: a framework and a brief history*. Springer.

Schönström, M. (2005). Creating Knowledge Networks: Lessons from Practice. *Journal of Knowledge Management*, *9*(6), 17–29. doi:10.1108/13673270510629936

Schuhmacher, Gassmann, O., & Hinder, M. (2016). Chasnging R&D Models in research-based pharmaceutical companies. *Journal of Translational Medicine*, *14*(1), 105. doi:10.118612967-016-0838-4 PMID:27118048

Schumacker, R. E., & Lomax, R. G. (2010). *A Beginner's Guide to Structural Equation Modeling* (3rd ed.). New York: Routledge, Taylor & Francis.

Schumpeter, J. A. (1934). *The theory of economic development*. Cambridge, MA: Harvard University Press.

Schwartz, S. L., & Austin, M. J. (2008). Leading and Managing Nonprofit Organizations: Mapping the Knowledge Base of Nonprofit Management in the Human Services. *Nonprofit Management in the Human Services*, 1-94. Retrieved from http://mackcenter.berkeley.edu/assets/files/articles/Leading%20and%20Managing%20Nonprofit%20Organizations%20Mapping%20the%20Knowledge%20Base.pdf

Sedkaoui, S. (2017). The Internet, Data Analytics and Big Data. In Internet Economics: Models, Mechanisms and Management (pp. 144-166). Gottinger: eBook Bentham Science Publishers.

Sedkaoui, S., & Monino, J. L. (2016). *Big data, Open Data and Data Development*. New York: ISTE-Wiley.

Seltzer, E., & Mahmoudi, D. (2013). Citizen Participation, Open Innovation, and Crowdsourcing Challenges and Opportunities for Planning. *Journal of Planning Literature, 28*(1), 3–18. doi:10.1177/0885412212469112

SETI@home. (n.d.). Retrieved May 29, 2017, from http://setiathome.berkeley.edu/

Shani, A.B., & Sena, J. A. (2016). *Knowledge Management and New Product Development: Learning from a Software Development Firm*. Available at: http://ceurws.org/Vol-34/shani_sena.pdf

Sharifi, M., Fink, E., & Carbonell, J. G. (2011). *Smartnotes: Application of crowdsourcing to the detection of web threats*. Paper presented at the Systems, Man, and Cybernetics (SMC), 2011 IEEE International Conference on. 10.1109/ICSMC.2011.6083845

Sharma, R., Yetton, P., & Crawford, J. (2009). Estimating the Effect of Common Method Variance: The Method - Method Pair Technique with an Illustration from TAM Research. *Management Information Systems Quarterly, 33*(3), 473–490. doi:10.2307/20650305

Sharp, P. (2006). MaKE: A Knowledge Management Method. *Journal of Knowledge Management, 10*(6), 100–109. doi:10.1108/13673270610709242

Shaw, A. D., Horton, J. J., & Chen, D. L. (2011). Designing incentives for inexpert human raters. *Proceedings of the ACM 2011 conference on Computer supported cooperative work.*

Sherman, A. (2011). *How 3 Cities Are Crowdsourcing for Community Revitalization*. Retrieved December 1, 2017, from http://mashable.com/2011/07/20/crowdsourcing-city-tech/

Shih, C.-S., Chen, L.-J., Lin, C.-J., & Chung, W.-H. (2012). Open Information Gateway for Disaster management. *IEEE International Conference on Communications (ICC).*

Shroff, G. (2013). *The Intelligent Web, Search, Smart Algorithms and Big Data*. Oxford, UK: Oxford Univ. Press.

Siegel, E. (2013). *Predictive analytics: The power to predict who will click, buy, lie, or die*. John Wiley & Sons.

Siegel, E. (2016). *Predictive Analytics*. New York: Wiley.

Simon, H. (1977). *The New Science of Management Decision*. Englewood Cliffs, NJ: Prentice Hall.

Simon, H. (1997). *Administrative behavior: A study of decision-making processes in administrative orgnizations*. New York: Free Press.

Singh, M. D., Shankar, R., Narain, R., & Kumar, A. (2006). Survey of Knowledge Management Practices in Indian Manufacturing Industries. *Journal of Knowledge Management, 10*(6), 110–128. doi:10.1108/13673270610709251

Sivula, A., & Kantola, J. (2015). Ontology focused crowdsourcing management. *Procedia Manufacturing, 3*, 632–638. doi:10.1016/j.promfg.2015.07.286

Sloane, P. (2011). *A Guide to Open Innovation and Crowdsourcing: Advice from Leading Experts*. Kogan Page Publishers.

Smith, J. G., & Lumba, P. M. (2008). Knowledge Management Practices and Challenges in International Networked NGOs: The Case of One World International. *Electronic Journal of Knowledge Management, 6*(2), 167–176.

Smith, M. L., & Seward, R. (2017). Openness as social praxis. *First Monday, 22*(4). doi:10.5210/fm.v22i4.7073

Söldner, J.-H., Haller, J., Bullinger, A. C., & Möslein, K. M. (2009). *Supporting Research Collaboration-On the Needs of Virtual Research Teams*. Paper presented at the Wirtschaftsinformatik (1).

Sotrender. (2017a). *Facebook Trends Poland.* Retrieved April, from https://www.sotrender.com/trends/facebook/poland/201702/porownanie-branz, DC: Author.

Sotrender. (2017b). *Poznaj swoich odbiorców i zrozum ich zachowanie*. Retrieved from https://www.sotrender.com/pl/audience/, DC: Author.

Stańczyk-Hugiet, E. (2007). Strategiczny kontekst zarządzania wiedzą. Wydawnictwo Akademii Ekonomicznej we Wrocławiu, Wrocław.

Stankowsky, M. A. (2005). Advances in Knowledge Management: University Research Toward an Academic Discipline. In *Creating the Discipline of Knowledge Management: The Latest in University Research*. Burlington: Elsevier Butterworth-Heinemann. doi:10.1016/B978-0-7506-7878-0.50005-3

Staw, B., & Epstein, L. (2000). What bandwagons bring: Effects of popular management techniques on corporate performance, reputation, and CEO pay. *Administrative Science Quarterly, 45*(3), 553–556. doi:10.2307/2667108

Steadman, I. (2013). *Big data and the death of the theorist*. Available at: http://www.wired.co.uk/news/archive/2013-01/25/big-data-end-of-theory

Steinmacher, I., Conte, T., Gerosa, M. A., & Redmiles, D. (2015). Social barriers faced by newcomers placing their first contribution in open source software projects. *Proceedings of the 18th ACM conference on Computer supported cooperative work & social computing*. 10.1145/2675133.2675215

Stieger, D., Matzler, K., Chatterjee, S., & Ladstaetter-Fussenegger, F. (2012). Democratizing Strategy: How Crowdsourcing Can be Used for Strategy Dialogues. *California Management Review*, *54*(4), 44–68. doi:10.1525/cmr.2012.54.4.44

Strang, D., & Soule, S. A. (1998). Diffusion in Organizations and Social Movements: From Hybrid Corn to Poison Pills. *Annual Review of Sociology*, *24*(1), 265–290. doi:10.1146/annurev.soc.24.1.265

Streeten, P. (1997). Nongovernmental Organizations and Development. *The Annals of the American Academy of Political and Social Science*, *554*(1), 193–210. doi:10.1177/0002716297554001012

Sturdy, A. (1997). The consultancy process – An insecure business? *Journal of Management Studies*, *34*(3), 389–413. doi:10.1111/1467-6486.00056

Surma, K., Krzycki, M., Prokurat, S., & Kubisiak, P. (2012). *Raport z badania Polskie firmy w mediach społecznościowych*. Retrieved from https://www.hbrp.pl/b/raport-z-badania-polskie-firmy-w-mediach-spolecznosciowych/b9PFjezh

Surowiecki, J. (2004). *The Wisdom of Crowds: Why the Many Are Smarter Than the Few and How Collective Wisdom Shapes Business, Economies, Societies, and Nations*. New York: Doubleday.

Swanson, E. B., & Ramiller, N. C. (1997). The organizing vision in information systems innovation. *Organization Science*, *8*(5), 458–474. doi:10.1287/orsc.8.5.458

Tarrell, A., Tahmasbi, N., Kocsis, D., Tripathi, A., Pedersen, J., Xiong, J., ... (2013). *Crowdsourcing: A Snapshot of Published Research*. Paper presented at the Nineteenth Americas Conference on Information Systems, Chicago, IL.

Tavakoli, A., Schlagwein, D., & Schoder, D. (2017). Open strategy: Literature review, re-analysis of cases and conceptualisation as a practice. *The Journal of Strategic Information Systems*, *26*(3), 163–184. doi:10.1016/j.jsis.2017.01.003

Tek, N. D. (2002). *The role of Non-Governmental Organisations in the improvement of livelihood in Nepal*. Tampere University Press.

Thuan, N. H., Antunes, P., & Johnstone, D. (2017). A process model for establishing business process crowdsourcing. *AJIS. Australasian Journal of Information Systems*, 21.

Tiwana, A. (2003). *Przewodnik po zarządzaniu wiedzą: e-biznes i zastosowania CRM*. Warszawa: Placet.

Tokhi, A., & Rauh, C. (2015). Die schiere Menge sagt noch nichts. Big Data in den Sozialwissenschaften. *WZB Mitteilungen*, *150*, 6–9.

Tomczak, A., & Brem, A. (2013). A conceptualized investment model of crowdfunding. *Venture Capital*, *15*(4), 335–359. doi:10.1080/13691066.2013.847614

Tripathi, A., Tahmasbi, N., Khazanchi, D., & Najjar, L. (2014). Crowdsourcing typology: a review of is research and organizations. *Proceedings of the Midwest Association for Information Systems (MWAIS)*.

Trudell, E. (2014). *Crowdsourcing as a Tool for Knowledge Management*. Retrieved from https://web.jinfo.com/go/blog/71903

Tsai, H.-S., Jiang, M., Alhabash, S., LaRose, R., Rifon, N. J., & Cotten, S. R. (2016). Understanding online safety behaviors: A protection motivation theory perspective. *Computers & Security*, *59*, 138–150. doi:10.1016/j.cose.2016.02.009

Tseng, T. L., Huang, C. C., Fan, Y. N., & Lee, C. H. (2015). Quality Control Using Agent Based Framework. In *Encyclopedia of Information Science and Technology* (3rd ed., pp. 5211–5223). Hershey, PA: IGI Global.

Tucker, E. (2013). *APQC's Knowledge Management Program Framework: A Road Map for Your KM Journey*. Houston, TX: Academic Press.

Turban, E., Liang, T. P., & Wu, S. P. (2011). A framework for adopting collaboration 2.0 tools for virtual group decision making. *Group Decision and Negotiation*, *20*(2), 137–154. doi:10.100710726-010-9215-5

UNCF and Regional Office for South Asia. (2008). *Learning from KM Experiences: Case studies on KM initiatives in UNICEF South Asia*. UN Regional Offices and Selected Agencies Possible. Retrieved from http://www.unicef.org/rosa/Learning_from_KM_Experiences.pdf

United Nation Volunteers (UNV). (2012). *Volunteering in India: Contexts, Perspectives and Discourses*. New Delhi: United Nations Development Programme. Retrieved from http://www.in.undp.org/content/dam/india/docs/UNV/volunteering-in-india-contexts-perspectives-and-discourses.pdf?download

Uriarte, F. A. (2008). *Introduction to Knowledge Management.* Jakarta: ASEAN Foundation.

USAID. (2013). *Crowdsourcing Applications For Agricultural Development in Africa.* USAID.

Väätäjä, H. (2012). Readers' motivations to participate in hyperlocal news content creation. *Proceedings of the 17th ACM international conference on Supporting group work.* 10.1145/2389176.2389234

Van Dyne, L., & Pierce, J. L. (2004). Psychological ownership and feelings of possession: Three field studies predicting employee attitudes and organizational citizenship behaviour. *Journal of Organizational Behavior, 25*(4), 439–459. doi:10.1002/job.249

Vance, A., Lowry, P., & Eggett, D. (2015). *Increasing Accountability through the User Interface Design Artifacts: A New Approach to Addressing the Problem of Access-Policy Violations.* Academic Press.

Vasilescu, B., Serebrenik, A., Devanbu, P., & Filkov, V. (2014). How social Q&A sites are changing knowledge sharing in open source software communities. *Proceedings of the 17th ACM conference on Computer supported cooperative work & social computing.* 10.1145/2531602.2531659

Venkatesh, V., & Bala, H. (2008). Technology acceptance model 3 and a research agenda on interventions. *Decision Sciences, 39*(2), 273–315. doi:10.1111/j.1540-5915.2008.00192.x

Voluntary Action Network India. (2012). *Status of the Voluntary Sector in India: A Study Report.* New Delhi: Voluntary Action Network India (VANI). Retrieved from http://www.vaniindia.org/update/Inside%20Pages%20-Status%20Voluntary%20Sector%20dt%2022-6-13.pdf

Vukovic & Bartolini. (2010). Towards a research agenda for enterprise crowdsourcing. *Leveraging applications of formal methods, verification, and validation*, 425-434.

Vukovic, M. (2009). Crowdsourcing for Enterprises. In SERVICES '09 Proceed of the 2009 Congr on Services - I (pp. 686-692). Los Angeles, CA: Academic Press.

Walczak, S. (2008). Knowledge Management and Organizational Learning: An International Research Perspective. *The Learning Organization, 15*(6), 486–494. doi:10.1108/09696470810907392

Waldron, R. F. (2012). *Open Innovation in Pharma – Defining Dialogue*. Retrieved from http://www.pharmexec.com/pharmexec/article/articleDetail.jsp?id=788391&pageID=1&sk=&date=

Wang, S., & Noe, R. A. (2010). Knowledge sharing: A review and directions for future research. *Human Resource Management Review*, *20*(2), 115–131. doi:10.1016/j.hrmr.2009.10.001

Wasko, M. M., & Faraj, S. (2005). Why should I share? Examining social capital and knowledge contribution in electronic networks of practices. *Management Information Systems Quarterly*, *29*(1), 35. doi:10.2307/25148667

Weather forecasting. (n.d.). Retrieved June 2, 2017, from https://en.wikipedia.org/wiki/Weather_forecasting

Wegner, D. M., Erber, R., & Raymond, P. (1991). Transactive Memory in Close Relationships. *Journal of Personality and Social Psychology*, *61*(6), 923–929. doi:10.1037/0022-3514.61.6.923 PMID:1774630

Wernerfelt, B. (1984). 'The resource-based view of the firm'. *Strategic Management Journal*, *5*(2), 171–180. doi:10.1002mj.4250050207

Wesselink, A., Hoppe, R., & Lemmens, R. (2015). Not just a tool. Taking context into account in the development of a mobile app for rural water supply in Tanzania. *Water Alternatives*, *8*(2).

Westin, A. (1967). *Privacy and Freedom*. New York: Atheneum Publishers.

West, J., Salter, A., Vanhaverbeke, W., & Chesbrough, H. (2014). Open innovation: The next decade. *Research Policy*, *43*(5), 805–811. doi:10.1016/j.respol.2014.03.001

Wexler, M. N. (2011). Reconfiguring the sociology of the crowd: Exploring crowdsourcing. *The International Journal of Sociology and Social Policy*, *31*(1/2), 6–20. doi:10.1108/01443331111104779

Whelan, E. (2007). Exploring knowledge exchange in electronic networks of practice. *Journal of Information Technology*, *22*(1), 5–12. doi:10.1057/palgrave.jit.2000089

Whitla, P. (2009). Crowdsourcing and its application in marketing activities. *Contemporary Management Research*, *5*(1). doi:10.7903/cmr.1145

Wiele, van der A. (1998). *Beyond Fads: Management Fads and Organizational Change with Reference to Quality Management*. Delft: Eburon Publishers.

Wiig, K. M. (1997). Knowledge Management: An Introduction and Perspective. *Journal of Knowledge Management*, *1*(1), 6–14. doi:10.1108/13673279710800682

Wikhamn, B. R., & Wikhamn, W. (2013). Structuring of the Open Innovation Field. *Journal of Technology Management & Innovation*, *8*(3), 173–185.

Wilhelm, H., & Bort, S. (2013). How managers talk about their consumption of popular management concepts: Identity, rules and situations. *British Journal of Management*, *24*(3), 428–444. doi:10.1111/j.1467-8551.2012.00813.x

Wilson, H. J., Guinan, P. J., Parise, S., & Weinberg, B. D. (2011, July). *What's Your Social Media Strategy? Harvard Business Review*.

Wiślicki, W., Bednarski, T., Białas, P., Czerwiński, E., Kapłon, Ł., Kochanowski, A., & Silar, M. (2014). *Computing support for advanced medical data analysis and imaging*. Bio-Algorithms and Med-Systems.

Wolfson, S. M., & Lease, M. (2011). Look before you leap: Legal pitfalls of crowdsourcing. *American Society for Information Science and Technology*, *48*(1), 1–10.

Wong, K. Y. (1989). Critical success factors for implementing knowledge management in small and medium enterprises. *Industrial Management & Data Systems*, *105*(3/4), 261–279.

Wood, R., & Bandura, A. (1989). Social cognitive theory of organizational management. Academy of management. *Academy of Management Review*, *14*(3), 361–384.

Workshop, J. J. (2013). *Big Data and Disaster Management.* NSF & JST Workshop.

World Bank and Civil Society Collaboration. (2002). *Non-Governmental Organizations and Civil Society Engagement in World Bank Supported Projects: Lessons from OED Evaluations*. Retrieved from http://lnweb90.worldbank.org/oed/oeddoclib.nsf/DocUNIDViewForJavaSearch/851D373F39609C0B85256C230057A3E3/$file/LP18.pdf

World Community Grid. (n.d.). Retrieved May 29, 2017, from https://www.worldcommunitygrid.org/discover.action#curent-projects

Yan, J., & Wang, X. (2013). *From Open Source to Commercial Software Development-the Community Based Software Development Model*. Academic Press.

Yang, H.-L., & Lai, C.-Y. (2010). Motivations of Wikipedia content contributors. *Computers in Human Behavior*, *26*(6), 1377–1383. doi:10.1016/j.chb.2010.04.011

Yang, J., Adamic, L., & Ackerman, M. (2008). Crowdsourcing and knowledge sharing: strategic user behavior on Taskcn. *Proceedings of the 9th ACM International Conference on Electronic Commerce*. 10.1145/1386790.1386829

Your Encore. (n.d.). We are a talent community of experts united in our pursuit to make an impact. *Your Encore.* Retrieved from: www.yourencore.com

Yu, L. L., & Nickerson, J. V. (2011). *Generating creative ideas through crowds: An experimental study of combination*. Academic Press.

Yu, C., Yu, T., & Yu, C. (2013). KS, organizational climate, and innovative behavior: A cross-level analysis of effects. *Social Behavior and Personality, 41*(1), 143–156. doi:10.2224bp.2013.41.1.143

Zaei, M. E., & Kapil, P. (2016). The Role of Intellectual Capital in Promoting Knowledge Management Initiatives. *Knowledge Management & E-Learning: An International Journal, 8*(2), 317-333.

Zapata Cantu, L. E., & Mondragon, C. E. (2016). Knowledge Management in Mexican NPOs: A Comparative Study in Organizations with a Local and National Presence. *Journal of Knowledge Management, 20*(1), 69–87. doi:10.1108/JKM-12-2014-0494

Zeng, Z., Tang, J., & Wang, T. (2017). Motivation mechanism of gamification in crowdsourcing projects. *International Journal of Crowd Science, 1*(1), 71–82. doi:10.1108/IJCS-12-2016-0001

Zhang, A. (2017). *Data analytics: Practical guide to leveraging the power of Algorithms, data science, data mining, statistics, big data, and predictive analysis to improve business, work, and life*. Kindle edition.

Zhang, X., & Zhu, F. (2006). *Intrinsic motivation of open content contributors: The case of Wikipedia.* Paper presented at the Workshop on Information Systems and Economics.

Zhao, Y., & Zhu, Q. (2012a). *A Conceptual Model for Participant's Motivation in Crowdsourcing Contest*. Academic Press.

Zhao, Y., & Zhu, Q. (2012b). *Exploring the motivation of participants in crowdsourcing contest*. Academic Press.

Zhao, Y. Ch., & Zhu, Q. (2014). Effects of Extrinsic and Intrinsic Motivation on Participation in Crowdsourcing Contest. *Online Information Review, 38*(7), 896–917. doi:10.1108/OIR-08-2014-0188

Zhao, Y., & Zhu, Q. (2012). *Exploring the Motivation of Participants in Crowdsourcing Contest.* ICIS Association for Information Systems.

Zhao, Y., & Zhu, Q. (2014). Evaluation on crowdsourcing research: Current status and future direction. *Information Systems Frontiers, 16*(3), 417–434. doi:10.100710796-012-9350-4

Zheng, H., Li, D., & Hou, W. (2011). Task design, motivation, and participation in crowdsourcing contests. *International Journal of Electronic Commerce*, *15*(4), 57–88. doi:10.2753/JEC1086-4415150402

Zogaj, S., Bretschneider, U., & Leimeister, J. M. (2014). Managing crowdsourced software testing: A case study based insight on the challenges of a crowdsourcing intermediary. *Journal of Business Economics*, *84*(3), 375–405. doi:10.100711573-014-0721-9

Zou, L., Ke, W., Zhang, J., & Wei, K. K. (2014). *User Creativity in Crowdsourcing Community: From Extrinsic Motivation Perspective.* Paper presented at the 18th Pacific Asia Conference on Information Systems (PACIS 2014), Chengdu, China.

Zwass, V. (2010). Co-creation: Toward a taxonomy and an integrated research perspective? *International Journal of Electronic Commerce*, *15*(1), 11–48. doi:10.2753/JEC1086-4415150101

Related References

To continue our tradition of advancing information science and technology research, we have compiled a list of recommended IGI Global readings. These references will provide additional information and guidance to further enrich your knowledge and assist you with your own research and future publications.

Abtahi, M. S., Behboudi, L., & Hasanabad, H. M. (2017). Factors Affecting Internet Advertising Adoption in Ad Agencies. *International Journal of Innovation in the Digital Economy*, *8*(4), 18–29. doi:10.4018/IJIDE.2017100102

Agrawal, S. (2017). The Impact of Emerging Technologies and Social Media on Different Business(es): Marketing and Management. In O. Rishi & A. Sharma (Eds.), *Maximizing Business Performance and Efficiency Through Intelligent Systems* (pp. 37–49). Hershey, PA: IGI Global. doi:10.4018/978-1-5225-2234-8.ch002

Alnoukari, M., Razouk, R., & Hanano, A. (2016). BSC-SI: A Framework for Integrating Strategic Intelligence in Corporate Strategic Management. *International Journal of Social and Organizational Dynamics in IT*, *5*(2), 1–14. doi:10.4018/IJSODIT.2016070101

Alnoukari, M., Razouk, R., & Hanano, A. (2016). BSC-SI, A Framework for Integrating Strategic Intelligence in Corporate Strategic Management. *International Journal of Strategic Information Technology and Applications*, *7*(1), 32–44. doi:10.4018/IJSITA.2016010103

Altındağ, E. (2016). Current Approaches in Change Management. In A. Goksoy (Ed.), *Organizational Change Management Strategies in Modern Business* (pp. 24–51). Hershey, PA: IGI Global. doi:10.4018/978-1-4666-9533-7.ch002

Alvarez-Dionisi, L. E., Turner, R., & Mittra, M. (2016). Global Project Management Trends. *International Journal of Information Technology Project Management, 7*(3), 54–73. doi:10.4018/IJITPM.2016070104

Anantharaman, R. N., Rajeswari, K. S., Angusamy, A., & Kuppusamy, J. (2017). Role of Self-Efficacy and Collective Efficacy as Moderators of Occupational Stress Among Software Development Professionals. *International Journal of Human Capital and Information Technology Professionals, 8*(2), 45–58. doi:10.4018/IJHCITP.2017040103

Aninze, F., El-Gohary, H., & Hussain, J. (2018). The Role of Microfinance to Empower Women: The Case of Developing Countries. *International Journal of Customer Relationship Marketing and Management, 9*(1), 54–78. doi:10.4018/IJCRMM.2018010104

Arsenijević, O. M., Orčić, D., & Kastratović, E. (2017). Development of an Optimization Tool for Intangibles in SMEs: A Case Study from Serbia with a Pilot Research in the Prestige by Milka Company. In M. Vemić (Ed.), *Optimal Management Strategies in Small and Medium Enterprises* (pp. 320–347). Hershey, PA: IGI Global. doi:10.4018/978-1-5225-1949-2.ch015

Aryanto, V. D., Wismantoro, Y., & Widyatmoko, K. (2018). Implementing Eco-Innovation by Utilizing the Internet to Enhance Firm's Marketing Performance: Study of Green Batik Small and Medium Enterprises in Indonesia. *International Journal of E-Business Research, 14*(1), 21–36. doi:10.4018/IJEBR.2018010102

Atiku, S. O., & Fields, Z. (2017). Multicultural Orientations for 21st Century Global Leadership. In N. Baporikar (Ed.), *Management Education for Global Leadership* (pp. 28–51). Hershey, PA: IGI Global. doi:10.4018/978-1-5225-1013-0.ch002

Atiku, S. O., & Fields, Z. (2018). Organisational Learning Dimensions and Talent Retention Strategies for the Service Industries. In N. Baporikar (Ed.), *Global Practices in Knowledge Management for Societal and Organizational Development* (pp. 358–381). Hershey, PA: IGI Global. doi:10.4018/978-1-5225-3009-1.ch017

Ávila, L., & Teixeira, L. (2018). The Main Concepts Behind the Dematerialization of Business Processes. In M. Khosrow-Pour, D.B.A. (Ed.), Encyclopedia of Information Science and Technology, Fourth Edition (pp. 888-898). Hershey, PA: IGI Global. doi:10.4018/978-1-5225-2255-3.ch076

Bartens, Y., Chunpir, H. I., Schulte, F., & Voß, S. (2017). Business/IT Alignment in Two-Sided Markets: A COBIT 5 Analysis for Media Streaming Business Models. In S. De Haes & W. Van Grembergen (Eds.), *Strategic IT Governance and Alignment in Business Settings* (pp. 82–111). Hershey, PA: IGI Global. doi:10.4018/978-1-5225-0861-8.ch004

Bashayreh, A. M. (2018). Organizational Culture and Organizational Performance. In W. Lee & F. Sabetzadeh (Eds.), *Contemporary Knowledge and Systems Science* (pp. 50–69). Hershey, PA: IGI Global. doi:10.4018/978-1-5225-5655-8.ch003

Bedford, D. A. (2018). Sustainable Knowledge Management Strategies: Aligning Business Capabilities and Knowledge Management Goals. In N. Baporikar (Ed.), *Global Practices in Knowledge Management for Societal and Organizational Development* (pp. 46–73). Hershey, PA: IGI Global. doi:10.4018/978-1-5225-3009-1.ch003

Benmoussa, F., Nakara, W. A., & Jaouen, A. (2016). The Use of Social Media by SMEs in the Tourism Industry. In I. Lee (Ed.), *Encyclopedia of E-Commerce Development, Implementation, and Management* (pp. 2159–2170). Hershey, PA: IGI Global. doi:10.4018/978-1-4666-9787-4.ch155

Berger, R. (2016). Indigenous Management and Bottom of Pyramid Countries: The Role of National Institutions. In U. Aung & P. Ordoñez de Pablos (Eds.), *Managerial Strategies and Practice in the Asian Business Sector* (pp. 107–123). Hershey, PA: IGI Global. doi:10.4018/978-1-4666-9758-4.ch007

Bharwani, S., & Musunuri, D. (2018). Reflection as a Process From Theory to Practice. In M. Khosrow-Pour, D.B.A. (Ed.), Encyclopedia of Information Science and Technology, Fourth Edition (pp. 1529-1539). Hershey, PA: IGI Global. doi:10.4018/978-1-5225-2255-3.ch132

Bhatt, G. D., Wang, Z., & Rodger, J. A. (2017). Information Systems Capabilities and Their Effects on Competitive Advantages: A Study of Chinese Companies. *Information Resources Management Journal, 30*(3), 41–57. doi:10.4018/IRMJ.2017070103

Bhushan, M., & Yadav, A. (2017). Concept of Cloud Computing in ESB. In R. Bhadoria, N. Chaudhari, G. Tomar, & S. Singh (Eds.), *Exploring Enterprise Service Bus in the Service-Oriented Architecture Paradigm* (pp. 116–127). Hershey, PA: IGI Global. doi:10.4018/978-1-5225-2157-0.ch008

Bhushan, S. (2017). System Dynamics Base-Model of Humanitarian Supply Chain (HSCM) in Disaster Prone Eco-Communities of India: A Discussion on Simulation and Scenario Results. *International Journal of System Dynamics Applications, 6*(3), 20–37. doi:10.4018/IJSDA.2017070102

Biswas, A., & De, A. K. (2017). On Development of a Fuzzy Stochastic Programming Model with Its Application to Business Management. In S. Trivedi, S. Dey, A. Kumar, & T. Panda (Eds.), *Handbook of Research on Advanced Data Mining Techniques and Applications for Business Intelligence* (pp. 353–378). Hershey, PA: IGI Global. doi:10.4018/978-1-5225-2031-3.ch021

Bücker, J., & Ernste, K. (2018). Use of Brand Heroes in Strategic Reputation Management: The Case of Bacardi, Adidas, and Daimler. In A. Erdemir (Ed.), *Reputation Management Techniques in Public Relations* (pp. 126–150). Hershey, PA: IGI Global. doi:10.4018/978-1-5225-3619-2.ch007

Bureš, V. (2018). Industry 4.0 From the Systems Engineering Perspective: Alternative Holistic Framework Development. In R. Brunet-Thornton & F. Martinez (Eds.), *Analyzing the Impacts of Industry 4.0 in Modern Business Environments* (pp. 199–223). Hershey, PA: IGI Global. doi:10.4018/978-1-5225-3468-6.ch011

Buzady, Z. (2017). Resolving the Magic Cube of Effective Case Teaching: Benchmarking Case Teaching Practices in Emerging Markets – Insights from the Central European University Business School, Hungary. In D. Latusek (Ed.), *Case Studies as a Teaching Tool in Management Education* (pp. 79–103). Hershey, PA: IGI Global. doi:10.4018/978-1-5225-0770-3.ch005

Campatelli, G., Richter, A., & Stocker, A. (2016). Participative Knowledge Management to Empower Manufacturing Workers. *International Journal of Knowledge Management, 12*(4), 37–50. doi:10.4018/IJKM.2016100103

Căpusneanu, S., & Topor, D. I. (2018). Business Ethics and Cost Management in SMEs: Theories of Business Ethics and Cost Management Ethos. In I. Oncioiu (Ed.), *Ethics and Decision-Making for Sustainable Business Practices* (pp. 109–127). Hershey, PA: IGI Global. doi:10.4018/978-1-5225-3773-1.ch007

Carneiro, A. (2016). Maturity in Health Organization Information Systems: Metrics and Privacy Perspectives. *International Journal of Privacy and Health Information Management, 4*(2), 1–18. doi:10.4018/IJPHIM.2016070101

Chan, R. L., Mo, P. L., & Moon, K. K. (2018). Strategic and Tactical Measures in Managing Enterprise Risks: A Study of the Textile and Apparel Industry. In K. Strang, M. Korstanje, & N. Vajjhala (Eds.), *Research, Practices, and Innovations in Global Risk and Contingency Management* (pp. 1–19). Hershey, PA: IGI Global. doi:10.4018/978-1-5225-4754-9.ch001

Chandan, H. C. (2016). Motivations and Challenges of Female Entrepreneurship in Developed and Developing Economies. In N. Baporikar (Ed.), *Handbook of Research on Entrepreneurship in the Contemporary Knowledge-Based Global Economy* (pp. 260–286). Hershey, PA: IGI Global. doi:10.4018/978-1-4666-8798-1.ch012

Charlier, S. D., Burke-Smalley, L. A., & Fisher, S. L. (2018). Undergraduate Programs in the U.S: A Contextual and Content-Based Analysis. In J. Mendy (Ed.), *Teaching Human Resources and Organizational Behavior at the College Level* (pp. 26–57). Hershey, PA: IGI Global. doi:10.4018/978-1-5225-2820-3.ch002

Chaudhuri, S. (2016). Application of Web-Based Geographical Information System (GIS) in E-Business. In U. Panwar, R. Kumar, & N. Ray (Eds.), *Handbook of Research on Promotional Strategies and Consumer Influence in the Service Sector* (pp. 389–405). Hershey, PA: IGI Global. doi:10.4018/978-1-5225-0143-5.ch023

Choudhuri, P. S. (2016). An Empirical Study on the Quality of Services Offered by the Private Life Insurers in Burdwan. In U. Panwar, R. Kumar, & N. Ray (Eds.), *Handbook of Research on Promotional Strategies and Consumer Influence in the Service Sector* (pp. 31–55). Hershey, PA: IGI Global. doi:10.4018/978-1-5225-0143-5.ch002

Dahlberg, T., Kivijärvi, H., & Saarinen, T. (2017). IT Investment Consistency and Other Factors Influencing the Success of IT Performance. In S. De Haes & W. Van Grembergen (Eds.), *Strategic IT Governance and Alignment in Business Settings* (pp. 176–208). Hershey, PA: IGI Global. doi:10.4018/978-1-5225-0861-8.ch007

Damnjanović, A. M. (2017). Knowledge Management Optimization through IT and E-Business Utilization: A Qualitative Study on Serbian SMEs. In M. Vemić (Ed.), *Optimal Management Strategies in Small and Medium Enterprises* (pp. 249–267). Hershey, PA: IGI Global. doi:10.4018/978-1-5225-1949-2.ch012

Daneshpour, H. (2017). Integrating Sustainable Development into Project Portfolio Management through Application of Open Innovation. In M. Vemić (Ed.), *Optimal Management Strategies in Small and Medium Enterprises* (pp. 370–387). Hershey, PA: IGI Global. doi:10.4018/978-1-5225-1949-2.ch017

Daniel, A. D., & Reis de Castro, V. (2018). Entrepreneurship Education: How to Measure the Impact on Nascent Entrepreneurs. In A. Carrizo Moreira, J. Guilherme Leitão Dantas, & F. Manuel Valente (Eds.), *Nascent Entrepreneurship and Successful New Venture Creation* (pp. 85–110). Hershey, PA: IGI Global. doi:10.4018/978-1-5225-2936-1.ch004

David, F., van der Sijde, P., & van den Besselaar, P. (2016). Enterpreneurial Incentives, Obstacles, and Management in University-Business Co-Operation: The Case of Indonesia. In J. Saiz-Álvarez (Ed.), *Handbook of Research on Social Entrepreneurship and Solidarity Economics* (pp. 499–518). Hershey, PA: IGI Global. doi:10.4018/978-1-5225-0097-1.ch024

David, R., Swami, B. N., & Tangirala, S. (2018). Ethics Impact on Knowledge Management in Organizational Development: A Case Study. In N. Baporikar (Ed.), *Global Practices in Knowledge Management for Societal and Organizational Development* (pp. 19–45). Hershey, PA: IGI Global. doi:10.4018/978-1-5225-3009-1.ch002

Delias, P., & Lakiotaki, K. (2018). Discovering Process Horizontal Boundaries to Facilitate Process Comprehension. *International Journal of Operations Research and Information Systems*, *9*(2), 1–31. doi:10.4018/IJORIS.2018040101

Denholm, J., & Lee-Davies, L. (2018). Success Factors for Games in Business and Project Management. In *Enhancing Education and Training Initiatives Through Serious Games* (pp. 34–68). Hershey, PA: IGI Global. doi:10.4018/978-1-5225-3689-5.ch002

Deshpande, M. (2017). Best Practices in Management Institutions for Global Leadership: Policy Aspects. In N. Baporikar (Ed.), *Management Education for Global Leadership* (pp. 1–27). Hershey, PA: IGI Global. doi:10.4018/978-1-5225-1013-0.ch001

Deshpande, M. (2018). Policy Perspectives for SMEs Knowledge Management. In N. Baporikar (Ed.), *Knowledge Integration Strategies for Entrepreneurship and Sustainability* (pp. 23–46). Hershey, PA: IGI Global. doi:10.4018/978-1-5225-5115-7.ch002

Dezdar, S. (2017). ERP Implementation Projects in Asian Countries: A Comparative Study on Iran and China. *International Journal of Information Technology Project Management*, *8*(3), 52–68. doi:10.4018/IJITPM.2017070104

Domingos, D., Martinho, R., & Varajão, J. (2016). Controlled Flexibility in Healthcare Processes: A BPMN-Extension Approach. In M. Cruz-Cunha, I. Miranda, R. Martinho, & R. Rijo (Eds.), *Encyclopedia of E-Health and Telemedicine* (pp. 521–535). Hershey, PA: IGI Global. doi:10.4018/978-1-4666-9978-6.ch040

Domingos, D., Respício, A., & Martinho, R. (2017). Reliability of IoT-Aware BPMN Healthcare Processes. In C. Reis & M. Maximiano (Eds.), *Internet of Things and Advanced Application in Healthcare* (pp. 214–248). Hershey, PA: IGI Global. doi:10.4018/978-1-5225-1820-4.ch008

Dosumu, O., Hussain, J., & El-Gohary, H. (2017). An Exploratory Study of the Impact of Government Policies on the Development of Small and Medium Enterprises in Developing Countries: The Case of Nigeria. *International Journal of Customer Relationship Marketing and Management, 8*(4), 51–62. doi:10.4018/IJCRMM.2017100104

Durst, S., Bruns, G., & Edvardsson, I. R. (2017). Retaining Knowledge in Smaller Building and Construction Firms. *International Journal of Knowledge and Systems Science, 8*(3), 1–12. doi:10.4018/IJKSS.2017070101

Edvardsson, I. R., & Durst, S. (2017). Outsourcing, Knowledge, and Learning: A Critical Review. *International Journal of Knowledge-Based Organizations, 7*(2), 13–26. doi:10.4018/IJKBO.2017040102

Edwards, J. S. (2018). Integrating Knowledge Management and Business Processes. In M. Khosrow-Pour, D.B.A. (Ed.), Encyclopedia of Information Science and Technology, Fourth Edition (pp. 5046-5055). Hershey, PA: IGI Global. doi:10.4018/978-1-5225-2255-3.ch437

Ejiogu, A. O. (2018). Economics of Farm Management. In *Agricultural Finance and Opportunities for Investment and Expansion* (pp. 56–72). Hershey, PA: IGI Global. doi:10.4018/978-1-5225-3059-6.ch003

Ekanem, I., & Abiade, G. E. (2018). Factors Influencing the Use of E-Commerce by Small Enterprises in Nigeria. *International Journal of ICT Research in Africa and the Middle East, 7*(1), 37–53. doi:10.4018/IJICTRAME.2018010103

Ekanem, I., & Alrossais, L. A. (2017). Succession Challenges Facing Family Businesses in Saudi Arabia. In P. Zgheib (Ed.), *Entrepreneurship and Business Innovation in the Middle East* (pp. 122–146). Hershey, PA: IGI Global. doi:10.4018/978-1-5225-2066-5.ch007

El Faquih, L., & Fredj, M. (2017). Ontology-Based Framework for Quality in Configurable Process Models. *Journal of Electronic Commerce in Organizations, 15*(2), 48–60. doi:10.4018/JECO.2017040104

El-Gohary, H., & El-Gohary, Z. (2016). An Attempt to Explore Electronic Marketing Adoption and Implementation Aspects in Developing Countries: The Case of Egypt. *International Journal of Customer Relationship Marketing and Management, 7*(4), 1–26. doi:10.4018/IJCRMM.2016100101

Entico, G. J. (2016). Knowledge Management and the Medical Health Librarians: A Perception Study. In J. Yap, M. Perez, M. Ayson, & G. Entico (Eds.), *Special Library Administration, Standardization and Technological Integration* (pp. 52–77). Hershey, PA: IGI Global. doi:10.4018/978-1-4666-9542-9.ch003

Faisal, M. N., & Talib, F. (2017). Building Ambidextrous Supply Chains in SMEs: How to Tackle the Barriers? *International Journal of Information Systems and Supply Chain Management, 10*(4), 80–100. doi:10.4018/IJISSCM.2017100105

Fernandes, T. M., Gomes, J., & Romão, M. (2017). Investments in E-Government: A Benefit Management Case Study. *International Journal of Electronic Government Research, 13*(3), 1–17. doi:10.4018/IJEGR.2017070101

Fouda, F. A. (2016). A Suggested Curriculum in Career Education to Develop Business Secondary Schools Students' Career Knowledge Management Domains and Professional Thinking. *International Journal of Technology Diffusion, 7*(2), 42–62. doi:10.4018/IJTD.2016040103

Gallardo-Vázquez, D., & Pajuelo-Moreno, M. L. (2016). How Spanish Universities are Promoting Entrepreneurship through Your Own Lines of Teaching and Research? In L. Carvalho (Ed.), *Handbook of Research on Entrepreneurial Success and its Impact on Regional Development* (pp. 431–454). Hershey, PA: IGI Global. doi:10.4018/978-1-4666-9567-2.ch019

Gao, S. S., Oreal, S., & Zhang, J. (2018). Contemporary Financial Risk Management Perceptions and Practices of Small-Sized Chinese Businesses. In I. Management Association (Ed.), Global Business Expansion: Concepts, Methodologies, Tools, and Applications (pp. 917-931). Hershey, PA: IGI Global. doi:10.4018/978-1-5225-5481-3.ch041

Garg, R., & Berning, S. C. (2017). Indigenous Chinese Management Philosophies: Key Concepts and Relevance for Modern Chinese Firms. In B. Christiansen & G. Koc (Eds.), *Transcontinental Strategies for Industrial Development and Economic Growth* (pp. 43–57). Hershey, PA: IGI Global. doi:10.4018/978-1-5225-2160-0.ch003

Gencer, Y. G. (2017). Supply Chain Management in Retailing Business. In U. Akkucuk (Ed.), *Ethics and Sustainability in Global Supply Chain Management* (pp. 197–210). Hershey, PA: IGI Global. doi:10.4018/978-1-5225-2036-8.ch011

Giacosa, E. (2016). Innovation in Luxury Fashion Businesses as a Means for the Regional Development. In L. Carvalho (Ed.), *Handbook of Research on Entrepreneurial Success and its Impact on Regional Development* (pp. 206–222). Hershey, PA: IGI Global. doi:10.4018/978-1-4666-9567-2.ch010

Giacosa, E. (2018). The Increasing of the Regional Development Thanks to the Luxury Business Innovation. In L. Carvalho (Ed.), *Handbook of Research on Entrepreneurial Ecosystems and Social Dynamics in a Globalized World* (pp. 260–273). Hershey, PA: IGI Global. doi:10.4018/978-1-5225-3525-6.ch011

Gianni, M., & Gotzamani, K. (2016). Integrated Management Systems and Information Management Systems: Common Threads. In P. Papajorgji, F. Pinet, A. Guimarães, & J. Papathanasiou (Eds.), *Automated Enterprise Systems for Maximizing Business Performance* (pp. 195–214). Hershey, PA: IGI Global. doi:10.4018/978-1-4666-8841-4.ch011

Gianni, M., Gotzamani, K., & Linden, I. (2016). How a BI-wise Responsible Integrated Management System May Support Food Traceability. *International Journal of Decision Support System Technology*, *8*(2), 1–17. doi:10.4018/IJDSST.2016040101

Glykas, M., & George, J. (2017). Quality and Process Management Systems in the UAE Maritime Industry. *International Journal of Productivity Management and Assessment Technologies*, *5*(1), 20–39. doi:10.4018/IJPMAT.2017010102

Glykas, M., Valiris, G., Kokkinaki, A., & Koutsoukou, Z. (2018). Banking Business Process Management Implementation. *International Journal of Productivity Management and Assessment Technologies*, *6*(1), 50–69. doi:10.4018/IJPMAT.2018010104

Gomes, J., & Romão, M. (2017). The Balanced Scorecard: Keeping Updated and Aligned with Today's Business Trends. *International Journal of Productivity Management and Assessment Technologies*, *5*(2), 1–15. doi:10.4018/IJPMAT.2017070101

Gomes, J., & Romão, M. (2017). Aligning Information Systems and Technology with Benefit Management and Balanced Scorecard. In S. De Haes & W. Van Grembergen (Eds.), *Strategic IT Governance and Alignment in Business Settings* (pp. 112–131). Hershey, PA: IGI Global. doi:10.4018/978-1-5225-0861-8.ch005

Grefen, P., & Turetken, O. (2017). Advanced Business Process Management in Networked E-Business Scenarios. *International Journal of E-Business Research, 13*(4), 70–104. doi:10.4018/IJEBR.2017100105

Haider, A., & Saetang, S. (2017). Strategic IT Alignment in Service Sector. In S. Rozenes & Y. Cohen (Eds.), *Handbook of Research on Strategic Alliances and Value Co-Creation in the Service Industry* (pp. 231–258). Hershey, PA: IGI Global. doi:10.4018/978-1-5225-2084-9.ch012

Haider, A., & Tang, S. S. (2016). Maximising Value Through IT and Business Alignment: A Case of IT Governance Institutionalisation at a Thai Bank. *International Journal of Technology Diffusion, 7*(3), 33–58. doi:10.4018/IJTD.2016070104

Hajilari, A. B., Ghadaksaz, M., & Fasghandis, G. S. (2017). Assessing Organizational Readiness for Implementing ERP System Using Fuzzy Expert System Approach. *International Journal of Enterprise Information Systems, 13*(1), 67–85. doi:10.4018/IJEIS.2017010105

Haldorai, A., Ramu, A., & Murugan, S. (2018). Social Aware Cognitive Radio Networks: Effectiveness of Social Networks as a Strategic Tool for Organizational Business Management. In H. Bansal, G. Shrivastava, G. Nguyen, & L. Stanciu (Eds.), *Social Network Analytics for Contemporary Business Organizations* (pp. 188–202). Hershey, PA: IGI Global. doi:10.4018/978-1-5225-5097-6.ch010

Hall, O. P. Jr. (2017). Social Media Driven Management Education. *International Journal of Knowledge-Based Organizations, 7*(2), 43–59. doi:10.4018/IJKBO.2017040104

Hanifah, H., Halim, H. A., Ahmad, N. H., & Vafaei-Zadeh, A. (2017). Innovation Culture as a Mediator Between Specific Human Capital and Innovation Performance Among Bumiputera SMEs in Malaysia. In N. Ahmad, T. Ramayah, H. Halim, & S. Rahman (Eds.), *Handbook of Research on Small and Medium Enterprises in Developing Countries* (pp. 261–279). Hershey, PA: IGI Global. doi:10.4018/978-1-5225-2165-5.ch012

Hartlieb, S., & Silvius, G. (2017). Handling Uncertainty in Project Management and Business Development: Similarities and Differences. In Y. Raydugin (Ed.), *Handbook of Research on Leveraging Risk and Uncertainties for Effective Project Management* (pp. 337–362). Hershey, PA: IGI Global. doi:10.4018/978-1-5225-1790-0.ch016

Hass, K. B. (2017). Living on the Edge: Managing Project Complexity. In Y. Raydugin (Ed.), *Handbook of Research on Leveraging Risk and Uncertainties for Effective Project Management* (pp. 177–201). Hershey, PA: IGI Global. doi:10.4018/978-1-5225-1790-0.ch009

Hassan, A., & Privitera, D. S. (2016). Google AdSense as a Mobile Technology in Education. In J. Holland (Ed.), *Wearable Technology and Mobile Innovations for Next-Generation Education* (pp. 200–223). Hershey, PA: IGI Global. doi:10.4018/978-1-5225-0069-8.ch011

Hassan, A., & Rahimi, R. (2016). Consuming "Innovation" in Tourism: Augmented Reality as an Innovation Tool in Digital Tourism Marketing. In N. Pappas & I. Bregoli (Eds.), *Global Dynamics in Travel, Tourism, and Hospitality* (pp. 130–147). Hershey, PA: IGI Global. doi:10.4018/978-1-5225-0201-2.ch008

Hawking, P., & Carmine Sellitto, C. (2017). Developing an Effective Strategy for Organizational Business Intelligence. In M. Tavana (Ed.), *Enterprise Information Systems and the Digitalization of Business Functions* (pp. 222–237). Hershey, PA: IGI Global. doi:10.4018/978-1-5225-2382-6.ch010

Hawking, P., & Sellitto, C. (2017). A Fast-Moving Consumer Goods Company and Business Intelligence Strategy Development. *International Journal of Enterprise Information Systems, 13*(2), 22–33. doi:10.4018/IJEIS.2017040102

Hawking, P., & Sellitto, C. (2017). Business Intelligence Strategy: Two Case Studies. *International Journal of Business Intelligence Research, 8*(2), 17–30. doi:10.4018/IJBIR.2017070102

Haynes, J. D., Arockiasamy, S., Al Rashdi, M., & Al Rashdi, S. (2016). Business and E Business Strategies for Coopetition and Thematic Management as a Sustained Basis for Ethics and Social Responsibility in Emerging Markets. In M. Al-Shammari & H. Masri (Eds.), *Ethical and Social Perspectives on Global Business Interaction in Emerging Markets* (pp. 25–39). Hershey, PA: IGI Global. doi:10.4018/978-1-4666-9864-2.ch002

Hee, W. J., Jalleh, G., Lai, H., & Lin, C. (2017). E-Commerce and IT Projects: Evaluation and Management Issues in Australian and Taiwanese Hospitals. *International Journal of Public Health Management and Ethics, 2*(1), 69–90. doi:10.4018/IJPHME.2017010104

Hernandez, A. A. (2018). Exploring the Factors to Green IT Adoption of SMEs in the Philippines. *Journal of Cases on Information Technology, 20*(2), 49–66. doi:10.4018/JCIT.2018040104

Hernandez, A. A., & Ona, S. E. (2016). Green IT Adoption: Lessons from the Philippines Business Process Outsourcing Industry. *International Journal of Social Ecology and Sustainable Development, 7*(1), 1–34. doi:10.4018/IJSESD.2016010101

Hollman, A., Bickford, S., & Hollman, T. (2017). Cyber InSecurity: A Post-Mortem Attempt to Assess Cyber Problems from IT and Business Management Perspectives. *Journal of Cases on Information Technology, 19*(3), 42–70. doi:10.4018/JCIT.2017070104

Igbinakhase, I. (2017). Responsible and Sustainable Management Practices in Developing and Developed Business Environments. In Z. Fields (Ed.), *Collective Creativity for Responsible and Sustainable Business Practice* (pp. 180–207). Hershey, PA: IGI Global. doi:10.4018/978-1-5225-1823-5.ch010

Ilahi, L., Ghannouchi, S. A., & Martinho, R. (2016). A Business Process Management Approach to Home Healthcare Processes: On the Gap between Intention and Reality. In M. Cruz-Cunha, I. Miranda, R. Martinho, & R. Rijo (Eds.), *Encyclopedia of E-Health and Telemedicine* (pp. 439–457). Hershey, PA: IGI Global. doi:10.4018/978-1-4666-9978-6.ch035

Iwata, J. J., & Hoskins, R. G. (2017). Managing Indigenous Knowledge in Tanzania: A Business Perspective. In P. Jain & N. Mnjama (Eds.), *Managing Knowledge Resources and Records in Modern Organizations* (pp. 198–214). Hershey, PA: IGI Global. doi:10.4018/978-1-5225-1965-2.ch012

Jabeen, F., Ahmad, S. Z., & Alkaabi, S. (2016). The Internationalization Decision-Making of United Arab Emirates Family Businesses. In N. Zakaria, A. Abdul-Talib, & N. Osman (Eds.), *Handbook of Research on Impacts of International Business and Political Affairs on the Global Economy* (pp. 1–22). Hershey, PA: IGI Global. doi:10.4018/978-1-4666-9806-2.ch001

Jain, P. (2017). Ethical and Legal Issues in Knowledge Management Life-Cycle in Business. In P. Jain & N. Mnjama (Eds.), *Managing Knowledge Resources and Records in Modern Organizations* (pp. 82–101). Hershey, PA: IGI Global. doi:10.4018/978-1-5225-1965-2.ch006

Jamali, D., Abdallah, H., & Matar, F. (2016). Opportunities and Challenges for CSR Mainstreaming in Business Schools. *International Journal of Technology and Educational Marketing, 6*(2), 1–29. doi:10.4018/IJTEM.2016070101

James, S., & Hauli, E. (2017). Holistic Management Education at Tanzanian Rural Development Planning Institute. In N. Baporikar (Ed.), *Management Education for Global Leadership* (pp. 112–136). Hershey, PA: IGI Global. doi:10.4018/978-1-5225-1013-0.ch006

Janošková, M., Csikósová, A., & Čulková, K. (2018). Measurement of Company Performance as Part of Its Strategic Management. In R. Leon (Ed.), *Managerial Strategies for Business Sustainability During Turbulent Times* (pp. 309–335). Hershey, PA: IGI Global. doi:10.4018/978-1-5225-2716-9.ch017

Jean-Vasile, A., & Alecu, A. (2017). Theoretical and Practical Approaches in Understanding the Influences of Cost-Productivity-Profit Trinomial in Contemporary Enterprises. In A. Jean Vasile & D. Nicolò (Eds.), *Sustainable Entrepreneurship and Investments in the Green Economy* (pp. 28–62). Hershey, PA: IGI Global. doi:10.4018/978-1-5225-2075-7.ch002

Jha, D. G. (2016). Preparing for Information Technology Driven Changes. In S. Tiwari & L. Nafees (Eds.), *Innovative Management Education Pedagogies for Preparing Next-Generation Leaders* (pp. 258–274). Hershey, PA: IGI Global. doi:10.4018/978-1-4666-9691-4.ch015

Joia, L. A., & Correia, J. C. (2018). CIO Competencies From the IT Professional Perspective: Insights From Brazil. *Journal of Global Information Management, 26*(2), 74–103. doi:10.4018/JGIM.2018040104

Juma, A., & Mzera, N. (2017). Knowledge Management and Records Management and Competitive Advantage in Business. In P. Jain & N. Mnjama (Eds.), *Managing Knowledge Resources and Records in Modern Organizations* (pp. 15–28). Hershey, PA: IGI Global. doi:10.4018/978-1-5225-1965-2.ch002

K., I., & A, V. (2018). Monitoring and Auditing in the Cloud. In K. Munir (Ed.), *Cloud Computing Technologies for Green Enterprises* (pp. 318-350). Hershey, PA: IGI Global. doi:10.4018/978-1-5225-3038-1.ch013

Kabra, G., Ghosh, V., & Ramesh, A. (2018). Enterprise Integrated Business Process Management and Business Intelligence Framework for Business Process Sustainability. In A. Paul, D. Bhattacharyya, & S. Anand (Eds.), *Green Initiatives for Business Sustainability and Value Creation* (pp. 228–238). Hershey, PA: IGI Global. doi:10.4018/978-1-5225-2662-9.ch010

Kaoud, M. (2017). Investigation of Customer Knowledge Management: A Case Study Research. *International Journal of Service Science, Management, Engineering, and Technology, 8*(2), 12–22. doi:10.4018/IJSSMET.2017040102

Kara, M. E., & Fırat, S. Ü. (2016). Sustainability, Risk, and Business Intelligence in Supply Chains. In M. Erdoğdu, T. Arun, & I. Ahmad (Eds.), *Handbook of Research on Green Economic Development Initiatives and Strategies* (pp. 501–538). Hershey, PA: IGI Global. doi:10.4018/978-1-5225-0440-5.ch022

Katuu, S. (2018). A Comparative Assessment of Enterprise Content Management Maturity Models. In N. Gwangwava & M. Mutingi (Eds.), *E-Manufacturing and E-Service Strategies in Contemporary Organizations* (pp. 93–118). Hershey, PA: IGI Global. doi:10.4018/978-1-5225-3628-4.ch005

Khan, M. A. (2016). MNEs Management Strategies in Developing Countries: Establishing the Context. In M. Khan (Ed.), *Multinational Enterprise Management Strategies in Developing Countries* (pp. 1–33). Hershey, PA: IGI Global. doi:10.4018/978-1-5225-0276-0.ch001

Khan, M. A. (2016). Operational Approaches in Organizational Structure: A Case for MNEs in Developing Countries. In M. Khan (Ed.), *Multinational Enterprise Management Strategies in Developing Countries* (pp. 129–151). Hershey, PA: IGI Global. doi:10.4018/978-1-5225-0276-0.ch007

Kinnunen, S., Ylä-Kujala, A., Marttonen-Arola, S., Kärri, T., & Baglee, D. (2018). Internet of Things in Asset Management: Insights from Industrial Professionals and Academia. *International Journal of Service Science, Management, Engineering, and Technology*, *9*(2), 104–119. doi:10.4018/IJSSMET.2018040105

Klein, A. Z., Sabino de Freitas, A., Machado, L., Freitas, J. C. Jr, Graziola, P. G. Jr, & Schlemmer, E. (2017). Virtual Worlds Applications for Management Education. In L. Tomei (Ed.), *Exploring the New Era of Technology-Infused Education* (pp. 279–299). Hershey, PA: IGI Global. doi:10.4018/978-1-5225-1709-2.ch017

Kożuch, B., & Jabłoński, A. (2017). Adopting the Concept of Business Models in Public Management. In M. Lewandowski & B. Kożuch (Eds.), *Public Sector Entrepreneurship and the Integration of Innovative Business Models* (pp. 10–46). Hershey, PA: IGI Global. doi:10.4018/978-1-5225-2215-7.ch002

Kumar, J., Adhikary, A., & Jha, A. (2017). Small Active Investors' Perceptions and Preferences Towards Tax Saving Mutual Fund Schemes in Eastern India: An Empirical Note. *International Journal of Asian Business and Information Management*, *8*(2), 35–45. doi:10.4018/IJABIM.2017040103

Lassoued, Y., Bouzguenda, L., & Mahmoud, T. (2016). Context-Aware Business Process Versions Management. *International Journal of e-Collaboration*, *12*(3), 7–33. doi:10.4018/IJeC.2016070102

Lavassani, K. M., & Movahedi, B. (2017). Applications Driven Information Systems: Beyond Networks toward Business Ecosystems. *International Journal of Innovation in the Digital Economy*, *8*(1), 61–75. doi:10.4018/IJIDE.2017010104

Lazzareschi, V. H., & Brito, M. S. (2017). Strategic Information Management: Proposal of Business Project Model. In G. Jamil, A. Soares, & C. Pessoa (Eds.), *Handbook of Research on Information Management for Effective Logistics and Supply Chains* (pp. 59–88). Hershey, PA: IGI Global. doi:10.4018/978-1-5225-0973-8.ch004

Lederer, M., Kurz, M., & Lazarov, P. (2017). Usage and Suitability of Methods for Strategic Business Process Initiatives: A Multi Case Study Research. *International Journal of Productivity Management and Assessment Technologies*, *5*(1), 40–51. doi:10.4018/IJPMAT.2017010103

Lee, I. (2017). A Social Enterprise Business Model and a Case Study of Pacific Community Ventures (PCV). In V. Potocan, M. Üngan, & Z. Nedelko (Eds.), *Handbook of Research on Managerial Solutions in Non-Profit Organizations* (pp. 182–204). Hershey, PA: IGI Global. doi:10.4018/978-1-5225-0731-4.ch009

Lee, L. J., & Leu, J. (2016). Exploring the Effectiveness of IT Application and Value Method in the Innovation Performance of Enterprise. *International Journal of Enterprise Information Systems*, *12*(2), 47–65. doi:10.4018/IJEIS.2016040104

Lee, Y. (2016). Alignment Effect of Entrepreneurial Orientation and Marketing Orientation on Firm Performance. *International Journal of Customer Relationship Marketing and Management*, *7*(4), 58–69. doi:10.4018/IJCRMM.2016100104

Leon, L. A., Seal, K. C., Przasnyski, Z. H., & Wiedenman, I. (2017). Skills and Competencies Required for Jobs in Business Analytics: A Content Analysis of Job Advertisements Using Text Mining. *International Journal of Business Intelligence Research*, *8*(1), 1–25. doi:10.4018/IJBIR.2017010101

Leu, J., Lee, L. J., & Krischke, A. (2016). Value Engineering-Based Method for Implementing the ISO14001 System in the Green Supply Chains. *International Journal of Strategic Decision Sciences*, *7*(4), 1–20. doi:10.4018/IJSDS.2016100101

Levy, C. L., & Elias, N. I. (2017). SOHO Users' Perceptions of Reliability and Continuity of Cloud-Based Services. In M. Moore (Ed.), *Cybersecurity Breaches and Issues Surrounding Online Threat Protection* (pp. 248–287). Hershey, PA: IGI Global. doi:10.4018/978-1-5225-1941-6.ch011

Levy, M. (2018). Change Management Serving Knowledge Management and Organizational Development: Reflections and Review. In N. Baporikar (Ed.), *Global Practices in Knowledge Management for Societal and Organizational Development* (pp. 256–270). Hershey, PA: IGI Global. doi:10.4018/978-1-5225-3009-1.ch012

Lewandowski, M. (2017). Public Organizations and Business Model Innovation: The Role of Public Service Design. In M. Lewandowski & B. Kożuch (Eds.), *Public Sector Entrepreneurship and the Integration of Innovative Business Models* (pp. 47–72). Hershey, PA: IGI Global. doi:10.4018/978-1-5225-2215-7.ch003

Lhannaoui, H., Kabbaj, M. I., & Bakkoury, Z. (2017). A Survey of Risk-Aware Business Process Modelling. *International Journal of Risk and Contingency Management*, *6*(3), 14–26. doi:10.4018/IJRCM.2017070102

Li, J., Sun, W., Jiang, W., Yang, H., & Zhang, L. (2017). How the Nature of Exogenous Shocks and Crises Impact Company Performance?: The Effects of Industry Characteristics. *International Journal of Risk and Contingency Management*, *6*(4), 40–55. doi:10.4018/IJRCM.2017100103

Lu, C., & Liu, S. (2016). Cultural Tourism O2O Business Model Innovation-A Case Study of CTrip. *Journal of Electronic Commerce in Organizations*, *14*(2), 16–31. doi:10.4018/JECO.2016040102

Machen, B., Hosseini, M. R., Wood, A., & Bakhshi, J. (2016). An Investigation into using SAP-PS as a Multidimensional Project Control System (MPCS). *International Journal of Enterprise Information Systems*, *12*(2), 66–81. doi:10.4018/IJEIS.2016040105

Malega, P. (2017). Small and Medium Enterprises in the Slovak Republic: Status and Competitiveness of SMEs in the Global Markets and Possibilities of Optimization. In M. Vemić (Ed.), *Optimal Management Strategies in Small and Medium Enterprises* (pp. 102–124). Hershey, PA: IGI Global. doi:10.4018/978-1-5225-1949-2.ch006

Malewska, K. M. (2017). Intuition in Decision-Making on the Example of a Non-Profit Organization. In V. Potocan, M. Ünğan, & Z. Nedelko (Eds.), *Handbook of Research on Managerial Solutions in Non-Profit Organizations* (pp. 378–399). Hershey, PA: IGI Global. doi:10.4018/978-1-5225-0731-4.ch018

Maroofi, F. (2017). Entrepreneurial Orientation and Organizational Learning Ability Analysis for Innovation and Firm Performance. In N. Baporikar (Ed.), *Innovation and Shifting Perspectives in Management Education* (pp. 144–165). Hershey, PA: IGI Global. doi:10.4018/978-1-5225-1019-2.ch007

Martins, P. V., & Zacarias, M. (2017). A Web-based Tool for Business Process Improvement. *International Journal of Web Portals*, *9*(2), 68–84. doi:10.4018/IJWP.2017070104

Matthies, B., & Coners, A. (2017). Exploring the Conceptual Nature of e-Business Projects. *Journal of Electronic Commerce in Organizations, 15*(3), 33–63. doi:10.4018/JECO.2017070103

McKee, J. (2018). Architecture as a Tool to Solve Business Planning Problems. In M. Khosrow-Pour, D.B.A. (Ed.), Encyclopedia of Information Science and Technology, Fourth Edition (pp. 573-586). Hershey, PA: IGI Global. doi:10.4018/978-1-5225-2255-3.ch050

McMurray, A. J., Cross, J., & Caponecchia, C. (2018). The Risk Management Profession in Australia: Business Continuity Plan Practices. In N. Bajgoric (Ed.), *Always-On Enterprise Information Systems for Modern Organizations* (pp. 112–129). Hershey, PA: IGI Global. doi:10.4018/978-1-5225-3704-5.ch006

Meddah, I. H., & Belkadi, K. (2018). Mining Patterns Using Business Process Management. In R. Hamou (Ed.), *Handbook of Research on Biomimicry in Information Retrieval and Knowledge Management* (pp. 78–89). Hershey, PA: IGI Global. doi:10.4018/978-1-5225-3004-6.ch005

Mendes, L. (2017). TQM and Knowledge Management: An Integrated Approach Towards Tacit Knowledge Management. In D. Jaziri-Bouagina & G. Jamil (Eds.), *Handbook of Research on Tacit Knowledge Management for Organizational Success* (pp. 236–263). Hershey, PA: IGI Global. doi:10.4018/978-1-5225-2394-9.ch009

Mnjama, N. M. (2017). Preservation of Recorded Information in Public and Private Sector Organizations. In P. Jain & N. Mnjama (Eds.), *Managing Knowledge Resources and Records in Modern Organizations* (pp. 149–167). Hershey, PA: IGI Global. doi:10.4018/978-1-5225-1965-2.ch009

Mokoqama, M., & Fields, Z. (2017). Principles of Responsible Management Education (PRME): Call for Responsible Management Education. In Z. Fields (Ed.), *Collective Creativity for Responsible and Sustainable Business Practice* (pp. 229–241). Hershey, PA: IGI Global. doi:10.4018/978-1-5225-1823-5.ch012

Muniapan, B. (2017). Philosophy and Management: The Relevance of Vedanta in Management. In P. Ordóñez de Pablos (Ed.), *Managerial Strategies and Solutions for Business Success in Asia* (pp. 124–139). Hershey, PA: IGI Global. doi:10.4018/978-1-5225-1886-0.ch007

Muniapan, B., Gregory, M. L., & Ling, L. A. (2016). Marketing Education in Sarawak: Looking at It from the Employers' Viewpoint. In B. Smith & A. Porath (Eds.), *Global Perspectives on Contemporary Marketing Education* (pp. 112–130). Hershey, PA: IGI Global. doi:10.4018/978-1-4666-9784-3.ch008

Murad, S. E., & Dowaji, S. (2017). Using Value-Based Approach for Managing Cloud-Based Services. In A. Turuk, B. Sahoo, & S. Addya (Eds.), *Resource Management and Efficiency in Cloud Computing Environments* (pp. 33–60). Hershey, PA: IGI Global. doi:10.4018/978-1-5225-1721-4.ch002

Mutahar, A. M., Daud, N. M., Thurasamy, R., Isaac, O., & Abdulsalam, R. (2018). The Mediating of Perceived Usefulness and Perceived Ease of Use: The Case of Mobile Banking in Yemen. *International Journal of Technology Diffusion*, *9*(2), 21–40. doi:10.4018/IJTD.2018040102

Naidoo, V. (2017). E-Learning and Management Education at African Universities. In N. Baporikar (Ed.), *Management Education for Global Leadership* (pp. 181–201). Hershey, PA: IGI Global. doi:10.4018/978-1-5225-1013-0.ch009

Naidoo, V., & Igbinakhase, I. (2018). Opportunities and Challenges of Knowledge Retention in SMEs. In N. Baporikar (Ed.), *Knowledge Integration Strategies for Entrepreneurship and Sustainability* (pp. 70–94). Hershey, PA: IGI Global. doi:10.4018/978-1-5225-5115-7.ch004

Nayak, S., & Prabhu, N. (2017). Paradigm Shift in Management Education: Need for a Cross Functional Perspective. In N. Baporikar (Ed.), *Management Education for Global Leadership* (pp. 241–255). Hershey, PA: IGI Global. doi:10.4018/978-1-5225-1013-0.ch012

Ndede-Amadi, A. A. (2016). Student Interest in the IS Specialization as Predictor of the Success Potential of New Information Systems Programmes within the Schools of Business in Kenyan Public Universities. *International Journal of Information Systems and Social Change*, *7*(2), 63–79. doi:10.4018/IJISSC.2016040104

Nedelko, Z., & Potocan, V. (2016). Management Practices for Processes Optimization: Case of Slovenia. In G. Alor-Hernández, C. Sánchez-Ramírez, & J. García-Alcaraz (Eds.), *Handbook of Research on Managerial Strategies for Achieving Optimal Performance in Industrial Processes* (pp. 545–561). Hershey, PA: IGI Global. doi:10.4018/978-1-5225-0130-5.ch025

Nedelko, Z., & Potocan, V. (2017). Management Solutions in Non-Profit Organizations: Case of Slovenia. In V. Potocan, M. Üngan, & Z. Nedelko (Eds.), *Handbook of Research on Managerial Solutions in Non-Profit Organizations* (pp. 1–22). Hershey, PA: IGI Global. doi:10.4018/978-1-5225-0731-4.ch001

Nedelko, Z., & Potocan, V. (2017). Priority of Management Tools Utilization among Managers: International Comparison. In V. Wang (Ed.), *Encyclopedia of Strategic Leadership and Management* (pp. 1083–1094). Hershey, PA: IGI Global. doi:10.4018/978-1-5225-1049-9.ch075

Nedelko, Z., Raudeliūnienė, J., & Črešnar, R. (2018). Knowledge Dynamics in Supply Chain Management. In N. Baporikar (Ed.), *Knowledge Integration Strategies for Entrepreneurship and Sustainability* (pp. 150–166). Hershey, PA: IGI Global. doi:10.4018/978-1-5225-5115-7.ch008

Nguyen, H. T., & Hipsher, S. A. (2018). Innovation and Creativity Used by Private Sector Firms in a Resources-Constrained Environment. In S. Hipsher (Ed.), *Examining the Private Sector's Role in Wealth Creation and Poverty Reduction* (pp. 219–238). Hershey, PA: IGI Global. doi:10.4018/978-1-5225-3117-3.ch010

Nycz, M., & Pólkowski, Z. (2016). Business Intelligence as a Modern IT Supporting Management of Local Government Units in Poland. *International Journal of Knowledge and Systems Science*, *7*(4), 1–18. doi:10.4018/IJKSS.2016100101

Obaji, N. O., Senin, A. A., & Olugu, M. U. (2016). Supportive Government Policy as a Mechanism for Business Incubation Performance in Nigeria. *International Journal of Information Systems and Social Change*, *7*(4), 52–66. doi:10.4018/IJISSC.2016100103

Obicci, P. A. (2017). Risk Sharing in a Partnership. In *Risk Management Strategies in Public-Private Partnerships* (pp. 115–152). Hershey, PA: IGI Global. doi:10.4018/978-1-5225-2503-5.ch004

Obidallah, W. J., & Raahemi, B. (2017). Managing Changes in Service Oriented Virtual Organizations: A Structural and Procedural Framework to Facilitate the Process of Change. *Journal of Electronic Commerce in Organizations*, *15*(1), 59–83. doi:10.4018/JECO.2017010104

Ojasalo, J., & Ojasalo, K. (2016). Service Logic Business Model Canvas for Lean Development of SMEs and Start-Ups. In N. Baporikar (Ed.), *Handbook of Research on Entrepreneurship in the Contemporary Knowledge-Based Global Economy* (pp. 217–243). Hershey, PA: IGI Global. doi:10.4018/978-1-4666-8798-1.ch010

Ojo, O. (2017). Impact of Innovation on the Entrepreneurial Success in Selected Business Enterprises in South-West Nigeria. *International Journal of Innovation in the Digital Economy*, *8*(2), 29–38. doi:10.4018/IJIDE.2017040103

Okdinawati, L., Simatupang, T. M., & Sunitiyoso, Y. (2017). Multi-Agent Reinforcement Learning for Value Co-Creation of Collaborative Transportation Management (CTM). *International Journal of Information Systems and Supply Chain Management*, *10*(3), 84–95. doi:10.4018/IJISSCM.2017070105

Ortner, E., Mevius, M., Wiedmann, P., & Kurz, F. (2016). Design of Interactional Decision Support Applications for E-Participation in Smart Cities. *International Journal of Electronic Government Research, 12*(2), 18–38. doi:10.4018/IJEGR.2016040102

Pal, K. (2018). Building High Quality Big Data-Based Applications in Supply Chains. In A. Kumar & S. Saurav (Eds.), *Supply Chain Management Strategies and Risk Assessment in Retail Environments* (pp. 1–24). Hershey, PA: IGI Global. doi:10.4018/978-1-5225-3056-5.ch001

Palos-Sanchez, P. R., & Correia, M. B. (2018). Perspectives of the Adoption of Cloud Computing in the Tourism Sector. In J. Rodrigues, C. Ramos, P. Cardoso, & C. Henriques (Eds.), *Handbook of Research on Technological Developments for Cultural Heritage and eTourism Applications* (pp. 377–400). Hershey, PA: IGI Global. doi:10.4018/978-1-5225-2927-9.ch018

Parry, V. K., & Lind, M. L. (2016). Alignment of Business Strategy and Information Technology Considering Information Technology Governance, Project Portfolio Control, and Risk Management. *International Journal of Information Technology Project Management, 7*(4), 21–37. doi:10.4018/IJITPM.2016100102

Pashkova, N., Trujillo-Barrera, A., Apostolakis, G., Van Dijk, G., Drakos, P. D., & Baourakis, G. (2016). Business Management Models of Microfinance Institutions (MFIs) in Africa: A Study into Their Enabling Environments. *International Journal of Food and Beverage Manufacturing and Business Models, 1*(2), 63–82. doi:10.4018/IJFBMBM.2016070105

Patiño, B. E. (2017). New Generation Management by Convergence and Individual Identity: A Systemic and Human-Oriented Approach. In N. Baporikar (Ed.), *Innovation and Shifting Perspectives in Management Education* (pp. 119–143). Hershey, PA: IGI Global. doi:10.4018/978-1-5225-1019-2.ch006

Pawliczek, A., & Rössler, M. (2017). Knowledge of Management Tools and Systems in SMEs: Knowledge Transfer in Management. In A. Bencsik (Ed.), *Knowledge Management Initiatives and Strategies in Small and Medium Enterprises* (pp. 180–203). Hershey, PA: IGI Global. doi:10.4018/978-1-5225-1642-2.ch009

Pejic-Bach, M., Omazic, M. A., Aleksic, A., & Zoroja, J. (2018). Knowledge-Based Decision Making: A Multi-Case Analysis. In R. Leon (Ed.), *Managerial Strategies for Business Sustainability During Turbulent Times* (pp. 160–184). Hershey, PA: IGI Global. doi:10.4018/978-1-5225-2716-9.ch009

Perano, M., Hysa, X., & Calabrese, M. (2018). Strategic Planning, Cultural Context, and Business Continuity Management: Business Cases in the City of Shkoder. In A. Presenza & L. Sheehan (Eds.), *Geopolitics and Strategic Management in the Global Economy* (pp. 57–77). Hershey, PA: IGI Global. doi:10.4018/978-1-5225-2673-5.ch004

Pereira, R., Mira da Silva, M., & Lapão, L. V. (2017). IT Governance Maturity Patterns in Portuguese Healthcare. In S. De Haes & W. Van Grembergen (Eds.), *Strategic IT Governance and Alignment in Business Settings* (pp. 24–52). Hershey, PA: IGI Global. doi:10.4018/978-1-5225-0861-8.ch002

Perez-Uribe, R., & Ocampo-Guzman, D. (2016). Conflict within Colombian Family Owned SMEs: An Explosive Blend between Feelings and Business. In J. Saiz-Álvarez (Ed.), *Handbook of Research on Social Entrepreneurship and Solidarity Economics* (pp. 329–354). Hershey, PA: IGI Global. doi:10.4018/978-1-5225-0097-1.ch017

Pérez-Uribe, R. I., Torres, D. A., Jurado, S. P., & Prada, D. M. (2018). Cloud Tools for the Development of Project Management in SMEs. In R. Perez-Uribe, C. Salcedo-Perez, & D. Ocampo-Guzman (Eds.), *Handbook of Research on Intrapreneurship and Organizational Sustainability in SMEs* (pp. 95–120). Hershey, PA: IGI Global. doi:10.4018/978-1-5225-3543-0.ch005

Petrisor, I., & Cozmiuc, D. (2017). Global Supply Chain Management Organization at Siemens in the Advent of Industry 4.0. In L. Saglietto & C. Cezanne (Eds.), *Global Intermediation and Logistics Service Providers* (pp. 123–142). Hershey, PA: IGI Global. doi:10.4018/978-1-5225-2133-4.ch007

Pierce, J. M., Velliaris, D. M., & Edwards, J. (2017). A Living Case Study: A Journey Not a Destination. In N. Silton (Ed.), *Exploring the Benefits of Creativity in Education, Media, and the Arts* (pp. 158–178). Hershey, PA: IGI Global. doi:10.4018/978-1-5225-0504-4.ch008

Radosavljevic, M., & Andjelkovic, A. (2017). Multi-Criteria Decision Making Approach for Choosing Business Process for the Improvement: Upgrading of the Six Sigma Methodology. In J. Stanković, P. Delias, S. Marinković, & S. Rochhia (Eds.), *Tools and Techniques for Economic Decision Analysis* (pp. 225–247). Hershey, PA: IGI Global. doi:10.4018/978-1-5225-0959-2.ch011

Radovic, V. M. (2017). Corporate Sustainability and Responsibility and Disaster Risk Reduction: A Serbian Overview. In M. Camilleri (Ed.), *CSR 2.0 and the New Era of Corporate Citizenship* (pp. 147–164). Hershey, PA: IGI Global. doi:10.4018/978-1-5225-1842-6.ch008

Raghunath, K. M., Devi, S. L., & Patro, C. S. (2018). Impact of Risk Assessment Models on Risk Factors: A Holistic Outlook. In K. Strang, M. Korstanje, & N. Vajjhala (Eds.), *Research, Practices, and Innovations in Global Risk and Contingency Management* (pp. 134–153). Hershey, PA: IGI Global. doi:10.4018/978-1-5225-4754-9.ch008

Raman, A., & Goyal, D. P. (2017). Extending IMPLEMENT Framework for Enterprise Information Systems Implementation to Information System Innovation. In M. Tavana (Ed.), *Enterprise Information Systems and the Digitalization of Business Functions* (pp. 137–177). Hershey, PA: IGI Global. doi:10.4018/978-1-5225-2382-6.ch007

Rao, Y., & Zhang, Y. (2017). The Construction and Development of Academic Library Digital Special Subject Databases. In L. Ruan, Q. Zhu, & Y. Ye (Eds.), *Academic Library Development and Administration in China* (pp. 163–183). Hershey, PA: IGI Global. doi:10.4018/978-1-5225-0550-1.ch010

Ravasan, A. Z., Mohammadi, M. M., & Hamidi, H. (2018). An Investigation Into the Critical Success Factors of Implementing Information Technology Service Management Frameworks. In K. Jakobs (Ed.), *Corporate and Global Standardization Initiatives in Contemporary Society* (pp. 200–218). Hershey, PA: IGI Global. doi:10.4018/978-1-5225-5320-5.ch009

Renna, P., Izzo, C., & Romaniello, T. (2016). The Business Process Management Systems to Support Continuous Improvements. In W. Nuninger & J. Châtelet (Eds.), *Handbook of Research on Quality Assurance and Value Management in Higher Education* (pp. 237–256). Hershey, PA: IGI Global. doi:10.4018/978-1-5225-0024-7.ch009

Rezaie, S., Mirabedini, S. J., & Abtahi, A. (2018). Designing a Model for Implementation of Business Intelligence in the Banking Industry. *International Journal of Enterprise Information Systems, 14*(1), 77–103. doi:10.4018/IJEIS.2018010105

Riccò, R. (2016). Diversity Management: Bringing Equality, Equity, and Inclusion in the Workplace. In J. Prescott (Ed.), *Handbook of Research on Race, Gender, and the Fight for Equality* (pp. 335–359). Hershey, PA: IGI Global. doi:10.4018/978-1-5225-0047-6.ch015

Romano, L., Grimaldi, R., & Colasuonno, F. S. (2017). Demand Management as a Success Factor in Project Portfolio Management. In L. Romano (Ed.), *Project Portfolio Management Strategies for Effective Organizational Operations* (pp. 202–219). Hershey, PA: IGI Global. doi:10.4018/978-1-5225-2151-8.ch008

Rostek, K. B. (2016). Risk Management: Role and Importance in Business Organization. In D. Jakóbczak (Ed.), *Analyzing Risk through Probabilistic Modeling in Operations Research* (pp. 149–178). Hershey, PA: IGI Global. doi:10.4018/978-1-4666-9458-3.ch007

Rouhani, S., & Savoji, S. R. (2016). A Success Assessment Model for BI Tools Implementation: An Empirical Study of Banking Industry. *International Journal of Business Intelligence Research*, *7*(1), 25–44. doi:10.4018/IJBIR.2016010103

Ruan, Z. (2016). A Corpus-Based Functional Analysis of Complex Nominal Groups in Written Business Discourse: The Case of "Business". *International Journal of Computer-Assisted Language Learning and Teaching*, *6*(2), 74–90. doi:10.4018/IJCALLT.2016040105

Ruhi, U. (2018). Towards an Interdisciplinary Socio-Technical Definition of Virtual Communities. In M. Khosrow-Pour, D.B.A. (Ed.), Encyclopedia of Information Science and Technology, Fourth Edition (pp. 4278-4295). Hershey, PA: IGI Global. doi:10.4018/978-1-5225-2255-3.ch371

Ryan, J., Doster, B., Daily, S., & Lewis, C. (2016). A Case Study Perspective for Balanced Perioperative Workflow Achievement through Data-Driven Process Improvement. *International Journal of Healthcare Information Systems and Informatics*, *11*(3), 19–41. doi:10.4018/IJHISI.2016070102

Safari, M. R., & Jiang, Q. (2018). The Theory and Practice of IT Governance Maturity and Strategies Alignment: Evidence From Banking Industry. *Journal of Global Information Management*, *26*(2), 127–146. doi:10.4018/JGIM.2018040106

Sahoo, J., Pati, B., & Mohanty, B. (2017). Knowledge Management as an Academic Discipline: An Assessment. In B. Gunjal (Ed.), *Managing Knowledge and Scholarly Assets in Academic Libraries* (pp. 99–126). Hershey, PA: IGI Global. doi:10.4018/978-1-5225-1741-2.ch005

Saini, D. (2017). Relevance of Teaching Values and Ethics in Management Education. In N. Baporikar (Ed.), *Management Education for Global Leadership* (pp. 90–111). Hershey, PA: IGI Global. doi:10.4018/978-1-5225-1013-0.ch005

Sambhanthan, A. (2017). Assessing and Benchmarking Sustainability in Organisations: An Integrated Conceptual Model. *International Journal of Systems and Service-Oriented Engineering*, *7*(4), 22–43. doi:10.4018/IJSSOE.2017100102

Sambhanthan, A., & Potdar, V. (2017). A Study of the Parameters Impacting Sustainability in Information Technology Organizations. *International Journal of Knowledge-Based Organizations*, *7*(3), 27–39. doi:10.4018/IJKBO.2017070103

Sánchez-Fernández, M. D., & Manríquez, M. R. (2018). The Entrepreneurial Spirit Based on Social Values: The Digital Generation. In P. Isaias & L. Carvalho (Eds.), *User Innovation and the Entrepreneurship Phenomenon in the Digital Economy* (pp. 173–193). Hershey, PA: IGI Global. doi:10.4018/978-1-5225-2826-5.ch009

Sanchez-Ruiz, L., & Blanco, B. (2017). Process Management for SMEs: Barriers, Enablers, and Benefits. In M. Vemić (Ed.), *Optimal Management Strategies in Small and Medium Enterprises* (pp. 293–319). Hershey, PA: IGI Global. doi:10.4018/978-1-5225-1949-2.ch014

Sanz, L. F., Gómez-Pérez, J., & Castillo-Martinez, A. (2018). Analysis of the European ICT Competence Frameworks. In V. Ahuja & S. Rathore (Eds.), *Multidisciplinary Perspectives on Human Capital and Information Technology Professionals* (pp. 225–245). Hershey, PA: IGI Global. doi:10.4018/978-1-5225-5297-0.ch012

Sarvepalli, A., & Godin, J. (2017). Business Process Management in the Classroom. *Journal of Cases on Information Technology*, *19*(2), 17–28. doi:10.4018/JCIT.2017040102

Satpathy, B., & Muniapan, B. (2016). Ancient Wisdom for Transformational Leadership and Its Insights from the Bhagavad-Gita. In U. Aung & P. Ordoñez de Pablos (Eds.), *Managerial Strategies and Practice in the Asian Business Sector* (pp. 1–10). Hershey, PA: IGI Global. doi:10.4018/978-1-4666-9758-4.ch001

Saygili, E. E., Ozturkoglu, Y., & Kocakulah, M. C. (2017). End Users' Perceptions of Critical Success Factors in ERP Applications. *International Journal of Enterprise Information Systems*, *13*(4), 58–75. doi:10.4018/IJEIS.2017100104

Saygili, E. E., & Saygili, A. T. (2017). Contemporary Issues in Enterprise Information Systems: A Critical Review of CSFs in ERP Implementations. In M. Tavana (Ed.), *Enterprise Information Systems and the Digitalization of Business Functions* (pp. 120–136). Hershey, PA: IGI Global. doi:10.4018/978-1-5225-2382-6.ch006

Seidenstricker, S., & Antonino, A. (2018). Business Model Innovation-Oriented Technology Management for Emergent Technologies. In M. Khosrow-Pour, D.B.A. (Ed.), Encyclopedia of Information Science and Technology, Fourth Edition (pp. 4560-4569). Hershey, PA: IGI Global. doi:10.4018/978-1-5225-2255-3.ch396

Senaratne, S., & Gunarathne, A. D. (2017). Excellence Perspective for Management Education from a Global Accountants' Hub in Asia. In N. Baporikar (Ed.), *Management Education for Global Leadership* (pp. 158–180). Hershey, PA: IGI Global. doi:10.4018/978-1-5225-1013-0.ch008

Sensuse, D. I., & Cahyaningsih, E. (2018). Knowledge Management Models: A Summative Review. *International Journal of Information Systems in the Service Sector*, *10*(1), 71–100. doi:10.4018/IJISSS.2018010105

Sensuse, D. I., Wibowo, W. C., & Cahyaningsih, E. (2016). Indonesian Government Knowledge Management Model: A Theoretical Model. *Information Resources Management Journal*, *29*(1), 91–108. doi:10.4018/irmj.2016010106

Seth, M., Goyal, D., & Kiran, R. (2017). Diminution of Impediments in Implementation of Supply Chain Management Information System for Enhancing its Effectiveness in Indian Automobile Industry. *Journal of Global Information Management*, *25*(3), 1–20. doi:10.4018/JGIM.2017070101

Seyal, A. H., & Rahman, M. N. (2017). Investigating Impact of Inter-Organizational Factors in Measuring ERP Systems Success: Bruneian Perspectives. In M. Tavana (Ed.), *Enterprise Information Systems and the Digitalization of Business Functions* (pp. 178–204). Hershey, PA: IGI Global. doi:10.4018/978-1-5225-2382-6.ch008

Shaikh, A. A., & Karjaluoto, H. (2016). On Some Misconceptions Concerning Digital Banking and Alternative Delivery Channels. *International Journal of E-Business Research*, *12*(3), 1–16. doi:10.4018/IJEBR.2016070101

Shams, S. M. (2016). Stakeholder Relationship Management in Online Business and Competitive Value Propositions: Evidence from the Sports Industry. *International Journal of Online Marketing*, *6*(2), 1–17. doi:10.4018/IJOM.2016040101

Shamsuzzoha, A. (2016). Management of Risk and Resilience within Collaborative Business Network. In R. Addo-Tenkorang, J. Kantola, P. Helo, & A. Shamsuzzoha (Eds.), *Supply Chain Strategies and the Engineer-to-Order Approach* (pp. 143–159). Hershey, PA: IGI Global. doi:10.4018/978-1-5225-0021-6.ch008

Shaqrah, A. A. (2018). Analyzing Business Intelligence Systems Based on 7s Model of McKinsey. *International Journal of Business Intelligence Research*, *9*(1), 53–63. doi:10.4018/IJBIR.2018010104

Sharma, A. J. (2017). Enhancing Sustainability through Experiential Learning in Management Education. In N. Baporikar (Ed.), *Management Education for Global Leadership* (pp. 256–274). Hershey, PA: IGI Global. doi:10.4018/978-1-5225-1013-0.ch013

Shetty, K. P. (2017). Responsible Global Leadership: Ethical Challenges in Management Education. In N. Baporikar (Ed.), *Innovation and Shifting Perspectives in Management Education* (pp. 194–223). Hershey, PA: IGI Global. doi:10.4018/978-1-5225-1019-2.ch009

Sinthupundaja, J., & Kohda, Y. (2017). Effects of Corporate Social Responsibility and Creating Shared Value on Sustainability. *International Journal of Sustainable Entrepreneurship and Corporate Social Responsibility*, *2*(1), 27–38. doi:10.4018/IJSECSR.2017010103

Škarica, I., & Hrgović, A. V. (2018). Implementation of Total Quality Management Principles in Public Health Institutes in the Republic of Croatia. *International Journal of Productivity Management and Assessment Technologies*, *6*(1), 1–16. doi:10.4018/IJPMAT.2018010101

Smuts, H., Kotzé, P., Van der Merwe, A., & Loock, M. (2017). Framework for Managing Shared Knowledge in an Information Systems Outsourcing Context. *International Journal of Knowledge Management*, *13*(4), 1–30. doi:10.4018/IJKM.2017100101

Soares, E. R., & Zaidan, F. H. (2016). Information Architecture and Business Modeling in Modern Organizations of Information Technology: Professional Career Plan in Organizations IT. In G. Jamil, J. Poças Rascão, F. Ribeiro, & A. Malheiro da Silva (Eds.), *Handbook of Research on Information Architecture and Management in Modern Organizations* (pp. 439–457). Hershey, PA: IGI Global. doi:10.4018/978-1-4666-8637-3.ch020

Sousa, M. J., Cruz, R., Dias, I., & Caracol, C. (2017). Information Management Systems in the Supply Chain. In G. Jamil, A. Soares, & C. Pessoa (Eds.), *Handbook of Research on Information Management for Effective Logistics and Supply Chains* (pp. 469–485). Hershey, PA: IGI Global. doi:10.4018/978-1-5225-0973-8.ch025

Spremic, M., Turulja, L., & Bajgoric, N. (2018). Two Approaches in Assessing Business Continuity Management Attitudes in the Organizational Context. In N. Bajgoric (Ed.), *Always-On Enterprise Information Systems for Modern Organizations* (pp. 159–183). Hershey, PA: IGI Global. doi:10.4018/978-1-5225-3704-5.ch008

Steenkamp, A. L. (2018). Some Insights in Computer Science and Information Technology. In *Examining the Changing Role of Supervision in Doctoral Research Projects: Emerging Research and Opportunities* (pp. 113–133). Hershey, PA: IGI Global. doi:10.4018/978-1-5225-2610-0.ch005

Studdard, N., Dawson, M., Burton, S. L., Jackson, N., Leonard, B., Quisenberry, W., & Rahim, E. (2016). Nurturing Social Entrepreneurship and Building Social Entrepreneurial Self-Efficacy: Focusing on Primary and Secondary Schooling to Develop Future Social Entrepreneurs. In Z. Fields (Ed.), *Incorporating Business Models and Strategies into Social Entrepreneurship* (pp. 154–175). Hershey, PA: IGI Global. doi:10.4018/978-1-4666-8748-6.ch010

Sun, Z. (2016). A Framework for Developing Management Intelligent Systems. *International Journal of Systems and Service-Oriented Engineering*, *6*(1), 37–53. doi:10.4018/IJSSOE.2016010103

Swami, B., & Mphele, G. T. (2016). Problems Preventing Growth of Small Entrepreneurs: A Case Study of a Few Small Entrepreneurs in Botswana Sub-Urban Areas. In N. Baporikar (Ed.), *Handbook of Research on Entrepreneurship in the Contemporary Knowledge-Based Global Economy* (pp. 479–508). Hershey, PA: IGI Global. doi:10.4018/978-1-4666-8798-1.ch020

Tabach, A., & Croteau, A. (2017). Configurations of Information Technology Governance Practices and Business Unit Performance. *International Journal of IT/Business Alignment and Governance*, *8*(2), 1–27. doi:10.4018/IJITBAG.2017070101

Talaue, G. M., & Iqbal, T. (2017). Assessment of e-Business Mode of Selected Private Universities in the Philippines and Pakistan. *International Journal of Online Marketing*, *7*(4), 63–77. doi:10.4018/IJOM.2017100105

Tam, G. C. (2017). Project Manager Sustainability Competence. In *Managerial Strategies and Green Solutions for Project Sustainability* (pp. 178–207). Hershey, PA: IGI Global. doi:10.4018/978-1-5225-2371-0.ch008

Tambo, T. (2018). Fashion Retail Innovation: About Context, Antecedents, and Outcome in Technological Change Projects. In I. Management Association (Ed.), Fashion and Textiles: Breakthroughs in Research and Practice (pp. 233-260). Hershey, PA: IGI Global. doi:10.4018/978-1-5225-3432-7.ch010

Tambo, T., & Mikkelsen, O. E. (2016). Fashion Supply Chain Optimization: Linking Make-to-Order Purchasing and B2B E-Commerce. In S. Joshi & R. Joshi (Eds.), *Designing and Implementing Global Supply Chain Management* (pp. 1–21). Hershey, PA: IGI Global. doi:10.4018/978-1-4666-9720-1.ch001

Tandon, K. (2016). Innovative Andragogy: The Paradigm Shift to Heutagogy. In S. Tiwari & L. Nafees (Eds.), *Innovative Management Education Pedagogies for Preparing Next-Generation Leaders* (pp. 238–257). Hershey, PA: IGI Global. doi:10.4018/978-1-4666-9691-4.ch014

Tantau, A. D., & Frăţilă, L. C. (2018). Information and Management System for Renewable Energy Business. In *Entrepreneurship and Business Development in the Renewable Energy Sector* (pp. 200–244). Hershey, PA: IGI Global. doi:10.4018/978-1-5225-3625-3.ch006

Teixeira, N., Pardal, P. N., & Rafael, B. G. (2018). Internationalization, Financial Performance, and Organizational Challenges: A Success Case in Portugal. In L. Carvalho (Ed.), *Handbook of Research on Entrepreneurial Ecosystems and Social Dynamics in a Globalized World* (pp. 379–423). Hershey, PA: IGI Global. doi:10.4018/978-1-5225-3525-6.ch017

Trad, A., & Kalpić, D. (2016). The E-Business Transformation Framework for E-Commerce Architecture-Modeling Projects. In I. Lee (Ed.), *Encyclopedia of E-Commerce Development, Implementation, and Management* (pp. 733–753). Hershey, PA: IGI Global. doi:10.4018/978-1-4666-9787-4.ch052

Trad, A., & Kalpić, D. (2016). The E-Business Transformation Framework for E-Commerce Control and Monitoring Pattern. In I. Lee (Ed.), *Encyclopedia of E-Commerce Development, Implementation, and Management* (pp. 754–777). Hershey, PA: IGI Global. doi:10.4018/978-1-4666-9787-4.ch053

Trad, A., & Kalpić, D. (2018). The Business Transformation Framework, Agile Project and Change Management. In M. Khosrow-Pour, D.B.A. (Ed.), Encyclopedia of Information Science and Technology, Fourth Edition (pp. 620-635). Hershey, PA: IGI Global. doi:10.4018/978-1-5225-2255-3.ch054

Trad, A., & Kalpić, D. (2018). The Business Transformation and Enterprise Architecture Framework: The Financial Engineering E-Risk Management and E-Law Integration. In B. Sergi, F. Fidanoski, M. Ziolo, & V. Naumovski (Eds.), *Regaining Global Stability After the Financial Crisis* (pp. 46–65). Hershey, PA: IGI Global. doi:10.4018/978-1-5225-4026-7.ch003

Turulja, L., & Bajgoric, N. (2018). Business Continuity and Information Systems: A Systematic Literature Review. In N. Bajgoric (Ed.), *Always-On Enterprise Information Systems for Modern Organizations* (pp. 60–87). Hershey, PA: IGI Global. doi:10.4018/978-1-5225-3704-5.ch004

van Wessel, R. M., de Vries, H. J., & Ribbers, P. M. (2016). Business Benefits through Company IT Standardization. In K. Jakobs (Ed.), *Effective Standardization Management in Corporate Settings* (pp. 34–53). Hershey, PA: IGI Global. doi:10.4018/978-1-4666-9737-9.ch003

Vargas-Hernández, J. G. (2017). Professional Integrity in Business Management Education. In N. Baporikar (Ed.), *Management Education for Global Leadership* (pp. 70–89). Hershey, PA: IGI Global. doi:10.4018/978-1-5225-1013-0.ch004

Vasista, T. G., & AlAbdullatif, A. M. (2017). Role of Electronic Customer Relationship Management in Demand Chain Management: A Predictive Analytic Approach. *International Journal of Information Systems and Supply Chain Management, 10*(1), 53–67. doi:10.4018/IJISSCM.2017010104

Vergidis, K. (2016). Rediscovering Business Processes: Definitions, Patterns, and Modelling Approaches. In P. Papajorgji, F. Pinet, A. Guimarães, & J. Papathanasiou (Eds.), *Automated Enterprise Systems for Maximizing Business Performance* (pp. 97–122). Hershey, PA: IGI Global. doi:10.4018/978-1-4666-8841-4.ch007

Vieru, D., & Bourdeau, S. (2017). Survival in the Digital Era: A Digital Competence-Based Multi-Case Study in the Canadian SME Clothing Industry. *International Journal of Social and Organizational Dynamics in IT, 6*(1), 17–34. doi:10.4018/IJSODIT.2017010102

Vijayan, G., & Kamarulzaman, N. H. (2017). An Introduction to Sustainable Supply Chain Management and Business Implications. In M. Khan, M. Hussain, & M. Ajmal (Eds.), *Green Supply Chain Management for Sustainable Business Practice* (pp. 27–50). Hershey, PA: IGI Global. doi:10.4018/978-1-5225-0635-5.ch002

Vlachvei, A., & Notta, O. (2017). Firm Competitiveness: Theories, Evidence, and Measurement. In A. Vlachvei, O. Notta, K. Karantininis, & N. Tsounis (Eds.), *Factors Affecting Firm Competitiveness and Performance in the Modern Business World* (pp. 1–42). Hershey, PA: IGI Global. doi:10.4018/978-1-5225-0843-4.ch001

von Rosing, M., Fullington, N., & Walker, J. (2016). Using the Business Ontology and Enterprise Standards to Transform Three Leading Organizations. *International Journal of Conceptual Structures and Smart Applications, 4*(1), 71–99. doi:10.4018/IJCSSA.2016010104

von Rosing, M., & von Scheel, H. (2016). Using the Business Ontology to Develop Enterprise Standards. *International Journal of Conceptual Structures and Smart Applications, 4*(1), 48–70. doi:10.4018/IJCSSA.2016010103

Walczak, S. (2016). Artificial Neural Networks and other AI Applications for Business Management Decision Support. *International Journal of Sociotechnology and Knowledge Development, 8*(4), 1–20. doi:10.4018/IJSKD.2016100101

Wamba, S. F., Akter, S., Kang, H., Bhattacharya, M., & Upal, M. (2016). The Primer of Social Media Analytics. *Journal of Organizational and End User Computing, 28*(2), 1–12. doi:10.4018/JOEUC.2016040101

Wang, C., Schofield, M., Li, X., & Ou, X. (2017). Do Chinese Students in Public and Private Higher Education Institutes Perform at Different Level in One of the Leadership Skills: Critical Thinking?: An Exploratory Comparison. In V. Wang (Ed.), *Encyclopedia of Strategic Leadership and Management* (pp. 160–181). Hershey, PA: IGI Global. doi:10.4018/978-1-5225-1049-9.ch013

Wang, F., Raisinghani, M. S., Mora, M., & Wang, X. (2016). Strategic E-Business Management through a Balanced Scored Card Approach. In I. Lee (Ed.), *Encyclopedia of E-Commerce Development, Implementation, and Management* (pp. 361–386). Hershey, PA: IGI Global. doi:10.4018/978-1-4666-9787-4.ch027

Wang, J. (2017). Multi-Agent based Production Management Decision System Modelling for the Textile Enterprise. *Journal of Global Information Management, 25*(4), 1–15. doi:10.4018/JGIM.2017100101

Wiedemann, A., & Gewald, H. (2017). Examining Cross-Domain Alignment: The Correlation of Business Strategy, IT Management, and IT Business Value. *International Journal of IT/Business Alignment and Governance, 8*(1), 17–31. doi:10.4018/IJITBAG.2017010102

Wolf, R., & Thiel, M. (2018). Advancing Global Business Ethics in China: Reducing Poverty Through Human and Social Welfare. In S. Hipsher (Ed.), *Examining the Private Sector's Role in Wealth Creation and Poverty Reduction* (pp. 67–84). Hershey, PA: IGI Global. doi:10.4018/978-1-5225-3117-3.ch004

Wu, J., Ding, F., Xu, M., Mo, Z., & Jin, A. (2016). Investigating the Determinants of Decision-Making on Adoption of Public Cloud Computing in E-government. *Journal of Global Information Management, 24*(3), 71–89. doi:10.4018/JGIM.2016070104

Xu, L., & de Vrieze, P. (2016). Building Situational Applications for Virtual Enterprises. In I. Lee (Ed.), *Encyclopedia of E-Commerce Development, Implementation, and Management* (pp. 715–724). Hershey, PA: IGI Global. doi:10.4018/978-1-4666-9787-4.ch050

Yablonsky, S. (2018). Innovation Platforms: Data and Analytics Platforms. In *Multi-Sided Platforms (MSPs) and Sharing Strategies in the Digital Economy: Emerging Research and Opportunities* (pp. 72–95). Hershey, PA: IGI Global. doi:10.4018/978-1-5225-5457-8.ch003

Yusoff, A., Ahmad, N. H., & Halim, H. A. (2017). Agropreneurship among Gen Y in Malaysia: The Role of Academic Institutions. In N. Ahmad, T. Ramayah, H. Halim, & S. Rahman (Eds.), *Handbook of Research on Small and Medium Enterprises in Developing Countries* (pp. 23–47). Hershey, PA: IGI Global. doi:10.4018/978-1-5225-2165-5.ch002

Zanin, F., Comuzzi, E., & Costantini, A. (2018). The Effect of Business Strategy and Stock Market Listing on the Use of Risk Assessment Tools. In *Management Control Systems in Complex Settings: Emerging Research and Opportunities* (pp. 145–168). Hershey, PA: IGI Global. doi:10.4018/978-1-5225-3987-2.ch007

Zgheib, P. W. (2017). Corporate Innovation and Intrapreneurship in the Middle East. In P. Zgheib (Ed.), *Entrepreneurship and Business Innovation in the Middle East* (pp. 37–56). Hershey, PA: IGI Global. doi:10.4018/978-1-5225-2066-5.ch003

About the Contributors

Regina Lenart-Gansiniec is an Assistant Professor at Jagiellonian University, Institute of Public Affairs, Faculty of Management and Social Communication (Krakow, Poland). She is expert in open innovation, knowledge management, clusters and public management of the Ministry of Economic Development (Poland) and Ministry of Economy (Poland). She has been an expert witness (areas: sales, marketing). Regina is a member of the editorial board of the Journal of Economic Processes Management (Sumy State University), International Journal of Contemporary Management (Jagiellonian University), Journal of Management and Marketing (Publishing Society Ltd., Zilina, Slovakia), Business and Management Studies (Redfame Publishing). Her research interests include open innovation, social innovation, crowdsourcing, knowledge management, and organisational learning in public organisations.

* * *

Edyta Abramek is an Assistant Professor at the University of Economics in Katowice (Poland) where she studies the role of informatics and information systems in management and the role of prosumption in computer systems. She is interested in social media and social network analysis. She holds two master's degrees and a doctorate in Economics and Management from the University of Economics in Katowice. In addition to publishing and presenting her research in scholarly venues, Edyta shares her knowledge with students. She has the tutor certificate.

Alireza Amrollahi holds a PhD in Information Systems as well as a Master of Information Technology Management (MITM) degree. Ali has been involved in teaching a variety of units in Australia since 2013. Recently, he has taught courses such as Electronic Commerce Systems, System Analysis and Design (undergraduate and postgraduate), Computer Control Auditing and Security, and Accounting Information Systems. In terms of research, Ali has more than 25 papers published in high-ranked, peer reviewed conferences and journals. His most recent publications were published in journals such as Information and Management (ranked A*), Information Technology and People (ranked A), Communications of the Association for Information Systems (ranked A), and conferences such as HICSS, AMCIS, PACIS, and ACIS. Ali is actively collaborating with researchers in USA, Canada, UK, and Australia.

Ravi Chaudhary holds an MBA from Indian Institute of Management Ahmedabad and carries around 10 years of experience in Strategy and Consulting. He has extensively worked in knowledge management domain. Ravi has handled several assignments with central and state governments in India, international development agencies e.g. Asian Development Bank, World Bank, Japan Fund for Poverty Reduction.

Prasenjit Choudhury is an Assistant Professor in the Department of Computer Science and Engineering at National Institute of Technology, Durgapur, India. He has completed his PhD in Computer Science and Engineering from the same institute. He has published more than 40 research papers in international journals and conferences. His research interest includes Wireless Network, Data Analytics, and Recommendation systems.

Shubhendu Dutta is currently an Executive Fellow at Indian Institute of Management, Kashipur in Information Systems area. He is working as Director-IT at Sistema Shyam TeleServices Ltd (which operates as MTS brand in India). He holds a Bachelor of Engineering degree from B.I.T Mesra and an MBA from VGSoM, IIT Kharagpur and carries over 20 years of industry experience across various domains.

Pijush Dutta Pramanik is a PhD Research Scholar in the Department of Computer Science and Engineering at National Institute of Technology, Durgapur, India. He has acquired a range of professional qualifications namely MIT, MCA, MBA(IT), MTech(CSE) & MPhil(CS). His active research areas include Internet of Things, Grid Computing, Fog Computing, Crowd Computing and Semantic Web. He is passionate about technical writing.

Mansour Esmaeil Zaei is a research scholar at the Department of Public Administration, Panjab University, India. His major research areas are knowledge management, youth entrepreneurship, innovation, public policy, voluntary organisations and SMEs. His recent research has been published in Knowledge Management & E-Learning. He has been involved as a guest editor in the International Journal of Entrepreneurship and Small Business (Inderscience Publishers). He also serves on the editorial board of several international journals including International Business Research and Public Administration Research.

Kadeghe Fue received his Master of Science degree from the University of Florida in 2014. He studied precision agriculture, information systems and automation. He was sponsored by iAGRI under USAID. He received Borlaug LEAP fellowship award in the Fall 2013 offered by the University of California Davis. After then, He received the Pan African Conference on Science, Computing and Telecommunications (PACT) 2014 best student paper award in Arusha, Tanzania for the paper entitled "A Solar-powered, Wi-Fi Re-programmable Precision Irrigation Controller" on 17th July, 2014.

Dhrubajit Goswami carries over 9 years of experience in Training Delivery & Management towards improving productivity and quality. He possesses expertise in managing Learning Management System and Training operations across India. Dhrubajit has exposure of Insurance, Education and Automobile sectors and has worked with Fortune 500 companies like Metlife, General Motors and Ford Motor Company.

Igor Hawryszkiewycz currently works on developing design thinking environments to provide business solutions in complex environments by integrating processes, knowledge, and social networking. Facilitating agility and evolution of business systems through collaboration. Creating models that require the close integration of social networks and business processes including social media in business applications to support large-scale collaboration. Developing and supporting community structures that promote sustainability within constantly changing environments. Over 200 research publications and 6 books. Most recent book "Designing Creative Organizations: Tools, Processes and Practice" Emerald books.

Fredy T. M. Kilima is Associate Professor and Head of Department of Agricultural Economics and Agribusiness. He holds a PhD in Agricultural Economics from Oklahoma State University and is well experienced in applied and action research as well as consultancy services. He has a strong background in quantitative economics (micro-economics, mathematics and econometrics) with a long-term teaching experience in this specialty. He has researched extensively in agricultural marketing, price transmission, food and safety standards, commodity value chains and livelihoods. His most recent research has been on:1) consumer behaviour and decision making through a regional project involving researcher from Kansas State in the United States of America, Lilongwe University of Agriculture Natural Resources in Malawi, Sokoine University of Agriculture (SUA) in Tanzania and University of Zambia; 2) adoption of nano technologies to enhance fruit freshness through an international project implemented in India, Sri Lanka, Trinidad and Tobago, Kenya and Tanzania; 3) Migration, access to credit and urbanization through a project involving researchers from Copenhagen University and SUA;4) Urban dairying and poverty reduction and, innovative communication and marketing in Tanzania. In the recent past Prof. Kilima has been contracted as lead or collaborating consultant by several clients including 1) BirldLife International to undertake comparative costs benefit analysis comparing soda ash mining with promotion of ecotourism and sustainable use of natural resources in the lake Natron basin,2) Tanzania; Japan International Cooperation Agency (JICA) to devise a methodology for computing farm gate prices as ratios of Free On Board (FOB) prices for coffee and cashew nuts; Seed Policy Action Node (SPAN) Project at SUA to prepare a monitoring and evaluation (M&E) manual; eoVision and Frieland to undertake impact assessment for a dam construction project in Tanzania. At SUA Prof. Kilima has participated in the Programme for Agricultural and Natural Resources Transformation for Improved Livelihood (PANTIL) as a Research Impact Assessment Expert. Prof. Kilima served as component leader of programme titled Enhancing Pro-poor Innovations in Natural Resources and Agricultural Value-chains (EPINAV) and was responsible for monitoring and evaluation of 21 research projects. In terms of publication Prof. Kilima has published on agricultural credit, biodiversity conservation, market reforms, livelihoods, value chain, production efficiency, gender, food choices, market choices, project monitoring and evaluation as well as price integration and volatility.

Maulilio Kipanyula is a specialist in Neuroscience, with enormous experience in research.

Neema Nicodemus Lyimo is a Lecturer in Informatics Department at Sokoine University of Agriculture, Tanzania. She has Masters in Computer Sc from the University of Dar es Salaam and Bachelor degree in Information and Communication Technology Management from Mzumbe University. Her research interest is in ICT for development, data Science, remote sensing and precision agriculture. She has published in the International Journal of Interdisciplinary Studies on Information Technology and Business. Ms. Nicodemus has a long-term teaching and practical experience in programming, web design, software engineering, database and operating system. She has taught both undergraduate and non-degree programs.

Saurabh Pal is an Assistant Professor at Bengal Institute of Technology, India and has been teaching Computer science in the Department of Computer Science and Engineering and Information Technology for last 10 years. He received his B.Sc from University of Calcutta in 1998, M.Sc - IT from Allahabad Agricultural Institute

- Deemed University in 2006, Advanced Diploma in Computer Application from Department of Information Technology, Govt of India in 2007 and M.Tech - IT from Jadavpur University in 2010. Presently he is pursuing his Ph.D in CSE from National Institute of Technology, Durgapur. His primary research areas are Context Aware Mobile Learning, Recommender System, IoT and Pervasive Computing. Besides being interested in programming and paintings he like to write technical articles.

Gaurav Pareek is with Department of Computer Science and Engineering at National Institute of Technology Goa, India. His areas of interest include Security, Privacy, Cloud Computing, Crowd Computing, Public key Cryptography, Wireless Sensor Networks, etc.

Dong Phung has a background in information system designs and education management. His corporate background of 15+ years is mainly in information system and education management where he managed and deployed information systems in higher education. Currently, he works on knowledge management to provide a method to improve knowledge sharing.

Elzbieta Pohulak-Zoledowska, PhD, assistant professor at the Department of Microeconomics at the Faculty of Regional Development and Tourism, Wroclaw University of Economics, Poland. Research interests include: knowledge based economy, academic sources of innovation, R&D activity of universities, financing sources of academic R&D, public sector economics.

Shilohu Rao currently designated as General Manager, National e-Governance Division (NeGD). He has 19 years of experience at Senior Management Level. Shilohu is heading KMS and LMS projects Under Digital India Program initiated by Govt of India. Shilohu has been recognised as top 50 Knowledge Management Professionals by World Educational Congress.

Camilius Sanga is Associate Professor from the Department of Informatics at Sokoine University of Agriculture (SUA), Tanzania. He is a head of the Department of Informatics at the Faculty of Science, SUA. He has PhD in Computer Science from the University of the Western Cape, South Africa. He holds MSc. Computer Science and BSc. in Computer Science from Osmania University and University of Dar es Salaam respectively. His great research interest is in the area of Information and Communication Technology for Development (ICT4D). He has published papers in a number of International journals. He has also published papers in local and International conferences. Furthermore, he has co-authored two books as well as book chapters. Some of the research projects which he has been involved are:

Development of Monitoring and Evaluation system for Projects under Enhancing Pro-poor Innovations in Natural Resources and Agricultural Value-chains (EPINAV) at SUA and Farmer Voice Radio (FVR) Project - Building a radio - based, impact driven small farmer extension service system. Currently, he is an assistant project leader for the research titled "The role of mobile phones towards improving coverage of agricultural extension services: a case study of maize value chain". Finally, he is also involved in the project titled "Assessing the impacts of climate variability and change on agricultural systems in Eastern Africa while enhancing the region's capacity to undertake integrated assessment of vulnerabilities to future changes in climate" (2012-2014). It is one of the projects jointly conducted with researchers from four East and Horn of Africa -Ethiopia, Kenya, Tanzania and Uganda and it is funded by AgMIP through the support from UKaid (http://www.agmip.org/).

Soraya Sedkaoui is a Senior Lecturer at the department of Economics, Khemis Miliana University (Algeria) and Researcher at TRIS laboratory in the University of Montpellier (France). Ph.D in Economic Analysis and Habilitation to Conduct Researches in Economic and Applied Statistics. Her research Interests include: econometrics, statistics, big data and data analytics, data science, forecasting, E-business and Entrepreneurship, and IT acceptance and uses. Her prior books and research has been published in several refereed editions and journals, including Wiley, Iste, Bentham science, Springer, Advances in Distributed Computing and Artificial Intelligence Journal, l'Harmattan, Chinese Business Review and Ed Universitaires européennes. She is presently a data analyst in "SRY-Consulting" at Montpellier (France).

Index

Stay Current on the Latest Emerging Research Developments

Become an IGI Global Reviewer for Authored Book Projects

The overall success of an authored book project is dependent on quality and timely reviews.

In this competitive age of scholarly publishing, constructive and timely feedback significantly decreases the turnaround time of manuscripts from submission to acceptance, allowing the publication and discovery of progressive research at a much more expeditious rate. Several IGI Global authored book projects are currently seeking highly qualified experts in the field to fill vacancies on their respective editorial review boards:

Applications may be sent to:
development@igi-global.com

Applicants must have a doctorate (or an equivalent degree) as well as publishing and reviewing experience. Reviewers are asked to write reviews in a timely, collegial, and constructive manner. All reviewers will begin their role on an ad-hoc basis for a period of one year, and upon successful completion of this term can be considered for full editorial review board status, with the potential for a subsequent promotion to Associate Editor.

If you have a colleague that may be interested in this opportunity, we encourage you to share this information with them.

www.ingramcontent.com/pod-product-compliance
Lightning Source LLC
LaVergne TN
LVHW081339300926
849161LV00008B/2024